About the Cover

Information philosophy can now suggest plausible solutions for a number of well-known problems in philosophy and physics.

The philosophical problems include metaphysics - what is there?, the problem of knowledge - how do we know what exists?, a theory of mind and the mind/body problem - can an *immaterial* mind move the material body?, the "hard problem" of consciousness, freedom of the will, theories of ethics - is there an objective universal Good?, what is Evil?, and problems from theology - does God exist?, is God responsible for the evil in the world, what is immortality?

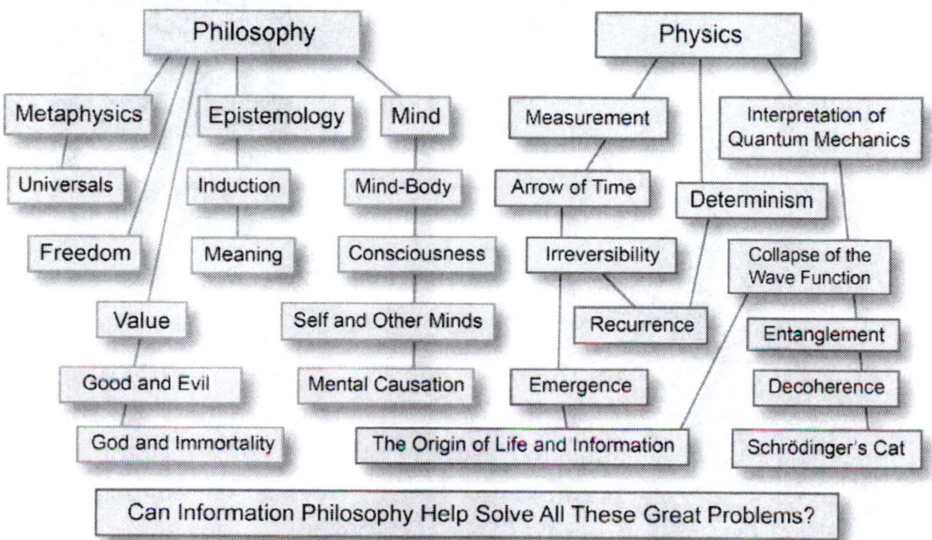

Another set of problems with plausible solutions comes from physics and the philosophy of science. They include an information interpretation of quantum mechanics to clarify the muddled Copenhagen interpretation, the collapse of the wave function, entanglement, decoherence and the quantum-to-classical transition, the universe expansion as the fundamental arrow of arrow of time, which requires microscopic irreversibility, the emergence of the biological and mental from the physical and chemical, and the creative process behind the origin of cosmic information structures that made biology possible.

What Philosophers Are Saying about Free Will

"How Free Are You?", asks the well-known determinist philosopher TED HONDERICH, in his best-selling book. Though he is its foremost champion, Honderich frankly characterizes determinism as a "black thing" and an "incubus" which gives him dismay.

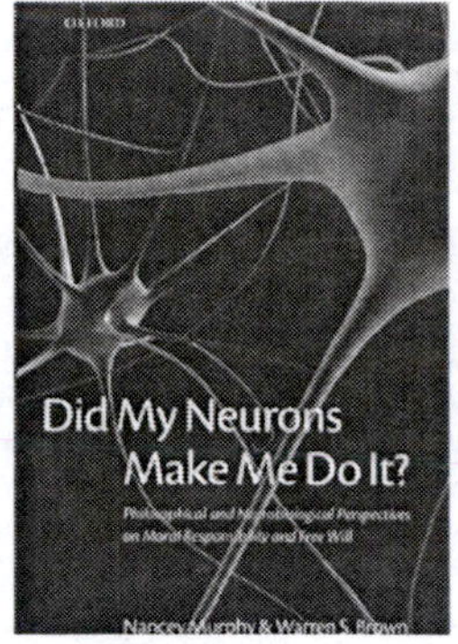

"Did My Neurons Make Me Do It?", asks NANCEY MURPHY, summarizing the concern of philosophers who think neuroscience will reveal us to be just biological machines that are running programs determined by our heredity and environment, by our genes and our upbringing,

"Is Conscious Will an Illusion?" Harvard psychologist DANIEL WEGNER thinks so. We think we do things freely for good reasons, but Wegner finds we often confabulate reasons after the fact, when we are challenged to provide the motivations for our actions.

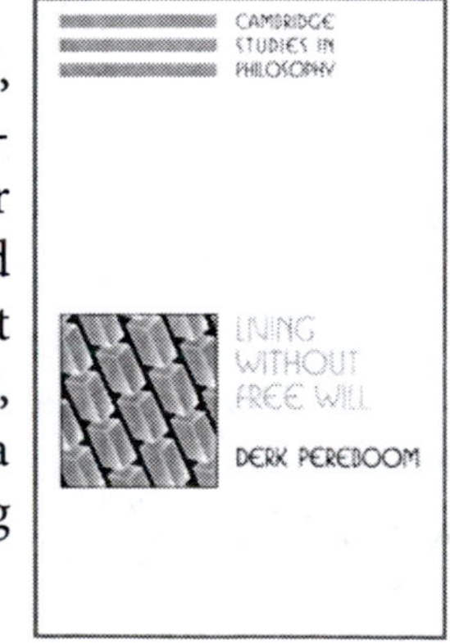

"Living Without Free Will" is required, according to hard incompatibilist philosopher DERK PEREBOOM. And philosopher GALEN STRAWSON provides a logical and "basic" argument to prove that we cannot possibly be responsible for our actions, because they are the consequences of a causal chain that goes back to times long before we were born.

Why The Free Will Scandal Should Matter to You

Academic philosophers, psychologists, and neuroscientists teach their students to believe that their actions may be determined and beyond their control, that free will is an illusion.

Like the workers in Charlie Chaplin's *Modern Times*, humans are seen as cogs in a vast biological machine. If scientists could show that this is so, and give us reasonable evidence for it, we would have little choice but to accept the science. Or, we could do as IMMANUEL KANT did in his great *Critique of Pure Reason*. We might doubt Reason to make room for Belief in Free Will.

But physical and biological science can produce no such evidence. Iron-clad proof that determinism is true is beyond the reach of empirical science, since evidence is always prone to observational errors, and physics today is indeterministic.

Nevertheless, some philosophers accept the faulty reasoning that freedom exists only on some metaphysical plane. If you accept freedom as a mystery beyond explanation, a gift of God beyond understanding by our finite minds, perhaps you need not worry and may not need this book.

But this ivory-tower thinking should still matter to you. Why? Because we have good evidence that telling young people they are determined beings, and that they are not responsible for their actions, actually makes them behave less morally, more willing to cheat their colleagues in innocent games, for example.

Whether you are one of those young students, or one of the older generation sending your children to school, or perhaps one of the faculty teaching our young, you should be concerned about what we are doing to the life hopes and moral fibre of our youth.

If you see something scandalous in this situation, this book provides you with the resources you need to do something to change what we are teaching in our schools.

La Trahison des Philosophes...
In a world full of problems, they sat doing puzzles.

Qui docet doctores?

Tantum philosophia potuit suadere malorum.

Werte ohne Freiheit sind nutzlos,
Freiheit ohne Werte ist absurd.

Ich mußte also den Determinismus und den Indeterminismus aufheben, um für die Freiheit Platz zu bekommen.

Our thoughts are free. Our actions are willed.

FREE WILL

The Scandal in Philosophy

Online updates are available here:
informationphilosopher.com/books/scandal
Send comments to bobdoyle@informationphilosopher.com

Bob Doyle
The Information Philosopher
"beyond logic and language"

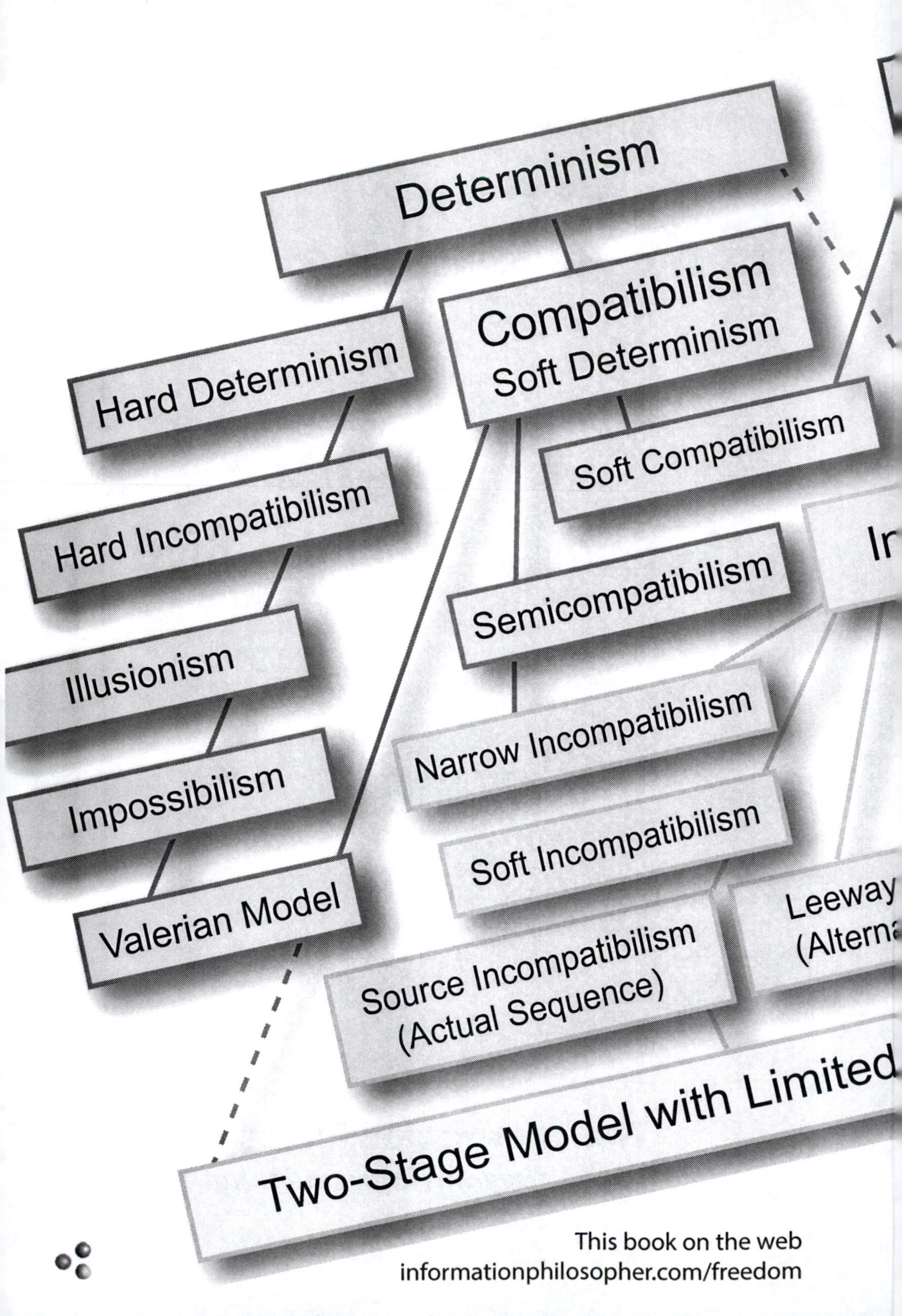

This book on the web
informationphilosopher.com/freedom

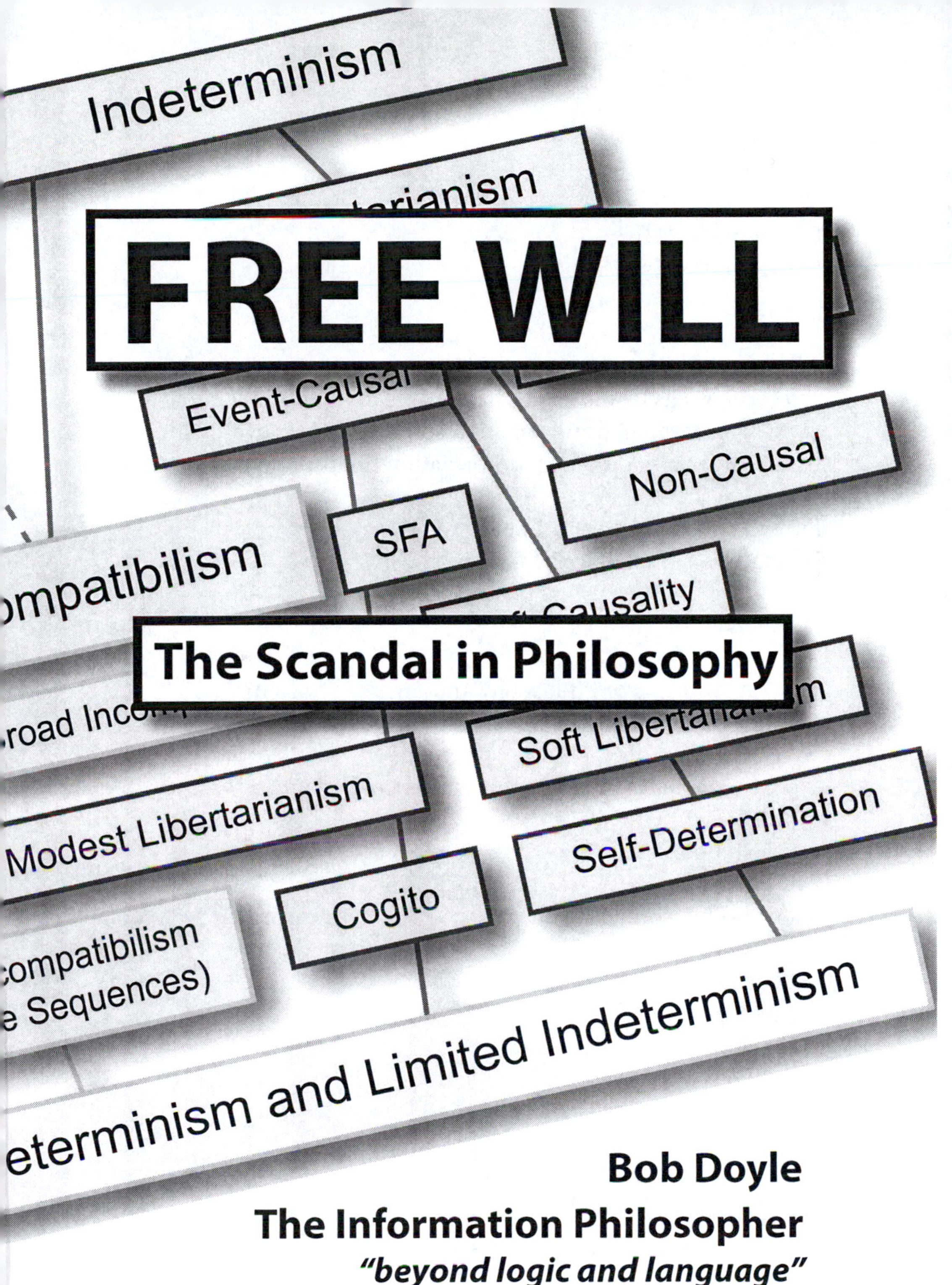

FREE WILL

The Scandal in Philosophy

Bob Doyle
The Information Philosopher
"beyond logic and language"

First edition, 2016

Publisher's Cataloging-in-Publication data
(Prepared by The Donohue Group)

Doyle, Bob. 1936–

Great Problems of Philosophy and Physics - Solved? / Bob Doyle. – Cambridge, Mass. : I-Phi Press, 2016.

p. ; cm. Includes bibliographic references and index.
ISBN: 978-0-9835802-8-7
ISBN(eBook): 978-0-9835802-9-4
1. Philosophy. 2. Physics. 3. Information science--Philosophy. I. Title.

BD21.Dxx 2016
123.5—dc22

I-Phi Press
Cambridge, MA, USA

Dedication

To the hundreds of philosophers and scientists with web pages on the INFORMATION PHILOSOPHER website.

After collecting and reading their works for the past six decades, I have tried to capture their essential contributions to philosophy and physics, as much as practical with excerpts in their own words.

Special thanks to many who have sent suggestions and corrections to ensure that their work is presented as accurately as possible for the students and young professionals who use the I-Phi website as an entry point into some great intellectual problems that they may help to solve in the coming decades.

As a scientist and inventor, the author has contributed some modest tools to help individuals and communities communicate, to share information. So he would like also to dedicate this work to some of the creators of the world's fundamental information-sharing technologies.

Alexander Graham Bell, Alan Turing, Claude Shannon, John von Neumann, Norbert Wiener, Steve Jobs, Tim Berners-Lee, Mark Zuckerberg, Jimmy Wales, Larry Page, Sergei Brin.

Information philosophy builds on the intersection of computers and communications. These two technologies will facilitate the sharing of knowledge around the world in the very near future, when almost everyone will have a smartphone and affordable access to the Internet and the World-Wide Web.

Information is like love. Giving it to others does not reduce it. It is not a scarce economic good. Sharing it increases the *Sum* of information in human minds.

Information wants to be free.

Bob Doyle

Cambridge, MA

August, 2016

Contents

List of Figures

List of Sidebars

Preface
Determinism
Compatibilism
Soft Determinism
Hard Determinism
Hard Incompatibilism
Preface
Semicompatibilism
Illusionism
Impossibilism
Valerian Model
Narrow Incompatibilism
Soft Incompatibilism
Source Incompatibilism
(Actual Sequence)
Two-Stage Model with Limite

My goal for this book is to provide you with a textbook/guide to the hundreds of pages on my Information Philosopher website (www.informationphilosopher.com). Information philosophy (I like to call it I-Phi) provides insights into some classical unsolved philosophical problems,[1] but of these the most important to society may well be the question of **free will**.

The free will problem has been uppermost in my mind since 1957, when I first read Arthur Stanley Eddington's 1927 book *The Nature of the Physical World*. Quantum mechanics had in that year just invalidated the deterministic physics of previous centuries, and Eddington thought that Werner Heisenberg's Uncertainty Principle might offer support for human freedom.

Eddington's hopes were dashed by his philosopher contemporaries. Quantum randomness is no more of a help to free will than Epicurus' ancient notion of a "swerve" of the atoms, they said. If our willed decisions are made at random, we cannot be **morally responsible** for our actions.

In the 1960's I studied quantum physics. My Ph.D. thesis was on collisions of hydrogen, the simplest of atoms. I came to believe that the philosophers might be wrong, that quantum physics might do no harm to human responsibility. Random thoughts need not make our actions random, as most philosophers argued, and even Eddington had reluctantly accepted.

I began a serious study of all the philosophers and scientists that had written on the problem of free will. My library now has over 150 books specifically on free will, and I have access to many more through Harvard's Widener Library. David Chalmers' PhilPapers.org website provides access to over 2000 articles on free will.

In recent years I moved all my research onto the web, where it is open source and freely available. Information Philosopher has about 140 web pages on philosophers and 65 on scientists, with critical analyses of their views. My I-Phi website now shows up on the first Google page for many search terms, and is used in a number of philosophy courses.

1 See Chapter 31 for some of my I-Phi problems.

When I create new web pages, if the philosophers are alive, I write and ask for their criticisms, to ensure that my account of their views is as accurate as I can make it. In many cases, I add new material to their Wikipedia page, or create a page.

My email exchanges with dozens of philosophers have greatly enhanced my appreciation for the wide variety of their views, which you see I have arranged in a taxonomy of two dozen or so basic positions. Sadly, I can report little progress in changing the fundamental opinions of any philosopher over these years.

Most well-known philosophers have made up their minds long ago, and have been teaching their views for decades. But by corresponding with them for years, by writing and rewriting their positions, I have come to understand how they fit with one another in their various intellectual niches. And by meeting many in person in the last year or so, I now think my web site presents as comprehensive an overview of the free will problem as is available anywhere today.

My hope is that philosophy students who read this book, or the I-Phi website, will be more likely to arrive at their own views on free will, different from that of their professors.

I hope to publish a second volume titled *Free Will: The Philosophers and Scientists*, with extended analyses of over 200 thinkers. But to give you a picture of my methods, this volume will focus on my interactions with just four philosophers - Robert Kane, the world's leading **libertarian** on free will, Ted Honderich, the leading **determinist**, who denies free will, Daniel Dennett, the leading **compatibilist**, who thinks that determinism gives us as much free will as we should want, and Alfred Mele, one of whose free will models is much like my own.

Although I started building the information management tools for my I-Phi website in 1999, and began writing pages in earnest in 2004, my first philosophical publication appeared only in June of 2009, in Nature magazine.[2] I was responding to a May 2009 essay in Nature, "Is Free Will an Illusion," by the German neuro-

2 Doyle (2009)

geneticist MARTIN HEISENBERG. Heisenberg described two-stage freedom in lower animals that he thought might be the basis for free will in humans. I agreed, and noted that the two-stage idea had been put forward by a dozen thinkers since William James in 1884.

My second publication appeared in *William James Studies* in June 2010.[3] It traced James' extraordinary insight into free will, as independently discovered by other philosophers and scientists down to Heisenberg. This paper led to an invitation to lead a 90-minute seminar at the William James Symposium (on the 100th anniversary of James' death) in August, 2010 at Chocorua, NH, and at Harvard.

Having seen my *Jamesian Free Will* paper, DANIEL DENNETT kindly invited me to participate in his graduate seminar on free will in the Fall term at Tufts University.

Then in October, 2010, an "Experts Meeting" on the question "Is Science Compatible with Our Desire for Freedom" was convened by the Social Trends Institute in Barcelona, Spain. Organized by ANTOINE SUAREZ of the Center for Quantum Philosophy in Zurich, Switzerland, the "experts" included several quantum physicists working with the exotic phenomena of nonlocality and entanglement to develop quantum cryptography, quantum computing, and possibly explain consciousness and free will.

The philosophers invited to Barcelona included myself, ROBERT KANE, the editor of the *Oxford Handbook on Free Will*, ALFRED MELE, who leads a four-year, $4.4-million research effort at Florida State University on the Big Questions in Free Will, funded by the Templeton Foundation. MARTIN HEISENBERG attended by video conference from his lab in Würzburg, Germany.

My Harvard talk and all the Barcelona talks were videotaped and posted to YouTube in January, 2011.[4] I then turned my attention to producing this printed book and e-book versions of the FREEDOM section of the I-PHI website.

3 Doyle (2010)

4 http://www.socialtrendsinstitute.org/Activities/Bioethics/Is-Science-Compatible-with-Our-Desire-for-Freedom/Free-Will-Debate-on-YouTube.axd

After the introductory Chapter 1, Chapter 2 makes the case why the current situation is a scandal in philosophy, not only because of the lack of progress, but because of grave implications for **moral responsibility** and **creativity** in young people.

Chapter 3 explores the reasons why the free will problem has been so intractable for millennia. In chapter 4, I identify the main reason for intractability as a **standard argument against free will** that has been used for centuries, but which is flawed.

The standard argument has two parts, each of which independently denies free will. It follows that each needs to be addressed on its merits, and this gives rise to two independent **requirements** that any satisfactory model of libertarian free will must meet. These are set out in Chapter 5.

Chapter 6 gives names and brief descriptions for the most common positions on free will taken over the centuries. This prepares us for a lengthy history of the free-will problem in Chapter 7, where we can put up milestones and signposts giving credit to the original thinkers behind the different positions we identified in Chapter 6.

Chapter 8 introduces actualism, possibilism, and probabilism, with a discussion of quantum probabilities.

Chapters 9 and 10 review the many different kinds of **determinism** that have been invented, and what it means for the different kinds of compatibilist "free will" that they entail.

In Chapter 11, I consider some theories of **libertarian** free will that postulate noumenal realms, non-causal events, and metaphysical or supernatural mystical gifts of freedom that remain mysteries, even for their proponents.

When the two requirements for libertarian free will of Chapter 5 are satisfied by a theory, it results in a **two-stage model**, each stage satisfying one of the requirements. The dozen or so thinkers who have proposed such a two-stage model are described in Chapter 12, and the most plausible and practical current version that I call the **Cogito** model is developed in Chapter 13.

Chapter 14 is a blow-by-blow discussion of the many objections levelled by philosophers against the two-stage model

Chapters 15 to 17 investigate the physics, the biology, and the neuroscience of free will. All three are being actively used to develop strong arguments in favor of **determinism**. They deserve careful examination. Chapter 18 explores the significance of the **Cogito** model for the traditional problem of consciousness.

From the very first debates, free will has been connected tightly to **moral responsibility**. Many modern thinkers equate, or at least conflate the two, making free will nothing but the control condition for moral responsibility. Chapter 19 describes the problem of moral responsibility and Chapter 20 makes the case for separating free will from moral responsibility. Indeed, I also propose separating "moral" from "responsibility," like the clear separation of "free" from "will" in my two-stage model.

Chapter 21 is devoted to Naturalism, a well-intentioned but misled movement that emphasizes the animal nature of human beings. Naturalists properly reject anything supernatural that separates humans from animals. But they also reject the idea of free will, perhaps because it is often said to be a gift of God, and therefore nonexistent for naturalists, who are atheists.

Free will involves bringing new **information** into the universe. I argue in Chapter 22 that **creativity** would not be possible in a deterministic universe, where the future is "already out there." Free will is a precondition for creativity.

Chapters 23, 24, 25, and 26 discuss my exchanges with Ted Honderich on determinism, Robert Kane on libertarianism, Daniel Dennett on compatibilism, and Alfred Mele on his modest libertarianism. In all these chapters, the fundamental question is the role of quantum **indeterminacy** in these philosophers' models for free will.

In Chapter 27, I imagine how different the history of free will would have been if Dennett and Kane had reached a compromise position. Instead of helping to make the history of philosophy today, I would be just writing the history of philosophy.

In Chapter 28, I make the case for reconciling free will with the **indeterminism** of quantum physics. Here I follow in the footsteps of David Hume, who reconciled freedom with the determinism of classical physics. Hume's **compatibilism** is fine if by **determinism** we mean the "**adequate determinism**" of classical physics, the one that emerges as the asymptotic limit of quantum mechanics in objects with large numbers of material particles.

I therefore invite all compatibilist philosophers to consider a new "**comprehensive compatibilism**" that reconciles free will with *both* limited determinism *and* limited indeterminism.

Most philosophers today think of themselves as compatibilists, and for understandable if somewhat misguided reasons. As R. E. Hobart wrote in his 1934 *Mind* article, "Free Will As Involving Determination, and Inconceivable Without It," our character, values, motives, and feelings must determine our willed decisions, or we could not be morally responsible for our actions.[5] But Hume was not happy with his determinism, and Hobart, if we read him carefully, did not deny the existence of irreducible **chance**, although he could not see, as we can today, how it is that **indeterminacy** helps to solve the problem of free will.

Chapter 29 summarizes the key points that you can use to help end the scandal of teaching that free will is an illusion.

Chapter 30 examines the cosmic information creation process that underlies information processing in the body and mind.

Chapter 31 has brief comments on some more unsolved problems in philosophy and in physics that may yield to an information philosophy analysis.

Join me on the I-Phi website to explore the work in progress on these problems. I look forward to your critical comments on problems that interest you. Your input will help to make the Information Philosopher as accurate a resource for twenty-first-century philosophy as we together can make it.

bobdoyle@informationphilosopher.com
Cambridge, MA
June, 2011

5 See the Hobart's Determination sidebar on page 23.

How To Use This Book With The I-Phi Website

The content of the book comes primarily from the Freedom section of the Information Philosopher website. Please refer to the website for more details than there is room for here.

You will find multiple entry points into the website from this book, with URLs for the chapters and in many of the footnotes. I hope that you agree that the combination of printed book and online website is a powerful way to do philosophy in the twenty-first century.

The Freedom section has a drop-down menu for the major sub-sections - Problem, History, Physics, Biology, etc.

In the left-hand navigation of the Freedom section there are links to the core concepts needed to understand the free will debates. These are followed by links to the hundreds of philosophers and scientists who have contributed to the history of free will.

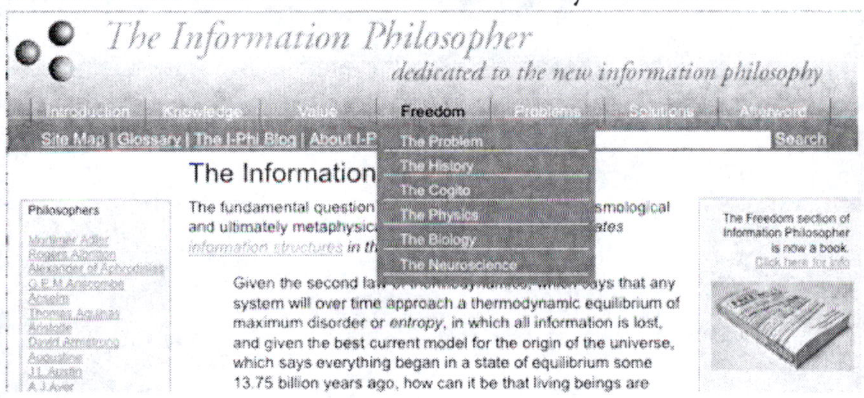

Words in **boldface** in the text refer to core concepts. Many of these have entries in the Glossary and are good Google search terms.

You will find a list of these core concepts on page 441.

Names in Small Caps are the philosophers and scientists with web pages on the I-Phi website. They are listed on page 440.

It is not easy to navigate any website, and I-Phi is no exception. A fast way to find things of interest is to use the Search box on every page. Once on a page, a "Cite this page" function generates a citation with the URL and the date the page was retrieved in APA format.

Chapter 1
Determinism
Compatibilism
Soft Determinism
Hard Determinism
mpatibilism
Hard Incompatibilism
Introduction
Semicompatibilism
Ir
Illusionism
Narrow Incompatibilism
Impossibilism
Soft Incompatibilism
Valerian Model
Leeway
(Altern
Source Incompatibilism
(Actual Sequence)
Two-Stage Model with Limited

Introduction

Of all the problems that information philosophy may help to solve, none is more important than the question of **free will**. There is little in philosophy more dehumanizing than the logic chopping and sophisticated linguistic analysis that denies the possibility of human freedom.

Many philosophers go further. They claim deterministic laws of nature deny even the possibility of **alternative possibilities**. Only the actual is possible, there is only one possible future, say some philosophical voices over the twenty-two centuries from Diodorus Cronus to Daniel Dennett.

Even the Cartesian dualism that reduced the bodies of all animals to living machines left room for a non-mechanistic, immaterial, and indeterministic mind above and beyond the deterministic limits set by the laws of nature.

Information philosophy hopes to show that information is itself that immaterial "substance" above and beyond matter and energy that Descartes and Kant were looking for.

What is Information?

Information is neither Matter nor Energy,
But it needs Matter for its Embodiment,
And it needs Energy for its Communication.
Information is the modern Spirit.
It is the Ghost in the Machine
It is the Mind in the Body.
It is the Soul, and when we Die,
It is our Information that Perishes.

Please go to the Information Philosopher website for more on information. (www.informationphilosopher.com/introduction/information)

To understand the role of information in human freedom, you need to know that information cannot be created without an **indeterministic** quantum process known as the "collapse of the wave function." I explain more about information creation in the universe in Chapters 1 and 31, and more about information physics, wave-function collapses, and free will in Chapter 15.

Quantum physics in the twentieth century opened a crack in the wall of physical **determinism**, through which a "chink of daylight" could be seen by ARTHUR STANLEY EDDINGTON in 1927. But academic philosophy reacted to **quantum indeterminacy** the same way as the Academics and Stoics had reacted to the idea of an Epicurean "swerve" of the atoms.

Ancient and modern academics were appalled at the idea that **chance** could play a role in generating **alternative possibilities** for **adequately determined** decisions that are "**up to us**," as Aristotle called them.

Chance is atheistic, said the Stoics. It denies the omnipotence of Nature and Nature's God - Reason. How could humans be exempt from universal laws that govern the macrocosmos and microcosmos, from the stars and planets down to the atoms themselves?

The illusion of chance is a consequence of human ignorance, the product of finite minds, say many ancient and modern thinkers. Chance is *epistemic* and not *ontologically* real, they say.

An infinite and omniscient mind can comprehend everything, and foresee the future with a God's-eye view, as clearly as it sees the present and the past. But our human and finite mind's-I views are limited. You will find this anti-humanistic thought in much theologically inspired philosophy.

Note that JOHN DUNS SCOTUS preferred a God capable of random miracles to THOMAS AQUINAS' vision of a God constrained by his own Reason, like the Nature/God of the deterministic Stoics. See the sidebar on omniscience and omnipotence.

On Omniscience, Omnipotence, Benevolence

In passing, it is worth noting that the idea of God as an omniscient and omnipotent being has an internal logical contradiction that is rarely discussed by the theologians.[1] If such a being had perfect knowledge of the future, like **Laplace's demon**, who knows the positions, velocities, and forces for all the particles, it would be perfectly impotent. Because if God had the power to change even one thing about the future, his presumed perfect knowledge would have been imperfect. Omniscience entails impotence. Omnipotence some ignorance. Prayer is useless.

As to benevolence, Archibald MacLeish said in J.B, "If God is Good, He is not God. If God is God, He is Not Good."

1 Anselm was an exception. See Sorabji (1980). p. 126.

With so much talk of **probability** and statistics after Pierre-Simon Laplace in the nineteenth century, it was becoming more respectable to discuss the possibility of absolute **chance**. Charles Darwin's theory of evolution included chance variations that could be inherited by an organism's offspring to allow the natural selection of new species. Genuine novelty in the universe needs chance to generate those new possibilities. Otherwise, the existing species would be the **pre-determined** consequence of laws of nature and events in the distant past. Determinism accommodates the view of an omniscient intelligent designer.

In Cambridge at Harvard, Charles Sanders Peirce and his colleague William James followed the Darwinian arguments closely. Peirce was undoubtedly more familiar than James with the statistical arguments of the physicists. Peirce's main attack was on the idea of logical and necessary truths about the physical world. Peirce was the strongest philosophical voice for absolute and objective chance since Epicurus. For Peirce, **chance** was ontological and real, not epistemic and merely human ignorance.

Peirce argued that chance liberated the will from determinism, but he gave no definite model, and in the end he compromised and wanted to manage and control the chance with a form of rationality that he called "synechism" or continuity. He dreamed of "evolutionary love" and a God who kept the chance in Darwin's "greedy" evolution in check.

Although Peirce is famous for promoting the reality of chance with his Tychism, his overall opinion of the role of chance was negative. We shall see that it is WILLIAM JAMES who in the end found a measured and constructive role for chance in his attempt to defend freedom of the will. Where Peirce saw chance as a negative force, James, like Darwin, saw it as a positive and creative one.

About the same time Darwin was introducing chance into biological evolution, JAMES CLERK MAXWELL and LUDWIG BOLTZMANN were applying the ideas of probability and statistics to a model of gases as untold numbers of particles, the atoms of the ancients DEMOCRITUS and EPICURUS.

Social scientists like the mathematician Joseph Fourier in France, the astronomer ADOLPH QUÉTELET in Belgium, and the historian HENRY THOMAS BUCKLE in England applied the calculus of probabilities to the statistics of social phenomena like marriages and suicides. They found regularities scattered about mean values (often following the bell curve of a normal distributions). The mean values seemed constant from year to year. They concluded that these regularities were proof of rigorous, though unknown, laws controlling chance.

Scientists like Maxwell and Boltzmann, inspired by the collective properties of many random social events, showed that the same distribution applied to physical properties, like the velocities of individual particles in a gas. (The word "gas" was coined from the "chaos" of the particles.) Unlike the social scientists, Maxwell and Boltzmann did not assume that the gross regularities meant the constituent particles were determined by unknown laws.

Instead, they had shown that trillions of trillions of trillions of atoms moving randomly average out to produce the regular laws of large bodies. Deterministic classical mechanics became indeterminate statistical mechanics. Once the microscopic world was found in the 20th century to include quantum indeterminacy, the regular laws of nature for macroscopic systems were seen to be irreducibly statistical laws. Nature is fundamentally stochastic. But how do we reconcile such indeterminate chaos with the regularities of nature and the rational operations of the human mind?

Contemporaries of EPICURUS would have been appalled by these developments. The Stoic CHRYSIPPUS wrote:

> "Everything that happens is followed by something else which depends on it by causal necessity. Likewise, everything that happens is preceded by something with which it is causally connected. For nothing exists or has come into being in the cosmos without a cause. The universe will be disrupted and disintegrate into pieces and cease to be a unity functioning as a single system, if any uncaused movement is introduced into it."

This perfect causal necessity of CHRYSIPPUS is still the ideal of many philosophers today. Although they no longer think they can *prove* Laplacian determinism, sobered by the indeterminacy of quantum physics, they reserve judgment and call themselves agnostics on determinism.

The disruption and disintegration of the universe predicted by CHRYSIPPUS if atoms were to swerve randomly was in some ways realized by the discovery of the second law of thermodynamics in the mid-19th century. The confirmation of the ancient idea that matter, and chaotic gases in particular, is made of atoms forever swerving, looks in many ways like a universe disintegrating.

Boltzmann's statistical mechanics explained how probabilistic processes would lead to the rise of entropy. Orderly systems would run down into disorder. Information would be lost.

The deep challenge for information philosophy is to explain the emergence and maintenance of so many rich macroscopic information structures when the microscopic world is as utterly chaotic as Chrysippus could have possibly imagined.

About Information Philosophy and Physics

By information we mean a quantity that can be understood mathematically and physically. It corresponds to the common-sense meaning of information, in the sense of communicating or informing. It is like the information stored in books and computers. But it also measures the information in any physical object, like a recipe, blueprint, or production process, as well as the information in biological systems, including the genetic code, the cell structures, and the developmental learning of the phenotype.

> Information is mathematically the opposite of entropy. It is sometimes called negative entropy. The same formula is used for the quantity of entropy or information.
>
> $$S = k\Sigma\, p_n \log p_n.$$
>
> where k is Boltzmann's constant, p_n is the probability of the state n, and the summation is over all states.

It is of the deepest philosophical significance that information is based on the mathematics of probability. If all outcomes were certain, there would be no "surprises" in the universe. Information would be conserved and a universal constant, as some mathematicians mistakenly believe. Information philosophy requires the ontological uncertainty and probabilistic outcomes of modern quantum physics to produce new information.

But at the same time, without the extraordinary stability of quantized information structures over cosmological time scales, life and the universe we know would not be possible. Quantum mechanics reveals the architecture of the universe to be discrete rather than continuous, to be digital rather than analog.

Creation of information structures means that in parts of the universe the local entropy is actually going down. Creation of a low-entropy system is always accompanied by radiation of energy and entropy away from the local structure to distant parts of the universe, into the night sky for example.

From Newton's time to the start of the 19th century, the Laplacian view coincided with the notion of the divine foreknowledge of an omniscient God. On this view, complete, perfect and constant information exists at all times that describes the designed evolution of the universe and of the creatures inhabiting the world.

In this God's-eye view, information is a constant of nature. Some mathematicians today argue that information must be a conserved quantity, like matter and energy.

We represent this picture of constant information in Figure 1-1.

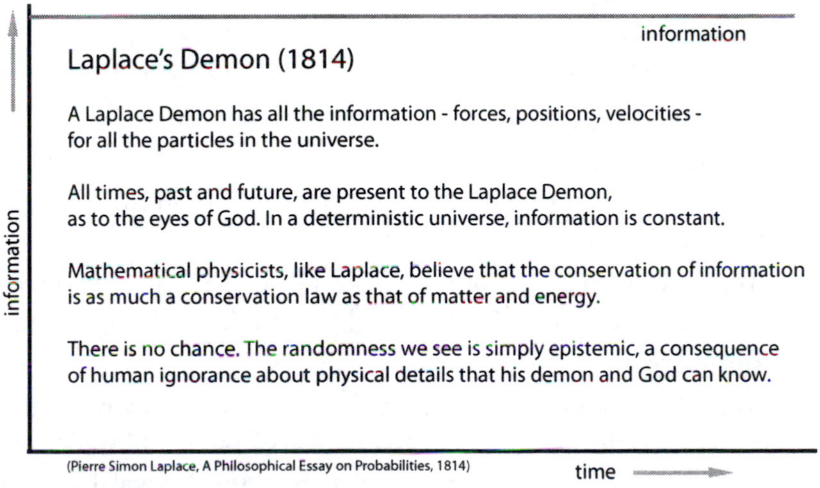

information

Laplace's Demon (1814)

A Laplace Demon has all the information - forces, positions, velocities - for all the particles in the universe.

All times, past and future, are present to the Laplace Demon, as to the eyes of God. In a deterministic universe, information is constant.

Mathematical physicists, like Laplace, believe that the conservation of information is as much a conservation law as that of matter and energy.

There is no chance. The randomness we see is simply epistemic, a consequence of human ignorance about physical details that his demon and God can know.

information

(Pierre Simon Laplace, A Philosophical Essay on Probabilities, 1814)

time

Figure 1-1. For a Laplace demon, information is a constant of nature.

If information were a universal constant, there would be "nothing new under the sun." Every past and future event can in principle be known by the super-intelligent demon of PIERRE SIMON LAPLACE, with its access to such a fixed totality of information.

But midway through the 19th century, Lord Kelvin (WILLIAM THOMSON) realized that the newly discovered second law of thermodynamics required that information could not be constant, but would be destroyed as the entropy (disorder) increased. Hermann Helmholtz described this as the "heat death" of the universe.

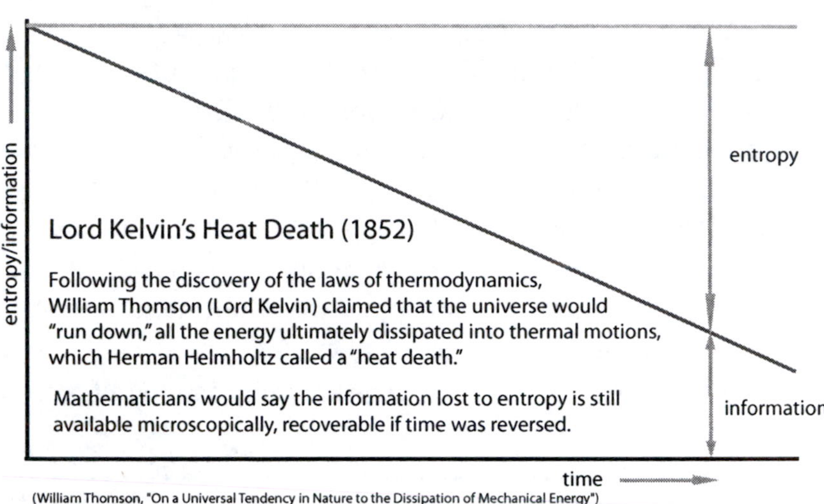

Figure 1-2. The second law requires information to decrease in a closed system.

Mathematicians who are convinced that information is always conserved argue that macroscopic order is disappearing into microscopic order, but the information could in principle be recovered, if time could only be reversed.

This raises the possibility of some connection between the increasing entropy and what Arthur Stanley Eddington called "Time's Arrow." [1]

Kelvin's claim that information must be destroyed when entropy increases would be correct if the universe were a closed system. But in our open and expanding universe, my Harvard colleague David Layzer showed that the maximum possible entropy is increasing faster than the actual entropy. The difference between maximum possible entropy and the current entropy is called negative entropy, opening the possibility for complex and stable information structures to develop.[2]

In Figure 1-3, we see that it is not only entropy that increases in the direction of the arrow of time, but also the information content of the universe.

1 www.informationphilosopher.com/problems/arrow_of_time/

2 Roger Penrose described this as 'standard." Penrose (1989) p. 328-9

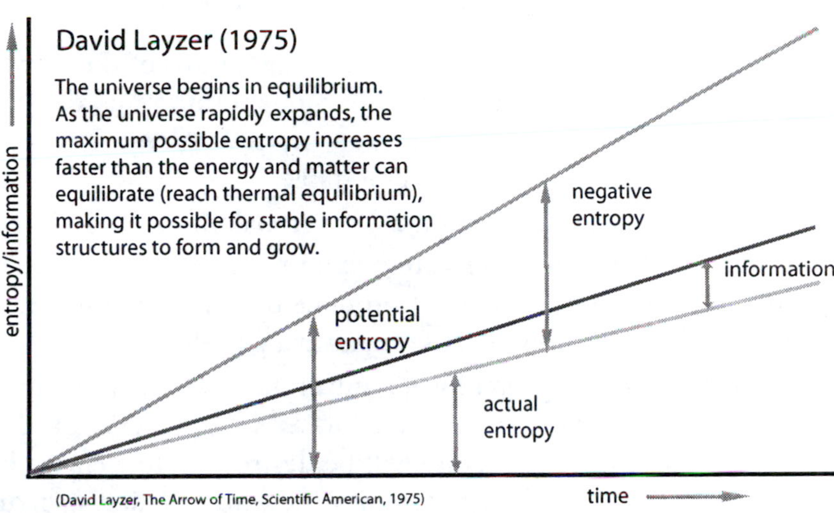

Figure 1-3. Information increases as entropy increases in our universe.

Despite the second law of thermodynamics, stable and lawlike information structures evolved out of the chaos. First, quantum processes formed microscopic particulate matter – quarks, baryons, nuclei, and electrons. Eventually these became atoms,. Later, under the influence of gravitation – macroscopic galaxies, stars, and planets form. Every new information structure reduces the entropy locally, so the second law requires an equal (or generally much greater) amount of entropy to be carried away. Without the expansion of the universe, this would be impossible.

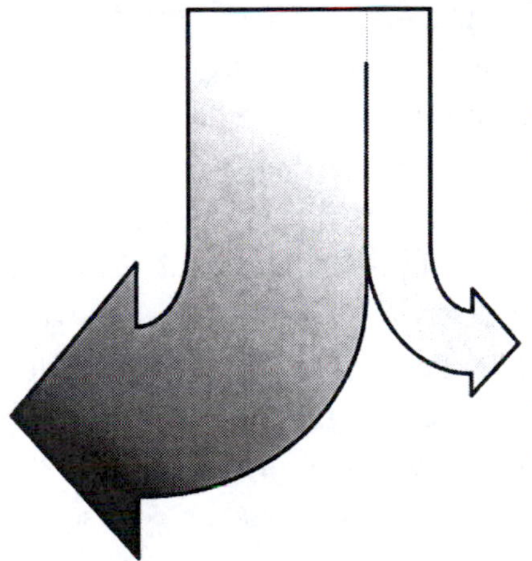

The positive entropy carried away (the big dark arrow on the left) is always greater than and generally orders of magnitude larger than the negative entropy in the created information structure (the smaller light arrow on the right). See Chapter 30 for more details.

Figure 1-4. Entropy/Information Flows

The Two-Step Cosmic Creation Process

Every material object created since the origin of the universe has involved two physical steps, first quantum events that form structures, then thermodynamical energy/entropy flows away from the structures so they can be stable.

The first step is the collapse of a probability-amplitude wave function.[3] Wave-function collapses are usually associated with measurements. Measurements produce new **information**. So the new structure is in some sense "measuring itself."

In the second step, binding energy of the new structure must be radiated, conducted, or convected away, carrying some positive entropy, or the new structure will be destroyed. In a closed box, thermal equilibrium will destroy any new information structure.

These two steps are found in all creative processes, from elementary particles to ideas in our minds.

With the emergence of teleonomic (purposive) information in self-replicating systems, the same two-step core process underlies all biological creation. But in biology some information structures are rejected by purposive natural selection, while others reproduce and maintain their low entropy states.

Finally, with the emergence of self-aware organisms and the creation of extra-biological information, the same process underlies communication, **consciousness**, **free will**, and **creativity**.

By creation we mean the coming into existence of recognizable information structures from a prior chaotic state in which there was no recognizable order or information.

Creation of information structures means that today there is more information or order in the universe than there was at any earlier time. Of course there is also more entropy or disorder, as Layzer's picture (Figure 1-3) and entropy flows (Figure 1-4) shows.

This fact of increasing information describes very well an undetermined universe with an open future that is still creating itself. In this universe, stars are still forming, biological systems are

3 informationphilosopher.com/solutions/experiments/wave-function_collapse.

creating new species, and intelligent human beings are co-creators of the world we live in.

All this creation is the result of the one core creative process. Understanding this process is as close as we are likely to come to understanding the creator of the universe, a still-present divine providence, the cosmic source of everything good and evil.

The creative ideas of individual human beings are a miniscule part of the cosmic information, but they can have enormous impact. And William James has a message we need young people to hear. As momentous as our ideas are, the neuroscientists will never see them in our brain scans.

> "Although such quickening of one idea might be morally and historically momentous, if considered dynamically, it would be an operation amongst those physiological infinitesimals which calculation must forever neglect." [4]

Information and Predictability

The future is now unpredictable for *two* basic reasons.

First, quantum mechanics has shown that some events are not predictable. The world is causal, but not **pre-determined**.

But second, and this is new and philosophically significant, the early universe does not contain the **information** of later times, just as early primates do not contain the information structures for intelligence and verbal communication that humans do, and infants do not contain the knowledge and remembered experience they will have as adults.

This second reason for unpredictability means that complete information or knowledge about our choices does not exist in the human brain/mind until the will has actually made a decision.[5]

In this simple fact lies human freedom.

---

4 James (2007) vol.2, ch.XXVI, p. 576

5 Thus the Frankfurt-style cases of an intervening demon (discussed in Chapter 7) are complete nonsense, as first noted by Robert Kane (1985) *fn*, p. 51

This chapter on the web
informationphilosopher.com/freedom/scandal.html

The Free Will Scandal

JOHN SEARLE says it is a scandal that philosophers have not made more progress on the problem of free will.

> "The persistence of the free will problem in philosophy seems to me something of a **scandal**. After all these centuries of writing about free will, it does not seem to me that we have made very much progress." [1]

Two centuries ago, IMMANUEL KANT called it a scandal that academic philosophers were so out of touch with the common sense of the masses when they doubted the existence of the external world.[2] DAVID HUME had criticized the Theory of Ideas of his fellow British empiricists JOHN LOCKE and GEORGE BERKELEY. If they are right that knowledge is limited to perceptions of sense data, we cannot "know" anything about external objects, even our own bodies. Kant's main change in the second edition of the *Critique of Pure Reason* was an attempted refutation of this idealism. He thought he had a proof of the existence of the external world. Kant thought it a scandal in philosophy that we must accept the existence of things outside of ourselves merely as a belief, with no proof.

> "However innocent idealism may be considered with respect to the essential purposes of metaphysics (without being so in reality), it remains a **scandal** to philosophy, and to human reason in general, that we should have to accept the existence of things outside us (from which after all we derive the whole material for our knowledge, even for that of our inner sense) merely on trust, and have no satisfactory proof with which to counter any opponent who chooses to doubt it." [3]

Kant said "speculative reason" must be investigated

> "to prevent the scandal which metaphysical controversies are sure, sooner or later, to cause even to the masses." [4]

---

1 Searle (2007) p. 37
2 Kant (1962) p. 11
3 Kant (1962) p. 12
4 Kant (1962) p. 11

Martin Heidegger commented on Kant's scandal:

> The "scandal of philosophy" is not that this proof has yet to be given, but that *such proofs are expected and attempted again and again.* [5]

Bertrand Russell said this was an unsatisfactory state,

> "Philosophy, from the earliest times, has made greater claims, and achieved fewer results, than any other branch of learning." [6]

This knowledge scandal is closely related to the free will scandal, in that so many philosophers and scientists have thought that they could *prove* that free will, because of several imagined determinisms, does not exist. Free will is an illusion, they say.

Moritz Schlick calls this scandal a "pseudo-problem,"

> "this pseudo-problem has long since been settled by the efforts of certain sensible persons; and, above all...— with exceptional clarity by Hume. Hence it is really one of the greatest scandals of philosophy that again and again so much paper and printer's ink is devoted to this matter... I shall, of course, say only what others have already said better; consoling myself with the thought that in this way alone can anything be done to put an end at last to that scandal." [7]

This most common proof that free will cannot exist is based on the two-part **standard argument** against free will, which we examine in Chapter 4.

The Standard Argument ***Against*** Free Will

1) If our actions are determined, we are not free.

2) If our actions are directly caused by chance, they are simply random, and we cannot be responsible for them.

Despite more than twenty-three centuries of philosophizing, I believe that the main reason that no progress has been made is

5 Heidegger (1962) p. 249.
6 Russell (196) p. 11.
7 Schlick (2008) Chapter VII, "The Pseudo-Problem of Freedom of the Will"

that most modern thinkers have not moved significantly beyond the second part, the problem of reconciling **indeterminism** and **free will**. They assume that choosing from random **alternative possibilities** makes the choice itself random. This is the mistaken idea that "free" actions are caused directly by a random event.

A Moral Scandal?

But there is a deeper and darker reason that failure to provide a plausible explanation for free will has become a scandal.

Ever since Hume, libertarian philosophers have expressed concerns that determinism implies a lack of moral responsibility and might, like a form of fatalism, even encourage irresponsibility.

In the past few decades, the "logical" standard argument against free will has been used by some philosophers - the hard determinists, illusionists, and impossibilists - to deny the existence of **moral responsibility**.

Others have reacted to these developments with an ancient concern - that people who are told they have no free will may behave less responsibly. Some recent psychological studies have actually confirmed such a laxity in moral behavior..[8]

Despite this concern, several philosophers and psychologists have openly called for our legal and judicial systems to recognize that advances in neuroscience ultimately will show that all human action is causally pre-determined, and that no one should be held morally responsible for their crimes.

One would hope that philosophers who are skeptical about the truth of modern physics, and claim to be agnostic about the truth of determinism or indeterminism, would be more circumspect and cautious about recommending drastic and unjustifiable changes in social policies based on little or no empirical evidence.

Beyond Searle's scandal of little progress made, it is this moral scandal that I hope this book may help to resolve, in part by simply making some modest progress after all this time.

8 Vohs and Schooler (2008)

This chapter on the web
informationphilosopher.com/freedom

Freedom

Freedom is the property of being free from constraints, especially from external constraints on our actions, but also from internal constraints such as physical disabilities or addictions. Political freedoms, such as the right to speak, to assemble, and the limits to government constraints on associations and organizations such as media and religions, are examples of external freedom.

Isaiah Berlin called this kind of freedom "negative" in his essay Two Concepts of Liberty.

> I am normally said to be free to the degree to which no man or body of men interferes with my activity. Political liberty in this sense is simply the area within which a man can act unobstructed by others. If I am prevented by others from doing what I could otherwise do, I am to that degree unfree. [1]

Philosophers call this absence of external and internal constraints "**freedom of action**." But there is another, more philosophical form of liberty that Berlin called "positive freedom."

> I wish to be the instrument of my own, not of other men's, acts of will. I wish to be a subject, not an object; to be moved by reasons, by conscious purposes, which are my own... I wish, above all, to be conscious of myself as a thinking, willing, active being, bearing responsibility for my choices and able to explain them by references to my own ideas and purposes.[2]

This kind of positive liberty raises the ancient question of "freedom of the will." One can be free to act, that is, be free of constraints, but one's will might be **pre-determined** by events in the past and the laws of nature.

Quite apart from whether we are free to act, are we free to will our actions?

This is the question that philosophers have not been able to resolve in twenty-two centuries of philosophical analysis.

---

1 Berlin (1990) p. 122. This is sometimes called "freedom from."
2 Berlin (1990) p. 131. Sometimes called "freedom to."

This book is based on parts of the Freedom section of the website INFORMATION PHILOSOPHER, a critical study of the "problem of free will." (www.informationphilosopher.com/freedom)

Those parts of the Freedom section that could not fit in this book will appear in two forthcoming volumes. *Free Will: The Core Concepts* will include the web pages devoted to over 60 critically important concepts needed to understand the free will debates. *Free Will: The Philosophers and Scientists* will excerpt the I-PHI web pages on 135 philosophers and 65 scientists.

There I have researched the arguments of hundreds of philosophers and scientists on the question of free will, from the original philosophical debates among the ancient Greeks down to the current day. They are presented on my I-PHI web pages, with some source materials in the original languages, for use by students and scholars everywhere, without asking me for permission to quote.

Some readers might want to skip ahead to Chapter 7, the History of the Free Will Problem. There you can try to develop your own ideas on how and why this problem has been thought insoluble, even unintelligible, for over two millennia.

If you don't mind being biased a bit, and would like a little guidance as you try to make more sense of the problem than hundreds of great thinkers have been able to do, I present briefly in this and the next chapter two of my ideas that you may want to study first and have in mind as you read the History chapter.

The First Idea - *against* libertarian free will

The first is a very strong logical argument against libertarian free will that I have found again and again in philosophy since ancient times. I call it the **standard argument** *against* free will.

If you fully master the standard argument, and perhaps even learn to detect its flaws, you will be more likely to recognize it in its various forms, and under a wide variety of names.

I believe that the standard argument was the main stumbling block to a coherent solution of the free will problem long ago.

In the next chapter, I provide examples of the standard argument taken from the work of over thirty philosophers, from CICERO to ROBERT KANE, over twenty-two centuries. I am sure there are others. Perhaps you will come across them in your readings. If so, I would very much like to hear from you about them.

The Second Idea - *for* libertarian free will

The second thing you might want to keep in mind is what looks to me to be, after twenty-two centuries of sophisticated discussion, the most plausible and practical solution to the free-will problem.

Please excuse my hubris to think that *I* have solved a 2200-year old problem, one that has escaped so many great minds. Despite JOHN SEARLE's cry of no progress, I have found steps toward the solution in nearly twenty fine minds. They just failed to convince their contemporaries, and I find that few of them have read their predecessors as carefully as I have. [3]

If you don't want to be aware of my opinions before you begin, just skip ahead to Chapter 4 for more on the **standard argument**.

Almost all philosophers and scientists have a preferred solution to any problem. It very likely biases their work. You almost certainly bring your own views to all your reading and research. If you want to read the free will history unbiased by my views, skip to Chapter 7. If you want a brief introduction to my libertarian free-will model before proceeding, read on.

---

3 If you don't remember the past, you don't deserve to be remembered by the future

Two Requirements for Free Will

Any plausible model for free will must separately attack the two branches of the **standard argument** against **libertarian** free will.

The foremost libertarian, Robert Kane, says that anyone wanting to show that free will is **incompatible** with **determinism** must successfully climb over what he calls "Incompatibilist Mountain." I take the liberty of time-reversing Kane's ascending and descending stages here, for reasons that will become clear later.

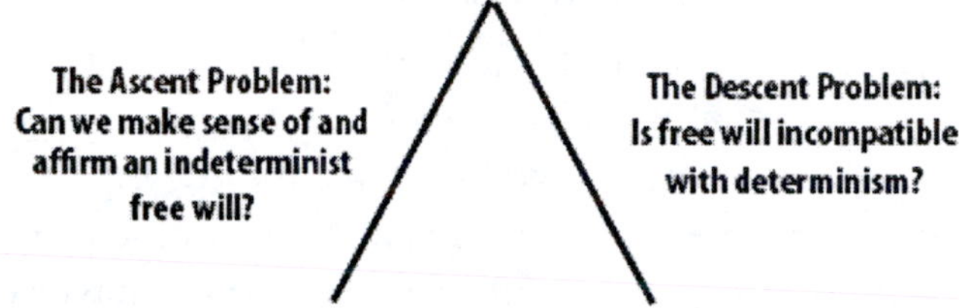

Figure 3-1. Robert Kane's Incompatibilist Mountain (reversed)

I like Kane's division of the one "incompatibilism" problem into two.[4] Although we will see that Kane thinks libertarian free will is focused in a single moment at the end of the decision process, his diagram shows that the upward and downward climbs of his metaphorical mountain deserve separate treatment.

First Requirement

The first, ascent, requirement is for a limited indeterminism. It must provide randomness enough to break the causal chain of determinism. Even more critical, it must be the indeterminism needed to generate creative thoughts and **alternative possibilities** for action. So why and how must it be limited? Because the indeterminism must not destroy our **moral responsibility**, by making our actions random.

So to make sense of indeterminist free will as we ascend the reversed incompatibilist mountain, we must demand that the indeterministic **alternative possibilities** are not normally the **direct cause of our actions**.

4 But I don't like the term "incompatibilism," as explained on p. 60 in Chapter 6. Why define human freedom by saying that it conflicts with something that does not exist, except as a philosophical ideal?

Second Requirement

The second, descent, requirement is to have enough determinism to say that our actions are "determined" by our character, our values, our motives, and feelings. Again, how and why is this determinism limited? It must not be so much that our actions are **pre-determined** from well before we began deliberation, or even from before we were born.[5]

So for our descent of Incompatibilist Mountain, we can say that free will is not incompatible with a limited determinism or **determination**, but it is definitely incompatible with pre-determinism.

Our deliberations, both evaluations and selections, are "adequately" determined. We can be responsible for choices that are "up to us," choices not determined from before deliberations.

Hobart's Determination

R. E. Hobart (the pseudonym of Dickinson Miller, the student and colleague of William James) is often misquoted as requiring **determinism**. He only advocated **determination**.

Hobart did not deny **chance** in his famous *Mind* article of 1934, entitled "Free Will as Involving Determination, and Inconceivable Without It." (It's my second requirement.)

Philippa Foot added to the misquote confusion in the title and in the footnotes for her 1957 *Philosophical Review* article, "Free Will as Involving Determinism." Most philosophers continue to misquote this important title.

Determinist and compatibilist philosophers, eager to support their unsupportable claims of a deterministic world, have been misquoting Hobart ever since, showing me that they do not always read the titles of their sources, never mind the original articles. If they did, they would be surprised to find that neither Hobart nor Foot was a determinist.

---

5 As claimed by the incompatibilist Peter van Inwagen's Consequence Argument and by the impossibilist Galen Strawson's Basic Argument.

Hobart on Indeterminism

Hobart was nervous about indeterminism. He explicitly does not endorse strict logical or physical determinism, and he explicitly does endorse the existence of **alternative possibilities**, which he says may depend on absolute chance. Remember that Hobart is writing about six years after the discovery of quantum indeterminacy, and he also refers back to the ancient philosopher Epicurus' "swerve" of the atoms.

> "I am not maintaining that determinism is true...it is not here affirmed that there are no small exceptions, no slight undetermined swervings, no ingredient of absolute chance." [6]

> "We say,' I can will this or I can will that, whichever I choose '. Two courses of action present themselves to my mind. I think of their consequences, I look on this picture and on that, one of them commends itself more than the other, and I will an act that brings it about. I knew that I could choose either. That means that I had the power to choose either." [7]

Here Hobart seems to agree with his mentor and colleague William James that there are ambiguous futures. And note that Hobart, like James and using his phrase, argues that courses of action "present themselves." Our thoughts appear to "come to us" - and the will's power to choose brings the act about - our actions "come from us."

Despite his moderate position on chance, Hobart finds fault with the indeterminist's position. He gives the typical overstatement by a determinist critic, that any chance will be the direct cause of our actions, which would clearly be a loss of freedom and responsibility

> "Indeterminism maintains that we need not be impelled to action by our wishes, that our active will need not be determined by them. Motives "incline without necessitating". We choose amongst the ideas of action before us, but need not choose solely according to the attraction of desire, in however wide a sense

6 Hobart (1934) p. 2

7 Hobart (1934) p. 8

> that word is used. Our inmost self may rise up in its autonomy and moral dignity, independently of motives, and register its sovereign decree.
>
> "Now, in so far as this "interposition of the self" is undetermined, the act is not its act, it does not issue from any concrete continuing self; it is born at the moment, of nothing, hence it expresses no quality; it bursts into being from no source". [8]

Hobart is clearly uncomfortable with raw indeterminism. He says chance would produce "freakish" results if it were directly to cause our actions. He is right.

> "In proportion as an act of volition starts of itself without cause it is exactly, so far as the freedom of the individual is concerned, as if it had been thrown into his mind from without — "suggested" to him — by a freakish demon. It is exactly like it in this respect, that in neither case does the volition arise from what the man is, cares for or feels allegiance to; it does not come out of him. In proportion as it is undetermined, it is just as if his legs should suddenly spring up and carry him off where he did not prefer to go. Far from constituting freedom, that would mean, in the exact measure in which it took place, the loss of freedom". [9]

It is very likely that Hobart has William James in mind as "the indeterminist." If so, despite knowing James very well, he is mistaken about James' position. James would not have denied that our will is an act of determination, consistent with, and in some sense "caused by" our character and values, our habits, and our current feelings and desires. James simply wanted chance to provide a break in the causal chain of strict determinism and alternative possibilities for our actions.

8 Hobart (1934) p. 6
9 Hobart (1934) p. 7

The Standard Argument *Against* Free Will

This chapter on the web
informationphilosopher.com/freedom/standard_argument.html

The Standard Argument *Against* Free Will

The **standard argument** has two parts.

1) If determinism is the case, the will is not free.
We call this the **Determinism Objection**.

2) If indeterminism and real chance exist, our will would not be in our control. We could not be responsible for our actions if they are random.
We call this the **Randomness Objection**.

Together, these objections can be combined as a single **Responsibility Objection**, namely that no Free Will model has yet provided us an intelligible account of the agent control needed for **moral responsibility**.

Both parts are logically and practically flawed, partly from abuse of language that led some 20th-century philosophers to call free will a "pseudo-problem," and partly from claims to knowledge that are based on faulty evidence (Kant's Scandal). We shall consider the evidence for each part and try to expose errors in the reasoning.

If you would like to examine the arguments of over thirty philosophers from ancient times to the present before reading my critical comments, skip to the examples starting on page 30. Later you can return to compare your conclusions to mine on the next two pages.

Part One - The Determinism Objection

Determinism is true. All events are caused by the fixed past and the laws of nature. All our actions are therefore pre-determined. There is no free will or moral responsibility.

Let's consider the evidence and the possible errors...

- Determinism is not "true." If one physical thing is "true," it is indeterminism.
- Physical determinism is not "true" because physics is empirical, not logical. And the empirical evidence has never justified the assumption of strict determinism.
- Quantum mechanical indeterminism is extremely well established. While also not logically "true," the evidence for quantum mechanics is better established than any other physical theory, including classical mechanics and determinism.
- Just because some events, like the motions of the planets, are adequately determined does not justify the widespread belief in an absolute universal determinism.
- Some events are unpredictable from prior events. They are ***causa sui***, starting new causal chains.
- The "chain" of events behind a particular cause may go back to inherited characteristics before we were born, others may go back to environmental and educational factors, but some may go back to uncaused events in our minds during our deliberations. Decisions have many contributing causes.
- We say correctly that our actions are "determined" by our (adequately determined) will. This **determination** does not imply universal strict determinism (as R. E. Hobart and Philippa Foot have shown).
- Our will chooses among free alternative possibilities, at least some of which are creative and unpredictable.
- The will itself is indeed not "free" (in the sense of uncaused), but we are free.

Part Two - The Randomness Objection

Chance exists. If our actions are caused by chance, we lack control. We can not call that free will, because we could not be held morally responsible for random actions.

Errors and evidence...

- Randomness in some microscopic quantum events is indeed chance.
- But microscopic chance does little to affect adequate macroscopic determinism.
- Just because some events are undetermined and involve chance does not justify the widespread fear that all events are undetermined and random.
- Chance only generates alternative possibilities for thought and action. It is not the direct cause of actions.
- We are free, in control, and morally responsible for our choices and actions, when they are adequately determined, in the normal cases of a two-stage decision process.
- But there are some cases where the two-stage model does not result in a self-determined decision. The alternative possibilities do not narrow down to a single possibility.
- In this case, if the remaining possibilities are simple everyday practical decisions with no moral or prudential significance, the agent can essentially "flip a coin" and still take responsibility for the choice.
- However, when the decision has important moral or prudential implications, and the agent must put effort into resolving the decision process, it is not appropriate to describe such choices as "flipping a coin." Robert Kane notes that the effort that goes into making these "torn" decisions is what deserves the credit for the decision. The underlying indeterminism may tip the scales away from some possible actions, making them fail, but the main cause of the action that succeeds should be seen as a result of the agent's effort.

Examples of the Standard Argument

Collected here are a few dozen examples of the standard argument from antiquity to the present day. You are invited to examine them for the appearance of the two objections.

Cicero's Version

> "Epicurus saw that if the atoms travelled downwards by their own weight; we should have no freedom of the will [*nihil fore in nostra potestate*], since the motion of the atoms would be determined by necessity. He therefore invented a device to escape from determinism (the point had apparently escaped the notice of Democritus): he said that the atom while travelling vertically downward by the force of gravity makes a very slight swerve to one side. (70) This defence discredits him more than if he had had to abandon his original position." [1]

Notice that Cicero's argument already appears in the form of a logical proposition, one or the other of determinism or randomness must be true. He claims that Epicurus must be denying such logical disjunctions. He and Aristotle did, for future events.

> (70) XXV. "He does the same in his battle with the logicians. Their accepted doctrine is that in every disjunctive proposition of the form' so-and-so either is or is not,' one of the two alternatives must be true. Epicurus took alarm; if such a proposition as 'Epicurus either will or will not be alive to-morrow' were granted, one or other alternative would be necessary. Accordingly he denied the necessity of a disjunctive proposition altogether. Now what could be stupider than that?" [2]

John Fiske's Version

> "Volitions are either caused or they are not. If they are not caused, an inexorable logic brings us to the absurdities just mentioned. If they are caused, the free-will doctrine is annihilated." [3]

1 Cicero (1951) Book I, sect. XXV, ¶¶ 69-70, Loeb Classical Library, v. 40, p. 67

2 *ibid.*

3 Outline of Cosmic Philosophy, part. H. Chap.xvii, cited in James (2007) p. 577

Max Planck's Version

"Let us ask for a moment whether the human will is free or whether it is determined in a strictly causal way. These two alternatives seem definitely to exclude one another. And as the former has obviously to be answered in the affirmative, so the assumption of a law of strict causality operating in the universe seems to be reduced to an absurdity in at least this one instance. In other words, if we assume the law of strict dynamic causality as existing throughout the universe, how can we logically exclude the human will from its operation?... "Recent developments in physical science [viz., quantum indeterminacy] have come into play here, and the freedom of the human will has been put forward as offering logical grounds for the acceptance of only a statistical causality operative in the physical universe. As I have already stated on other occasions, I do not at all agree with this attitude. If we should accept it, then the logical result would be to reduce the human will to an organ which would be subject to the sway of mere blind chance." [4]

Arthur Stanley Eddington's Version

"There is no half-way house between random and correlated behavior. Either the behavior is wholly a matter of chance, in which case the precise behavior within the Heisenberg limits of uncertainty depends on chance and not volition. Or it is not wholly a matter of chance, in which case the Heisenberg limits... are irrelevant." [5]

L. Susan Stebbing's Version

"If previous physical events completely determine all the movements of my body, then the movements of my pen are also completely determined by previous physical events....But if the movements of my pen are completely determined by previous physical events, how can it be held that my mental processes have anything to do with the movements made by my

4 Planck (1981) p. 101-105
5 Eddington (1939) p. 182.

pen....I do not think that it can reasonably be maintained that physical indeterminism is capable of affording any help in this problem." [6]

NORBERT WIENER's Version

Wiener sees no advantage in quantum mechanical indeterminism.

> "Tyche [chance] is as relentless a mistress as Ananke [necessity]." [7]

A. J. AYER's Version

Ayer is extremely clear that the "truth" of determinism cannot be proved. He says that the determinist's

> "belief that all human actions are subservient to causal laws still remains to be justified. If, indeed, it is necessary that every event should have a cause, then the rule must apply to human behaviour as much as to anything else. But why should it be supposed that every event must have a cause? The contrary is not unthinkable. Nor is the law of universal causation a necessary presupposition of scientific thought. But nevertheless he states the standard argument succinctly: But now we must ask how it is that I come to make my choice. Either it is an accident that I choose to act as I do or it is not. If it is an accident, then it is merely a matter of chance that I did not choose otherwise; and if it is merely a matter of chance that I did not choose otherwise, it is surely irrational to hold me morally responsible for choosing as I did. But if it is not an accident that I choose to do one thing rather than another, then presumably there is some causal explanation of my choice: and in that case we are led back to determinism." [8]

J. J. C. SMART's Version

Smart states two definitions - one for determinism and one for randomness and declares them to be exhaustive of all possibilities.

---

6 Stebbing (1958) pp. 216-7
7 Wiener (1965) p. 49.
8 Ayer (1954) p. 275.

"Dl. I shall state the view that there is 'unbroken causal continuity' in the universe as follows. It is in principle possible to make a sufficiently precise determination of the state of a sufficiently wide region of the universe at time to, and sufficient laws of nature are in principle ascertainable to enable a superhuman calculator to be able to predict any event occurring within that region at an already given time t.

"D2. I shall define the view that 'pure chance' reigns to some extent within the universe as follows. There are some events that even a superhuman calculator could not predict, however precise his knowledge of however wide a region of the universe at some previous time.

"For the believer in free will holds that no theory of a deterministic sort or of a pure chance sort will apply to everything in the universe: he must therefore envisage a theory of a type which is neither deterministic nor indeterministic in the senses of these words which I have specified by the two definitions D1 and D2; and I shall argue that no such theory is possible." [9]

P. F. Strawson's Version

"...the notions of moral guilt, of blame, of moral responsibility are inherently confused and that we can see this to be so if we consider the consequences either of the truth of determinism or of its falsity. The holders of this opinion agree with the pessimists that these notions lack application if determinism is true, and add simply that they also lack it if determinism is false." [10]

Roderick Chisholm's Version

"The metaphysical problem of human freedom might be summarized in the following way: "Human beings are responsible agents; but this fact appears to conflict with a deterministic view of human action (the view that every event that is involved in an act is caused by some other event); and it also appears to conflict with an indeterministic view of human action (the

9 Smart (1961) p. 294.
10 Strawson (1962) p. 1.

> view that the act, or some event that is essential to the act, is not caused at all)." To solve the problem, I believe, we must make somewhat far-reaching assumptions about the self of the agent — about the man who performs the act." [11]

Richard Taylor's Version

Here Taylor clearly states what his student Peter van Inwagen made famous as the Consequence Argument.

> "If determinism is true, as the theory of soft determinism holds it to be, all those inner states which cause my body to behave in what ever ways it behaves must arise from circumstances that existed before I was born; for the chain of causes and effects is infinite, and none could have been the least different, given those that preceded. Both determinism and simple indeterminism are loaded with difficulties, and no one who has thought much on them can affirm either of them without some embarrassment. Simple indeterminism has nothing whatever to be said for it, except that it appears to remove the grossest difficulties of determinism, only, however, to imply perfect absurdities of its own."

Taylor sees the asymmetry in favor of determinism over indeterminism as a popular belief.

> "Determinism, on the other hand, is at least initially plausible. Men seem to have a natural inclination to believe in it; it is, indeed, almost required for the very exercise of practical intelligence. And beyond this, our experience appears always to confirm it, so long as we are dealing with everyday facts of common experience, as distinguished from the esoteric researches of theoretical physics. But determinism, as applied to human behavior, has implications which few men can casually accept, and they appear to be implications which no modification of the theory can efface." [12]

David Wiggins' Version

> "If it were false that every event and every action were causally determined then the causally undetermined events and actions would surely, to that extent, be simply random. So the argument

11 Chisholm (1964), in Lehrer (1966) p. 11.

12 Taylor (1963) p. 46.

> goes. That a man could have done x would mean no more than it might have turned out that way - at random."

Wiggins also prefers determinism to indeterminism, to ensure that actions are caused by character.

> "It will be asked if it makes any better sense to hold the man responsible for actions which happen at random that for ones which arise from his character. Surely then, if it doesn't, we ought to prefer that our actions be caused?" [13]

Thomas Nagel's Version

> "Once we see an aspect of what we or someone else does as something that happens, we lose our grip on the idea that it has been done and that we can judge the doer and not just the happening. This explains why the absence of determinism is no more hospitable to the concept of agency than is its presence — a point that has been noticed often. Either way the act is viewed externally, as part of the course of events." [14]

Robert Nozick's Version

> "Without free will, we seem diminished, merely the playthings of external forces. How, then, can we maintain an exalted view of ourselves? Determinism seems to undercut human dignity, it seems to undermine our value. Some would deny what this question accepts as given, and save free will by denying determinism of (some) actions. Yet if an uncaused action is a random happening, then this no more comports with human value than does determinism. Random acts and caused acts alike seem to leave us not as the valuable originators of action but as an arena, a place where things happen, whether through earlier causes or spontaneously." [15]

Peter van Inwagen's Version

> "Here is an argument that I think is obvious (I don't mean it's obviously right; I mean it's one that should occur pretty quickly

13 Wiggins (1973) p. 50.
14 Nagel (1979) p. 37.
15 Nozick (1981) pp. 291-2

to any philosopher who asked himself what arguments could be found to support incompatibilism):

> "If determinism is true, then our acts are the consequences of the laws of nature and events in the remote past. But it is not up to us what went on before we were born, and neither is it up to us what the laws of nature are. Therefore, the consequences of these things (including our present acts) are not up to us.

"I shall call this argument the Consequence Argument." [16]

Note that van Inwagen's Consequence Argument includes only the Determinist Objection, just one part of the standard argument. He also presented the Randomness Objection, and called it the Mind Argument. (Not referring to the human mind, but to the journal *Mind*, where many arguments of this type can be found, notably the 1934 article of R. E. Hobart.)

> "[It] proceeds by identifying indeterminism with chance and by arguing that an act that occurs by chance, if an event that occurs by chance can be called an act, cannot be under the control of its alleged agent and hence cannot have been performed freely. Proponents of [this argument] conclude, therefore, that free will is not only compatible with determinism but entails determinism." [17]

Van Inwagen dramatized his understanding of the indeterministic brain events needed for agent causation by imagining God "replaying" a situation to create exactly the same circumstances and then arguing that decisions would reflect the indeterministic probabilities.

> "If God caused Marie's decision to be replayed a very large number of times, sometimes (in thirty percent of the replays, let us say) Marie would have agent-caused the crucial brain event and sometimes (in seventy percent of the replays, let us say) she would not have... I conclude that even if an episode of agent causation is among the causal antecedents of every voluntary human action, these episodes do nothing to undermine the prima facie impossibility of an undetermined free act." [18]

---

16 Van Inwagen (1983) p. 16.

17 *ibid.*

18 Van Inwagen (2004) p. 227.

John Searle's Version

Searle argues that individual particles have statistically predictable paths.

> "As far as human freedom is concerned, it doesn't matter whether physics is deterministic, as Newtonian physics was, or whether it allows for an indeterminacy at the level of particle physics, as contemporary quantum mechanics does. Indeterminism at the level of particles in physics is really no support at all to any doctrine of the freedom of the will; because first, the statistical indeterminacy at the level of particles does not show any indeterminacy at the level of the objects that matter to us – human bodies, for example. And secondly, even if there is an element of indeterminacy in the behaviour of physical particles – even if they are only statistically predictable – still, that by itself gives no scope for human freedom of the will; because it doesn't follow from the fact that particles are only statistically determined that the human mind can force the statistically-determined particles to swerve from their paths. Indeterminism is no evidence that there is or could be some mental energy of human freedom that can move molecules in directions that they were not otherwise going to move. So it really does look as if everything we know about physics forces us to some form of denial of human freedom." [19]

Galen Strawson's Version

Strawson notes the argument is familiar and cites Henry Sidgwick's 1874 *Methods of Ethics*. Actually Sidgwick, who held the 19th-century view that freedom is metaphysical, was a firm determinist and only cites the Determinist Objection to free will.

> "It is a compelling objection. Surely we cannot be free agents, in the ordinary, strong, true-responsibility-entailing sense, if determinism is true and we and our actions are ultimately wholly determined by "causes anterior to [our] personal existence"* And surely we can no more be free if determinism is false and it is, ultimately, either wholly or partly a matter of chance or random outcome that we and our actions are as they are?

19 Searle (1984) pp. 86-7

* H. Sidgwick, *The Methods of Ethics*, p. 66. This familiar objection to the claim that we can be truly responsible agents is of course disputed (and indeed scorned) by compatibilists, but it is entirely sufficient for establishing the structure of the present discussion. Cf. also An Essay on Free Will, by P. van Inwagen." [20]

Colin McGinn's Version

"The argument is exceedingly familiar, and runs as follows. Either determinism is true or it is not. If it is true, then all our chosen actions are uniquely necessitated by prior states of the world, just like every other event. But then it cannot be the case that we could have acted otherwise, since this would require a possibility determinism rules out. Once the initial conditions are set and the laws fixed, causality excludes genuine freedom. On the other hand, if indeterminism is true, then, though things could have happened otherwise, it is not the case that we could have chosen otherwise, since a merely random event is no kind of free choice. That some events occur causelessly, or are not subject to law, or only to probabilistic law, is not sufficient for those events to be free choices. Thus one horn of the dilemma represents choices as predetermined happenings in a predictable causal sequence, while the other construes them as inexplicable lurches to which the universe is randomly prone. Neither alternative supplies what the notion of free will requires, and no other alternative suggests itself. Therefore freedom is not possible in any kind of possible world. The concept contains the seeds of its own destruction." [21]

Paul Russell's Version

"...the well-known dilemma of determinism. One horn of this dilemma is the argument that if an action was caused or necessitated, then it could not have been done freely, and hence the agent is not responsible for it. The other horn is the argument that if the action was not caused, then it is inexplicable and random, and thus it cannot be attributed to the agent, and

20 Strawson, G. (1986) p. 25
21 McGinn (1995) p. 80.

> hence, again, the agent cannot be responsible for it. In other words, if our actions are caused, then we cannot he responsible for them; if they are not caused, we cannot be responsible for them. Whether we affirm or deny necessity and determinism, it is impossible to make any coherent sense of moral freedom and responsibility." [22]

Derk Pereboom's Version

Pereboom focuses on the Randomness and Responsibility Objections

> "Let us now consider the libertarians, who claim that we have a capacity for indeterministically free action, and that we are thereby morally responsible. According to one libertarian view, what makes actions free is just their being constituted (partially) of indeterministic natural events. Lucretius, for example, maintains that actions are free just in virtue of being made up partially of random swerves in the downward paths of atoms. These swerves, and the actions they underlie, are random (at least) in the sense that they are not determined by any prior state of the universe. If quantum theory is true, the position and momentum of micro-particles exhibit randomness in this same sense, and natural indeterminacy of this sort might also be conceived as the metaphysical foundation of indeterministically free action. But natural indeterminacies of these types cannot, by themselves, account for freedom of the sort required for moral responsibility. As has often been pointed out, such random physical events are no more within our control than are causally determined physical events, and thus, we can no more be morally responsible for them than, in the indeterminist opinion, we can be for events that are causally determined." [23]

Steven Pinker's One-sentence Version

> "a random event does not fit the concept of free will any more than a lawful one does, and could not serve as the long-sought locus of moral responsibility." [24]

---

22 Russell, P (1995) p. 14.
23 Pereboom (1997) p. 252.
24 Pinker (1997) p. 54.

Ishtiyaque Haji's Version

"Among the grandest of philosophical puzzles is a riddle about moral responsibility. Almost all of us believe that each one of us is, has been, or will be responsible for at least some of our behavior. But how can this be so if determinism is true and all our thoughts, decisions, choices, and actions are simply droplets in a river of deterministic events that began its flow long, long before we were ever born? The specter of determinism, as it were, devours agents, for if determinism is true, then arguably we never initiate or control our actions; there is no driver in the driver's seat; we are simply one transitional link in an extended deterministic chain originating long before our time. The puzzle is tantalizingly gripping and ever so perplexing — because even if determinism is false, responsibility seems impossible: how can we be morally accountable for behavior that issues from an "actional pathway" in which there is an indeterministic break? Such a break might free us from domination or regulation by the past, but how can it possibly help to ensure that the reins of control are now in our hands?" [25]

Bernard Berofsky's Version

"Basically, the compatibilists charged the opposition with two confusions. Causation, which is not freedom undermining even in its deterministic forms, is confused with compulsion or coercion, which, of course, is freedom-undermining. A physical barrier or even an internal compulsion or addiction can be an impediment to action; but when one acts simply because one wants to, one is not being impeded from acting otherwise. Hence, one is expressing one's freedom by doing what one wants. Second, although determinism entails that all human behavior is subsumable under universal law, freedom is not thereby threatened, for the sorts of laws involved are merely descriptive (natural, scientific), not prescriptive, like the laws of a legislative body. They just describe the way in which people behave; they do not force or constrain adherence. Finally, the compatibilists argued that indeterminism would not be more desirable

25 Haji (1998) p. vii.

since, under indeterminism, behavior is random and not under the control of the agent, a situation actually antithetical to freedom." [26]

Owen Flanagan's Version

"Free actions, if there are any, are not deterministically caused nor are they caused by random processes of the sort countenanced by quantum physicists or complexity theorists. Free actions need to be caused by me, in a nondetermined and nonrandom manner." [27]

Randolph Clarke's Version

"Accounts of free will purport to tell us what is required if we are to be free agents, individuals who, at least sometimes when we act, act freely. Libertarian accounts, of course, include a requirement of indeterminism of one sort or another somewhere in the processes leading to free actions. But while proponents of such views take determinism to preclude free will, indeterminism is widely held to be no more hospitable. An undetermined action, It is said would be random or arbitrary. It could not be rational or rationally explicable. The agent would lack control over her behavior. At best, indeterminism in the processes leading to our actions would be superfluous, adding nothing of value even if it did not detract from what we want." [28]

"If the truth of determinism would preclude free will, it is far from obvious how indeterminism would help." [29]

Mark Balaguer's Version

"Any event that's undetermined is uncaused and, hence, accidental. That is, it just happens; i.e., happens randomly. Thus, if our decisions are undetermined, then they are random, and so they couldn't possibly be "appropriately non-random". Or to put the point the other way around, if our decisions are

26 Berofsky, "Ifs, Cans, and Free Will," in Kane (2002) p. 182.
27 Flanagan (2003) p.135
28 Clarke (2003) p. xiii.
29 Clarke, Incompatibilist (Nondeterministic) Theories of Free Will. Stanford Encyclopedia of Philosophy, retrieved September 2008

> appropriately non-random, then they are authored and controlled by us; that is, we determine what we choose and what we don't choose, presumably for rational reasons. Thus, if our decisions are appropriately non-random, then they couldn't possibly be undetermined. Therefore, libertarianism is simply incoherent: it is not possible for a decision to be undetermined and appropriately non-random at the same time." [30]

Later, Balaguer reduces his argument to J.J.C.Smart's exhaustive determinism or indeterminism. He calls it "D-or-R-ism."

> "Determined-or-Randomism (D-or-R-ism): None of our decisions is both undetermined and appropriately nonrandom; that is, all of our decisions are either (i) causally determined by prior events or (ii) random in the sense that they're not appropriately nonrandom." [31]

Thomas Pink's Version

> "There are but these two alternatives. Either an action is causally determined. Or, to the extent that it is causally undetermined, its occurrence depends on chance. But chance alone does not constitute freedom. On its own, chance comes to nothing more than randomness. And one thing does seem to be clear. Randomness, the operation of mere chance, clearly excludes control." [32]

Peter Lipton's Version

> "First, everything that happens in the world is either determined or not. Second, if everything is determined, there is no free will. For then every action would be fixed by earlier events, indeed events that took place before the actor was born. Third, if on the other hand not everything is determined, then there is no free will either. For in this case any given action is either determined, which is no good, or undetermined. But if what you do is undetermined then you are not controlling it, so it is not an exercise of free will. Finally, we have the conclusion: there is no free will." [33]

30 Balaguer (2004) p. 380.
31 Balaguer (2009) p. 8.
32 Pink (2004) p. 16.
33 Lipton (2004) p. 89.

John Martin Fischer's Version

Fischer mistakenly attributes this dilemma to William James's *Dilemma of Determinism*, which was actually a dilemma about regret in a deterministic world.

> "Either causal determinism is true, or it is not. If it is true, then we would lack freedom (in the alternative-possibilities and source senses). If it is false, then we would lack freedom in that we would not select the path into the future — we would not be the source of our behavior. Indeterminism appears to entail that it is not the agent who is the locus of control." [34]

Joshua Greene and Jonathan Cohen's Version

> "There are three standard responses to the problem of free will. The first, known as 'hard determinism', accepts the incompatibility of free will and determinism ('incompatibilism'), and asserts determinism, thus rejecting free will. The second response is libertarianism (again, no relation to the political philosophy), which accepts incompatibilism, but denies that determinism is true. This may seem like a promising approach. After all, has not modern physics shown us that the universe is indeterministic? The problem here is that the sort of indeterminism afforded by modern physics is not the sort the libertarian needs or desires. If it turns out that your ordering soup is completely determined by the laws of physics, the state of the universe 10,000 years ago, and the outcomes of myriad subatomic coin flips, your appetizer is no more freely chosen than before. Indeed, it is randomly chosen, which is no help to the libertarian." [35]

Kadri Vihvelin's Version

> "Either determinism is true or it's not. If determinism is true, then my choices are ultimately caused by events and conditions outside my control, so I am not their first cause and therefore...I am neither free nor responsible. If determinism is false, then something that happens inside me (something that I call "my choice" or "my decision") might be the first event in a causal chain leading to a sequence of body movements that I call "my

34 Fischer (2005) p. xxix.
35 Greene and Cohen (2004) p. 1776.

> action". But since this event is not causally determined, whether or not it happens is a matter of chance or luck. Whether or not it happens has nothing to do with me; it is not under my control any more than an involuntary knee jerk is under my control. Therefore, if determinism is false, I am not the first cause or ultimate source of my choices and...I am neither free nor responsible." [36]

Robert Kane's Ascent and Descent Version

Kane offers what may be the most attractive version of the standard argument against free will, with a memorable diagram. He describes the usual determinism and randomness objections (the two horns of the Libertarian Dilemma) as the ascent and descent of what he calls "Incompatibilism Mountain."

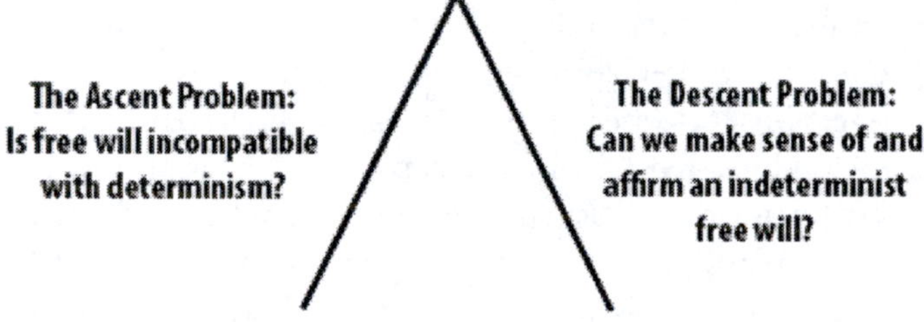

Figure 4-1. Kane's Incompatibilist Mountain.

The ascent problem is to show free will is incompatible with determinism. The descent problem is to show that free will is compatible with indeterminism.

Kane says that if free will is not compatible with **determinism,** it does not seem to be compatible with **indeterminism** either.

> "Let us call this the 'Libertarian Dilemma.' Events that are undetermined, such as quantum jumps in atoms, happen merely by chance. So if free actions must be undetermined, as libertarians claim, it seems that they too would happen by chance. But how can chance events be free and responsible actions? To solve the Libertarian Dilemma, libertarians must not only show that free will is incompatible with determinism, they must also show how free will can be compatible with indeterminism." [37]

36 Vihvelin (2007) Arguments for Incompatibilism. Stanford Encyclopedia of Philosophy, retrieved March 2011.

37 Kane (2005) p. 34.

An Important Asymmetry

Note that the compatibilism of free will with determinism has always been a great deal easier to accept than compatibilism with indeterminism.[38]

"Agnostics" on the truth of determinism and indeterminism implicitly equate the two difficulties, whereas there is a great asymmetry between the two parts of the standard argument.

Indeterminism (non-rational chance) is much more difficult to reconcile with freedom than is (causal and rational) determinism.

Most philosophers are comfortable with the idea that their actions are determined by their reasons and motives, their character and values, and their feelings and desires. As they should be.

Thus it was relatively easy for David Hume to reconcile freedom with determinism by defining freedom as "freedom from" coercions, primarily external forces but also internal constraints.

But this **freedom of action** is not what libertarians think is the essential freedom from **pre-determinism** needed to make us the authors of our own lives.

Two-stage models for free will (see Chapter 12) accomplish the more difficult reconciliation of free will with indeterminism.

Thus where Hume's freedom of action is sometimes called "compatibilist free will," we can say that a two-stage model gives us a more **comprehensive compatibilism**, a free will that is compatible both with some (limited) determinism and with some (limited) indeterminism. See Chapter 28.

38 As Richard Taylor indicated, p. 34 above.

What's Wrong with the Standard Argument?

The most straightforward way to attack the standard argument is to see that the three objections - determinism, randomness, and responsibility - really need to become three requirements for free will. I will discuss these requirements in the next chapter. But to conclude our examples of the standard argument, let's consider some of the ways that philosophers have gone wrong in their uses of the standard argument against free will

How Determinists and Compatibilists Go Wrong

Determinists and Compatibilists go wrong when they mistakenly assume that any chance or indeterminism will lead directly to random actions for which we cannot be morally responsible.

Although they are often metaphysical determinists, they lack confidence in the personal determination of the will, which we see is provided by the adequate physical determinism of our macroscopic minds. And as William James said, they have an "antipathy to chance."

Our **adequately determined** will gives us adequate control of microscopic chaos and chance. Just as Chrysippus thought the universe would fall apart if a single uncaused event were to occur,[39] some modern philosophers are equally frightened by the idea of objective chance, especially quantum indeterminacy.

Some of the compatibilists' fears of randomness are quite funny.

> "Indeterminism does not confer freedom on us: I would feel that my freedom was impaired if I thought that a quantum mechanical trigger in my brain might cause me to leap into the garden and eat a slug." (J. J. C. Smart) [40]

> "For the simplest actions could not be performed in an indeterministic universe. If I decide, say, to eat a piece of fish, I cannot do so if the fish is liable to turn into a stone or to disintegrate in mid-air or to behave in any other utterly unpredictable manner." (P.H.Nowell-Smith) [41]

39 See p. 7.
40 Smart (2003) p. 63.
41 Nowell-Smith (1948) p. 47.

How Libertarians Go Wrong

Libertarians go wrong when they fear that "determination" of the will by an agent's character, values, motives, and desires is somehow equivalent to "**determinism**," in the sense of **pre-determined** before the agent began deliberations, perhaps even back before the agent was born, as Richard Taylor and Peter van Inwagen have speculated.

Some critics of libertarianism suspect that libertarians also go wrong when they try to keep some "freedom" (i.e., indeterminism) "centered" in the moment of the will's determination. Critics say that this is at best an **undetermined liberty**, where the choice is made at random from two or more equally valued possibilities that are themselves **adequately determined**.

Libertarians say that an agent must be able to do something different in exactly the **same circumstances**. Agents could not **do otherwise**, they say, if they are determined by any preceding events, including the results of their immediately prior "free" deliberations.

Robert Kane calls this "The Indeterminist Condition:"

> "the agent should be able to act and act otherwise (choose different possible futures), given the same past circumstances and laws of nature." [42]

Although **self-determination** is not pre-determination by a strict causal chain of metaphysical determinism going back to the big bang, some extreme libertarians over-react. They have what William James might have called an "antipathy to determinism."

Despite advice from Daniel Dennett and Alfred Mele to keep indeterminism in the early pre-deliberation stages, libertarians like Kane, Peter van Inwagen, Laura Waddell Ekstrom, and Mark Balaguer want indeterminism in the decision itself.

Self-determination of the will only means that one is acting consistently, in character, and according to values expressed in one's habits and customs, when one does the same thing in the same circumstances.

42 Kane (2005) p. 38.

And since truly identical circumstances are essentially impossible, given the information of the past stored in the world and in the agent's memory, this worry of the libertarians is not too serious a problem.

But let's grant the possibility that an agent might be in exactly the same circumstances in order to understand what the libertarian is worried about. Here is how LAURA WADDELL EKSTROM describes her concern,

> "Consider an agent whose act is, in such a sense, "libertarian free." Now a duplicate agent in exactly similar circumstances governed by the same natural laws and subject to the same occurrence of considerations at the same points in the deliberative process will form exactly the same judgment concerning the best thing to do and will act accordingly. But then, given the consideration pattern that occurs (but might not have), there is no "wiggle room" for the agent in forming an evaluative judgment — it simply falls out, of necessity, from the consideration pattern. Hence such an account does not leave sufficient room for free agency." [43]

And ROBERT KANE thinks that the early-stage chance offered by Dennett and Mele does not provide the agent with all of the control over actions that the libertarian is looking for.

> "Mike does not have complete control over what chance images and other thoughts enter his mind or influence his deliberation. They simply come as they please. Mike does have some control after the chance considerations have occurred. But then there is no more chance involved. What happens from then on, how he reacts, is determined by desires and beliefs he already has. So it appears that he does not have control in the libertarian sense of what happens after the chance considerations occur as well. Libertarians require more than this for full responsibility and free will. What they would need for free will is for the agent to be able to control which of the chance events occur rather than merely reacting to them in a determined way once they have occurred." [44]

---

43 Ekstrom (2000) p. 121

44 Kane (2005) p. 65.

Finally, let's look at how the libertarian Peter van Inwagen deals with randomness. He says that "libertarianism is the conjunction of incompatibilism and the thesis that we have free will." [45] But all this means is that determinism is not true, that indeterminism is the case, that randomness and chance exist.

Given all the objections to randomness that we have just seen, including van Inwagen's own "Mind Objection" (page 36), it is clearly not enough to simply say that randomness exists. The hard problem for free will is to understand what work it is that indeterminism does for freedom.

We need to see where the indeterminism fits into a plausible model for free will, that is to say, exactly when and where indeterminism can enter and help the problem, while doing minimal or no harm to agent control, as Kane says.

In the coming chapters we shall see that there are plenty of sources of randomness in the world, for example, in the process that drives chance variations in the gene pool and the subsequent new species that result from natural selection.

Randomness shows up in our best computers and communications systems. It introduces errors, misunderstandings, and mistakes in our everyday lives all the time. These errors are occasionally the source of new creative ideas.

Libertarians go wrong when they fear that their idea of freedom will be equated with randomness and chance. Chance is only the enabling factor that breaks the causal chain of determinism.

Libertarians need to embrace chance in the world, in the actions of other persons, and most importantly, in their minds.

We shall see that this indeterminism can be either in the early stages of deliberation where new **alternative possibilities** for action are generated, or even at the moment of choice itself where multiple **undetermined liberties** are possible, as Robert Kane has long maintained for his Self-Forming Actions.

---

45 Van Inwagen (1983) p. 13.

The Standard Argument in Antiquity

In view of the basic conflict between human freedom and physical causal determinism, it is hard to believe that one of the inventors of determinism, DEMOCRITUS (c. 5th century BCE), intended it to liberate humans from the arbitrary interventions of the gods in human affairs.

But Democritus apparently saw divine intervention and foreknowledge as a grave threat to moral responsibility.

On his view, his reduction of mind to atoms and a void, working by natural laws, was such a gain over the traditional view of arbitrary fate and capricious gods determining our actions, that he simply insisted that determinism provided humans more control for moral responsibility.

The First Determinist

Democritus was the first **determinist**.

This means that the **determinist objection**, the first part of the standard argument against free will, was recognized at the creation of determinism, but the creator (Democritus) simply did not appreciate its importance.

The First Libertarians

The first indeterminist was ARISTOTLE. In his Physics and Metaphysics he said there were "accidents" caused by "chance (τυχῆ)." In his *Physics*, he clearly reckoned chance among the causes. Aristotle might have added chance as a fifth cause - an uncaused or self-caused cause - one that happens when two causal chains come together by accident (συμβεβεκός). He noted that the early physicists found no place for chance among the causes.

Aristotle's solution to the problem of free will (though he very likely did not see any problem, since Democritus' determinism was for material things and Aristotle thought living things were different) was likely to have been metaphysical. He probably assumed that the human mind was somehow exempt from the materialist laws of nature, whether causally determined or accidental chance, so that our actions can depend on us (ἐφ ἡμῖν). In this respect, we can call Aristotle the first **agent-causal** free-will **libertarian**.

One generation after Aristotle, Epicurus (c. 4th century BCE), proposed a physical explanation for free choice as a better basis for moral responsibility. His solution was a random "swerve" of the atoms to break the causal chain of determinism, giving us more control than was possible in Democritus' strict determinism.

Summarizing Aristotle's position, Epicurus saw three possibilities for causes - necessity, chance, and autonomous human agency (a "*tertium quid*").

> "...some things happen of necessity, others by chance, others through our own agency. For he sees that necessity destroys responsibility and that chance is inconstant; whereas our own actions are autonomous, and it is to them that praise and blame naturally attach. It were better, indeed, to accept the legends of the gods than to bow beneath that yoke of destiny which the natural philosophers have imposed. The one holds out some faint hope that we may escape if we honor the gods, while the necessity of the naturalists is deaf to all entreaties." [46]

Epicurus wanted a purely materialist solution to the conflict with determinism. He proposed that his random swerves could happen at any time and place. As long as there were some uncaused events in the past, there would no longer be a chain of causes back before our births limiting human agency.

Many subsequent philosophers argued mistakenly that Epicurus wanted a swerve to happen at the moment of decision - one swerve for each decision. But this is implausible. That would make our actions random. Epicurus could not explain when and where randomness could occur in his idea of free will to explain moral responsibility.

Although Epicurus' physical model for chance is ingenious and anticipated twentieth-century quantum mechanics, it provides

46 Epicurus, Letter to Menoeceus

little of deep significance for free will and moral responsibility that is not already implicit in Aristotle.

Nevertheless, we can say that Epicurus was the first event-causal libertarian.

We can also say that the **randomness objection**, the second part of the standard argument against free will, was recognized at the creation of indeterminism. His Stoic critics, and Epicurus himself provide us no specific idea of how his free will model might have met the objection.

The First Compatibilist

The first **compatibilist** was the Stoic Chryssipus (c. 3rd century BCE). He strongly objected to Epicurus' suggestion of randomness, arguing that it would only undermine moral responsibility if chance was the direct cause of action. Chryssipus was also aware of the charge that physical determinism had been equated with a necessitarianism that denied any human freedom. He sought a solution to both these objections to free will and moral responsibility.

So we can also say that the **responsibility objection**, implicit in both parts of the standard argument against free will, was recognized at the creation of compatibilism, with its creator Chryssipus rejecting Epicurean randomness but also claiming that there is no Leucippean necessity for our human decisions.

Chryssipus agreed with Aristotle that our decisions depend on us (πάρ' ἡμᾶς). They need our assent or choice (ἀιρήσις) to act or not act, even if our actions are fated.

Chryssipus felt that his compatibilism handled both objections, and it continues to this day as the most common model for free will among professional philosophers.

A generation later, Carneades, the head of the Platonic Academy in the 2nd century BCE, chastised Epicurus for suggesting the swerve of the atoms as a physical solution to the free will problem. It would be better, he said, for Epicurus to have given a special power to the mind than giving it to the atoms. In this regard, CARNEADES was favoring the metaphysical agent causalism that ARISTOTLE very likely preferred.

But as we will see below, today we know far more about the atoms than we know about the mind. And the power that Epicurus imagined in the atoms provides the mind with all the randomness, and independence from any deterministic physical laws of nature, that it needs to be creative and free.

Summary

The vast majority of philosophers and scientists who have thought deeply about free will have been unable to confront and overcome the **standard argument** against it.

Compatibilists and determinists have simply accepted the implications of the **determinist objection** and chosen to describe the resulting degree of freedom as good enough for them. I believe this is because their motives and desires, shaped by their character and values, at least play a part in their "determined" decisions.

When they consider indeterminism - the only apparent alternative in an "exhaustive" logical argument - they find that totally unacceptable.

Surprisingly, even the libertarians, who nominally accept the need for indeterminism somewhere to break the causal chain back to the beginning of the universe, cannot find an intelligible location for chance in the mind/brain.

In the next chapter, I turn the two component objections of the standard argument into two explicit requirements that any coherent and intelligible model of free will must satisfy.

Determinism

Hard Determinism

Compatibilism
Soft Determinism

Soft Compatibilism

Hard Incompatibilism

Illusionis

Impossibi

Requirements for Libertarian Free Will

Narrow Incompatibilism

Soft Incompatibilism

Valerian Model

Source Incompatibilism
(Actual Sequence)

Leewa
(Alter

Two-Stage Model with Limite

This chapter on the web
informationphilosopher.com/freedom/requirements.html

Free Will Requirements

The major and minor requirements for human free will must deal explicitly with the determinist objection and the randomness objection that are the core issues in the **standard argument** against free will in the previous chapter.

We need one requirement to defeat the **determinism** objection and another distinct requirement to defeat the **randomness** objection.

If we can meet these two requirements, we may have also eliminated the **responsibility** objection, but some philosophers think we can meet the responsibility objection whether or not we have free will, so this needs a bit more thought.

Part One - The Randomness Requirement

First, there must be a **Randomness Requirement**, unpredictable chance events that break the causal chain of determinism in an appropriate place and time. Without a chance break in the chain, our actions are simply the consequences of events in the remote past. There would be but one possible future.

This randomness must be located in a place and time that enhances free will, not one that reduces it to pure **chance**. If we can find this place and time, it will defeat the **determinism objection**.

Determinists do not like this requirement!

Any mention of randomness threatens to make everything random. (See CHRYSIPPUS' fears on p. 7.)

Note that strong libertarians (e.g., ROBERT KANE) say that indeterminism, centered in the decision itself, is needed for human freedom that provides ultimate responsibility.

Some randomness - chance or indeterminism - is required. The problem is how to prevent that randomness from making our decisions themselves random.

Part Two - The Determinism Requirement

Next, there is a **Determinism Requirement** - that our actions be **adequately determined** by our character and values, our feelings, motives, and desires.

Randomness can not be the direct and primary cause of our actions if we are to defeat the randomness objection and satisfy the determinism requirement.

Some libertarians do not like this requirement!

Determinists who think that determinism is all they need for **free will** call themselves compatibilists.

Part Three - The Responsibility Requirement

If we can meet these two requirements, can we automatically satisfy the **Responsibility Requirement?**

We can do this by showing

1. that the determinism we really have in the world is only adequate determinism and

2. that the randomness we have (especially quantum indeterminism) has negligible effect on that adequate determinism, but provides the alternative possibilities from which our determined will can choose, can make a selection for which we can be responsible.

These requirements should be such as to satisfy Libertarians, in that they ensure the unpredictable **alternative possibilities** needed for freedom.

They should also be such as to satisfy Determinists, in that they ensure the **adequate determinism** of the will and its actions, causal decisions that are needed for moral responsibility.

The requirements are straightforward, coherent, and intelligible, to guard against the centuries-old criticisms of free will as "unintelligible."

Let's summarize the implications of each requirement.

The Randomness (Freedom) Requirement

Over the centuries the freedom requirement has been described in many ways. We can explicitly clarify those descriptions that are in many cases equivalent.

- Chance exists.
- Indeterminism is True.
- Our Decisions are Unpredictable (even to ourselves)
- Our Actions are "Up to Us"
- We have Alternative Possibilities
- After the Fact, We Could Have Done Otherwise
- We Start New Causal Chains
- We Create New Information.

The Determinism (Will) Requirement

The will requirement has had many forms corresponding to the dogmatic forms of determinism.

Instead of a strict causal determinism, the world offers only adequate determinism and soft causality.

- Adequate Determinism Is True
- Chance Must Not Be The Direct Cause of Action
- Our Will is Adequately Determined by Reasons (Character, Values, Motives, Feelings, Desires, et.)
- Our Actions are Causally Determined by Our Will

The Moral Responsibility Requirement

The moral responsibility requirement is a joint consequence of randomness and adequate determinism.

- Since we always have Alternative Possibilities
- Since we can knowingly say , we Could Have Done Otherwise
- Since our Actions are Causally Determined by Our Will and are Up to Us
- We are Morally Responsible for our Actions

A Taxonomy of Free Will Positions

This chapter on the web
informationphilosopher.com/freedom/taxonomy.html

Taxonomy of Free Will Positions

The free will debates of the late 20th century tended to be monologues and diatribes defending narrow niche positions against many other possible positions on free will.

This too is part of the scandal in philosophy. Instead of carving out narrow niches and developing specialized new vocabularies of technical terminology, philosophy would be better served by an effort to standardize the jargon used in the dialectic. We may not be able to achieve the universal, ambiguity-free language that Leibniz dreamed of and logical positivists hoped for, but we could try to simplify rather than complicate.

The next best thing is to provide as complete a set of jargon terms as we can assemble (see the Glossary, and the I-Phi website version, which is of course a work in progress).

Of all the terms, the most important are those used to describe what might be loosely called major "schools" on free will. For me, there are three historically significant terms - determinism, libertarianism, and compatibilism. This last is the current name for William James' "soft" determinism, which is the logically contradictory notion that free will is compatible with determinism.

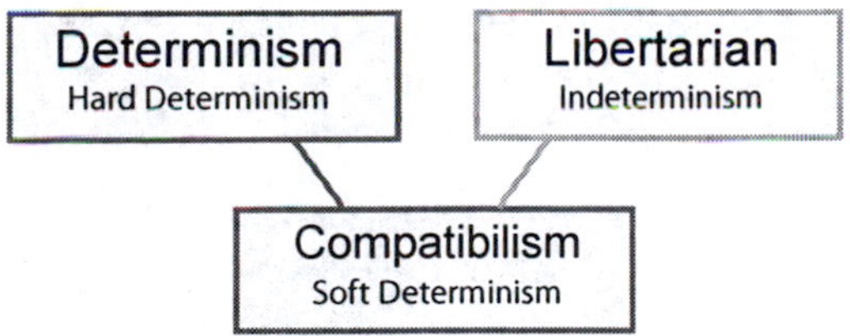

Figure 6-1. Traditional categories of the free will debates.

Compatibilism is an old idea, of course. Immanuel Kant found it in the work of the English thinkers Thomas Hobbes, John Locke, George Berkeley, and especially in David Hume. Kant described it in his 1788 *Critique of Practical Reason*,

> "although the actions of men are necessarily determined by causes which precede in time, we yet call then *free*, because these causes are ideas produced by our own faculties..."

> "This is a wretched subterfuge ["miserable substitute" is a better translation of *ein elender Behelf*, but the English phrase is now famous in philosophy] with which some persons still let themselves be put off, and so think they have solved, with a petty word-jugglery [again, "a little quibbling" is better for *einer kleinen Wortklauberei*], that difficult problem, at the solution of which centuries have laboured in vain, and which can therefore scarcely be found so completely on the surface." [1]

I agree that it is sophistry to solve the problem of free will and determinism by a language game that redefines freedom.

John Stuart Mill took up the notion and it was known as the Hume-Mill tradition of reconciling freedom with determinism.

William James thought this idea a "quagmire of evasion," a "eulogistic terminology," and a "mere word-grabbing game played by the soft determinists." He says "they make a pretense of restoring the caged bird to liberty with one hand, while with the other we anxiously tie a string to its leg to make sure it does not get beyond our sight." [2]

Incompatibilism Changes the Taxonomy

"Soft" determinism became "compatibilism" in the early 20th century. It was, and still is, the most popular view of philosophers, although it was challenged when Carl Ginet and later Peter van Inwagen argued for "incompatibilism." This incompatibilism was not simply arguing that determinism was not true, but that the presumed compatibilist premise - that free will involved, perhaps required, or even entailed, determinism - was not true.

As we saw in Chapter 3, R. E. Hobart had argued in 1934 that free will involves **determination**, otherwise our willed actions would be random. Ginet and van Inwagen used the first part of the **standard argument** to show that if we are determined, we are not free. Therefore, compatibilism is not true. Q.E.D.?

No. Logical philosophers say that the alternative is incompatibilism. And they note that there are two ways that determinism

1 Kant (1962) p. 332.
2 James (1956) p. 149.

and free will can be incompatible. The first is the normal libertarian view. Free will is true. Determinism is false.

But there is another possibility. Free will is false and determinism is true. This is James' traditional "hard" determinism. Van Inwagen convinced many philosophers that a compatibilism-incompatibilism dichotomy made more sense than the traditional freedom-determinism dichotomy (with compatibilism their reconciliation). He wrote in 1983:

> "I shall argue that free will is incompatible with determinism. It will be convenient to call this thesis incompatibilism and to call the thesis that free will and determinism are compatible compatibilism.
>
> "I have no use for the terms 'soft determinism', 'hard determinism; and 'libertarianism'. I do not object to these terms on the ground that they are vague or ill-defined. They can be easily defined by means of the terms we shall use and are thus no worse in that respect than our terms.
>
> "Soft determinism is the conjunction of determinism and compatibilism; hard determinism is the conjunction of determinism and incompatibilism; libertarianism is the conjunction of incompatibilism and the thesis that we have free will.
>
> "I object to these terms because they lump together theses that should be discussed and analysed separately. They are therefore worse than useless and ought to be dropped from the working vocabulary of philosophers." [3]

In my view, it is van Inwagen's new terms that are "worse than useless" (though they have been accepted as the standard jargon in the current dialectic). They are useless because they also "lump together theses that should be discussed and analysed separately," namely they call both libertarians and determinists "incompatibilists." What could be more confusing? But van Inwagen's new jargon has succeeded. The old terms are seen less often today in the working vocabulary.

3 Van Inwagen (1983) p. 13.

If "soft" determinism was a "quagmire of evasion," van Inwagen's "incompatibilism is a deeper and darker "tarpit of confusion."

As KADRI VIHVELIN said in her Stanford Encyclopedia of Philosophy article on Incompatibilism,

> "Why an encyclopedia entry on arguments for incompatibilism? (Why not an entry on the problem of free will and determinism?)"[4]

It seems to me embarrassing for libertarians to have to describe themselves as "incompatibilists," especially since incompatibilism "lumps together" libertarians and determinists. RANDOLPH CLARKE's SEP article on free will thus has the convoluted and confusing title "Incompatibilist (Nondeterministic) Theories." [5]

The van Inwagen taxonomy then looks like this,

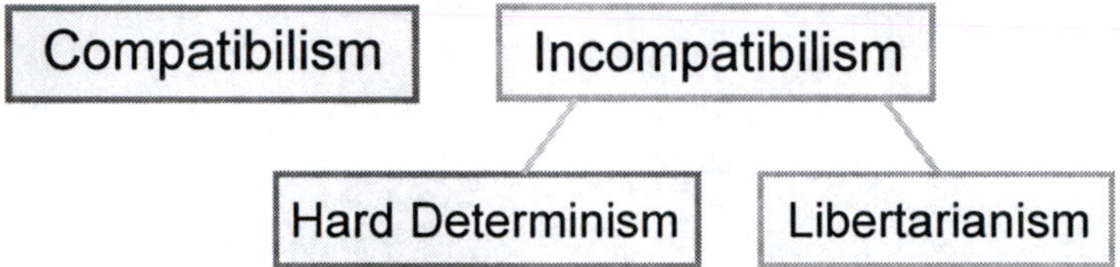

Figure 6-2. Van Inwagen's compatibilism-incompatibilism categories.

The fact that compatibilists are also determinists is obscured in this taxonomy. It helps the compatibilists to co-opt the term "free will" for their "compatibilist free will," in opposition to a supposed unintelligible "libertarian free will."

Free will is not a puzzle to be dis-solved by the logical paradoxes and language games of the philosophers, especially those analytic language philosophers who pride themselves on their clear conceptual analysis.

A New Taxonomy

So I have developed an extended version of the traditional taxonomy of free will positions. Positions are defined by what they are, rather than what they are not. It is based on the traditional (hard) determinism - libertarian (indeterminist) - compatibilism (soft determinist) distinctions that van Inwagen thought "useless."

4 plato.stanford.edu/entries/incompatibilism-arguments/
5 plato.stanford.edu/entries/incompatibilism-theories/

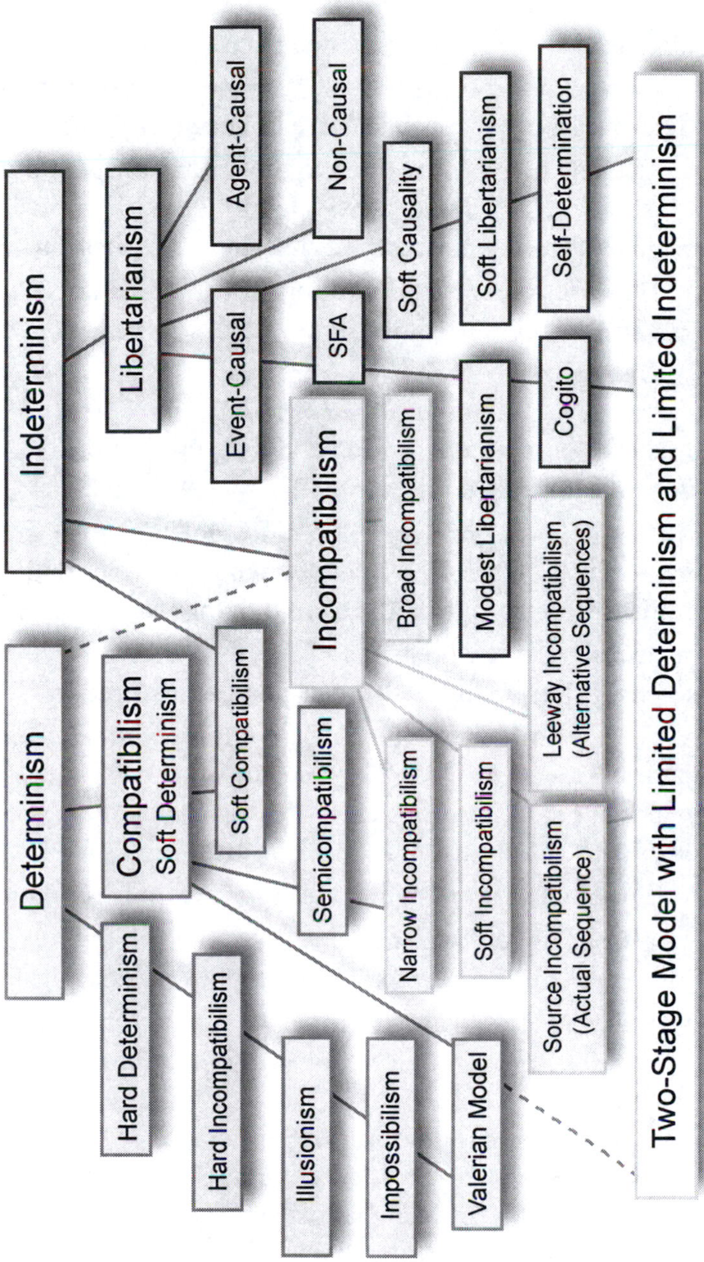

Figure 6-3. Taxonomy of Free Will Positions

My new taxonomy calls a determinist a determinist, and arranges other positions in their proper places in the hierarchy.

Libertarian incompatibilists are under indeterminism. Hard determinist incompatibilists are under determinism.

The new hierarchy is open to the criticism that it puts compatibilists at a disadvantage when claiming that their position is "free will," by showing clearly their deterministic position. So be it.

Here are some brief definitions for the positions in Figure 6-2. For still more interrelationships, see the Glossary.

Determinism is the position that every event is caused, in a chain of events with just one possible future. Historically, there are many kinds of determinisms or causes for the one possible future. They are discussed in Chapter 9.

"Hard" determinism and **"soft" determinism** are terms invented by William James who lamented the fact that some determinists were co-opting the term freedom for themselves. [6]

"Hard" determinists deny the existence of free will. **"Soft" determinists** baldly claim their position as "free will."

Compatibilism is the most common name used today for James's category of "soft" determinism. For compatibilists, free will is compatible with determinism, or would be, *if determinism were true*, the agnostics on determinism say.

This makes compatibilism today much more complicated...

We can divide two sub-categories of compatibilism, as we did for incompatibilsm, based on their view of determinism.

Today's sophisticated (and sophistical) compatibilists want to include both "the conjunction of compatibilism and the thesis that determinism is true" AND "the conjunction of compatibilism and the thesis that determinism is false." They want it both ways (or either way), because most compatibilists today are agnostic on the truth of determinism. (Most are cognizant of the indeterminism of quantum physics.)

It is thus difficult today to know what compatibilists are compatible with! We are being sucked deeper and deeper into William James' "quagmire of evasion," to a "tarpit of confusion."

6 James (1956) p. 149.

Semicompatibilists are agnostic about free will and determinism, but claim that **moral responsibility** is compatible with determinism, in any case. Narrow incompatibilism is a similar concept.

Hard incompatibilists think both free will and moral responsibility are incompatible with determinism, which is "true.".

Illusionists are hard incompatibilists, who say free will is an illusion and usually deny moral responsibility. Some say we should preserve moral responsibility in society by maintaining the illusion (i.e., keep the masses uninformed about the "truth" of determinism).

Impossibilists are also hard incompatibilists. They say moral responsibility is provably impossible.

Incompatibilism is the idea that free will and determinism are incompatible. Incompatibilists today include both hard determinists and libertarians. This confusion, created by analytic language philosophers who are normally committed to clear and unambiguous conceptualization, adds difficulties for new students of philosophy. See pp. 59-61.

Soft incompatibilists say that free will is incompatible with pre-determinism, and that pre-determinism is not true. It is preferable to the loose usage of the term "incompatibilist" to describe a libertarian, since "incompatibilist" is ambiguous and also used for determinists (hard incompatibilists).

Source and **Leeway** incompatibilists locate indeterminism in the **Actual Sequence** of events or **Alternative Sequences**. An **Actual Sequence** event breaks the causal chain. **Alternative Sequences** provide alternative possibilities.[7]

Indeterminism is the position that there are random (chance) events in a world with many possible futures.

Libertarians believe that indeterminism makes free will possible. But it is not enough. Many philosophers admit indeterminism may be true, but that it does not provide free will ("hard" indeterminists?). See the **standard argument** against free will in Chapter 4. If our actions are determined, we are not free. If they

---

7 See Timpe (2008) for a very clear account.

are random, we are not responsible for them. So indeterminism is not enough. We also need "**adequate determinism**" - Hobart's determination - in a second stage (See Chapter 13).

Agent-causal indeterminists are libertarians who think that agents originate causes for their actions. These causes are not events. So their actions do not depend on any prior causes. Some call this "metaphysical" freedom.

Non-causal indeterminists simply deny any causes whatsoever for libertarian free will.

Event-causal indeterminists generally accept the view that random events (most likely quantum mechanical events) occur in the world. Whether in the physical world, in the biological world (where they are a key driver of genetic mutations), or in the mind, randomness and uncaused events are real. They introduce the possibility of accidents, novelty, and both biological and human creativity.

Soft Causality is the idea that most events are adequately determined by normal causes, but that some events are not precisely predictable from prior events, because there are occasional quantum events that start new causal chains with unpredictable futures. These events are said to be *causa sui*.

Soft Libertarians accept some indeterminism in the Actual Sequence. They are source incompatibilists.

Self-Determination is the traditional name for decisions that are the result of our choices, determined by our character and values, etc., decisions that are "**up to us**."

SFA is the **Self-Forming Action** of ROBERT KANE's libertarian free-will model, with indeterminism centered in the choice itself.

Two-Stage Models that combine limited **Determinism** and **Indeterminism** have been discussed by many thinkers, including WILLIAM JAMES, HENRI POINCARÉ, ARTHUR HOLLY COMPTON, KARL POPPER, DANIEL DENNETT (**Valerian Model**), HENRY MARGENAU, ROBERT KANE, JOHN MARTIN FISCHER, ALFRED MELE (**Modest Libertarianism**), STEPHEN KOSSLYN, BOB DOYLE

(**Cogito Model**), and Martin Heisenberg. See Chapter 12 and these thinkers' personal pages on the I-Phi website for more details.

Two-stage models include both "**adequate determinism**" (which denies **pre-determinism**) and an **indeterminism** that is limited to generating **alternative possibilities** for action. It is only **pre-determinism** that is incompatible with free will.

Two-Stage Models in a Nutshell

Thoughts *come to us* freely. Actions *go from us* willfully.

First chance, then choice.

First "free," then "will."

I argue that because two-stage models reconcile free will with both determinism (as David Hume did in his compatibilism) and with indeterminism (as William James first did), we can say that this kind of freedom is even more compatible than standard compatibilism, and might be called "**comprehensive compatibilism**."

So why accept "comprehensive compatibilism?" I believe that compatibilists have all along had excellent reasons for insisting on some determinism in any intelligible model for free will. The **adequate determinism** in my Cogito model provides the kind of **determination** R. E. Hobart wanted, for example.

It gives compatibilists the determination of their will by character, values, motives, and desires that they need, but reconciliation with a limited indeterminism also gives them the generation of new ideas that makes them the authors of their lives and co-creators of the universe. See Chapter 28 for more details on the idea of a comprehensive compatibilism.

If widely discussed, the two-stage model might help us to end the "free will scandal in philosophy."

With this taxonomy of free will positions and the **standard argument** against free will in mind, we are now ready to turn to the history of the free will problem.

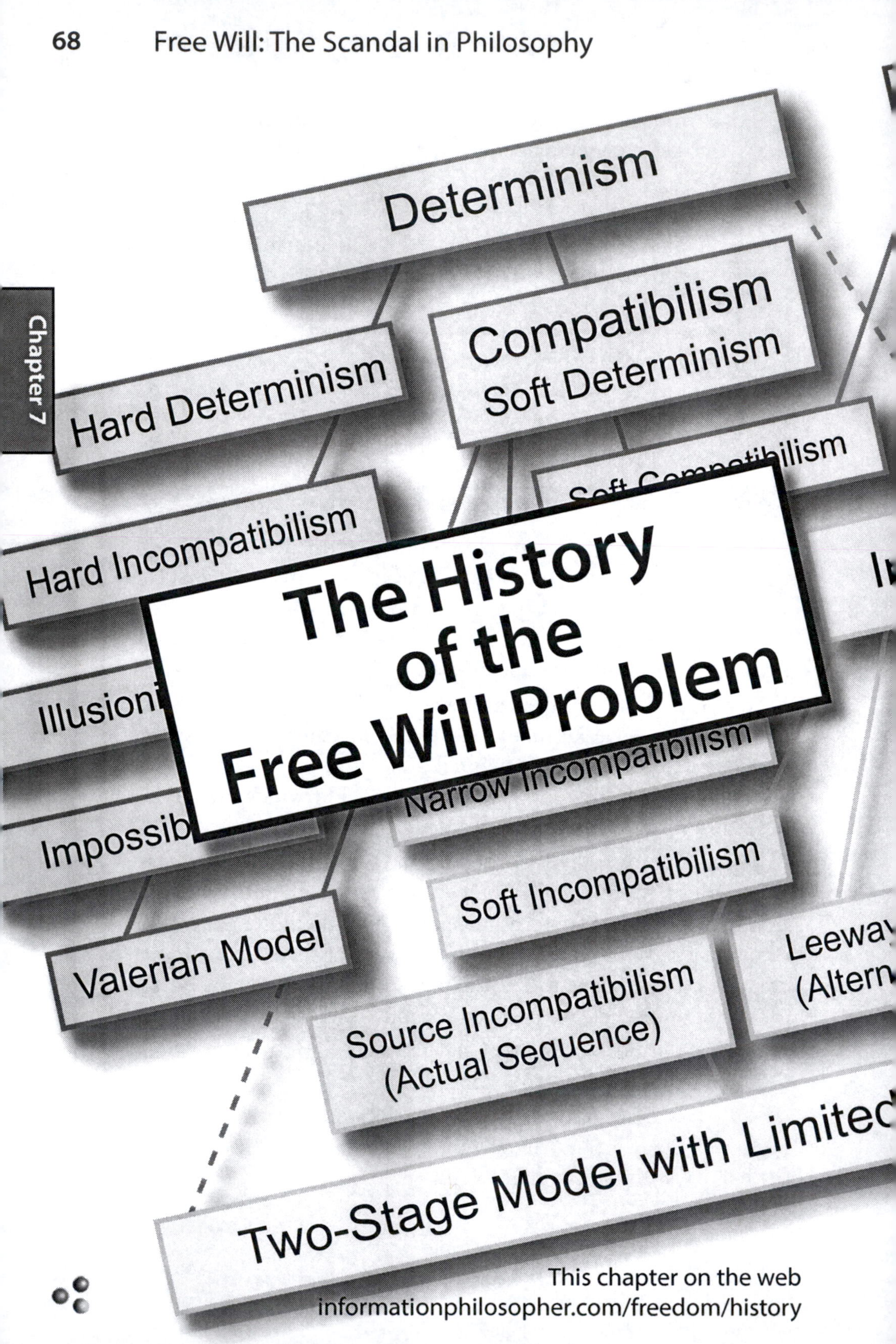

The History of the Free Will Problem

This chapter on the web
informationphilosopher.com/freedom/history

History of the Problem

From its earliest beginnings, the problem of "**free will**" has been intimately connected with the question of **moral responsibility**. Most of the ancient thinkers on the problem were trying to show that we humans have **control** over our decisions, that our actions "depend on us", and that they are not **pre-determined** by fate, by arbitrary gods, by logical **necessity**, or by a natural causal **determinism**.

Almost everything written about free will to date has been verbal and formal logical debate about the precise meaning of philosophical concepts like **causality**, necessity, and other dogmas of determinism.

The "problem of free will" is often described as a question of **reconciling** "free will" with one or more of the many kinds of determinism. As a result, the "problem of free will" depends on two things, the exact definition of free will and which of the determinisms is being reconciled.

There is also an even more difficult reconciliation for "**libertarian**" free will. How can a morally responsible will be reconciled with **indeterminism** or objective **chance**? The **standard argument** against free will is that it can not possibly be reconciled with either randomness or determinism, and that these two exhaust the logical possibilities.

Before there was anything called philosophy, religious accounts of man's fate explored the degree of human freedom permitted by superhuman gods. Creation myths often end in adventures of the first humans clearly making choices and being held responsible. But a strong **fatalism** is present in those tales that foretell the future, based on the idea that the gods have **foreknowledge** of future events. Anxious not to annoy the gods, the myth-makers rarely challenge the implausible view that the gods' foreknowledge is compatible with human freedom. This was an early form of today's **compatibilism**, the idea that causal determinism and logical necessity are compatible with free will.

The first thinkers to look for causes in natural phenomena (rather than gods controlling events) were the Greek physiologoi or cosmologists. The reasons (λόγοι) behind the physical (φύσις) world became the ideal "laws" governing material phenomena. The first cosmologist was ANAXIMANDER, who coined the term physis (φύσις). He also likely combined the words cosmos (κόσμος), as organized nature, and logos (λόγος), as the law behind nature, in cosmology.

The Greeks had a separate word for the laws (or conventions) of society, nomos (νόμος).

The Presocratics

HERACLITUS, the philosopher of change, agreed that there were laws or rules (the logos) behind all the change. The early cosmologists' intuition that their laws could produce an ordered cosmos out of chaos was prescient. Our current model of the universe begins with a state of minimal information and maximum disorder. Early cosmologists imagined that the universal laws were all-powerful and must therefore explain the natural causes behind all things, from regular motions of the heavens to the mind (νοῦς) of man.

The physiologoi transformed pre-philosophical arguments about gods controlling the human will into arguments about pre-existing causal laws controlling it. The cosmological problem became a psychological problem. Some saw a causal chain of events leading back to a first cause (later taken by many religious thinkers to be God). Other physiologoi held that although all physical events are caused, mental events might not be. This is mind/body dualism, the most important of all the great dualisms. If the mind (or soul) is a substance different from matter, it could have its own laws, different from the laws of nature for material bodies.

Determinism

The materialist philosophers DEMOCRITUS and LEUCIPPUS, again with extraordinary prescience, claimed that all things, including humans, were made of atoms in a void, with individual atomic motions strictly controlled by causal laws. DEMOCRITUS wanted to wrest control of man's fate from arbitrary gods and make us more responsible for our actions. But ironically, he and LEUCIPPUS originated two of the great dogmas of determinism, physical determinism and logical necessity, which lead directly to the modern problem of free will and determinism. LEUCIPPUS stated the first dogma, an absolute necessity which left no room in the cosmos for chance.

> "Nothing occurs at random, but everything for a reason and by necessity."
>
> οὐδὲν χρῆμα μάτην γίνεται, ἀλλὰ πάντα ἐκ λόγου τε καὶ ὑπ᾽ ἀνάγκης [1]

The consequence is a world with but one possible future, completely determined by its past. Some even argued for a great cycle of events (an idea borrowed from Middle Eastern sources) repeating themselves over thousands of years.

The Pythagoreans, SOCRATES, and PLATO attempted to reconcile human freedom with material determinism and causal law, in order to hold man responsible for his actions.

Aristotle

The first major philosopher to argue convincingly for some indeterminism was probably ARISTOTLE. First he described a causal chain back to a prime mover or first cause, and he elaborated the four possible causes (material, efficient, formal, and final). Aristotle's word for these causes was ἀιτία, which translates as causes in the sense of the multiple factors or explanations behind an event. Aristotle did not subscribe to the simplistic "every event has a (single) cause" idea that was to come later.

Then, in his Physics and Metaphysics, Aristotle also said there were "accidents" caused by "chance (τύχη)." In his Physics, he clearly reckoned chance among the causes. Aristotle might have added chance as a fifth cause - an uncaused or self-caused cause

1 Leucippus, Fragment 569 - from Fr. 2 Actius I, 25, 4

- one he thought happens when two causal chains come together by accident (συμβεβεκός).

He noted that the early physicists had found no place for chance among their causes.

Aristotle opposed his accidental chance to necessity:

> "Nor is there any definite cause for an accident, but only chance (τυχόν), namely an indefinite (ἀόριστον) cause. "[2]

> "It is obvious that there are principles and causes which are generable and destructible apart from the actual processes of generation and destruction; for if this is not true, everything will be of necessity: that is, if there must necessarily be some cause, other than accidental, of that which is generated and destroyed. Will this be, or not? Yes, if this happens; otherwise not."[3]

For Aristotle, a break in the causal chain allowed us to feel our actions "depend on us" (ἐφ' ἡμῖν). He knew that many of our decisions are quite predictable based on habit and character, but they are no less free nor we less responsible if our character itself and predictable habits were developed freely in the past and are changeable in the future.

> "If we are unable to trace conduct back to any other origins than those within ourselves, then actions of which the origins are within us (ἐν ἡμῖν), themselves depend upon us (ἐφ' ἡμῖν), and are voluntary (ekousia - will)."[4]

Some scholars say Aristotle did not see or confront the problem of free will versus determinism. But consider his arguments for some indeterminism, his "Sea-Battle" example against the Megarians claim that future contingency is logically impossible, and his belief that animals are exempt from laws of material determinism.

One generation after Aristotle, Epicurus argued that as atoms moved through the void, there were occasions when they would "swerve" from their otherwise determined paths, thus initiating new causal chains. Epicurus argued that these swerves would allow us to be more responsible for our actions, something impossible if

---

2 Aristotle (1935) Metaphysics, Book V, 1025a25

3 Aristotle (1935) Metaphysics, Book VI, 1027a29

4 Aristotle (1937) Nichomachean Ethics, III.v.6

every action was deterministically caused. For Epicurus, the occasional interventions of arbitrary gods would be preferable to strict determinism.

Epicurus did not say the swerve was directly involved in decisions. His critics, ancient and modern, have claimed mistakenly that Epicurus did assume "one swerve - one decision." Following Aristotle, Epicurus thought human agents have the ability to transcend necessity and chance.

> "...some things happen of necessity, others by chance, others through our own agency. ...necessity destroys responsibility and chance is inconstant; whereas our own actions are autonomous, and it is to them that praise and blame naturally attach." [5]

Parenthetically, we now know that atoms do not occasionally swerve, they move unpredictably whenever they are in close contact with other atoms. Everything in the material universe is made of atoms in unstoppable perpetual motion. Deterministic paths are only the case for very large objects, where the statistical laws of atomic physics average to become nearly certain dynamical laws for billiard balls and planets.

So Epicurus' intuition of a fundamental randomness was correct. We know Epicurus' work largely from the Roman Lucretius and his friend Cicero.

Lucretius saw the randomness as enabling free will, even if he could not explain how, beyond the fact that random swerves would break the causal chain of determinism.

> "If all motion is always one long chain, and new motion arises out of the old in order invariable, and if first-beginnings do not make by swerving a beginning of motion so as to break the decrees of fate, whence comes this free will [*libera*]?" [6]

Cicero unequivocally denies fate, strict causal determinism, and God's foreknowledge. Augustine quotes Cicero,

> "If there is free will, all things do not happen according to fate; if all things do not happen according to fate, there is not

5 Epicurus, Letter to Menoeceus, §133

6 Lucretius (1982) De Rerum Natura), book 2, lines 216-250

> a certain order of causes; and if there is not a certain order of causes, neither is there a certain order of things foreknown by God." [7]

The Stoics

It was the Stoic school of philosophy that solidified the idea of natural laws controlling all things, including the mind.[8] Their influence persists to this day, in philosophy and religion. Most of the extensive Stoic writings are lost, probably because their doctrine of fate, which identified God with Nature, was considered anathema to the Christian church. The church agreed that the laws of God were the laws of Nature, but that God and Nature were two different entities. In either case strict determinism follows by universal Reason (logos) from an omnipotent and omniscient God.

Stoic virtue called for men to resist futile passions like anger and envy. The fine Stoic morality that all men (including slaves and women) were equal children of God coincided with (or was adopted by) the church. Stoic logic and physics freed those fields from ancient superstitions, but strengthened the dogmas of determinism that dominate modern science and philosophy, especially when they explicitly denied Aristotle's chance as a cause.[9]

The major founder of Stoicism, CHRYSIPPUS, took the edge off strict determinism. Like Democritus, Aristotle, and Epicurus before him, he wanted to strengthen the argument for moral responsibility, in particular defending it from Aristotle's and Epicurus's indeterminate chance causes.

Whereas the past is unchangeable, CHRYSIPPUS argued that some future events that are possible do not occur by necessity from past external factors alone, but might depend on us. We have a choice to assent or not to assent to an action.

Chrysippus said our actions are determined (in part by ourselves as causes) and fated (because of God's foreknowledge), but he also said correctly that they are not necessitated. Chrysippus would be seen today as a compatibilist, as was the Stoic Epictetus.[10]

---

7 Augustine (1935) Bk V, Ch. 9, Cf. Cicero, De Divinatione Book II, x 25
8 Long (2000), Sorabji (1980) p. 70
9 Sambursky, (1988) p. 73-76.
10 Sharples (1983) p. 8, Long, (1986) p. 101, Sharples (1996) p. 8.

Hellenistic Thinking

ALEXANDER OF APHRODISIAS, the most famous commentator on Aristotle, wrote 500 years after Aristotle's death, at a time when Aristotle and Plato were rather forgotten minor philosophers in the age of Stoics, Epicureans, and Skeptics. Alexander defended a view of moral responsibility we would call libertarianism today. Greek philosophy had no precise term for "free will" as did Latin (liberum arbitrium or libera voluntas). The discussion was in terms of responsibility, what "depends on us" (in Greek ἐφ ἡμῖν).

Alexander believed that Aristotle was not a strict determinist like the Stoics, and Alexander himself argued that some events do not have predetermined causes. In particular, man is responsible for self-caused decisions, and can choose to do or not to do something. Alexander denied the foreknowledge of events that was part of the Stoic identification of God and Nature.[11]

Most of the ancient thinkers recognized the obvious difficulty with chance (or an uncaused cause) as the source of human freedom. Even Aristotle described chance as a "cause obscure to human reason" (ἀιτιάν ἄδελον ἀνθρωπίνῳ λογισμῷ).

Actions caused by chance are simply random and we cannot feel responsible for them. But we do feel responsible. Despite more than twenty-three centuries of philosophizing, most modern thinkers have not moved significantly beyond this core problem of randomness and free will for libertarians - the confused idea that free actions are caused directly by a random event.

Caught between the horns of a dilemma, with determinism on one side and randomness on the other, the standard argument against free will continues to make human freedom an unintelligible mystery. See Chapter 4.

Early Christians

A couple of centuries after ALEXANDER, a subtle argument for free will was favored by early Christian theologians. They wanted human free will in order to absolve an omnipotent God of

11 Sharples (1983) p. 21

responsibility for evil actions. This is called the problem of evil. Those who held God to be omniscient, AUGUSTINE for example, maintained that God's foreknowledge was compatible with human freedom, an illogical position still held today by most theologians. AUGUSTINE argued for free will, but only as compatible with God

> "God must needs have given free will to man. God's foreknowledge is not opposed to our free choice." [12]

Augustine's more sensible contemporary, the British monk PELAGIUS (Morgan) held, with Cicero, that human freedom prohibited divine foreknowledge. The success of Augustine's ideas led the church to judge Pelagius a heretic.[13]

Classicists on Free Will in Antiquity

Before we leave the ancients, it will be instructive to see how great classicists have understood what the ancients were saying about free will. Unfortunately, many of them are influenced by our modern ideas of free will, looking for specific modern theories like compatibilism and extreme libertarianism. I will try to point out these biases where they are obvious.

Carlo Giussani

In his 1896 *Studi lucreziani* (p.126), Giussani put forward the idea that Epicurus' atomic swerves are involved directly in every case of human free action, not just somewhere in the past that breaks the causal chain of determinism. This goes beyond

and leads to the mistaken conclusion that the swerves directly cause actions. This was the Stoics' view of Epicurus.

> "The complete conception of the will according to Epicurus comprises two elements, a complex atomic movement which has the characteristic of spontaneity, that is, is withdrawn from the necessity of mechanical causation: and then the sensus, or self-consciousness in virtue of which the will, illuminated by previous movements of sensation, thought, and emotion, profits by the peculiar liberty or spontaneity of the atomic motions,

12 Augustine, On Free Choice of the Will. Book Two, I, 7, Book Three, IV, 38

13 Augustine, On Free Choice of the Will. Book Three, IV, 40

to direct or not to direct these in a direction seen or selected." [14] (Cyril Bailey translation)

Cyril Bailey

In 1928 Bailey agreed with Giussani that the atoms of the mind-soul provide a break in the continuity of atomic motions, otherwise actions would be necessitated. Bailey imagined complexes of mind-atoms that work together to form a consciousness that is not determined, but also not susceptible to the pure randomness of individual atomic swerves, something that could constitute Epicurus' idea of actions being "up to us" (πὰρ' ἡμάς).

> "It is a commonplace to state that Epicurus, like his follower Lucretius, intended primarily to combat the 'myths' of the orthodox religion, to show by his demonstration of the unfailing laws of nature the falseness of the old notions of the arbitrary action of the gods and so to relieve humanity from the terrors of superstition. But it is sometimes forgotten that Epicurus viewed with almost greater horror the conception of irresistible 'destiny' or 'necessity', which is the logical outcome of the notion of natural law pressed to its conclusion. This conclusion had been accepted in its fulness by Democritus, but Epicurus conspicuously broke away from him: 'it were better to follow the myths about the gods than to become a slave to the "destiny" of the natural philosophers: for the former suggests a hope of placating the gods by worship, whereas the latter involves a necessity which knows no placation'. " [15]

> "The 'swerve' of the atoms is, no doubt, as the critics have always pointed out, a breach of the fundamental laws of cause and effect, for it is the assertion of a force for which no cause can be given and no explanation offered... But it was no slip or oversight on Epicurus' part which a more careful consideration of his principles might have rectified. On the contrary it was a very deliberate breach in the creed of 'necessity' and is in a sense the hinge on which the whole of his system turns. He wished to secure 'freedom' as an occasional breach of 'natural law'." [16]

---

14 Giussani (1896) *Studi lucreziani*, p. 126

15 Bailey (1964) p. 318.

16 Bailey (1964) p. 320

David Furley

In 1967, Furley examined the ideas of Giussani and Bailey and de-emphasized the importance of the swerve in both Epicurus and Lucretius so as to defend Epicurus from the extreme view that our actions are caused directly by random swerves. (Bailey had denied this "traditional interpretation" of the swerve.) Furley argues for a strong connection between the ideas of Aristotle and Epicurus on autonomous actions that are "up to us."

> "If we now put together the introduction to Lucretius' passage on voluntas and Aristotle's theory of the voluntary, we can see how the swerve of atoms was supposed to do its work. Aristotle's criterion of the voluntary was a negative one: the source of the voluntary action is in the agent himself, in the sense that it cannot be traced back beyond or outside the agent himself. Lucretius says that voluntas must be saved from a succession of causes which can be traced back to infinity. All he needs to satisfy the Aristotelian criterion is a break in the succession of causes, so that the source of an action cannot be traced back to something occurring before the birth of the agent. A single swerve of a single atom in the individual's psyche would be enough for this purpose, if all actions are to be referred to the whole of the psyche.
>
> "But there is no evidence about the number of swerves. One would be enough, and there must not be so many that the psyche exhibits no order at all; between these limits any number would satisfy the requirements of the theory.
>
> "The swerve, then, plays a purely negative part in Epicurean psychology. It saves voluntas from necessity, as Lucretius says it does, but it does not feature in every act of voluntas. There is no need to scrutinize the psychology of a voluntary action to find an uncaused or spontaneous element in it. The peculiar vulnerability of Epicurean freedom — that it seemed to fit random actions, rather than deliberate and purposive ones — is a myth, if this explanation is correct." [17]

---

17 Furley (1967) p. 232.

Pamela Huby

In the same year 1967, Huby suggested that EPICURUS was the original discoverer of the "freewill problem." Huby noted that there had been two main free will problems, corresponding to different determinisms, namely theological determinism (predestination and foreknowledge) and the physical causal determinism of Democritus.

> "In spite of the poverty of our evidence, it is quite clear that one main reason Epicurus had for introducing the swerve, or rather the swerve as a random, uncaused event, was as a solution to the problem of freewill. Unlike Aristotle, he fully appreciated that there was a problem. He believed in free will, because it seemed to him manifestly clear that men could originate action, but he could not, like Aristotle, regard this as the end of the matter.
>
> "...the fact remains, on the evidence of Cicero and Lucretius, that Epicurus still ultimately traced the freedom of the will to the swerve of the atoms. How exactly he did this remains a mystery." [18]

Richard Sorabji

Sorabji's 1980 *Necessity, Cause, and Blame* surveyed ARISTOTLE's positions on causation and necessity, comparing them to his predecessors and successors, especially the Stoics and Epicurus. Sorabji argues that Aristotle was an indeterminist, that real chance and uncaused events exist, but never that human actions are uncaused in the extreme libertarian sense that some commentators mistakenly attribute to Epicurus.

> "I shall be representing Aristotle as an indeterminist; but opinions on this issue have been diverse since the earliest times...
>
> "It is not always recognised that Aristotle gave any consideration to causal determinism, that is, to determinism based on causal considerations. But I shall argue that in a little-understood passage he maintains that coincidences lack causes. To understand why he thinks so; we must recall his view that a cause is one of four kinds of explanation. On both counts, I think he is right.

18 Huby (1967) pp. 353-62

> His account of cause, I believe, is more promising than any of those current today, and also justifies the denial that coincidences have causes." [19]

R. W. Sharples

Sharples' great translation and commentary *Alexander of Aphrodisias On Fate* appeared in 1983. He described ALEXANDER's De Fato as perhaps the most comprehensive treatment surviving from classical antiquity of the problem of responsibility (τὸ ἐφ' ἡμίν) and determinism. It especially shed a great deal of light on Aristotle's position on free will and on the Stoic attempt to make responsibility compatible with determinism.

Sharples thinks that the problem of determinism and responsibility was not realized, in the form in which it was eventually passed on to post-classical thinkers, until relatively late in the history of Greek thought - at least not until after Aristotle.

> "The mechanistic atomism of Democritus (born 460-457 B.C.) may well seem to us to raise difficulties for human responsibility, and it seemed to do so to Epicurus, but Democritus himself apparently felt no such problem." [20]

> "The Stoic position, given definitive expression by Chrysippus (c. 280-207 B.C.), the third head of the school, represents not the opposite extreme from that of Epicurus but an attempt to compromise, to combine determinism and responsibility." [21]

Don Fowler

In his 1983 thesis, "Lucretius on the Clinamen and 'Free Will,'" Fowler criticized Furley's limits on the swerve and defended the ancient - but seriously mistaken - claim that Epicurus proposed random swerves as directly causing our actions. This mistaken claim has become common in current interpretations of Epicurus.

> "I turn to the overall interpretation. Lucretius is arguing from the existence of voluntas to the existence of the clinamen;

19 Sorabji (1980) p. x.
20 Sharples (2007) p. 4.
21 Sharples (2007) p. 8.

nothing comes to be out of nothing, therefore voluntas must have a cause at the atomic level, viz. the clinamen. The most natural interpretation of this is that every act of voluntas is caused by a swerve in the atoms of the animal's mind."

This is not an interpretation that would have been acceptable to Epicurus, as Furley had argued. Fowler continues:

> "Furley, however, argued that the relationship between voluntas and the clinamen was very different; not every act of volition was accompanied by a swerve in the soul-atoms, but the clinamen was only an occasional event which broke the chain of causation."

A. A. Long and D. N. Sedley

In their great 1987 work *The Hellenistic Philosophers* (dedicated to David Furley), Long and Sedley discussed Epicurus and the free will problem at length, with references to the principal original Greek and Latin sources.

> "Epicurus' problem is this: if it has been necessary all along that we should act as we do, it cannot be up to us, with the result that we would not be morally responsible for our actions at all. Thus posing the problem of determinism he becomes arguably the first philosopher to recognize the philosophical centrality of what we know as the Free Will Question. His strongly libertarian approach to it can be usefully contrasted with the Stoics' acceptance of determinism.
>
> "It is perhaps the most widely known fact about Epicurus that he for this reason modified the deterministic Democritean system by introducing a slight element of indeterminacy to atomic motion, the 'swerve'. But taken in isolation such a solution is notoriously unsatisfactory. It promises to liberate us from rigid necessity only to substitute an alternative human mechanism, perhaps more undependable and eccentric but hardly more autonomous. Epicurus' remarks, where 'that which depends on us' (or 'that which is up to us') is contrasted with unstable fortune as well as with necessity, suggest that he meant to avoid this trap." [22]

22 Long and Sedley (1987) p. 107.

Julia Annas

In her 1992 book, *The Hellenistic Philosophy of Mind*, Annas finds it hard to see how random swerves can help to explain free action. But she sees clearly that randomness can provide alternative possibilities for the will to choose from.

> "...since swerves are random, it is hard to see how they help to explain free action. We can scarcely expect there to be a random swerve before every free action... The role of swerves is to provide alternative possibilities for volitions to choose between, for there would be no point in having free will if there were no genuinely open possibilities between which to select." [23]

Tim O'Keefe

In his 2005 study *Epicurus on Freedom*, O'Keefe concluded that Epicurus was mostly concerned with defending an open future against fatalism and the logical necessity of statements about future events. If it is true that there will be a sea battle on Monday, the future event is necessitated.

> "My own thesis is that Epicurus' main concern is not with justified praise and blame, but with preserving the rationality and efficacy of deliberating about one's future actions, although he thinks that determinism is incompatible with both. The reason for this is that a necessary condition on effective deliberation is the openness and contingency of the future, and determinism makes the future necessary." [24]

John Dudley

In his 2011 monograph Aristotle's Concept of Chance, Dudley makes it clear that Aristotle rejects determinism. He says that Aristotle offers three causes (ἀιτία) that are not themselves caused. These are human free choice (ἐφ' ἡμῖν), accidents (συμβεβεκός), and chance (τύχη for humans, and ταὐτόματον for animals and nature). These uncaused causes break the chain of "necessary" causes (ἀνάγκη), explain future contingency, and make the future inherently unpredictable (p. 268). He says in conclusion,

---

23 Annas (1992) p. 186.
24 O'Keefe (2005) p. 17.

> "It may be said, then, that Aristotle not only was not a determinist, but that he provided an epistemological and metaphysical explanation for the inadequacy of determinism. He argued profoundly not only that human free choices are not the only exception in an otherwise determined world, but that all events on earth are in the final analysis contingent, since they can all be traced back to a contingent starting-point. This contingent starting-point can be a free choice or a [sc. unusual] accident or chance, which can be based on both." [25]

Scholastics

The Scholastics were medieval theologians who tried to use Reason to establish the Truth of Religion. Because they used Reason, instead of accepting traditional views based on faith and scripture alone, they were called moderns. THOMAS AQUINAS maintained that man was free but also held there was a divine necessity in God's omniscience, that God himself was ruled by laws of Reason. DUNS SCOTUS took the opposite view, that God's own freedom demanded that God's actions not be necessitated, even by Reason. Both argued that human freedom was compatible with divine foreknowledge, using sophisticated arguments originally proposed by Augustine, that God's knowing was outside of time, arguments used again later in the Renaissance and by Immanuel Kant in the Enlightenment.

Great Jewish thinkers like Maimonides in his *Guide for the Perplexed* and *Chapters on Ethics* argued for human freedom, especially against the idea of omniscience in the Christian God, though in more popular commentaries he embraced a natural law and divine foreknowledge that controlled much human action.[26] Islamic thinkers hotly debated God's will, with the Sunni generally determinist and the Shia inclined toward freedom. Asian religions like Buddhism, which do not have the paradox of an omniscient God, embrace human freedom in Karma, which includes a person's character and values that tend to shape one's behavior, but can always be changed by acts of will.

25 Dudley (2011) p. 15.
26 Argument from Free Will in Wikipedia, retrieved October 2010

The Renaissance

Renaissance thinkers like Pico della Mirandola and Giordano Bruno questioned the teachings of the church and asserted a perfectibility of man that required the freedom to improve as well as to fail. Lorenzo Valla and Pietro Pomponazzi followed the Scholastics and argued that God's foreknowledge of human actions was outside of time. The Dutch humanist Erasmus and protestant reformer Martin Luther exchanged diatribes on free will. Luther's was frankly called "The Bondage of the Will." He saw nothing new in Erasmus' work, nor do I.

The Rationalists

Modern philosophy began with René Descartes and the other continental rationalists, Gottfried Leibniz and Baruch Spinoza. Again, they were called modern because they tried to use Reason to establish the certainty of Truth (including Religion). Descartes found the realm of human freedom in the Mind, which he thought was a separate substance from the material Body. He advocated a mind/body dualism in which matter or body is determined and spirit or mind is free and by its nature unconstrainable and indeterminate. Spinoza objected to Descartes's freedom. It involves an uncaused cause, which Spinoza felt was impossible. Spinoza's freedom was compatible with necessity.

Thomas Hobbes and John Bramhall were contemporaries of Descartes living in Europe as expatriates during the English Civil War. They debated Liberty and Necessity circa 1650. Hobbes held that liberty was simply the absence of external impediments to action (the modern "freedom of action"). The "voluntary" actions of a "free will" all have prior necessary causes and are thus determined. He equated necessity to the decree of God. Bramhall saw liberty as a freedom from inevitability and predetermination, but saw it consistent with the prescience of God. Both were compatibilists, Hobbes' freedom was compatible with causal determinism and Bramhall's with religious determinism.

The Empiricists

The British empiricist philosophers - George Berkeley, John Locke, and David Hume - all found chance or indeterminism unacceptable. Determinism was obviously required for us to be responsible for our actions.

John Locke liked the idea of Freedom and Liberty but was disturbed by the confusing debates about "free will". He thought it was inappropriate to describe the will itself as free. The will is a determination. It is the man who is free.

> "I think the question is not proper, whether the will be free, but whether a man be free."

> "This way of talking, nevertheless, has prevailed, and, as I guess, produced great confusion."[27]

The empiricists saw new evidence for strict causality and determinism in natural science. Isaac Newton's mathematical theory of motion (classical mechanics) could predict the motions of all things based on knowledge of their starting points, their velocities, and the forces between them. Surely the forces that controlled the heavenly bodies controlled everything else, including our minds. Thus the rationale for determinism was shifting from theological or religious determinism back to the physical/causal determinism of the Greek cosmologists and atomists. Leibniz imagined a scientist who could see the events of all times, just as all times are thought to be present to the mind of God.

> "Everything proceeds mathematically...if someone could have a sufficient insight into the inner parts of things, and in addition had remembrance and intelligence enough to consider all the circumstances and take them into account, he would be a prophet and see the future in the present as in a mirror."

Pierre-Simon Laplace particularized this Leibniz vision as an intelligent being who knows the positions and velocities of all the atoms in the universe and uses Newton's equations of motion to

27 Locke (1959) s. 21

predict the future. Laplace's Demon has become a cliché for physical determinism.

David Hume

Hume was a modern Skeptic. He doubted the existence of certain knowledge and questioned **causality**, but he thought (correctly, if inconsistently) that our actions proceeded from causes in our character. Free will is at best **compatible** with **determinism** in the sense that our will caused our actions, even though the willed action was the consequence of prior causes. An uncaused cause (the "*causa sui*" or self-cause), or a free action generated randomly with no regard for earlier conditions ("sui generis" or self-generated), was considered absurd and unintelligible. Hume said "'tis impossible to admit of any medium betwixt chance and an absolute necessity."[28]

I see Hume as a median between antiquity and the present, perhaps even an Archimedean point, a fulcrum on which the world of freedom pivoted decisively toward physical determinism and the limited freedom of action allowed by Hobbes.

There is no doubt that Hume's reconciliation of freedom and necessity was a great influence on most analytic and logical empiricist philosophers, through JOHN STUART MILL, G. E. MOORE, BERTRAND RUSSELL, A. J. AYER, and MORITZ SCHLICK, as well as physical scientists like ERNST MACH.

So what is it that distinguishes Hume's compatibilism from earlier compatibilists from CHRYSIPPUS to THOMAS HOBBES? The major difference can be traced to the work of empiricist philosophers JOHN LOCKE and GEORGE BERKELEY and of the scientist ISAAC NEWTON between Hobbes and Hume.

Locke's "Theory of Ideas," which limits human knowledge to that gathered through the senses (the mind starts as a blank slate with no innate ideas) was an enormous influence on Hume. Hume is often simply regarded as one of the three British empiricists who put knowledge of the "things themselves" with their "primary" qualities, beyond the reach of our perceptions. It is this standard

28 Hume (1978) A Treatise of Human Nature, p. 171.

view of Hume, as one denying unknowable concepts, particularly the notion of "causation," that inspired the positivists to declare such concepts "meaningless" and "metaphysical."

But Hume is much more complex, as a careful reading of the *Treatise* and especially the *Enquiry concerning Human Understanding* shows. Hume did not deny causation. He embraced it. What he did say is that empirical methods could not *prove* causality, as observations only show a "constant conjunction" of events, a "regular succession" of A followed by B, which leads the mind to the inference of cause and effect.

Thus we cannot "know" causation and "matters of fact" as we can know the "relations of ideas" such as mathematics and logic. But we have a natural belief in causation and in many matters of fact.

A major theme of Hume's work, perhaps his core contribution, is that "Reason" cannot motivate our Beliefs. Reason is an evaluative tool only. It is "Feeling" and "Passion" that motivates our "natural" beliefs, judgments, and actions.

Most earlier and later philosophers make the feelings and passions subject to reason. Hume turned this around and based his ideas of morality on sentiments and feelings. He denied that one could ever produce reasoned arguments to derive "ought" from "is," but that we naturally hold many of our moral beliefs simply based on our feelings and moral sentiments. And that only these Passions, not Reason, are capable of motivating us to action. In a most famous observation, he says..

> "I cannot forbear adding to these reasonings an observation, which may, perhaps, be found of some importance. In every system of morality, which I have hitherto met with, I have always remark'd, that the author proceeds for some time in the ordinary way of reasoning, and establishes the being of a God, or makes observations concerning human affairs; when of a sudden I am surpriz'd to find, that instead of the usual copulations of propositions, is, and is not, I meet with no proposition that is not connected with an ought, or an ought not. This change is imperceptible; but is, however, of the last consequence. For

> as this ought, or ought not, expresses some new relation or affirmation, 'tis necessary that it shou'd be observ'd and explain'd; and at the same time that a reason should be given, for what seems altogether inconceivable, how this new relation can be a deduction from others, which are entirely different from it." [29]

What is true in moral thinking is true in our physical understanding; we have a natural belief in causality, says Hume. Although it is not an empirically justified "idea" and thus not knowledge, we have a natural feeling about how one billiard ball causes a second one to move.

Similarly, we judge a person praiseworthy or blameworthy because we see the causal connection between a person's character, volition, and resulting actions. This agrees with Hobbes, and it will show up later in R. E. Hobart and Peter F. Strawson.

Hume's greatest contribution to the free will debates was to "reconcile" freedom and necessity.

> "But to proceed in this reconciling project with regard to the question of liberty and necessity; the most contentious question of metaphysics, the most contentious science; it will not require many words to prove, that all mankind have ever agreed in the doctrine of liberty as well as in that of necessity, and that the whole dispute, in this respect also, has been hitherto merely verbal...
>
> "By liberty, then, we can only mean a power of acting or not acting, according to the determinations of the will; this is, if we choose to remain at rest, we may; if we choose to move, we also may. Now this hypothetical liberty is universally allowed to belong to every one who is not a prisoner and in chains. Here, then, is no subject of dispute." [30]

For Hume, there was no such thing as chance. Human ignorance leads to all our ideas of probability. This was the view of all the great mathematicians who developed the calculus of probabilities - Abraham de Moivre before Hume and Pierre-Simon Laplace after him. And, following de Moivre, Hume called chance a mere word.

29 Hume (1978) *Treatise*, p. 469.
30 Hume (1975) *Enquiry*, p. 95.

> "Though there be no such thing as Chance in the world; our ignorance of the real cause of any event has the same influence on the understanding, and begets a like species of belief or opinion." [31]

Most compatibilists and determinists since Hobbes and Hume never mention the fact that a causal chain of events going back before our birth would not provide the kind of liberty they are looking for. But Hume frankly admits that such a causal chain would be a serious objection to his theory.

> "I pretend not to have obviated or removed all objections to this theory, with regard to necessity and liberty. I can foresee other objections, derived from topics which have not here been treated of. It may be said, for instance, that, if voluntary actions be subjected to the same laws of necessity with the operations of matter, there is a continued chain of necessary causes, preordained and pre-determined, reaching from the original cause of all to every single volition, of every human creature. No contingency anywhere in the universe; no indifference; no liberty. While we act, we are, at the same time, acted upon." [32]

To escape this objection, we must imagine that Hume wanted some kind of agent-causal freedom in voluntarist acts.

Hume knew the ancients better than most, and of the ancients, his favorite was Cicero.. His *Dialogues concerning Natural Religion* is on some level largely a paraphrase of Cicero's *De Natura Deorum*.

Probabilists

One might naively think that the development of modern probability theory and statistics would have encouraged acceptance of chance in human affairs, but surprisingly, the major theorists of probability were determinists. The mathematical distribution of possible outcomes in games of chance was formally derived independently by a number of great mathematicians in the eighteenth century - Abraham De Moivre (1667-1754), Daniel Bernoulli (1700-1782), Laplace (1749-1827), and Carl Friedrich Gauss (1777-1855). Laplace disliked the disreputable origins of this theory and renamed it the "calculus of probabilities."

31 Hume (1975) *Enquiry*, p. 56.
32 Hume (1975) *Enquiry*, p. 99.

Kant

IMMANUEL KANT's reaction to Newtonian determinism, and to DAVID HUME's criticism of obtaining certain knowledge based only on our sense perceptions, was to admit **determinism** as correct in the physical or phenomenal world, but he set limits on this determinism. Kant subsumed causality and determinism under his idea of Pure Reason. Indeed he made determinism a precondition for rational thought. But he set limits on what we can know by pure speculative Reason, in order to make room for belief in a timeless noumenal (or mental) world that includes God, freedom, and immortality.

> "I cannot even make the assumption – as the practical interests of morality require – of God, freedom, and immortality, if I do not deprive speculative reason of its pretensions to transcendent insight. For to arrive at these, it must make use of principles which, in fact, extend only to the objects of possible experience, and which cannot be applied to objects beyond this sphere without converting them into phenomena, and thus rendering the practical extension of pure reason impossible. I must therefore, abolish knowledge, to make room for belief." [33]

Kant's noumenal world is a variation on Plato's concept of Soul, Descartes' mental world, and the Scholastic idea of a world in which all times are present to the eye of God. His idea of free will is a most esoteric form of **compatibilism**. Our decisions are made in our souls outside of time and only appear determined to our senses, which are governed by our built-in a priori categories of understanding, like space and time.

> "We then see how it does not involve any contradiction to assert, on the one hand, that the will, in the phenomenal sphere – in visible action – is necessarily obedient to the law of nature, and, in so far, not free; and, on the other hand, that, as belonging to a thing in itself, it is not subject to that law, and, accordingly, is free." [34]

---

33 Kant (1952) "The Critique of Pure Reason." p. 10.
34 Kant (1952) "The Critique of Pure Reason." p. 9.

If Kant's *Critique of Pure Reason* can be seen as a reaction to David Hume's skeptical attitude toward knowledge that depends on sense data, the parallel between Hume and Kant is even stronger in Kant's *Critique of Practical Reason*.

Hume and Kant both sought a reconciling of freedom and necessity or causality. Where Hume said we could not reason to knowledge of causality, for example, but could have a natural belief in causality because of our moral sentiments and feelings, so Kant claims that his Practical Reason establishes freedom in a noumenal realm whose grounding principle is morality. Freedom is the condition for the moral law.

> "Freedom, however, is the only one of all the ideas of the speculative reason of which we know the possibility a priori (without, however, understanding it), because it is the condition of the moral law which we know." [35]

In an early letter to a friend, Kant described the workings of his mind as involving **chance**, and in terms that sound remarkably like my **Cogito** model, - "The mind must...lie open to any chance suggestion which may present itself." He described his method...

> "In mental labour of so delicate a character nothing is more harmful than preoccupation with extraneous matters. The mind, though not constantly on the stretch, must still, alike in its idle and in its favourable moments, lie uninterruptedly open to any chance suggestion which may present itself. Relaxations and diversions must maintain its powers in freedom and mobility, so that it may be enabled to view the object afresh from every side, and so to enlarge its point of view from a microscopic to a universal outlook that it adopts in turn every conceivable standpoint, verifying the observations of each by means of all the others." [36]

At the same time that Kant was inventing his most fanciful other-worldly explanation of free will, his contemporary Samuel Johnson uttered this brief analysis of the problem.

"We know our will is free, and there's an end on't."

---

35 Kant (1952) "The Critique of Practical Reason." p. 329.

36 Letter to Marcus Herz, February 21, 1772, Werke, x, p. 127 (cited by Norman Kemp Smith, Commentary to Kant's Critique of Pure Reason, p. xxii)

Five Post-Kantian Shocks to Determinism

Since the age of Newton and Kant, very few philosophers have offered genuinely new ideas for reconciling our sense of human freedom with physical determinism, which for most thinkers also implies causality, certainty, necessity, and predictability of the one possible future consistent with determinism.

This is despite three great advances in science that critically depend on the existence of real chance in the universe and two developments in logic and mathematics that question the status of philosophical certainty.

The history of the problem of free will cannot be addressed without being aware of these shocking developments in an eighty-year period that eroded the foundations of classical deterministic thinking in five areas of thought.

Evolution

Charles Darwin's explanation of biological evolution in 1859 requires chance to create variation in the gene pool. The alternative is a deterministic law controlling such change, which implies that information about all species has existed for all time. Or perhaps the idea that there is no real change. The "Great Chain of Being" from Plato's Timaeus to the middle ages maintained that all the species - from the smallest organisms, through man at the pinnacle of the natural world, then up to God through various types of supernatural angels - had existed for all time, at least since the creation. Darwin's work confirmed that Becoming was as real and important as Being (another great dualism).

Thermodynamics

Ludwig Boltzmann's attempts, starting in 1866, to derive the second law of thermodynamics (increasing entropy and irreversibility) from the classical mechanical motions of gas particles (atoms) failed until he introduced probability (chance) and treated the atoms statistically. He was ridiculed by his physicist colleagues in Germany, who rejected the idea of atoms, let alone real chance in the universe.

After Boltzmann, the presumed certain laws of physics became irreducibly statistical laws.

Logic

Aristotle's logic was accepted as the paradigm of truth for over 2000 years until Gottlob Frege in 1879 and BERTRAND RUSSELL's *Principia Mathematica* in 1910 failed to establish a logical basis for mathematics and found the first of the paradoxes that call logic into question.

Quantum Mechanics

WERNER HEISENBERG's indeterminacy principle in 1927 is believed by many thinkers to have put an end to the absolute determinism implied by Newton's laws, at least for atoms. Classical mechanics is now seen as simply the limiting case of quantum mechanics for macroscopic (large) systems. Even before Heisenberg, MAX BORN had shown in 1926 that in collisions of atomic particles we could only predict the probabilities for the atomic paths, confirming Boltzmann's requirement for microscopic randomness.

So the original two cases for irreducible randomness, implicit in the work of Darwin in 1859, explicitly made by Boltzmann in the 1870's, and espoused as philosopher CHARLES SANDERS PEIRCE's *Tychism* and WILLIAM JAMES' answer to determinism, have in the 20th century found an explanation in quantum indeterminacy.

Mathematics

Kurt Gödel's incompleteness theorem in 1937 proved there would always be true propositions that could not be proved in any consistent mathematical system complex enough to include the integers.

Determinists

Many modern philosophers admit to being "hard" determinists (as WILLIAM JAMES called them). They maintain that there is just one possible future, primarily because there is a single causal sequence of events from the beginning of time. Some argue that without "strict" causality knowledge would be impossible, since we could not be sure of our reasoning process and deduced truths. Note that there are many arguments for the truth of determinism. See Chapter 9.

Libertarians

Libertarians argue that free will is incompatible with any and all determinism. Many libertarians still hold a dualist view, with an immaterial Mind able to circumvent causal laws that constrain the physical Body. Critics call the libertarian view incoherent and unintelligible if it denies determinism and causality, which they take to be a basic requirement for modern science - for some it is the basis for logic and reason. And many libertarians admit their unhappiness with chance as the source of human freedom.

Compatibilists

WILLIAM JAMES' "soft" determinists claim that free will is compatible with determinism, since if determinism did not hold, they think that their will could not determine their actions, which would be random. Though our will is itself caused, these causes include our own character, and this is enough freedom for them, even if our character was itself determined by prior causes.

Broadly speaking, philosophers after Kant can be divided into four main groups,

- those who continued to accept compatibilism (or even determinism),
- those who simply asserted human freedom (some even admitting chance as a factor),

• those philosophers and scientists who reacted, most of them negatively, to the specific new form of chance and "indeterminism" introduced by quantum mechanics in the 1920's,

• and those active in recently renewed debates about free will, with lots of philosophical analysis and logic chopping, but virtually nothing new of substance.

Germans in the 19th century

Georg Wilhelm Friedrich Hegel's greatest contribution to philosophy was to stress the importance of time and process over mechanism, with its implicit predictability. Just as Aristotle was more this-worldly than his mentor Plato, so Hegel brings Kantian ideas down from the timeless noumenal realm into an evolving world. He spoke of an absolute freedom of the individual "in itself," a concept following Kant, the "*an sich*." But in his dialectical idealism, the individual subject (or being) goes on to see itself in the light of others as objects (the non-being). He calls this the "for itself," Kant's "*für sich*." The final stage of his "aufhebung" unites these to become the "in and for itself." At this point, Hegel's freedom is a will that is the will of a community (Being). He says, "Freedom and will are for us the unity of subjective and objective." "Freedom also lies neither in indeterminateness nor in determinateness, but in both." [37]

Hegel's idealist colleagues Johann Fichte and Friedrich Schelling were very enthusiastic about freedom for the individual, the "I," which was Kant's "transcendental subject." They wanted the I to be "unconditioned," an undetermined thing in itself (*unbedingtes Ding an sich*). For Schelling, this freedom was freedom from both Nature and God.

> "The defenders of Freedom usually only think of showing the independence of man from nature, which is indeed easy. But they leave alone man's inner independence from God, his Freedom even with respect to God, because this is the most difficult problem.

37 Hegel (1967) Introduction, Sect. 8. Two-stage model or contradiction?

> "Thus since man occupies a middle place between the non-being of nature and the absolute Being, God, he is free from both. He is free from God through having an independent root in nature; free from nature through the fact that the divine is awakened in him, that which in the midst of nature is above nature." [38]

ARTHUR SCHOPENHAUER's essay "On the Freedom of the Will" won the prize of the Royal Danish Academy of Sciences in 1839. His description of his predecessors' work (pp. 65-90) is extensive. He defined absolute freedom - the *liberum arbitrium indifferentiae* - as not being determined by prior grounds.

> "Under given external conditions, two diametrically opposed actions are possible."

Schopenhauer found this completely unacceptable.

> "If we do not accept the strict necessity of all that happens by means of a causal chain which connects all events without exception, but allow this chain to be broken in countless places by an absolute freedom, then all foreseeing of the future... becomes...absolutely impossible, and so inconceivable." [39]

The Rise of Statistical Thinking

In the 1820's the great French mathematician Joseph Fourier noticed that statistics on the number of births, deaths, marriages, suicides, and various crimes in the city of Paris had remarkably stable averages from year to year. The mean values in a "normal distribution" (one that follows the bell curve or "law of errors") of statistics took on the prestige of a social law. The Belgian astronomer and statistician ADOLPHE QUÉTELET did more than anyone to claim these statistical regularities were evidence of determinism.

Individuals might think marriage was their decision, but since the number of total marriages was relatively stable from year to year, Quételet claimed the individuals were determined to marry.

---

38 Schelling (1936) p. 458

39 Schopenhauer (1995) p 64.

Quételet used AUGUSTE COMTE's term "social physics" to describe his discovery of "laws of human nature," prompting Comte to rename his theory "sociology."

Quételet's argument for determinism in human events is quite illogical. It appears to go something like this:

- Perfectly random, unpredictable individual events (like the throw of dice in games of chance) show statistical regularities that become more and more certain with more trials (the law of large numbers).

- Human events show statistical regularities.

- Human events are determined.

Quételet might more reasonably have concluded that individual human events are unpredictable and random. Were they determined, they might be expected to show a non-random pattern, perhaps a signature of the Determiner.

In England, HENRY THOMAS BUCKLE developed the ideas of Quételet and also argued that statistical regularities proved that human free will was nonexistent.

A few thinkers questioned the idea that individual random events were actually determined simply because their statistical averages appeared to be determined. BERNARD BOLZANO (1781-1848) and FRANZ EXNER (1802-1880) were both professors at Prague in the 1830's and 40's. They had a famous correspondence in which they discussed the possibility of free will. Bolzano, a Catholic priest, was stripped of his teaching post because his ideas were anathema to the Catholic Austrian government that paid his salary. One outcome of the revolution of 1848 was a reform of Austrian education aimed at diminishing the power of the Catholic religion, especially in education. Exner was the principal architect of this curriculum reform, and a central secular tenet was to teach the concept of probability, to encourage students to take responsibility for their own lives.

In France, two philosophers, CHARLES RENOUVIER (1815-1903) and ALFRED FOUILLÉE (1838-1912), argued for human freedom and based it on the existence of absolute chance. In his *Essais de Critique Générale*, Renouvier generally followed Kant, but he moved human freedom from Kant's imaginary noumenal realm into the phenomenal world, which for Renouvier included contingent events. In *La Liberté et le Déterminisme,* Fouillée denied necessity and determinism.

Every philosopher after Charles Darwin's Origin of Species was affected by the explanation of evolution as random variation followed by natural selection. A few embraced it, and found that it gave support to their ideas of human freedom, based on the liberating notion of chance. But few offered a convincing idea of how exactly chance as a cause could be made consistent with moral responsibility.

Charles Sanders Peirce was deeply impressed by chance as a way to bring diversity and "progress" (in the form of increasingly complex organisms) to the world. Obviously modeling his thinking on the work of Darwin, Peirce was unequivocal that chance was a real property of the world. He named it *Tyche*, and made tychism the basis for the evolutionary growth of variety, of irregular departures from an otherwise mechanical universe, including life and Peirce's own original thoughts. But Peirce did not like Darwin's fortuitous variation and natural selection. He falsely associated it with the Social Darwinist thinking of his time and called it a "greed philosophy." Peirce also rejected the deterministic evolution scheme of Herbert Spencer, and proposed his own grand scheme for the evolution of everything including the laws of Nature! He called this synechism, a coined term for continuity, in clear contrast to the random events of his tychism.

Peirce (correctly) reads Aristotle as espousing absolute chance and offering a *tertium quid* beyond chance and necessity. Aristotle, he says, holds that events come to pass in three ways, namely

> "(1) by external compulsion, or the action of efficient causes, (2) by virtue of an inward nature, or the influence of final causes, and (3) irregularly without definite cause, but just by absolute chance." [40]

40 Peirce (1958) Vol. 6, p. 28

Peirce is boastful about his knowledge of early philosophers, and we know he was familiar with the ancient Stoic objection to chance (since at least Chrysippus and Cicero) as the cause of human actions. The Stoics objected that we cannot be responsible for chance actions. Peirce agrees, saying

> "To undertake to account for anything by saying baldly that it is due to chance would, indeed, be futile. But this I do not do. I make use of chance chiefly to make room for a principle of generalization, or tendency to form habits, which I hold has produced all regularities." [41]

William James, in *The Will to Believe*, simply asserted that his will was free. As his first act of freedom, he said, he chose to believe his will was free. He was encouraged to do this by reading Charles Renouvier.

James coined the terms "hard determinism" and "soft determinism" in his lecture on "The Dilemma of Determinism." He described chance as neither of these, but "indeterminism." He said,

> "The stronghold of the determinist argument is the antipathy to the idea of chance...This notion of alternative possibility, this admission that any one of several things may come to pass is, after all, only a roundabout name for chance." [42]

James was the first thinker to enunciate clearly a two-stage decision process, with chance in a present time of random alternatives, leading to a choice which grants consent to one possibility and transforms an equivocal future into an unalterable and simple past. There are undetermined alternatives followed by adequately determined choices.

> "What is meant by saying that my choice of which way to walk home after the lecture is ambiguous and matter of chance?...It means that both Divinity Avenue and Oxford Street are called but only one, and that one either one, shall be chosen." [43]

James very likely had the model of Darwinian evolution in mind. Unlike his colleague Charles Peirce, from whom he learned

41 *ibid.*
42 James (1956) p. 153
43 James (1956) p. 155

much about chance, James accepted Darwin's explanation of human evolution.

John Stuart Mill (1806-1873) did great work on probability in his System of Logic, but like the continental mathematicians was a confirmed determinist. His endorsement of Hume's reconciliation of free will with determinism came to be known as the Hume-Mill thesis. Mill accepted Hume's view that human actions would some day be explainable by laws of human nature as sure as Newton's laws of physical nature. If this were not so, he feared for science itself.

> "At the threshold of this inquiry we are met by an objection, which, if not removed, would be fatal to the attempt to treat human conduct as a subject of science. Are the actions of human beings, like all other natural events, subject to invariable laws?"
>
> "The question, whether the law of causality applies in the same strict sense to human actions as to other phenomena, is the celebrated controversy concerning the freedom of the will: which, from at least as far back as the time of Pelagius, has divided both the philosophical and the religious world. The affirmative opinion is commonly called the doctrine of a Necessity, as asserting human volitions and actions to be necessary and inevitable. The negative maintains that the will is not determined, like other phenomena, by antecedents, but determines itself; that our volitions are not, properly speaking, the effects of causes, or at least have no causes which they uniformly and implicitly obey.
>
> "I have already made it sufficiently 'apparent' that the former of these opinions is that which I consider the true one." [44]

Mill's godson Bertrand Russell also had no doubt that causality and determinism were needed to do science. "Where determinism fails, science fails," he said. Russell could not find in himself "any specific occurrence that I could call 'will.'"

Henri Bergson, in his "Time and Free Will," argued that time in the mind (he called it dureé or duration) was different from physical time. In particular, because minds were evolving living

44 A System of Logic, Bk VI, Ch II, Of Liberty and Necessity

things with memories of all their past experience, they could not be treated as collections of mechanical atoms with no such memories, so minds were not subject to deterministic laws.

Friedrich Nietzsche knew Darwin and perhaps knew of the debates in the German universities about probability and irreversibility. He may have been impressed by mechanistic explanations for everything including human affairs. His "eternal return" is consistent with microscopic particles (atoms) following deterministic paths that eventually repeat themselves. His aphoristic and polemical writing style makes his real position on free will hard to fathom. Nietzsche both denied the will and even more strongly claimed that as overmen we must choose to make ourselves. This choice has even greater weight because it would be repeated again and again in his vision of an eternal return.

Henri Poincaré describes a two-stage process in mathematical discoveries, in his lectures to the Paris Société de Psychologie around 1907. The first stage is random combinations, which he likens to Epicurus' "hooked atoms" ploughing through space in all directions, like a "swarm of gnats." He apologizes for the crude comparison, but says

> "the right combination is to be found by strict calculations [which] demand discipline, will, and consequently consciousness. In the subliminal ego, on the contrary, there reigns what I would call liberty, if one could give this name to the mere absence of discipline and to disorder born of chance." [45]

In 1937, at the Paris Centre de Synthése, a week of lectures was delivered on inventions of various kinds, including experimental science, mathematics, and poetry. The mathematician Jacques Hadamard described the conference in his book *The Psychology of Invention in the Mathematical Field* (1949) Hadamard's emphasis was on the discovery or invention of mathematical theories and his main subject was Henri Poincaré.

Hadamard assures us that Poincaré's observations do not impute discovery directly to pure chance. He says

45 Poincaré (2003) p. 60

> "Indeed, it is obvious that invention or discovery, be it in mathematics or anywhere else, takes place by combining ideas."
>
> "It cannot be avoided that this first operation takes place, to a certain extent, at random, so that the role of chance is hardly doubtful in this first step of the mental process. But we see that the intervention of chance occurs inside the unconscious." [46]

The first step is only the beginning of creation, for the following step, says Hadamard,

> "Invention is discernment, choice...it is clear that no significant discovery or invention can take place without the will of finding." [47]

Poincaré is apparently the second thinker, after WILLIAM JAMES, to see random combinations of ideas in the unconscious mind, followed by willful decisions or choices made consciously.

MORITZ SCHLICK (1882-1936) was a founder of the great Vienna Circle of Logical Empiricism, which included LUDWIG WITTGENSTEIN in its early years. Like Wittgenstein, Schlick thought some problems could be dis-solved by logical analysis. They were pseudo-problems, of which "the so-called problem of the freedom of the will" was an old one.

> "this pseudo-problem has long since been settled by the efforts of certain sensible persons; and, above all...— with exceptional clarity by Hume. Hence it is really one of the greatest scandals of philosophy that again and again so much paper and printer's ink is devoted to this matter... I shall, of course, say only what others have already said better; consoling myself with the thought that in this way alone can anything be done to put an end at last to that scandal." [48]

Quantum Indeterminacy

In 1925 MAX BORN, WERNER HEISENBERG, and PASCUAL JORDAN, formulated their matrix mechanics version of quantum

46 Hadamard (1945) pp. 29-30.
47 Hadamard (1945) p. 30.
48 Schlick (2008) Ch. VII.

mechanics as a superior formulation of NEILS BOHR's old quantum theory. Matrix mechanics confirmed discrete energy levels and random "quantum jumps" of electrons between the energy levels, with emission or absorption of photons accompanying the jump.

In 1926, ERWIN SCHRÖDINGER developed wave mechanics as an alternative formulation of quantum mechanics. Schrödinger disliked the abrupt jumps. His wave mechanics was a continuous, even deterministic, theory.

Within months of the new wave mechanics, MAX BORN showed that while Schrödinger's wave function evolved over time deterministically, it only predicted the positions and velocities of atomic particles probabilistically.

Heisenberg used Schrödinger's wave functions to calculate the "transition probabilities" for electrons to jump from one energy level to another. Schrödinger's wave mechanics was easier to visualize and much easier to calculate than Heisenberg's own matrix mechanics.

In early 1927, Heisenberg announced his **indeterminacy principle** limiting our knowledge of the simultaneous position and velocity of atomic particles, and declared that the new quantum theory disproved causality.

> "We cannot - and here is where the causal law breaks down - explain why a particular atom will decay at one moment and not the next, or what causes it to emit an electron in this direction rather than that." [49]

More popularly known as the Uncertainty Principle in quantum mechanics, it states that the exact position and momentum of an atomic particle can only be known within certain (sic) limits. The product of the position error and the momentum error is greater than or equal to Planck's constant h/2π.

$$\Delta p \Delta x \geq h/2\pi$$

Indeterminacy (*Unbestimmtheit*) was Heisenberg's original name for his principle. It is a better name than the more popular uncertainty, which connotes lack of knowledge. The Heisenberg

49 Heisenberg, W (1972) p. 119.

principle is an ontological and real lack of information, not merely an epistemic lack, a result of human ignorance.

Later in 1927, Bohr announced his complementarity principle and the Copenhagen interpretation of quantum mechanics that argued for a dualist combination of wave and particle aspects for atoms and electrons.

Schrödinger argued vociferously against the random quantum jumps of Bohr and Heisenberg and for a return to his easily visualized, deterministic, and continuous physics.

ALBERT EINSTEIN, MAX PLANCK, Schrödinger, and other leading physicists were appalled at Born's assertion that quantum mechanics was probabilistic and Heisenberg's claim that strict causality was no longer tenable. Einstein's famous reaction was "The Lord God does not play dice." Planck said,

> "the assumption of absolute chance in inorganic nature is incompatible with the working principle of physical science.
>
> "This means that the postulate of complete determinism is accepted as a necessary condition for the progress of psychological research." [50]

Just a few years earlier, in 1919, Schrödinger and his mentor FRANZ SERAFIN EXNER (son of the 19th-century educator) had been strong disciples of LUDWIG BOLTZMANN. They were convinced that Boltzmann's kinetic theory of gases required a microscopic world of random and chaotic atomic motions.

Why did Schrödinger switch from an indeterminist to a determinist philosophy, then adhere to it the rest of his life? Perhaps because his work now put him in the company of Einstein and Planck? Planck stepped down from his chair of theoretical physics at the University of Berlin and gave it to Schrödinger, who won the Nobel prize in 1933. It took nearly thirty more years and another world war before the Nobel committee gave Max Born the prize for his probabilistic interpretation of the wave function.

---

50 Planck (1981) pp. 154-5.

In his Gifford Lectures of 1927, Arthur Stanley Eddington had described himself as unable "to form a satisfactory conception of any kind of law or causal sequence which shall be other than deterministic." [51]

Eddington had already established himself as the leading interpreter of the new relativity and quantum physics. His astronomical measurements of light bending as it passes the sun had confirmed Einstein's general relativity theory.

A year later, in response to Heisenberg's uncertainty principle, Eddington revised his lectures for publication as *The Nature of the Physical World*. There he announced "It is a consequence of the advent of the quantum theory that physics is no longer pledged to a scheme of deterministic law," [52] and enthusiastically identified indeterminism with freedom of the will.

But Eddington left himself open to the charge since Epicurus' time, that chance could not be identified with freedom. He was apparently unaware of the work of William James or Henri Poincaré to make deliberation a two-stage process - first random possibilities, then a choice. A decade later, in his 1939 book *The Philosophy of Physical Science*, just a few years before his death, he reluctantly concluded there is no "halfway house" between randomness and determinism, [53] an echo of David Hume's claim that there is "no medium betwixt chance and an absolute necessity." [54]

Niels Bohr mentioned the free will and causality discussions in 1929, but he spoke vaguely, with his vision of complementarity, and likened them to subjective and objective views:

> "Just as the freedom of the will is an experiential category of our psychic life, causality may be considered as a mode of perception by which we reduce our sense impressions to order... the feeling of volition and the demand for causality are equally indispensable elements in the relation between subject and object which forms the core of the problem of knowledge." [55]

51 Eddington (1928) p. 294.
52 Eddington (1928) p.
53 Eddington (1939) p.
54 Hume (1978) p. 171.
55 Bohr (1936) p.

The German philosopher ERNST CASSIRER was close to many of the physicists in this debate and had a profound influence on some of them. Cassirer also influenced the predominantly deterministic views of other philosophers, themselves untrained in physics, who tried to understand the implications of quantum indeterminism for their philosophies. In his 1936 book *Determinism and Indeterminism in Modern Physics*, Cassirer made the case an ethical one, saying

> "all truly ethical action must spring from the unity and persistence of a definite ethical character. This in itself shows us that it would be fatal for ethics to tie itself to and, as it were, fling itself into the arms of a limitless indeterminism." [56]

MAX BORN had been first to see that chance and probability were essential to quantum mechanics, as they had been to the statistical laws of physics since Boltzmann. Unfortunately Born was strongly influenced by Cassirer, the non-scientist philosopher who said "we cannot do away with the guiding concept of determinism." Born concluded somewhat dialectically that free will was just a subjective phenomenon,

> "I think that the philosophical treatment of the problem of free will suffers often from an insufficient distinction between the subjective and objective aspect."[57]

Born approvingly quotes Cassirer, from the last chapter of *Determinism and Indeterminism in Modern Physics*,

> "whether causality in nature is regarded in the form of rigorous 'dynamical' laws or of merely statistical laws...In neither way does there remain open that sphere of 'freedom' which is claimed by ethics." [58]

Some biologists quickly objected to the idea of physical uncertainty in the human mind because large amounts of matter ensure adequate regularity of the statistical laws. [59]

---

56 Cassirer (1956), p. 209.
57 Born (1964) p. 127.
58 Original source, Cassirer (1956), p. 209.(Note: Standard Argument.)
59 C. G. Darwin, *Science*, 73, 653, June 19, 1931.

But physicist Arthur Holly Compton defended the Eddington suggestion, with the idea of an amplifier that would allow microscopic random events to produce macroscopic random events.[60] Four years earlier, the biologist Ralph Lillie had pointed out that natural selection was just such an amplifier of microscopic randomness.[61]

This naive model for free will came to be known as the massive switch amplifier. It was open to the ancient criticism that we can not take responsibility for random actions caused by chance. Compton defended the amplifier in his 1935 book *The Freedom of Man*, but like Eddington, later denied he was trying to show that human freedom was a direct consequence of the uncertainty principle. If physics were the sole source of our information, he said, we should expect men's actions to follow certain (sic) rules of chance.[62]

Much later, in the *Atlantic Monthly* of 1957, Compton saw the two-stage process of chance preceding choice.

> "When one exercises freedom, by his act of choice he is himself adding a factor not supplied by the [random] physical conditions and is thus himself determining what will occur." [63]

John Eccles, the great neurophysiologist, took Eddington's suggestions seriously and looked for places in the brain where quantum uncertainty might be important. He decided on the synapses, where the axon of one neuron communicates with the dendrite of another neuron across a narrow gap (less than 1000 Angstroms). In his 1953 book *The Neurophysiological Basis of Mind*, Eccles calculated the positional uncertainty of the tiny synaptic knob. He found it to be 20 Angstroms in 1 second, a relatively tiny but perhaps significant fraction of the synaptic gap or cleft.[64]

One other scientist and sometime philosopher, Henry Margenau, saw quantum uncertainty as necessary for free will, but that there were "more steps" needed to explain freedom. In his Wimmer Lecture of 1968, he said,

---

60 A. H. Compton, *Science*, 74, 1911, August 14, 1931.

61 Ralph Lillie, *Science*, 66, 139, 1927

62 The Human Meaning of Science, 1940

63 *Atlantic Monthly*, October, 1957; reprinted in Compton (1967)

64 Eccles (1953) pp. 271-286.

> "Freedom cannot appear in the domains of physiology and psychology if it is not already lodged in physics...embracing the belief that freedom is made possible by indeterminacies in nature will not solve the problem of freedom...it permits only one first step towards its solution."[65]

Instead of Ernst Cassirer's view "that it would be fatal for ethics to tie itself to and, as it were, fling itself into the arms of a limitless indeterminism," Margenau embraced indeterminism as just the first step toward a solution of the problem of human freedom.

Margenau lamented that his position

> "forces us to part company with many distinguished moral philosophers who see the autonomy of ethics threatened when a relation of any sort is assumed to exist between that august discipline and science."

Margenau clearly means his longtime mentor.

> "Ethics, says Cassirer, should not be forced to build its nests in the gaps of physical causation, but he fails to tell where else it should build them, if at all." [66]

Then in his 1982 book *Einstein's Space and Van Gogh's Sky*, Margenau condensed his model into a single paragraph, with two components - Compton's chance and choice.

> "Our thesis is that quantum mechanics leaves our body, our brain, at any moment in a state with numerous (because of its complexity we might say innumerable) possible futures, each with a predetermined probability. Freedom involves two components: chance (existence of a genuine set of alternatives) and choice. Quantum mechanics provides the chance, and we shall argue that only the mind can make the choice by selecting (not energetically enforcing) among the possible future courses." [67]

We note sadly that Margenau does not cite the earlier work of Compton (or the philosopher Karl Popper's 1977 adaptation of Compton - see below). Perhaps because free will was not a topic for mainstream scientific journals, he felt no need for rigorous

65 Margenau (1968)

66 Margenau (1968) p. 71.

67 Margenau and Leshan (1982) p. 240.

references and scrupulous priority of ideas. But Margenau pays a price, his own work does not get referred to by later thinkers.

Most other Nobel-prize-winning scientists and their philosophical interpreters could not reconcile quantum mechanics and the uncertainty principle with human freedom, concluding only that strict determinism was certainly not the case for the physical or phenomenal world.

Quantum Mysteries

We should mention a few bizarre suggestions by scientists on how some of the more mysterious properties of "quantum reality" might help explain consciousness and free will.

Roger Penrose claims, in his 1989 book *The Emperor's New Mind* that non-locality and quantum gravity are involved in the mind. Like Eccles, he speculates that single-quantum sensitive neurons are playing an important role deep inside the brain. But he says he needs large numbers of neurons to cooperate:

> "Such co-operation, I am maintaining, must be achieved quantum-mechanically; and the way that this is done is by many different combined arrangements of atoms being 'tried' simultaneously in linear superposition perhaps a little like the quantum computer...The selection of an appropriate (though probably not the best) solution to the minimizing problem must be achieved as the one-graviton criterion (or appropriate alternative) is reached - which would presumably only occur when the physical conditions are right"[68]

David Hodgson extended Penrose's ideas in his 1991 book *Mind Matters*. He claims that

> "My discussion of quantum mechanics has confirmed [the mind's] indeterministic character; and has also suggested that quantum mechanics shows that matter is ultimately 'non-material' and non-local, and that perhaps mind and matter are interdependent."[69]

68 Penrose (1989) p. 437
69 Hodgson (1991) p. 381

Penrose went further in 1994 in his book *Shadows of the Mind*, calculating that tens of thousands of neurons could exist in a coherent correlated superposition of states for one-fortieth of a second (the fundamental alpha-rhythm rate). He cites the idea of a dualistic "mind-stuff" influencing the "quantum choices" with its "free will."

> "With the possibility that quantum effects might indeed trigger much larger activities within the brain, some people have expressed the hope that, in such circumstances, quantum indeterminacy might be what provides an opening for the mind to influence the physical brain. Here, a dualistic viewpoint would be likely to be adopted, either explicitly or implicitly. Perhaps the 'free will' of an 'external mind' might be able to influence the quantum choices that actually result from such non-deterministic processes. On this view, it is presumably through the action of quantum theory's R-process that the dualist's 'mind-stuff' would have its influence on the behaviour of the brain."[70] (p. 349)

The idea that mental processes or even just macroscopic entities can "influence" quantum events (e.g., by changing probabilities) is called **downward causation**. JOHN ECCLES argued that wave functions might be influenced because they are neither matter nor energy and are thus an ideal vehicle for the interaction between non-physical mind and physical matter. Eccles thought this idea was first suggested by HENRY MARGENAU.

Penrose provides considerable evidence for correlated states in the microtubules within the cell's cytoskeleton, then describes chemical evidence for connecting the microtubules and consciousness in anaesthesia.[71]

HENRY STAPP is another physicist employing quantum strangeness. In his 2003 *Mind, Matter, and Quantum Mechanics*, Stapp argues that mental intentions and strong "mental efforts" can influence quantum wave functions and produce correlated behaviors over large regions of the brain. Resembling Penrose's arguments (without any reference), Stapp says:

---

70 Shadows of the Mind, p. 349.

71 Shadows of the Mind, p. 357-370.

> "It should be mentioned here that the actions P are nonlocal: they must act over extended regions, which can, and are expected to, cover large regions of the brain. Each conscious act is associated with a Process I action [collapse of the wave function] that coordinates and integrates activities in diverse parts of the brain. A conscious thought, as represented by the von Neumann Process I, effectively grasps as a whole an entire quasi-stable macroscopic brain activity."[72]

Behavioral Freedom

In 2009, the neurobiologist and geneticist MARTIN HEISENBERG, son of quantum physicist WERNER HEISENBERG, found evidence for a combination of random and lawful behavior in animals and unicellular bacteria. They can originate actions, so are not simply Cartesian stimulus-response mechanisms.

> Evidence of randomly generated action — action that is distinct from reaction because it does not depend upon external stimuli — can be found in unicellular organisms. Take the way the bacterium Escherichia coli moves. It has a flagellum that can rotate around its longitudinal axis in either direction: one way drives the bacterium forward, the other causes it to tumble at random so that it ends up facing in a new direction ready for the next phase of forward motion. This 'random walk' can be modulated by sensory receptors, enabling the bacterium to find food and the right temperature.

In higher organisms, Heisenberg finds that the brain still may include elements that do a random walk among options for action.

> As with a bacterium's locomotion, the activation of behavioural modules is based on the interplay between chance and lawfulness in the brain. Insufficiently equipped, insufficiently informed and short of time, animals have to find a module that is adaptive. Their brains, in a kind of random walk, continuously preactivate, discard and reconfigure their options, and evaluate their possible short-term and long-term consequences.[73]

---

72 Mind, Matter, and Quantum Mechanics, p. 252.

73 Nature, 14 May 2009, p. 165

Philosophers Specializing in Free Will

Mortimer Adler

In the late 1950's, MORTIMER ADLER compiled a massive two-volume history of *The Idea of Freedom*. It covers at great length ideas of political freedom and freedom from external constraints, as well as the central freedom of the individual will to choose from among possibilities that are not necessary or predictable.

In an attempt to classify types of freedom, Adler invents three categories that he hopes are "dialectically neutral" - the *circumstantial* freedom of **self-realization** (freedom from coercion, political end economic freedom, etc.), the *acquired* freedom of **self-perfection** (making decisions for moral reasons rather than desires and passions), and the *natural* freedom of **self-determination** (the normal freedom of the will).

Self-perfection is the idea from Plato to Kant that we are only free when our decisions are for reasons and we are not slaves to our passions. Adler also includes many theologically minded philosophers who argue that man is only free when following a divine moral law, which may have led to Hegel's freedom of a stone "falling freely" according to Newton's law of gravity.

Sinners, they say, do not have this free will, presumably to make sinners responsible for evil in the world despite an omniscient and omnipotent God.

Self-determination covers the classic problem of free will. Do our choices determine our will, or are they part of a causal chain?

Most of Adler's freedoms are actually compatible with classical physics. In his over 1400 pages, Adler devotes only six pages to brief comments on quantum mechanical indeterminism.[74] Adler depends heavily on the thoughts of MAX PLANCK and ERWIN SCHRÖDINGER, who along with major thinkers like Einstein, Louis de Broglie, and DAVID BOHM, rejected indeterminism.

Karl Popper

The philosopher KARL POPPER had a famous collaboration over some decades with the neuroscientist JOHN ECCLES. The two were

74 The Idea of Freedom, v. 1, p. 461-466.

mind/body or mind/brain dualists who hoped to discover the mind to be more than a mere "epiphenomenon" of the material brain. They considered quantum effects, initially to dismiss them, and later to reconsider them.

In their dialogue X, Eccles said, "It is not possible I think to utilize quantum indeterminacy." Popper replied,

> "I do of course agree that quantum theoretical indeterminacy in a sense cannot help, because this leads merely to probabilistic laws, and we do not wish to say that such things as free decisions are just probabilistic affairs. The trouble with quantum mechanical indeterminacy is twofold. First, it is probabilistic, and this doesn't help much with the free-will problem, which is not just a chance affair. Second, it gives us only indeterminism."[75]

To this point, Popper reflects the overall negative reaction of the scientific and philosophical communities to indeterminism. But in his 1965 Arthur Holly Compton memorial lecture *Of Clouds and Clocks*, Popper celebrated Compton's contributions to the question of human freedom, including the insufficient idea of the quantum uncertainty amplifier. But then he goes on to describe a two-stage decision process modeled on Darwinian natural selection. Can we doubt these were directly inspired by Compton's later remarks and Compton's 1931 references to Ralph Lillie and evolution?

Any intelligible explanation for free will must include both indeterminism and adequate determinism, resembling biological evolution, Popper says,

> "New ideas have a striking similarity to genetic mutations," "Mutations are, it seems, brought about by quantum theoretical indeterminacy (including radiation effects). On them there subsequently operates natural selection which eliminates inappropriate mutations. Now we could conceive of a similar process with respect to new ideas and to free-will decisions. That is to say, a range of possibilities is brought about by a probabilistic and quantum mechanically characterized set of proposals, as it were - of possibilities brought forward by the brain. On these there operates a kind of selective procedure which eliminates

---

75 Popper and Eccles, 1977,

> those proposals and those probabilities which are not acceptable to the mind." [76]

In 1977 Popper gave the first Darwin Lecture, at Darwin College, Cambridge. He called it *Natural Selection and the Emergence of Mind*. In it he said he had changed his mind (a rare admission by a philosopher) about two things. First he now thought that natural selection was not a "tautology" that made it an unfalsifiable theory. Second, he had come to accept the random variation and selection of ideas as a model of free will.

> "The selection of a kind of behavior out of a randomly offered repertoire may be an act of indeterminism; and in discussing indeterminism I have often regretfully pointed out that quantum indeterminacy does not seem to help us; for the amplification of something like, say, radioactive disintegration processes would not lead to human action or even animal action, but only to random movements."

This is the randomness objection of the standard argument..

> "I have changed my mind on this issue. A choice process may be a selection process, and the selection may be from some repertoire of random events, without being random in its turn. This seems to me to offer a promising solution to one of our most vexing problems, and one by downward causation." [77]

Karl Popper is thus the third thinker (or fourth, if we liberally interpret Compton) to describe a two-stage mental process, after William James and Henri Poincaré. He also solves the problem of indeterminism directly causing our decisions. Note Popper's not so subtle shift of the realm of chance to the material body (his "World 1") and the realm of determination to the mind (his "World 2"). The traditional dualism from the ancients to Kant made the material body the realm of phenomenal determinism and the mind or spirit the noumenal realm of freedom, God, and immortality.

---

76 Popper and Eccles, 1977, pp. 539-540

77 Darwin College Lecture, (1977) Parts of this lecture are available online as a rare audio recording of Popper.

http://www.spokenword.ac.uk/record_view.php?pbd=gcu-a0a0r2-b

Elizabeth Anscombe

The physicist RICHARD FEYNMAN also proposed a Compton-style Geiger-counter event followed by a bomb explosion. This caught the attention of Wittgenstein scholar ELIZABETH ANSCOMBE in her inaugural lecture at Cambridge University, where she said

> It has taken the inventions of indeterministic physics to shake the rather common dogmatic conviction that determinism is a presupposition or perhaps a conclusion, of scientific knowledge. Feynman's example of the bomb and Geiger counter smashes this conception; but as far as I can judge it takes time for the lesson to be learned. I find deterministic assumptions more common now among people at large, and among philosophers, than when I was an undergraduate. [78]

P. F. Strawson

In his 1962 landmark essay *Freedom and Resentment*, PETER F. STRAWSON changed the subject from free will itself to the question of moral responsibility.[79] Strawson said he could make no sense of the truth or falsity of determinism, indeterminism, or free will. But even if determinism were true, he argued, we would continue to act as if persons were morally responsible and deserving of praise and blame, gratitude and resentment.

Strawson was following DAVID HUME's naturalist arguments that our moral sentiments are simply given facts beyond the skepticism of logic and critical thought. Hume the Naturalist had no problem deriving Ought from Is - something shown logically impossible by Hume the Skeptic. See p. 86.

Strawson himself was optimistic that compatibilism could reconcile determinism with moral obligation and responsibility. He accepted the facts of determinism. He felt that determinism was true. But he was concerned to salvage the reality of our attitudes even for libertarians, whom he described as pessimists about determinism.

---

78 Anscombe (1971) p. 24.

79 Strawson, P.F. (1962) A pupil of H. P. Grice, Strawson belonged to the so-called "School of Ordinary Language Philosophy" under the leadership of J. L. Austin in post-war Oxford.

> "What I have called the participant reactive attitudes are essentially natural human reactions to the good or ill will or indifference of others towards us, as displayed in their attitudes and actions. The question we have to ask is: What effect would, or should, the acceptance of the truth of a general thesis of determinism have upon these reactive attitudes? More specifically, would, or should, the acceptance of the truth of the thesis lead to the decay or the repudiation of all such attitudes? Would, or should, it mean the end of gratitude, resentment, and forgiveness; of all reciprocated adult loves; of all the essentially personal antagonisms?
>
> "But how can I answer, or even pose, this question without knowing exactly what the thesis of determinism is? Well, there is one thing we do know; that if there is a coherent thesis of determinism, then there must be a sense of 'determined' such that, if that thesis is true, then all behaviour whatever is determined in that sense. Remembering this, we can consider at least what possibilities lie formally open; and then perhaps we shall see that the question can be answered without knowing exactly what the thesis of determinism is."[80]

Strawson felt that the truth of determinism would in no way repudiate such attitudes, even the feeling of resentment, unless what he called "participant" attitudes were universally replaced by "objective" attitudes.

Harry Frankfurt

In 1969 Harry Frankfurt changed the debate on free will and moral responsibility with a famous thought experiment that challenged the existence of **alternative possibilities** for action. The traditional argument for free will requires alternative possibilities so that an agent could have **done otherwise,** without which there is no moral responsibility.

Frankfurt posited a counterfactual demon who can intervene in an agent's decisions if the agent is about to do something different from what the demon wants the agent to do. Frankfurt's demon will block any alternative possibilities, but leave the agent to "freely choose" to do the one possibility desired by the demon.

80 Strawson (1962) p. 10

Frankfurt claimed the existence of the hypothetical control mechanisms blocking alternative possibilities would be irrelevant to the agent's free choice. This is true when the agent's choice agrees with the demon, but obviously false should the agent disagree. In that case, the demon would have to block the agent's will and the agent would surely notice.

Compatibilists had long been bothered by alternative possibilities, needed in order that agents "could have done otherwise." They knew that **determinism** allows only a single future - just one **actual** causal chain of events - and were delighted to get behind Frankfurt's examples as *proofs* that alternative possibilities, perhaps generated in part by random events, did not exist. Frankfurt, like Strawson, argued for **moral responsibility** without libertarian free will.

Note, however, that Frankfurt actually assumes that genuine alternative possibilities do exist. If not, there is nothing for his counterfactual intervening demon to block. John Martin Fischer called these alternative possibilities "flickers of freedom." Without these virtual alternatives, Frankfurt would have to admit that there is only one "actual sequence" of events leading to one possible future. "Alternative sequences" would be ruled out. Since Frankfurt's demon, much like Laplace's demon, has no way of knowing the actual information about future events - such as an agent's decisions - until that information comes into existence, such demons are not possible and Frankfurt-style thought experiments, entertaining as they are, cannot establish the compatibilist version of free will.

Richard Taylor's Fatalism

In 1962, the agent-causalist libertarian philosopher Taylor wrote a tongue-in-cheek article in the *Philosophical Review* entitled "Fatalism." It was not about fatalism exactly, but about the logical determinism that results from the truth conditions of certain propositions. It was the **Master Argument** of Diodorus Cronus that denies **future contingency**, also discussed by Aristotle in terms of a future "sea-batttle."

Taylor had five years earlier explained correctly that Aristotle did not deny future contingency. Statements about future events occurring are neither true nor false. The word is indeterminate about the open future.

Determinist philosophy being so popular, Taylor's Fatalism article was widely anthologized, and taken by many to be a *proof* of determinism. One of those taken in was the young DAVID FOSTER WALLACE, who wrote an undergraduate philosophy thesis in 1985 attempting to disprove Taylor's argument, with an elaborate symbolic logical argument developed with one of his professors.[81]

Wallace was arguably deeply discouraged by the deterministic fatalism promoted by academic philosophers. This view had driven the young WILLIAM JAMES near suicide in 1869, and may have contributed to the young Wallace's tragic death in 2008.

Daniel Dennett

DANIEL DENNETT, perhaps the leading spokesman for Compatibilism, is a strong critic of any genuine **indeterminism** in free will. Yet in his 1978 book *Brainstorms*, he proposed an influential "model of decision making" with a two-stage account of free will. In his chapter "On Giving Libertarians What They Say They Want," Dennett clearly separates random possibilities from determined choices.

But does Dennett, following James, Poincaré, and Popper, see that this solves the problem of indeterminism in free will that has plagued philosophy since EPICURUS' "swerve" of the atoms? He says, a bit sarcastically, that his model

> "puts indeterminism in the right place for the libertarian, *if there is a right place* at all [my emphasis]." [82]

And after giving six excellent reasons why his suggestion is what libertarians are looking for, Dennett then suggests that the randomness generator might as well have been a computer-generated pseudo-random number generator. He says

81 Wallace (2011)

82 Dennett (1978) p. 295.

> "Isn't it the case that the new improved proposed model for human deliberation can do as well with a random-but-deterministic generation process as with a causally undetermined process?" [83]

This completely misses the libertarian's point, which needs randomness that breaks the causal chain of pre-determinism back to the universe origin! But then Dennett's argument for libertarianism may just be a compatibilist's straw man. He does not pursue it in his later works, such as *Elbow Room, The Varieties of Free Will Worth Wanting* (Dennett, 1984) or the more recent *Freedom Evolves* (2003).

Dennett's model was inspired by many sources. One was David Wiggins' *Towards a Reasonable Libertarianism*, which cited Bertrand Russell and Arthur Stanley Eddington as suggesting quantum indeterminism. Another was Herbert Simon's 1969 two-stage "generate and test" model for a creating problem-solving computer.[84] Simon's model is itself a computer version of Darwin's random variation and natural selection model for biological evolution. Another source was Jacques Hadamard's book. Dennett quotes the poet Paul Valéry (as Hadamard quoted), who imagines two agents (in one mind?)

> "It takes two to invent anything. The one makes up combinations; the other one chooses."[85]

But as we have seen, this was Poincaré's idea which Valéry picked up at the 1937 Synthése conference. Some evidence now exists that Poincaré's work was in fact inspired by William James. They both say that **alternative possibilities** "present themselves."

Nevertheless, Dennett's article is so influential in the philosophical community that two-stage models for free will are sometimes called "Valerian." See Chapter 25 for more on Dennett.

83 Dennett (1978) p. 298.
84 Simon (1981)
85 Dennett (1978) p. 293, Hadamard (1945), p. 30.

Peter van Inwagen

In his 1983 "An Essay on Free Will," PETER VAN INWAGEN changed the taxonomy of free will positions. For the previous century, there were basically three positions - **determinist, libertarian**, and **compatibilist** (James's name for this was "soft" determinist). The compatibilists were usually described as following a traditional view handed down from Hobbes to Hume to Mill to Schlick.

Van Inwagen caused a stir by arguing that compatibilism is demonstrably false, even admitting Frankfurt's denial of alternative possibilities (which implies only one "actual sequence" of events), in what has come to be called his **Consequence Argument**.

In short, if compatibilism traces the causes of our actions, in the "actual sequence" of events, back to events before we existed, then our actions are simply the consequences of those earlier events and are "not up to us." Speaking as a logical philosopher, he concludes that

> "the free-will thesis and determinism are incompatible. That is, **incompatibilism** is true."

> "To deny the free-will thesis is to deny the existence of moral responsibility, which is absurd...Therefore, we should reject determinism." [86]

This has been obvious to libertarians since EPICURUS. It is the first half of the **standard argument against free will.** Van Inwagen called the second half his Mind Argument.

Van Inwagen called for a new position in the free will debates he called "Incompatibilism." It is more than just saying determinism is false. It is the assumed interdependence of free will and determinism that he claims is false. Unfortunately, there are two ways to be incompatibilist, the libertarian and the hard determinist. Incompatibilism lumps these opposites together.

Van Inwagen replaced the traditional dichotomy determinism-libertarian (with the reconciliation position compatibilism). His new scheme was compatibilism - incompatibilism, with incom-

86 Van Inwagen (1983) p. 223.

patibilism a messy category that lumps together hard determinism and libertarians - strange bedfellows indeed. See p. 60.

Robert Kane

ROBERT KANE is the leading spokesman for Libertarianism. Before Kane, in the late twentieth century, Anglo-American philosophers had largely dismissed libertarian free will as a "pseudoproblem." Most philosophers and scientists thought free will was compatible with determinism, or perhaps impossible because of determinism.

In his 1985 book *Free Will and Values*, aware of earlier proposals by Eccles, Popper, and Dennett, but working independently, Kane proposed an ambitious amplifier model for a quantum randomizer in the brain - a spinning wheel of fortune with probability bubbles corresponding to **alternative possibilities**, in the massive switch amplifier tradition of Compton and Gomes. Kane says:

> "neurological processes must exist corresponding to the randomizing activity of the spinning wheel and the partitioning of the wheel into equiprobable segments (red, blue, etc.) corresponding to the relevant R-alternatives." [87]

Kane was not satisfied with this early model. He explains that the main reason for failure is

> "locating the master switch and the mechanism of amplification...We do not know if something similar goes on in the brains of cortically developed creatures like ourselves, but I suspect it must if libertarian theories are to succeed."[88]

Unlike DANIEL DENNETT, who put randomness in the first stage of a two-stage model, Kane locates indeterminism in the final moment of choice, in the decision itself.

Kane's major accomplishment is to show that an agent can still claim moral responsibility for "torn" decisions that were made at indeterministically, provided there exist equally good reasons whichever way the decisions go. Critics who say that indeterminism necessarily destroys the kind of control needed for moral responsibility have been shown wrong by Kane.

87 Kane (1985) p. 147.
88 Kane (1985) p. 168.

Kane claims that the major criticism of all indeterminist libertarian models is explaining the power to **choose or do otherwise** in "exactly the same conditions," something he calls "dual rational self-control." Given that A is the rational choice, how can one defend doing B under exactly the **same circumstances**? [89] Kane's critics say that such a "dual power" is arbitrary, capricious, and irrational. But he disagrees

Apart from the fact that information-rich systems with a history are *never* in the exact same conditions, and ignoring the fact that random alternative possibilities are very unlikely to repeat, an adequately determined will might very likely make the same choice, for the same reasons, from the same set of **alternative possibilities**.

But this was not Kane's main interest. He says it is the agent's effort that is the main cause in cases of moral and prudential choices where the agent is "torn" between a moral and a self-interested alternative. Kane says that indeterminism might tip the scales against one option, making it fail, and in favor of another, making it succeed. But the main cause for the successful choice should not be the indeterminism, says Kane. It is the agent's effort that is the main cause, since the successful choice is brought about by that effort, for the reasons and desires that motivated the effort.

In 2005, Kane published *A Contemporary Introduction to Free Will*, a comprehensive survey of the recent positions on free will, perhaps the most comprehensive since MORTIMER ADLER. Kane adds two more freedom classifications to Adler's three categories.

Self-control is a variation on Adler's acquired freedom of **Self-perfection** to include the arguments of the many "New Compatibilists" who are more concerned about moral responsibility than free will, such as HARRY FRANKFURT and JOHN MARTIN FISCHER.

Self-formation is a variation of Adler's natural freedom of **Self-determination** to include Kane's own "self-forming actions" (SFA) that are a subset of self-determining actions.[90] Kane requires that an SFA is an indeterministic "will-setting action" that helps form

89 Kane (1985) p. 59.

90 Adler (1961) p. 122. **Self-realization** is Adler's third freedom.

our character. Later, other actions can be determined by our character, but we can still assert "ultimate responsibility" (UR) for those actions, to the extent they can be traced back to earlier SFAs.

Kane cites ELIZABETH ANSCOMBE's remark that determinism is becoming more common, and insightfully notes that

> "One may legitimately wonder why worries about determinism persist at all in the twenty-first century, when the physical sciences - once the stronghold of determinist thinking - seem to have turned away from determinism." [91]

Indeed, today it is determinism that is "metaphysical."

We shall see in Chapter 24 that Kane remains an ardent supporter of quantum indeterminism playing a major role in the solution to the free will problem. It is no longer a quantum event amplified by chaos that triggers a decision, but the general low-level noise in the brain that adds enough indeterminacy.

Richard Double

RICHARD DOUBLE, in his 1991 book *The Non-Reality of Free Will*, agrees with Kane that libertarian free will must have the "dual ability" to choose otherwise with rational control. But he says this is impossible:

> "My conclusion is that the deep reason why no libertarian view can satisfy all three conditions [ability-to-choose-otherwise, control, and rationality] is that the conditions are logically incompatible. Hence, libertarianism, despite its intuitive appeal, turns out to be incoherent." [92]

Two Classicists on Doing Otherwise

There is a rich history of linguistic and logical quibbles among compatibilists over the ability to **do otherwise**. G. E. MOORE and A. J. AYER said that one could have done otherwise, *if one had chosen to do so*, i.e., if things in the past had been different. But since the "fixed past" could never be different (in retrospect) one could not have so chosen, according to compatibilists (and determinists).

91 Kane (2002) p. 7.
92 Double (1991) p. 222.

In 1987 two classicists, ANTHONY LONG and DAVID SEDLEY, speculated that EPICURUS' swerve of the atoms might be limited to providing undetermined **alternative possibilities** for action, from which the mind's power of volition could choose in a way that reflects character and values, desires and feelings.

> "It does so, we may speculate, not by overriding the laws of physics, but by choosing between the alternative possibilities which the laws of physics leave open." [93]

Long and Sedley assume a non-physical (metaphysical) ability of the volition to affect the atoms, which is implausible. But the idea that a physical volition chooses - (consistent with and adequately determined by its character and values and its desires and feelings) from among **alternative possibilities** provided randomly by atomic indeterminacy - is plausible to Long and Sedley.

Ted Honderich

TED HONDERICH, the major spokesman for "Hard Determinism," in 1988 published his 750-page The Theory of Determinism, with excursions into quantum mechanics, neuroscience, and consciousness.

Unlike most of his colleagues specializing in free will, Honderich did not succumb to the easy path of **compatibilism**, by simply declaring that the free will we have (and should want, says Dennett) is completely consistent with **determinism**, namely a "voluntarism" in which our will is completely caused by prior events.

Nor does Honderich go down the path of **incompatibilism**, looking for non-physical substances, dualist forms of agency, or simply identifying freedom with Epicurean chance, as have many scientists with ideas of brain mechanisms amplifying quantum mechanical indeterminism to help with the uncaused "origination" of actions and decisions.

Honderich does not claim to have found a solution to the problem of free will or determinism, but he does claim to have confronted the problem of the consequences of determinism. He is "dismayed" because the truth of determinism requires that we give up "origination" with its promise of an open future, restricting - though not eliminating - our "life hopes."

93 Long and Sedley (1987) p. 111.

Though he is determinism's foremost champion, Honderich characterizes it as a "black thing." He passionately feels the real loss, when he follows his reason to accept the truth of determinism.

Honderich faults both Compatibilists and Incompatibilists on three counts. First, he says that moral responsibility is not all that is at stake, there are personal feelings, reactive attitudes, problems of knowledge, and rationalizing punishment with ideas of limited responsibility. Second, these problems can not be resolved by logical "proofs" nor by linguistic analyses of propositions designed to show "free" and "determined" are logically compatible. And third, he faults their simplistic idea that one or the other of them must be right. Although he does not call it a scandal, Honderich is describing the scandal in philosophy.

And unlike some of his colleagues, Honderich does not completely dismiss indeterminism and considers the suggestion of "near-determinism." He says,

> "Maybe it should have been called determinism-where-it-matters. It allows that there is or may be some indeterminism but only at what is called the micro-level of our existence, the level of the small particles of our bodies." [94]

Alfred Mele

Alfred Mele, in his 1995 book *Autonomous Agents*, argued, mostly following Dennett, that libertarians should admit that the final stages of deliberation are (adequately) determined and only allow indeterminism in the early stages of the decision process. While he himself has made no commitment to such indeterminism, and wonders how it could be physically possible, he offers the idea to others as a "modest libertarianism."[95] Mele's model satisfies the temporal sequence requirements for libertarian free will (see Chapter 5), even if he does not see the possible location of indeterminism in the brain.

> "Where compatibilists have no good reason to insist on determinism in the deliberative process as a requirement for autonomy, where internal indeterminism is, for all we know, a reality, and

94 Honderich (2002) p. 5.
95 Mele (1995) pp. 211-220

> where such indeterminism would not diminish the nonultimate control that real agents exert over their deliberation even on the assumption that real agents are internally deterministic — that is, at the intersection of these three locations — libertarians may plump for ultimacy-promoting indeterminism. Modest libertarians try to stake out their view at this intersection." [96]

Paul Russell

PAUL RUSSELL, also in 1995, suggested that the location of the break in the causal chain might be put between willings, which might be uncaused, and actions, which would be determined. This goes against the common sense use of the word "will," but Russell correctly puts something "free" before a final "will."

Randolph Clarke

In his 2003 book *Libertarian Accounts of Free Will*, RANDOLPH CLARKE assessed suggestions of DANIEL DENNETT and ALFRED MELE. He found them inadequate. His work, he says, was carried out by thinking alone and required no specialized knowledge of natural science. At best, he concludes, indeterminism in processes leading to our actions is superfluous, adding nothing of value and possibly detracting from what we want. In a 2000 article called "Modest Libertarianism," he ignores Mele's suggestion of early-stage indeterminism and "places indeterminism in the direct production of the decision," as does ROBERT KANE and other "event-causal" libertarians, such as LAURA WADDELL EKSTROM and MARK BALAGUER.

As we saw in Chapter 4, recent libertarian philosophers defend "incompatibilism" (note that they usually mean libertarianism)[97] but have not reached general agreement on an "intelligible" account of how, when, and perhaps most importantly, where indeterminism enters the picture - without making our actions purely random.

They include RANDOLPH CLARKE, LAURA WADDELL EKSTROM, CARL GINET, TIMOTHY O'CONNOR, PETER VAN INWAGEN, and DAVID WIGGINS. DAVID WIDERKER independently developed Kane's strong 1985 criticism of Frankfurt-style examples, in defense of incompatibilist (libertarian) free will.

---

96 Mele (1995), p. 235

97 Cf., Randolph Clarke's SEP article, awkwardly entitled "Incompatibilist (Nondeterminsitic) Theories of Free Will"

Unfortunately, their works are full of a dense jargon defining (sometimes obscuring) subtle differences in their views - agent causation, event causation, non-occurrent causation, reasons as causes, intentions, undefeated authorization of preferences as causes, non-causal accounts, dual control, plurality conditions, origination, actual sequences and alternative sequences, source and leeway compatibilism, revisionism, restrictivism, semicompatibilism, and narrow and broad incompatibilism. (See our Glossary of Terms in the appendix for some clarification of this dense terminology.)

Not a few compatibilist/determinist philosophers have, following Peter F. Strawson, turned the conversation away from the "unintelligible" free will problem to the problem of moral responsibility. Peter's son, Galen Strawson, is one. He accepts determinism outright on the grounds that a *causa sui* is simply impossible. Where Sir Peter says that the truth of determinism would not change our attitudes about **moral responsibility**, his son Galen says it makes moral responsibility impossible.

John Martin Fischer

John Martin Fischer calls his position **semicompatibilism**. Fischer says free will may or may not be incompatible with determinism, but his main interest, **moral responsibility**, is not incompatible. Fischer recently edited a four-volume, 46-contributor, 1300+ pages compendium of articles on moral responsibility - entitled *Free Will*, a reference work in the *Critical Concepts in Philosophy* series (Routledge 2005).

In it, Fischer explains that his colleagues are setting aside the "unintelligible" problem of free will.

> Some philosophers do not distinguish between freedom and moral responsibility. Put a bit more carefully, they tend to begin with the notion of moral responsibility, and "work back" to a notion of freedom; this notion of freedom is not given independent content (separate from the analysis of moral responsibility). For such philosophers, "freedom" refers to whatever conditions are involved in choosing or acting in such a way as to be morally responsible.[98]

98 Fischer (2005), Vol.1, p. xxiii.

Derk Pereboom, Saul Smilansky, and the psychologist Daniel Wegner follow many earlier thinkers and say that libertarian free will is incoherent and an illusion. Pereboom agrees with Galen Strawson that moral responsibility is impossible.

Smilansky may share the "dismay" that Ted Honderich sees in the apparent loss of control implicit in determinism. But unlike the others who find it uplifting and therapeutic to disabuse the public of illusions about free will, Smilansky thinks that we need to maintain the public illusion of free will, as did the 18th-century Lord Kames, because the illusion of libertarian free will is arguably positive, and probably even morally necessary.

The Garden of Forking Paths

Jorge Luis Borges' stories have proved fertile ground for philosophical metaphors. Robert Kane describes the "free will labyrinth" and John Martin Fischer and his colleagues created a popular blog on free will called the "Garden of Forking Paths." [99] I was a contributor to the GFP blog until it was closed in early 2010. Some of the bloggers created a new blog, with a more restricted membership. It too has a Fischer-inspired name - "Flickers of Freedom." [100] The new blog focuses on moral responsibility and the philosophy of action.

Experimental Philosophy

Experimental philosophy consists of opinion polls on common philosophical questions, intended to quantify the positions of the philosophically naive or untrained public, the so-called "folk" of "folk psychology." Experimental philosophers have a blog.[101]

One of the X-Phi surveys attempted to establish the "folk" intuitions on the classic philosophical question of **free will** and **determinism**. Unfortunately, experimental philosophers follow John Martin Fischer and define free will as the "control condition" for **moral responsibility**. So their questions are really about the moral responsibility of two kinds of agents, those completely determined and others assumed to have libertarian free will.

99 gfp.typepad.com
100 agencyandresponsibility.typepad.com/flickers-of-freedom
101 experimentalphilosophy.typepad.com

The earliest surveys, by Shaun Nichols,[102] tended to show that participants believed in agent causality, that "incompatibilism was true." Later surveys, notably by Eddy Nahmias,[103] tend to show the opposite, that the folk have compatibilist intuitions.

Note the convoluted, post van Inwagen, titles like that of Nahmias et al., "Is Incompatibilism Intuitive?"

The experimental philosophers established that many of those interviewed want to hold even the determined agents responsible for their crimes, especially when the crime raises emotions, either because it is a particularly heinous crime or because it harms someone close to the person being interviewed.

In relatively abstract situations, the idea that the agent was determined (by any number of determining factors) was enough to provide mitigating circumstances. But as the crime stirred up strong emotions in the person judging the action, the agent was more likely to be held morally responsible, even if the agent was clearly determined.

Sadly, experimental philosophers describe their results using Peter van Inwagen's distinction between "incompatibilist" or "compatibilist" intuitions, which makes interpretations difficult.

The results say very little about free will, but a lot about what Peter F. Strawson knew, that we would not easily give up natural feelings about praise and blame, gratitude and resentment.

What X-Phi has shown is that when their emotions rise up, those judging an action are more likely to react with an attitude of blame and seek punishment for the action. Holding an agent morally responsible is a function of how hurtful their action is to the one judging the action. This result is quite believable for normal persons. It is the reason jurors are selected from persons with no connections to the accused or the plaintiff.

---

102 Nichols (2004) Folk Psychology of Free Will *Mind & Language*, 19, 473-502.

103 Eddy Nahmias et al. (2006). Is Incompatibilism Intuitive? *Philosophy and Phenomenological Research* 73(1): 28-53.

Major Forks in the Garden Paths

We conclude our historical review with a diagram identifying some major turning points in the history of the free will problem. It is disappointing to see that many philosophers have turned away from liberty, from freedom, more particularly away from indeterminism and chance, away from alternative possibilities in an open future, to questions not about freedom directly, but about moral responsibility in the one possible actual future.

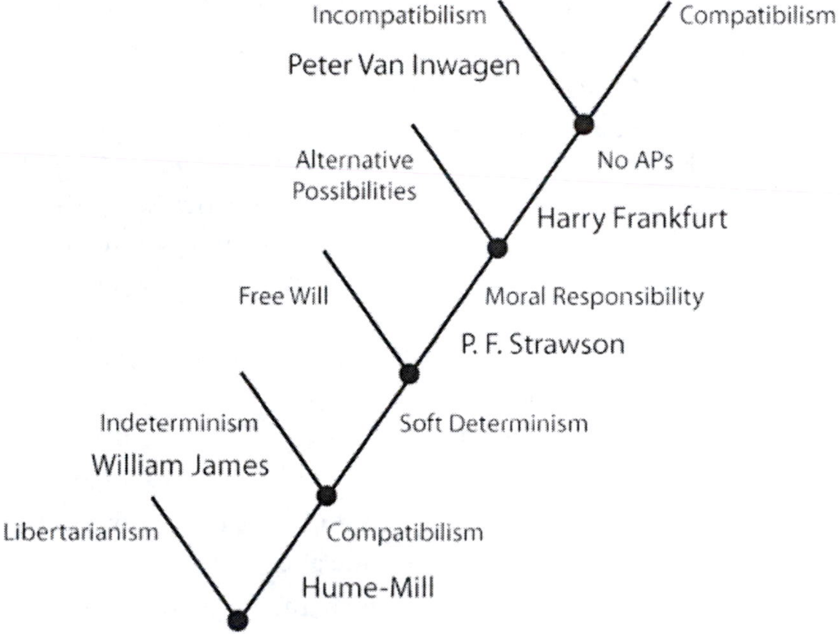

Figure 7-1. Forking paths in the free will debates.

The Scandal Today

The view of most philosophers over the history of philosophy seems to be something like this...

> "Science can never prove that indeterminism exists. Quantum physics may be wrong. So scientists cannot logically deny determinism. Objective chance would make us random. Therefore, compatibilists can teach students that we are determined, yet still morally responsible (or not, for hard determinists)."

As we noted in Chapter 2, John Searle recently wrote in his 2007 book *Freedom and Neurobiology*, "The persistence of the free will problem in philosophy seems to me something of a scandal." And in a breakthrough of sorts, Searle admits that he could never see, until now, the point of introducing quantum mechanics into discussions of consciousness and free will.

Now he says we know two things,

> "First we know that our experiences of free action contain both indeterminism and rationality...Second we know that quantum indeterminacy is the only form of indeterminism that is indisputably established as a fact of nature...it follows that quantum mechanics must enter into the explanation of consciousness."[104]

Indeed it does. Despite a century of failed attempts, can we convince Searle and other philosophers that quantum indeterminism followed by an adequate if not strict determinism is the most plausible and practical two-stage model for free will?

In the next few chapters we look more closely at determinism (actually many determinisms), libertarianism, and compatibilism.

Then in Chapter 12, we will look at a number of suggestions for two-stage models of free will, combinations of some limited indeterminism and limited determinism.

> - aye, chance, free will, and necessity - no wise incompatible - all interweavingly working together. The straight warp of necessity, not to be swerved from its ultimate course - its every alternating vibration, indeed, only tending to that; free will still free to ply her shuttle between given threads; and chance, though restrained in its play within the right lines of necessity, and sideways in its motions directed by free will, though thus prescribed to by both, chance by turns rules either, and has the last featuring blow at events.
>
> Herman Melville, *Moby-Dick*, Ch. 47, p. 213. Melville knew his Aristotle.[105]

104 Searle (2007) p. 74-75

105 Thanks to Robert Kane for this 1850 insight into the will as a *tertium quid*.

Determinism

Compatibilism
Soft Determinism

Hard Determinism

Soft Compatibilism

Hard Incompatibilism

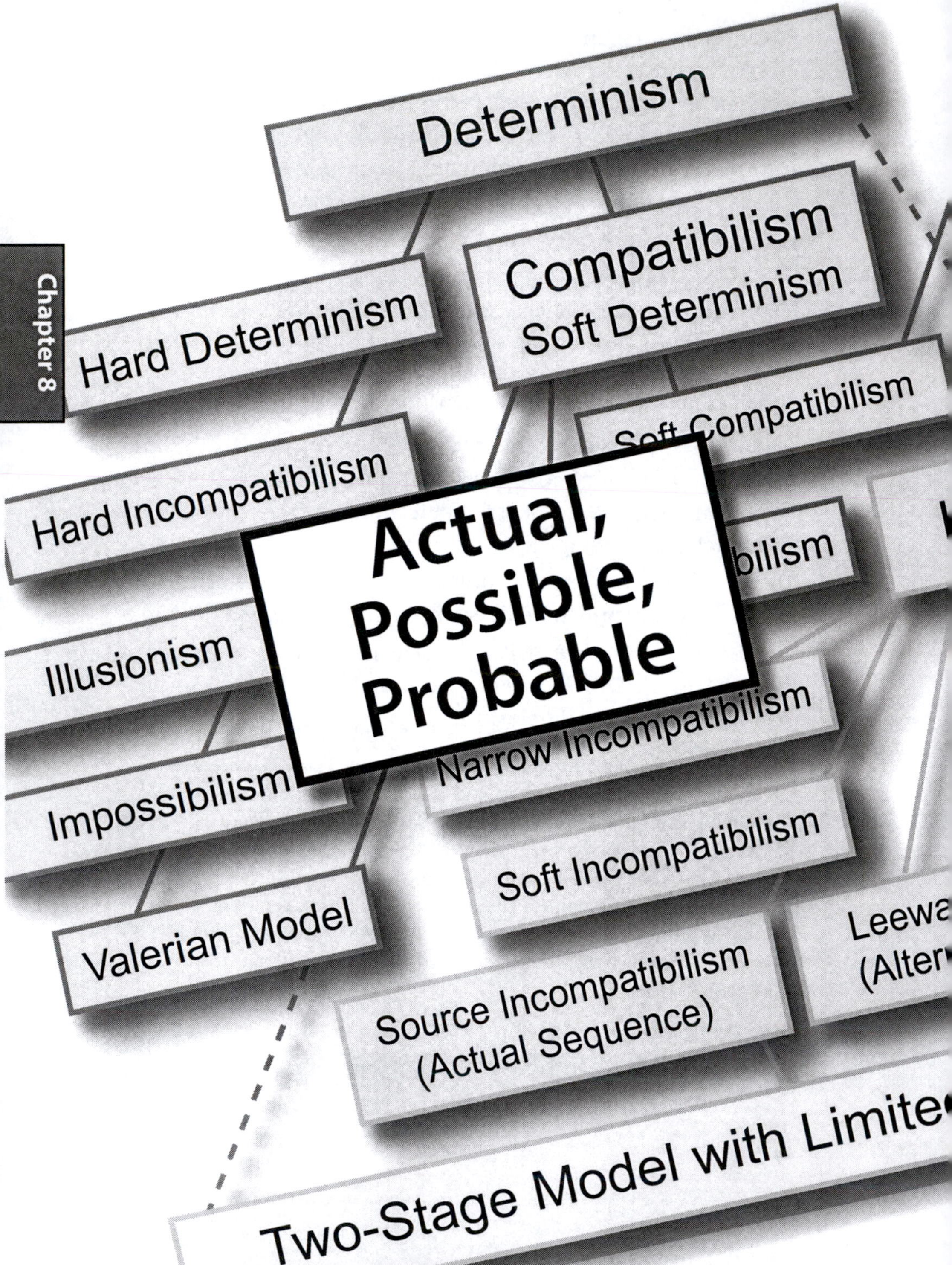

Actual, Possible, Probable

Illusionism

Narrow Incompatibilism

Impossibilism

Soft Incompatibilism

Valerian Model

Source Incompatibilism (Actual Sequence)

This chapter on the web
informationphilosopher.com/freedom/probability.html

Actual, Possible, Probable

As a philosopher who was trained in physics, I think I can see why philosophers trained in logic may be uncomfortable with libertarian solutions to the problem of free will that involve indeterminism and uncertainty, ontological and objective chance.

So, before we leave the history of our problem, let's take a brief look at the history of chance. I believe it can provide powerful insights for thinkers who work in logic and language alone.

At the very beginning of our problem, in the 5th century BCE, we find the first **determinist** philosopher, LEUCIPPUS, denying randomness and chance.

> "Nothing occurs by chance (μάτην), but there is a reason (λόγου) and necessity (ἀνάγκης) for everything." [1]

A century later, the first **indeterminist** philosopher, ARISTOTLE, embraced chance, but he worried that it was obscure and unintelligible. In the *Metaphysics,* Aristotle makes the case for chance and uncaused causes (*causa sui*).

> "Nor is there any definite cause for an accident, but only chance (τυχόν), namely an indefinite (ἀόριστον) cause." [2]

Aristotle's description of chance as "obscure" (ἄδηλος) to reason led centuries of philosophers to deny the existence of chance:

> "Causes from which chance results might happen are indeterminate; hence chance is obscure to human reason and is a cause by accident (συμβεβεκός)." [3]

And another century later, we find the first **compatibilist** philosopher, CHRYSIPPUS, warning of the calamity that would happen if even one chance event were to occur.

> "Everything that happens is followed by something else which depends on it by causal necessity. Likewise, everything that happens is preceded by something with which it is causally connected. For nothing exists or has come into being in the cosmos

1 Leucippus, Fragment 569 - from Fr. 2 Actius I, 25, 4
2 Metaphysics, Book V, 1025a25
3 Metaphysics, Book XI, 1065a33

> without a cause. The universe will be disrupted and disintegrate into pieces and cease to be a unity functioning as a single system, if any uncaused movement is introduced into it." [4]

The cosmos that we have is actually built on top of a microscopic chaos that was the case from the beginning of the universe. The challenge for philosophy - and physics, one that is addressed by information philosophy, is to understand the cosmic creative process that has generated and maintained the visible macroscopic order, in the continuous presence of noise and irreducible chance in the microcosmos.

We shall see that the order is the result of laws of nature, as the ancients thought. But today laws are only probabilistic and statistical (I will define the difference between probability and statistics).

The laws only appear to be certain and deterministic because of the law of large numbers in probability and the correspondence principle (or law of large quantum numbers) in physics.

We saw that Heraclitus wanted a law or an account (logos) behind all change and that Anaximander said the universe must have a "cosmos-logos." Philosophers divided on the question of whether change (becoming) was real (being). Plato sided with Parmenides on the idea that Truth could not change. Some concluded that logically true statements could have controlling power over the future. The "dialectical" philosopher Diodorus Cronus developed his language game to show that the future is determined by true statements about it. Diodorus specialized in puzzles like the sorites paradox - how many grains does it take to make a heap.

But future contingency seemed more like a problem than a puzzle. It remains actively discussed as a defense of **fatalism** by philosophers like Richard Taylor, Peter van Inwagen, and David Foster Wallace.

Diodorus is an "**actualist**." His Master Argument (κύριος λόγος) can be translated as the "authorized, proper, real, or actual" argument. According to it, there is only one possible future. The Master Argument is the granddaddy of all logical, nomological,

---

4 Chrysippus

and perhaps even theological arguments for determinism. The Greek for "Master" (κύριος) translates the Hebrew Ba'al (Lord) in the Bible.

The Actual

The first serious philosophical discussion of the actual and the possible was that of Aristotle, and it is the denial of the possible in Aristotle's sense (the potential) that forms the core of my argument that is a scandal to deny this kind of potential to our students. So let's look start with Aristotle's concepts for the actual.

Aristotle uses two words for the actual (one he invented). They both have the sense of "realized." The first is energeia (ἐνέργεια), which means an action that is the result of work (ἔργον) or a deed (as opposed to words - ἔπος). Energeia also has the meaning of modern energy (that does work). Its Indo-European root *werg-* is the source of our word for work (German Werk).

Aristotle's invented word for action is entelecheia (ἐντελεχεία). He built it from en (in) + telos (end or purpose) + echein (to have). An act then has fulfilled and realized its end.

Note that an action has normally happened. One can talk about a hypothetical action in the future, of course, but Aristotle's meaning carries the sense of something that is completed and is now in what modern philosophers call the "fixed past." The actual contrasts with the possible, which is something that has not yet happened.

Actualists believe that everything that is going to happen is already actual in some sense (because it is a true statement that it will happen, because its cause is already present, because it is physically determined, because God foreknows it, etc.)

The Possible

Aristotle's word for the possible was dynamis (δύναμις), power, capacity, or capability. The Romans translated it as *potentia*, thus our potential. Aristotle contrasts actuality to potentiality in Metaphysics, Book IX, saying that "we call a man a theorist even if he is not theorizing at the moment. He has the capacity to theorize.[5]

5 Metaphysics, IX, 1048a35

Aristotle chastises thinkers like Diodorus who say that an agent cannot act when he is not acting. They deny the potential for acting. They believe only the actual is possible. So an agent not acting cannot possibly act. Aristotle said it is easy to see the absurdity of this idea.

But ancient and modern actualists continued to pursue this absurd idea. Just as you cannot change the past, you cannot change the one possible future. "Change it from what to what?," asks Daniel Dennett, for example.

The Probable

The subtle difference between provable and probable marks a critical distinction between logical philosophers and mathematicians, on the one hand, and scientists on the other. The former is the realm of certainty, of absolute truths, of determinism. In the latter we find uncertainty, relative doubts, indeterminacy, and, above all, chance.

Both words derive from the same Latin verb, *probare*, to test, from the noun *probus*, good. The ancient Indo-European word is formed from two roots that mean pro (forward) and be (to be, to exist, to grow).

About the same time that Isaac Newton was discovering his laws that provided the foundation for physical determinism, mathematicians were discovering the laws of probability. One might think that studying the "doctrine of chances," they would have been circumspect about the certainty of their results. But, being mathematicians, they had no doubts whatsoever.

As hard as it seems to believe, the mathematicians who gave us probability did not think that objective, ontological chance was real. On the contrary, they believed deeply that chance was merely epistemic, human ignorance, the product of finite minds, by comparison with the infinite mind of God.

Chance is atheistic. It questions God's omniscience.

The Bernoullis, De Moivre, Laplace, Legendre, and Gauss all knew that random events are distributed in what CHARLES SANDERS PEIRCE first called a "normal distribution," the familiar bell-shaped curve.

Abraham de Moivre (1667-1754) was regarded by Newton as the greatest mathematician in England, but being a French Huguenot refugee, he could not find work, so made his living selling a gambler's handbook entitled *The Doctrine of Chances*, in which he derived most of the famous formulas of probability that are associated with better known mathematicians like Laplace and Gauss. His first sentence tells us everything we need to know.

> "The Probability of an Event is greater or less, according to the number of Chances by which it may happen, compared with the whole number of Chances by which it may happen or fail." [6]

De Moivre's assumption is that the events are random, independent of one another, and that they are equiprobable. Equiprobability means that no information exists to make one more probable than another. This is sometimes called the principle of indifference or the principle of insufficient reason.

If contrary information did exist, it could and would be revealed in large numbers of experimental trials, which provide "statistics" on the different "states."

Probabilities are *a priori* theories.
Statistics are *a posteriori*, the results of experiments.

In his book, de Moivre worked out the mathematics for the binomial expansion of $(p - q)^n$ by analyzing the tosses of a coin.

If p is the probability of a "heads" and q = 1 - p the probability of "tails," then the probability of k heads is

$$Pr(k) = (n!/(n - k)!\ k!)p^{(n - k)}q^k$$

He also was the first to approximate the factorial for large n as

$$n! \approx (\text{constant}) \sqrt{n}\ n^n e^{-n}$$

6 De Moivre (1756) p. 1.

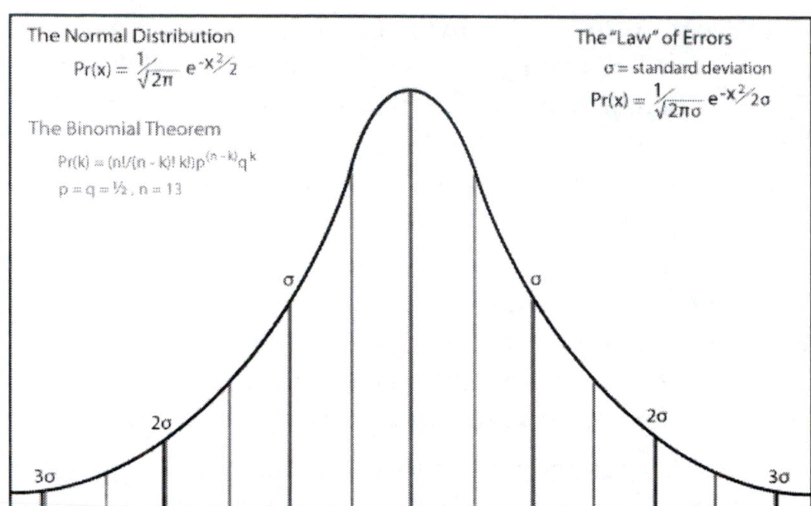

Figure 8-1. De Moivre's binomial expansion (vertical lines) and his continuous approximation, the normal distribution. This became the "law" of experimental errors.

De Moivre then fitted a smooth curve to the probabilities Pr(k) and was the first to derive the "normal" bell curve. [7] De Moivre also derived the "central limit theorem," that in the limit of large numbers of independent random events, the distribution asymptotically approaches the normal,

When social scientists started to collect statistics on various human activities like births, deaths, marriages, and suicides, they found distributions remarkably like the above curves. They might have concluded that individual human characteristics are distributed randomly, by chance. But they decided just the opposite. Perhaps seduced by the idea that the regularities they found were "lawlike," they illogically concluded that human characteristics must be determined, but some unknown laws, to produce these "lawlike" regularities.

Immanuel Kant argued this as early as 1784, suggesting that it undermines the concept of free will..

> "No matter what conception may form of the freedom of the will in metaphysics, the phenomenal appearances of the will, i.e., human actions, are determined by general laws of nature

7 For an animation of how discrete probabilities become continuous, see De Moivre's I-Phi web page. informationphilosopher.com/solutions/scientists/de_moivre

> like any other event of nature...Thus marriages, the consequent births and the deaths, since the free will seems to have such a great influence on them, do not seem to be subject to any law according to which one could calculate their number beforehand. Yet the annual (statistical) tables about them in the major countries show that they occur according to stable natural laws... Individual human beings, each pursuing his own ends according to his inclination and often one against another (and even one entire people against another) rarely unintentionally promote, as if it were their guide, an end of nature which is unknown to them."[8]

As we saw in Chapter 7 (p. 91) , the social scientists Adolphe Quételet and Henry Thomas Buckle developed this idea to claim that the "laws of human nature" are as deterministic as those of physical nature.

Then in the mid-nineteenth century, the scientists James Clerk Maxwell and Ludwig Boltzmann showed that, by analogy with the social laws, that the regular macroscopic properties of gases, including the "gas laws" describing pressure, volume, and temperature, could be derived on the assumption that the motions of individual gas particles were independent random events. The famous "Maxwell-Boltzmann distribution" is essentially identical to Figure 8-1.

At that point, some laws of classical physics appeared to be statistical laws only. And in the twentieth century, quantum mechanics showed that the laws of physics are irreducibly probabilistic.

So today, we can say that the laws of nature are fundamentally indeterministic, although chance shows up primarily in the microscopic world. Regularities that we see in the macroscopic world, including the laws of classical physics, are the results of the central limit theorem and the law of large numbers of independent physical events.

The information that we gain from probabilities in quantum physics turns out to be surprising and non-intuitive. Before we return to the subject of free will, we need to build on our

8 Idea for a Universal History with a Cosmopolitan Intent.

understanding of classical probabilities to explain the mysterious properties of quantum-mechanical wave functions, which some philosophers think can help us understand major philosophical problems like consciousness and free will.

Quantum Probabilities

The probabilistic nature of quantum physics is captured perfectly in the "wave function," which propagates in space and time to tell us the probability of finding a quantum particle at any given point and time. It is the quantum equivalent of Newton's equations of motion for a classical particle, which we imagine is localized at all times and is travelling in a well-defined path, like a billiard ball across a pool table.

The wave function, on the other hand, diffuses from a starting point where the particle is initially localized, travelling in many directions at the speed of light. In principle, given enough time, and without an experimental measurement that localizes the particle, the wave function fills all space. This means simply that there exists some probability of finding the particle anywhere within its relativistic light cone.

At the 1927 Solvay conference, Albert Einstein went to the chalkboard to complain that when a particle is measured, on the right side of the room, for example, the finite probability of finding it on the left side of the room, which existed an instant earlier, has collapsed at a speed faster than light to the right side.

Clearly, the new quantum mechanics violates his special theory of relativity, he said. Then, eight years later, he and his Princeton colleagues, Boris Podolsky and Nathan Rosen, argued that two particles initially localized at a central point and described by a single wave function propagating from that central point would have an even stranger property. If one particle was found, say again on the right side of the room, we would instantly know where the other particle was, on the left side.

How, they asked, could local information on the right side travel instantly to affect the distant particle on the left side, again, faster than the speed of light. Einstein suggested that quantum reality has a "non-local" property. Although Einstein never accepted this aspect of quantum theory, the non-locality has been confirmed in many experiments first suggested by John Bell as tests of his Bell's Theorem.

Let's see how information philosophy explains the apparent infinite speed of information transmission when a wave function "collapses. Figure 8-2 shows the famous "two-slit" experiment. The wave function for a particle is travelling through the two slits and interfering with itself, as waves do. The "interference pattern" at the screen predicts the likelihood of finding particles at different places along the screen. This pattern is statistically confirmed by thousands of experiments, one particle at a time.

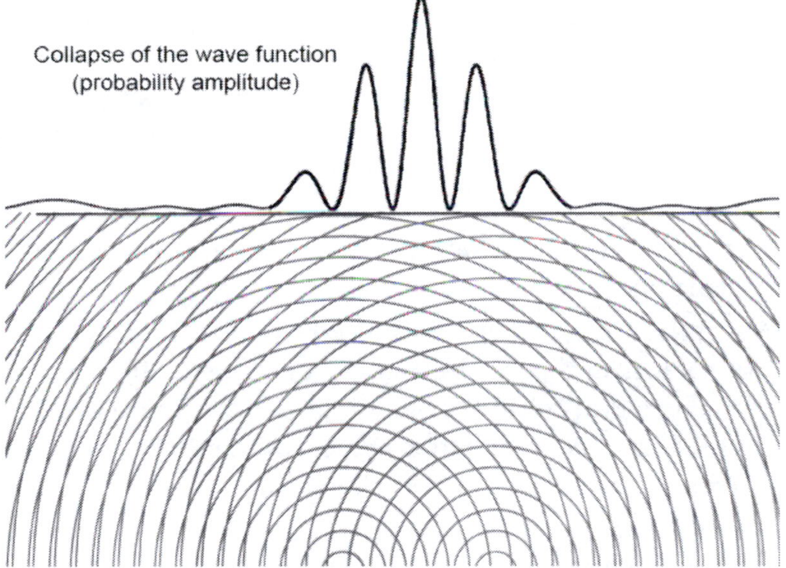

Figure 8-2. The two-slit experiment

Now what happens when the experiment captures a particle at a specific location on the screen, say on the right side somewhere. This experiment could be very large, in principle many miles across, as current tests of nonlocality are achieving. What happens to all that probability on the left side?

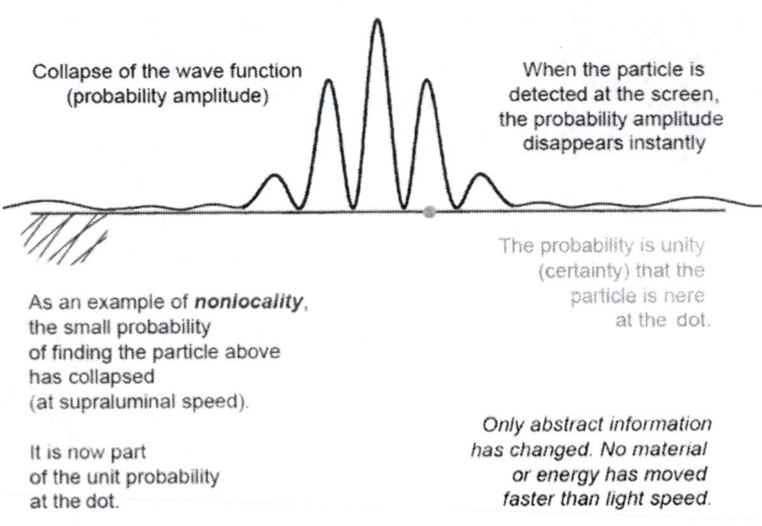

Figure 8-3. The wave function has collapsed.

The information philosophy explanation of the collapse of the wave function is that no matter or energy has been transferred from one place to another. It is only **information** about probabilities that changed. Note that the information has not been *transmitted* from one place to another. That would allow faster-than-light signalling.

New information enters the universe when a measurement is made that locates the particle at a specific point on the screen. At that moment, the probability of finding the particle anywhere else collapses to zero. We can better understand this by considering a macroscopic example. Consider a horse race.

When the nose of one horse crosses the finish line, its probability of winning goes to certainty, and the finite probabilities of the other horses, including the one in the rear, instantaneously drops to zero. This happens faster than the speed of light, since the last horse is in a "spacelike" separation from the first.

Figure 8-4. The probability of a trailing horse winning collapses instantly.

Note that probability, like information, is neither matter nor energy. When a wave function "collapses" or "goes through both slits" in the dazzling two-slit experiment, nothing physical is traveling faster than the speed of light or going through the slits. No messages or signals can be sent using this collapse of probability.

Actualism, Possibilism, and Probabilism

If actualism gives us only one possible future (and one universe), possibilism is the idea that there are an infinite number of possible futures, each with its own universe. It is ironic to find compatibilist philosophers who deny the **alternative possibilities** essential to libertarian free will, but who embrace David Lewis' picture of "nearby" possible worlds as philosophically important.

Probabilism is the idea that all our knowledge is contingent, based on empirical evidence, hence only statistical and probable. Without possibilities, there is no meaning to probabilities.

Information theory is based on the existence of different possibilities and their probabilities.

Can we see the history of the free will problem as being fought along the actualism-possibilism dimension? Looking back to the traditional determinism-libertarianism-compatibilism taxonomy[9] that we had before Peter van Inwagen changed it to compatibilism vs. incompatibilism, can we see this new dichotomy as justifying the traditional taxonomy?

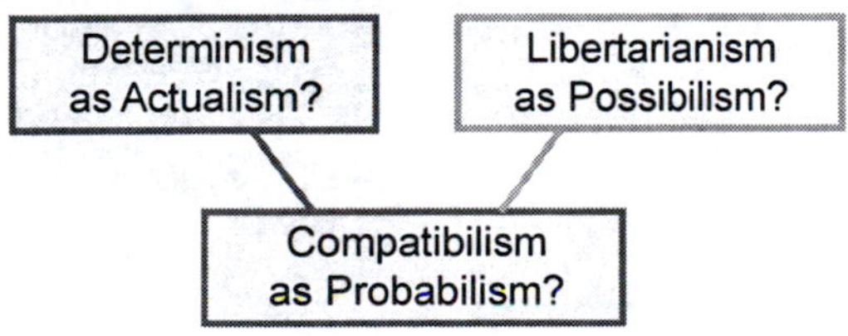

Figure 8-5. Justifying the traditional taxonomy.

In my view, libertarians need possibilism and the underlying indeterminism, uncertainty, and chance that provides our open futures. And compatibilists should consider probabilism.

---

9 See Chapter 6.

This chapter on the web
informationphilosopher.com/solutions/determinisms

Determinisms

Determinism is the idea that everything that happens, including all human actions, is completely determined by prior events. There is only one possible future, and it is completely predictable in principle, most famously by Laplace's Supreme Intelligent Demon, assuming perfect knowledge of the positions, velocities, and forces for all the atoms in the void.

More strictly, I strongly suggest that determinism should be distinguished from **pre-determinism**, the idea that the entire past (as well as the future) was determined at the origin of the universe.

Determinism is sometimes confused with **causality**, the idea that all events have causes. Despite David Hume's critical attack on the necessity of causes, and despite compatibilists' great respect for Hume as the modern founder of compatibilism, many philosophers embrace causality and determinism very strongly. Some even connect it to the very possibility of logic and reason. And Hume himself believed strongly, if inconsistently, in necessity. "'tis impossible to admit any medium betwixt chance and necessity," he said.

Bertrand Russell said "The law of causation, according to which later events can theoretically be predicted by means of earlier events, has often been held to be *a priori*, a necessity of thought, a category without which science would not be possible." [1]

But some events may themselves not be completely determined by prior events. This does not mean they are without causes, just that their causes are probabilistic. Such an event is then indeterminate. It might or might not have happened. It is sometimes called a "*causa sui*" or self-caused event. But a probabilistically caused event may in turn be the adequately deterministic cause for following events. These later events would therefore not be predictable from conditions before the uncaused event. We call this "soft" causality. Events are still caused, but they are not always predictable or completely pre-determined.

1 Russell (1960) p. 179

Uncaused events are said to break the "causal chain" of events back to a primordial cause or "unmoved mover." ARISTOTLE's "accidents" and EPICURUS' "swerve" are such uncaused causes.

There is only one basic form of indeterminism. There is only one irreducible freedom, based on a genuine randomness that provides for a world with breaks in the causal chain. Quantum mechanics is the fundamental source for irreducible objective indeterminacy and unpredictability in the physical, biological, and human worlds.

By contrast, there are many determinisms, depending on what pre-conditions are considered to be determinative of an event or action. This chapter identifies more than a dozen distinguishable determinisms, though they overlap a great deal.

Philosophers and religious thinkers may feel ill-equipped to discuss the conflict between a physical freedom based on quantum physics and their own particular (logical or physical) determinism. Because interpretations of quantum mechanics are difficult even for physicists, most recent philosophers dodge the issue and declare themselves agnostic on the truth of determinism or indeterminism.

Even some philosophers who accept the idea of human freedom are uncomfortable with the randomness implicit in quantum mechanics and the indeterminacy principle. True chance is problematic, even for many scientists. This included some, like MAX PLANCK, ALBERT EINSTEIN, and ERWIN SCHRÖDINGER, who discovered the quantum world. And for traditional philosophers in a religious tradition, chance has been thought to be an atheistic idea for millennia, since it denies God's foreknowledge. Chance, they say, is only epistemic, the result of human ignorance.

But quantum indeterminacy is real and ontological. There is objective chance in the physical world.

The Determinisms

Actualism is the idea that only whatever actually happens could ever have happened. It denies the existence of alternative possibilities for actions. This idea began with the logical sophistry of Diodorus Cronus' **Master Argument** for determinism. Statements about a future event that are true today necessitate the future event.

Sophisticated defenses of this idea include the so-called Frankfurt cases, which claim that an agent's actions can be free even if a hypothetical intervening controller can change the agent's decisions, preventing any alternative possibilities that might have appeared as what John Martin Fischer calls "flickers of freedom.".

Behavioral Determinism assumes that our actions are reflex reactions developed in us by environmental or operant conditioning. This is the Nurture side of the famous Nature/Nurture debate - note that both are determinisms. This view was developed to an extreme by B. F. Skinner in the early 20th century, who had great success "programming" the behaviors of animals, but never with perfect control of behavior. Many cognitive scientists are behaviorists who see the mind as a computer that has been programmed, by accident or deliberately, by education, for example.

Biological Determinism finds causes for our actions in our genetic makeup. This is the Nature side of the Nature/Nurture debate. Again, both sides are determinisms. There is little doubt that our genes pre-dispose us to certain kinds of behavior. But note that our genes contain a miniscule fraction of the information required to determine our futures. Most of the information in the adult brain is acquired through life experiences.

Causal Determinism assumes that every event has an antecedent cause, in an infinite causal chain going back to Aristotle's Prime Mover. Nothing is uncaused or self-caused (*causa sui*). Galen Strawson supports this view with his Basic Argument. Note that there are always multiple causes for any event. Basically, all the events that are in the past light-cone of an event can have a causal relationship with the event.

Cognitive Science Determinism results from a computational model of mind that sees the mind as a computer. The mind may be evolving its own computer programs, but the overall process is completely pre-determined, say cognitive scientists, and philosophers like DANIEL DENNETT.

Fatalism is the simple idea that everything is fated to happen, so that humans have no control over their future. Notice that fate might be an arbitrary power and need not follow any causal or otherwise deterministic laws. It can thus include the miracles of omnipotent gods, and thus be a theological fatalism. Some philosophers use the term fatalism loosely to cover other determinisms. RICHARD TAYLOR's well-known article, Fatalism, in the *Philosophical Review*, was about logical arguments denying future contingency. The Idle Argument claimed that since things are fated, it is "idle" to take any actions at all, since they can have no effect.

Historical Determinism is the dialectical idealism of Hegel or the dialectical materialism of Marx that are assumed to govern the course of future history. Marxists have often felt they could revise the past to suit their purposes, but claimed that the future is economically determined.

Logical Determinism reasons that a statement about a future event happening is either true or it is not true. This is the Principle of Bivalence and the Law of the Excluded Middle. If the statement is true, logical certainty then necessitates the event. ARISTOTLE's Sea Battle and DIODORUS CRONUS' Master Argument are the classical examples of this kind of determinism. If the statement about the future is false, the event it describes can not possibly happen. In logic, as in other formal systems, truth is outside of time, like the foreknowledge of God. Fortunately, logic can constrain our reasoning, but it cannot provide us with knowledge about the physical world nor can it constrain the world.

Linguistic Determinism claims that our language determines (at least limits) the things we can think and say and thus know. The Sapir-Whorf hypothesis claims that speech patterns in a language community constrain the conceptual categories of a linguistic community and thus determine thought.

Mechanical Determinism explains man as a machine. If Newton's laws of classical mechanics govern the workings of the planets, stars, and galaxies, goes the argument, surely they govern man the same way. Note that although René Descartes described human bodies and all animals as deterministic machines, he said that the human mind was free and undetermined (*indeterminata*).

Necessitarianism is a variation of logical and causal determinism that claims everything is simply necessary. This was Leucippus' view at the beginning of determinism. This was the most popular name for determinists in the 18th century, when they were opposed to libertarians.

Neuroscientific Determinism assumes that the neurons are the originators of our actions. "My neurons made me do it." The Libet experiments have been interpreted to show that decisions are made by the brain's neurons significantly before any action of conscious will.

Nomological Determinism is a broad term to cover determinism by laws, of nature, of human nature, etc.

Physical Determinism extends the laws of physics to every atom in the human mind and assumes that the mind will someday be perfectly predictable, once enough measurements are made. The paradigmatic case is that of Laplace's Demon. Knowing the positions, velocities, and forces acting on every particle in the world, the demon can know the entire past and future. All times are visible to such a super intelligence.

Psychological Determinism is the idea that our actions must be determined by the best possible reason or our greatest desire. Otherwise, our acts would be irrational. Since all the possible actions are presented to the mind, determined by prior actions, the choice is not really made by the agent.

Pre-determinism claims that everything that ever happens was pre-determined at the beginning of the universe. Theological predestination is similar, but if God is assumed to be omnipotent, the events may have been pre-destined more recently. Some theologians insist that God is unchanging and outside of time, in which case predestination reduces to pre-determinism.

Religious or **Theological Determinism** is the consequence of the presumed omniscience of God. God has foreknowledge of all events. All times are equally present to the eye of God (Aquinas' *totem simul*). Note the multiple logical inconsistencies in the idea of an omnipotent, omniscient, benevolent God. If God knows the future, he obviously lacks the power to change it. And if benevolence is assumed, it leads to the problem of evil.[2]

Spatio-temporal Determinism is a view based on special relativity. The "block universe" of HERMANN MINKOWSKI and ALBERT EINSTEIN is taken to imply that time is simply a fourth dimension that already exists, just like the spatial dimensions. The one possible future is already out there, up ahead of where we are now, just like the city blocks to our left and right. J. J. C. SMART is a philosopher who holds this view. He calls himself "somewhat of a fatalist."

Finally, **Compatibilism** is the idea that Free Will is compatible with Determinism. Compatibilists believe that as long as our Mind is one cause in the causal chain then we can be responsible for our actions, which is reasonable. But they think every cause, including our decisions, are **pre-determined**. Compatibilists are Determinists. Although some modern compatibilists say they are agnostic on the truth of determinism (and indeterminism).

Some of these determinisms (behavioral, biological, historical-economic, language, and psychological) have demonstrable evidence that they do in fact constrain behaviors and thus limit human freedom. But others are merely dogmas of determinism, believed primarily for the simple reason that they eliminate random chance in the universe.

Chance is anathema to most philosophers and many scientists. But without **indeterminacy**, there are simply no possibilities for the world to be different from what these many determinisms claim that it will be.

---

2 See page 5.

Do the Laws of Physics Deny Human Freedom?

Of all the determinisms listed here, physical determinism stands out as a special case.

All the fanciful logical, theological, and nomological determinisms described here are basically just ideas.

Isaac Newton's classical mechanics was also an idea at first, of course, just a theory.

But then it was confirmed experimentally, by observations that have grown more and more accurate with every passing decade.

To be sure, the theory has been revised and refined, first for the case of matter moving at velocities that are a significant fraction of the speed of light. Albert Einstein's special theory of relativity goes beyond classical mechanics, but it asymptotically approaches the classical theory as velocities go to zero.

The next grand refinement was Einstein's general theory, but it too corresponds to ordinary Newtonian physics in the limit.

The most important refinement is the quantum mechanics of Werner Heisenberg and Neils Bohr. Again, it corresponds to the classical theory, in the limit of large numbers of particles.

When Arthur Stanley Eddington revised his 1927 Gifford lectures for publication as *The Nature of the Physical World*, there he dramatically announced

> "It is a consequence of the advent of the quantum theory that physics is no longer pledged to a scheme of deterministic law." [1]

There is nothing in the laws of physics, or any wider "laws of nature," that in any way puts constraints on human freedom.

1 Eddington (2005)

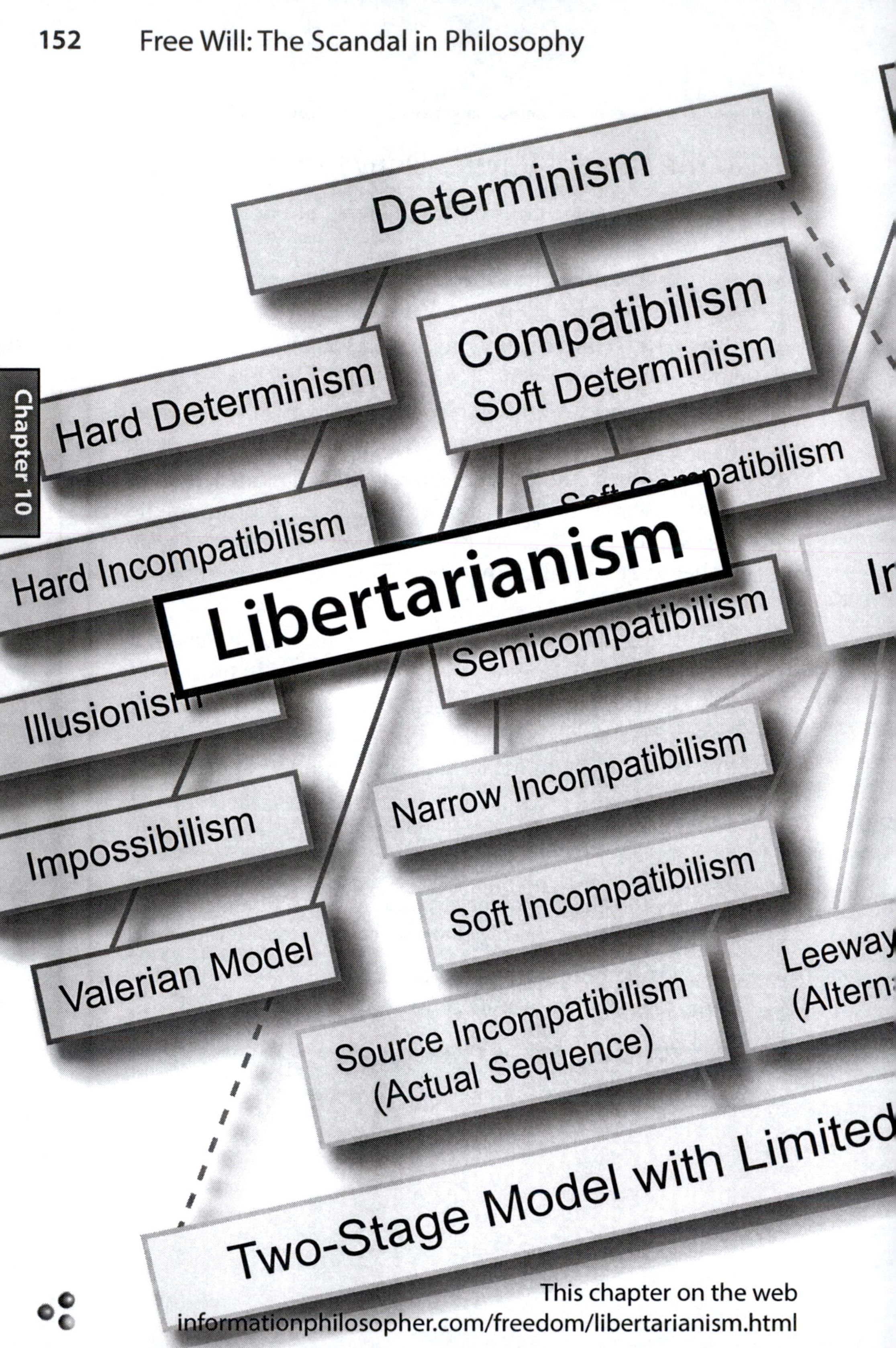

This chapter on the web
informationphilosopher.com/freedom/libertarianism.html

Libertarianism

Libertarianism is a school of thought that says humans are free, not only from physical determinism, but from all the other diverse forms of **determinism** described in chapter 9.

Libertarians believe that strict determinism and freedom are incompatible. Freedom seems to require some form of **indeterminism** somewhere in the decision process.

Most libertarians in the past have been mind/body dualists who, following RENÉ DESCARTES, explained human freedom by a separate mind substance that somehow manages to act indeterministically in the physical world. Some, especially IMMANUEL KANT, believed that our freedom only exists in a transcendental or noumenal world, leaving the physical world to be completely deterministic. How this works remains a mystery.

Religious libertarians say that God has given man a gift of freedom. But at the same time they say that God has foreknowledge of everything that man will do. Another mystery.

In recent free will debates, these dualist explanations are called "agent-causal libertarianism." The idea is that humans have some kind of metaphysical agency (an ability to act) that cannot be explained in terms of physical causes.

One alternative to dualism is "event-causal libertarianism," in which at least some physical or brain events are uncaused or indeterministically caused. Note that eliminating strict determinism does not eliminate **causality**.

We can still have events that are caused by indeterministic prior events. And these indeterministic events have prior causes, but those prior causes are not sufficient to determine the events precisely. In modern physics, for example, events are only statistical or probabilistic. We can call this "soft" causality, meaning not **pre-determined** but still having a causal explanation.

Still another libertarian position is to say that human freedom is uncaused or simply **non-causal**. This would eliminate causality.

Some philosophers like CARL GINET think "reasons" or "intentions" are not causes and describe their explanations of libertarian freedom as "**non-causal**."

But we do not have to avoid causes completely to provide freedom, just admit that some events are only probabilistically caused.

A conservative or "modest" event-causal libertarianism has been proposed by DANIEL DENNETT and ALFRED MELE. They and many other philosophers and scientists have proposed two-stage models of free will (discussed in Chapter 12) that keep indeterminism in the early stages of deliberation, limiting it to creating **alternative possibilities** for action.

Some strong event-causal libertarians believe that one's actions are caused but not completely "determined" by events prior to a decision, including one's character and values, reasons and motives, and one's feelings and desires. In the view of the leading libertarian philosopher ROBERT KANE, reasons and motives are contributing causes, but indeterminism "centered" in the moment of choice can also contribute to actions done "of one's own free will."

Critics of Kane's libertarianism attack his view as unintelligible. They argue that no coherent idea can be provided for such a late role for indeterminism. Kane's response is that this is not the case. In the "torn" decisions of his Self-Forming Actions (SFAs), the agent has excellent reasons, and chooses for those reasons, for whichever action is selected.

Until recently I too was a critic of Kane, worried that any randomness in the moment of choice would make chance the direct and primary cause of our actions. But I have changed my mind, as we will see in Chapter 13.

Kane's "torn" decisions are not completely random, They are those cases when previous deliberations in the two-stage model have not narrowed down options to a single choice. What remains are choices that are caused by the agent's reasons and motives, consistent with character and values, etc., but not yet fully decided despite the agent's best efforts to come to a decision.

When indeterminism makes one or more of the remaining options fail, Kane says that it is the effort of the agent that deserves to get the credit as the "cause" of the option that succeeds.

The first libertarian, EPICURUS, argued that as atoms moved through the void, there were occasions when they would "swerve" from their otherwise determined paths, thus initiating new causal chains.

The modern equivalent of the Epicurean swerve is quantum mechanical indeterminacy, again a property of atoms. We now know that atoms do not just occasionally swerve, they move unpredictably whenever they are in close contact with other atoms.

Everything in the material universe is made of atoms and subatomic particles in unstoppable perpetual motion. Deterministic paths are only the case for very large objects, where the statistical laws of atomic physics average to become nearly certain dynamical laws for billiard balls and planets.

Many determinists and compatibilists are now willing to admit that physics has shown there is real **indeterminism** in the universe. I believe that libertarians should agree with them, and accept their criticism that if nothing but chance was the direct cause of our actions, that would not be the freedom with responsibility that compatibilists are looking for.

Determinists and compatibilists might also agree that if **chance** is not a direct cause of our actions, it would do no harm. In which case, libertarians should be able to convince them that if chance provides real alternatives to be considered by the **adequately determined** will, it provides real **alternative possibilities** for thought and action. It provides freedom and creativity.

Libertarians can give the determinists, at least open-minded compatibilists agnostic about determinism, the kind of freedom they say they want, one that provides an **adequately determined** will and actions for which they can take **responsibility**.

This is the goal of the two-stage models of free will discussed in Chapters 12 and 13.

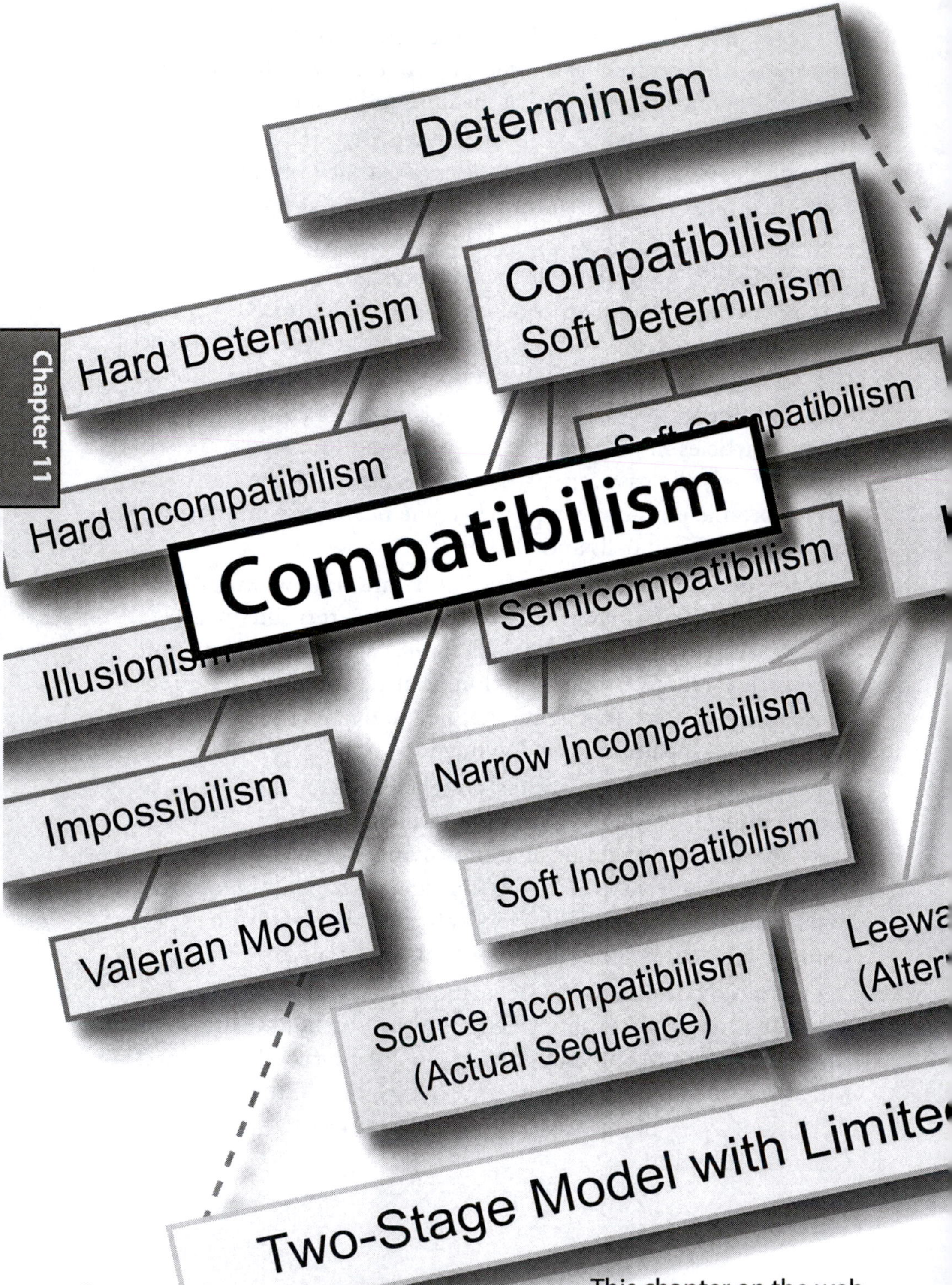

Chapter 11

Determinism

Hard Determinism

Compatibilism
Soft Determinism

Soft Compatibilism

Hard Incompatibilism

Compatibilism

Semicompatibilism

Illusionism

Impossibilism

Narrow Incompatibilism

Soft Incompatibilism

Valerian Model

Source Incompatibilism
(Actual Sequence)

Leewa
(Alter

Two-Stage Model with Limite

This chapter on the web
informationphilosopher.com/freedom/compatibilism.html

Compatibilism

Compatibilists argue that determinism is compatible with human freedom, and that indeterminism is not compatible or at best incoherent. They feel (correctly) that there must be a deterministic or causal connection between our will and our actions. This allows us to take responsibility for our actions, including credit for the good and blame for the bad.

As long as the agent is free from external coercion, they have freedom of action. This is the compatibilist freedom we have, according to THOMAS HOBBES and DAVID HUME. It is the "negative freedom" of ISAIAH BERLIN.

Compatibilists (or "soft determinists" as they have been known since WILLIAM JAMES) identify free will with freedom of action - the lack of external constraints. We are free, and we have free will, if we are not in physical chains. But freedom of the will is different from freedom of action.

And our wills can be free, even if we are in physical chains.

Many compatibilists accept the view of a causal chain of events going back indefinitely in time, consistent with the laws of nature, with the plan of an omniscient God, or with other determinisms. As long as our own will is included in that causal chain, we are free, they say. And they think causality in nature is related to the very possibility of reason and logic. Without causality, they say, we could not be certain of the truths of our arguments.

Compatibilists don't mind all their decisions being caused by a metaphysical chain of events, as long as they are not in physical chains.

We think compatibilists should be classified according to the particular determinisms they think are compatible with human freedom. It is one thing to claim compatibility with physics, another to claim compatibility with God's foreknowledge, etc.

An increasing number of compatibilists, often reluctantly, accept the view that random quantum mechanical events occur in the world. Whether in the physical world, in the biological world (where they are a key driver of genetic mutations), or in the mind, randomness and uncaused events are real.

Other compatibilists, DANIEL DENNETT, for example, simply insist that such genuine irreducible randomness is not needed for human freedom, or even for biological evolution. Others point out that even if strict **determinism** were true (which it isn't), compatibilist freedom of action, in DAVID HUME's sense, would still exist. I agree. This would be so.

Quantum events introduce the possibility of accidents, novelty, and human creativity. Compatibilists who admit that such **indeterminism** exists might very likely be convinced of a stronger argument for human freedom that still provides an **adequately determined** will.

I call this "**comprehensive compatibilism**," in which free will is compatible *both* with adequate determinism (limited to the real determinism that we have in the world) *and* with indeterminism (constrained to not causing any of our actions directly, but simply providing **alternative possibilities** for the **adequately determined** will to choose from).

Comprehensive compatibilism is developed in Chapter 28.

Giving Compatibilists What They Want

1. They Want Determinism, especially **determination** of their will by their motives and feelings, their character and values.

So let us ask them two simple questions:

> "First, Do you agree that there is some physical indeterminism in the universe?" By which of course we mean quantum mechanical indeterminacy.
>
> "And second, do you agree that quantum mechanical indeterminism normally has no observable effect on large physical structures?" By which we mean that the world is "adequately determined."

2. They Want Intelligible Freedom. Let's ask a third simple question,

> "If the indeterminism only provided genuine possible **alternatives** for action and thought, if it did not impair the **adequately determined** will in any way, if it does not directly cause any action, is such a freedom and element of unpredictability acceptable?"

3. They Want Moral Responsibility. So finally, let's ask one last question,

> "Would you agree that the adequately determined will, making its selection from among such unpredictable actions or thoughts, can be held morally responsible for its choices?"

If you are a compatibilist, what are your answers?

Incompatibilism

PETER VAN INWAGEN gave incompatibilism a new meaning in his 1983 *Essay on Free Will.* His new definition changed the taxonomy of free will positions (see Chapter 6). Van Inwagen accepts the lack of **alternative possibilities** (in what he calls the **Direct Argument** and others describe as the **Actual Sequence** of events), as compatibilists have done, especially since the 1969 work of HARRY FRANKFURT.

Incompatibilists of many stripes now appear - Source Incompatibilists, Leeway Incompatibilists, Hard and Soft Incompatibilists, and Broad and Narrow Incompatibilists. Libertarians - of many kinds as well - all get lumped together with Hard Determinists as Incompatibilists in van Inwagen's new catch-all category.

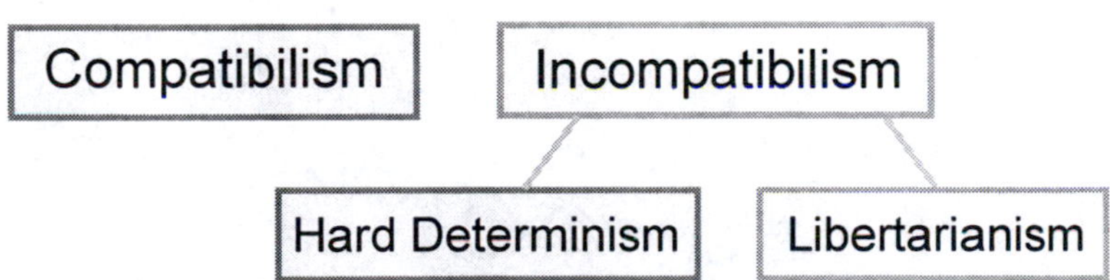

Figure 11-1. A compatibilist-incompatibilist taxonomy.

This chapter on the web
informationphilosopher.com/freedom/two-stage_models.html

Two-Stage Models of Free Will

In our history of the free will problem (Chapter 7), we found several thinkers who developed two-stage solutions to the classical problem of free will, among them William James (1884), Henri Poincaré (about 1906), the physicist Arthur Holly Compton (1931, 1955), the philosopher Mortimer Adler (1961), the mathematician Jacques Hadamard, the philosopher Karl Popper (1965, 1977), the physicist and philosopher Henry Margenau (1968, 1982), the philosophers Daniel Dennett (1978) and Robert Kane (1985), the classicists Anthony Long and David Sedley (1987), Roger Penrose (1989), Julia Annas (1990), Alfred Mele (1995), Benjamin Libet and Stephen Kosslyn (2004), John Searle (2007), and most recently, the neurogeneticist and biologist Martin Heisenberg (2009).

My own **Cogito** two-stage model has been in development since the 1970's, and will be discussed in the next chapter.

William James (1884)

The genius of the first two-stage model of free will is that James makes **indeterminism** the source for what he calls "**alternative possibilities**" and "ambiguous futures."

The chance generation of such alternative possibilities for action does not in any way limit his choice to one of them. For James, chance is not the direct cause of actions. James makes it clear that it is his choice that "grants consent" to one of them.

As James biographer Robert Richardson puts it,

> "Accepting the possibility of chance does not mean accepting a world that is random. It means realizing that chance is another word for freedom." [1]

In 1884 James asked some Harvard Divinity School students to consider his choice for walking home after his talk.

---

1 James (2010) p. 21.

> "What is meant by saying that my choice of which way to walk home after the lecture is ambiguous and matter of chance?...It means that both Divinity Avenue and Oxford Street are called but only one, and that one either one, shall be chosen." [2]

With this simple example, James was the first thinker to enunciate clearly a two-stage decision process, with chance in a present time of random alternatives, leading to a choice which grants consent to one possibility and transforms an equivocal ambiguous future into an unalterable and simple past. There is a temporal sequence of undetermined alternative possibilities followed by an adequately determined choice where chance is no longer a factor.

James also asked the students to imagine his actions repeated in exactly the **same circumstances**, a condition which is regarded today as one of the great challenges to libertarian free will. In the following passage, James anticipates much of modern philosophical modal reasoning and physical theories of multiple universes.

> "Imagine that I first walk through Divinity Avenue, and then imagine that the powers governing the universe annihilate ten minutes of time with all that it contained, and set me back at the door of this hall just as I was before the choice was made. Imagine then that, everything else being the same, I now make a different choice and traverse Oxford Street. You, as passive spectators, look on and see the two alternative universes,--one of them with me walking through Divinity Avenue in it, the other with the same me walking through Oxford Street. Now, if you are determinists you believe one of these universes to have been from eternity impossible: you believe it to have been impossible because of the intrinsic irrationality or accidentality somewhere involved in it. But looking outwardly at these universes, can you say which is the impossible and accidental one, and which the rational and necessary one? I doubt if the most ironclad determinist among you could have the slightest glimmer of light on this point." [3]

James's two-stage model effectively separates chance (the indeterministic free element) from choice (an arguably determinate decision that follows causally from one's character, values, and

2 James (1056) "The Dilemma of Determinism," p. 149.

3 *ibid.*, p. 155.

especially feelings and desires at the moment of decision). In his 1890 book *The Principles of Psychology*, James said there were five types of decision. In the first, the reasonable type,

> "arguments for and against a given course seem to settle themselves in the mind and to end by leaving a clear balance in favor of one alternative.... In this easy transition from doubt to assurance we seem to ourselves almost passive; the reasons which decide us appearing to flow in from the nature of things, and to owe nothing to our will. We have, however, a perfect sense of being free, in that we are devoid of any feeling of coercion.... It may be said in general that a great part of every deliberation consists in the turning over of all the possible modes of conceiving the doing or not doing of the act in point. The moment we hit upon a conception which lets us apply some principle of action which is a fixed and stable part of our Ego, our state of doubt is at an end." [4]

Where do the alternative possibilities for action come from? From past experiences - initially involuntary and later from observing the experiences of others, all these the results of chance - we build up a stock of possibilities in our memory.

> "We learn all our possibilities by the way of experience. When a particular movement, having once occurred in a random, reflex, or involuntary way, has left an image of itself in the memory, then the movement can be desired again, proposed as an end, and deliberately willed.
>
> "*A supply of ideas of the various movements that are possible left in the memory by experiences of their involuntary performance is thus the first prerequisite of the voluntary life.*" [5]

In the fifth kind of decision, James sees room for creativity that allows us to do something beyond what the given reasons would logically imply. Note that in a deterministic universe, there are no genuinely new creative acts. Determinism is "information-preserving." There is "nothing new under the sun."

---

4 James (2007) p. 531

5 James (2007) p. 487-8. The italics are in the original

"In the fifth and final type of decision, the feeling that the evidence is all in, and that reason has balanced the books, may be either present or absent. But in either case we feel, in deciding, as if we ourselves by our own wilful act inclined the beam; in the former case by adding our living effort to the weight of the logical reason which, taken alone, seems powerless to make the act discharge; in the latter by a kind of creative contribution of something instead of a reason which does a reason's work." [6]

James' "mental evolution" was clearly inspired by Charles Darwin's biological evolution.

"A remarkable parallel, which I think has never been noticed, obtains between the facts of social evolution on the one hand, and of zoölogical evolution as expounded by Mr. Darwin on the other...

["In mental evolution], if anywhere, it would seem at first sight as if that school must be right which makes the mind passively plastic, and the environment actively productive of the form and order of its conceptions; which, in a word, thinks that all mental progress must result from a series of adaptive changes, in the sense already defined of that word...It might, accordingly, seem as if there were no room for any agency other than this; as if the distinction we have found so useful between "spontaneous variation," as the producer of changed forms, and the environment, as their preserver and destroyer, did not hold in the case of mental progress; as if, in a word, the parallel with Darwinism might no longer obtain...

"But, in spite of all these facts, I have no hesitation whatever in holding firm to the Darwinian distinction even here...

"And I can easily show...that as a matter of fact the new conceptions, emotions, and active tendencies which evolve are originally produced in the shape of random images, fancies, accidental out-births of spontaneous variation in the functional activity of the excessively instable human brain." [7]

6 James (2007) p. 534.
7 James (1880) p. 441.

Henri Poincaré (about 1906)

Henri Poincaré was called the "last universalist" because he was a great contributor to so many fields in mathematics, but his work was also broad in physics, philosophy, and psychology. William James read Poincaré and the great thinker knew James work. There is some sign of direct influence.

Poincaré speculated on how his mind works when he is solving mathematical problems. He had the critical insight that random combinations and possibilities are generated, some in an unconscious way with chance involved, then they are selected among, perhaps initially also by an unconscious process, but then by a definite conscious process of validation.

> "It is certain that the combinations which present themselves to the mind in a kind of sudden illumination after a somewhat prolonged period of unconscious work are generally useful and fruitful combinations... all the combinations are formed as a result of the automatic action of the subliminal ego, but those only which are interesting find their way into the field of consciousness... A few only are harmonious, and consequently at once useful and beautiful, and they will be capable of affecting the geometrician's special sensibility I have been speaking of; which, once aroused, will direct our attention upon them, and will thus give them the opportunity of becoming conscious... In the subliminal ego, on the contrary, there reigns what I would call liberty, if one could give this name to the mere absence of discipline and to disorder born of chance." [8]

Poincaré was thus the second thinker to propose the two-stage process of random alternatives followed by selection of one choice.

Jacques Hadamard (1945)

In his 1945 book *Psychology of Invention in the Mathematical Field*, Hadamard described the Synthèse conference in Paris in 1936 organized to study creativity. The conference focused on Henri Poincare's two-stage approach to problem solving, in which the unconscious generates random combinations. In his book, Hadamard quoted the poet Valéry (as did Dennett later),

8 Poincaré (2003)

summarizing the conference opinion. For Hadamard, it captured Poincaré's description of how the combination of random ideas is followed by a choice of the best combination. Chance alone is not enough.

> "...it is obvious that invention or discovery, be it in mathematics or anywhere else, takes place by combining ideas.
>
> "However, to find these, it has been necessary to construct the very numerous possible combinations, among which the useful ones are to be found.
>
> "It cannot be avoided that this first operation take place, to a certain extent, at random, so that the role of chance is hardly doubtful in this first step of the mental process.
>
> "It is obvious that this first process, this building up of numerous combinations, is only the beginning of creation, even, as we should say, preliminary to it...Invention is discernment, choice.
>
> "*To Invent Is to Choose.* This very remarkable conclusion appears the more striking if we compare it with what Paul Valéry writes in the Nouvelle Revue Française: "It takes two to invent anything. The one makes up combinations; the other one chooses, recognizes what he wishes and what is important to him in the mass of the things which the former has imparted to him."
>
> "What we call genius is much less the work of the first one than the readiness of the second one to grasp the value of what has been laid before him and to choose it." [9]

Although Valéry describes two persons, this is clearly William James' temporal sequence of random chance ("free") followed by a determining choice ("will"). For James, chance and choice are part of a single mind.

Arthur Holly Compton (1931, 1955)

In 1931, Nobel prize-winning physicist Compton championed the idea of human freedom based on quantum uncertainty and invented the notion of amplification of microscopic quantum events to bring chance into the macroscopic world. In his rather

9 Hadamard (1945) p. 30.

bizarre mechanism, he imagined sticks of dynamite attached to his amplifier, anticipating the Schrödinger's Cat paradox.

Years later, Compton clarified the two-stage nature of his idea in an *Atlantic Monthly* article in 1955.

> "A set of known physical conditions is not adequate to specify precisely what a forthcoming event will be. These conditions, insofar as they can be known, define instead a range of possible events from among which some particular event will occur. When one exercises freedom, by his act of choice he is himself adding a factor not supplied by the physical conditions and is thus himself determining what will occur. That he does so is known only to the person himself. From the outside one can see in his act only the working of physical law. It is the inner knowledge that he is in fact doing what he intends to do that tells the actor himself that he is free." [10]

Mortimer Adler (1961)

In the second volume of his massive book *The Idea of Freedom*, Adler revisits the idea of a natural freedom of self-determination, which explicitly includes **alternative possibilities** and the self as a cause so our actions are "**up to us**." Note that the uncaused self decides from prior alternative possibilities.

"We have employed the following descriptive formula to summarize the understanding of self-determination." It is "only when at least two of the three following points are affirmed:

"(i) that the decision is intrinsically unpredictable, i.e., given perfect knowledge of all relevant causes, the decision cannot be foreseen or predicted with certitude;

"(ii) that the decision is not necessitated, i.e., the decision is always one of a number of alternative possible decisions any one of which it was simultaneously within the power of the self to cause, no matter what other antecedent or concurrent factors exercise a causal influence on the making of the decision;

"(iii) that the decision flows from the causal initiative of the self, i.e., on the plane of natural or finite causes, the self is the uncaused cause of the decision it makes." [11]

---

10 Compton (1967)

11 Adler (1961) p. 225.

Karl Popper (1965, 1977)

Compton's work was no doubt closely read by philosopher KARL POPPER, especially when Popper was selected to give the first ARTHUR HOLLY COMPTON Memorial Lecture in 1965.

At first Popper dismissed quantum mechanics as being no help with free will, but later he describes a **two-stage model** that parallels Darwinian evolution, with genetic mutations being probabilistic and involving quantum uncertainty. In his Compton lectures, he criticizes Compton's amplifier idea

> "The idea that the only alternative to determinism is just sheer chance was taken over by Schlick, together with many of his views on the subject, from Hume, who asserted that
>
>> 'the removal' of what he called 'physical necessity' must always result in 'the same thing with chance. As objects must either be conjoin'd or not, . . . 'tis impossible to admit of any medium betwixt chance and an absolute necessity'.
>
> "I shall later argue against this important doctrine according to which the alternative to determinism is sheer chance. Yet I must admit that the doctrine seems to hold good for the quantum-theoretical models which have been designed to explain, or at least to illustrate, the possibility of human freedom. This seems to be the reason why these models are so very unsatisfactory.
>
> "Compton himself designed such a model, though he did not particularly like it. It uses quantum indeterminacy, and the unpredictability of a quantum jump, as a model of a human decision of great moment. It consists of an amplifier which amplifies the effect of a single quantum jump in such a way that it may either cause an explosion or destroy the relay necessary for bringing the explosion about. In this way one single quantum jump may be equivalent to a major decision. But in my opinion the model has no similarity to any rational decision, being probabilistic and involving quantum uncertainty.
>
> "Hume's and Schlick's ontological thesis that there cannot exist anything intermediate between chance and determinism seems to me not only highly dogmatic (not to say doctrinaire) but clearly absurd; and it is understandable only on the assumption

> that they believed in a complete determinism in which chance has no status except as a symptom of our ignorance." [12]

Popper called for a combination of randomness and control to explain freedom, though not yet explicitly in two stages with random chance before the controlled decision.

> "freedom is not just chance but, rather, the result of a subtle interplay between something almost random or haphazard, and something like a restrictive or selective control." [13]

In his 1977 book with JOHN ECCLES, *The Self and its Brain*, Popper finally formulates the two-stage model in a temporal sequence, and makes the comparison with evolution and natural selection,

> "New ideas have a striking similarity to genetic mutations. Now, let us look for a moment at genetic mutations. Mutations are, it seems, brought about by quantum theoretical indeterminacy (including radiation effects). Accordingly, they are also probabilistic and not in themselves originally selected or adequate, but on them there subsequently operates natural selection which eliminates inappropriate mutations. Now we could conceive of a similar process with respect to new ideas and to free-will decisions, and similar things.
>
> "That is to say, a range of possibilities is brought about by a probabilistic and quantum mechanically characterized set of proposals, as it were - of possibilities brought forward by the brain. On these there then operates a kind of selective procedure which eliminates those proposals and those possibilities which are not acceptable to the mind."

In 1977 Popper gave the first Darwin Lecture, at Darwin College, Cambridge. He called it *Natural Selection and the Emergence of Mind*. In it he said he had changed his mind (a rare admission by a philosopher) about two things. First he now thought that natural selection was not a "tautology" that made it an unfalsifiable theory. Second, he had come to accept the random variation and selection of ideas as a model of free will.

> "The selection of a kind of behavior out of a randomly offered repertoire may be an act of choice, even an act of free will. I am

12 Popper (1972) p. 227ff..

13 *ibid.*

> an indeterminist; and in discussing indeterminism I have often regretfully pointed out that quantum indeterminacy does not seem to help us;[1] for the amplification of something like, say, radioactive disintegration processes would not lead to human action or even animal action, but only to random movements.
>
> "I have changed my mind on this issue.[2] A choice process may be a selection process, and the selection may be from some repertoire of random events, without being random in its turn. This seems to me to offer a promising solution to one of our most vexing problems, and one by downward causation."
>
> 1. Cf. my Objective Knowledge, chapter 6, pp. 226-29.
> 2. See p. 540 of J. C. Eccles and K. R. Popper, The Self and Its Brain.

Henry Margenau (1968, 1982)

In 1968, physicist Margenau was invited to give the Wimmer Lecture at St. Vincent College in Pennsylvania. His topic was *Scientific Indeterminism and Human Freedom*. Margenau embraced indeterminism as the first step toward a solution of the problem of human freedom.

Then in 1982, with co-author Lawrence LeShan, Margenau called his model of free will a "solution" to what had heretofore had been seen as mere "paradox and illusion." He very neatly separates "free" and "will" in a temporal sequence, as William James had done, naming them simply "chance" followed by "choice."

> "Our thesis is that quantum mechanics leaves our body, our brain, at any moment in a state with numerous (because of its complexity we might say innumerable) possible futures, each with a predetermined probability. Freedom involves two components: chance (existence of a genuine set of alternatives) and choice. Quantum mechanics provides the chance, and we shall argue that only the mind can make the choice by selecting (not energetically enforcing) among the possible future courses." [14]

Daniel Dennett (1978)

While he is a confirmed compatibilist, in "On Giving Libertarians What They Say They Want," chapter 15 of his 1978 book

14 Margenau and Leshan (1982) p. 240.

Brainstorms, Tufts philosopher Daniel Dennett articulated the case for a two-stage model of free will better than any libertarian.

Dennett named his model of decision-making "Valerian" after the poet Paul Valéry, who took part in a 1936 conference in Paris with Jacques Hadamard. He quotes Valéry,

> "It takes two to invent anything. The one makes up combinations; the other one chooses." [15]

Dennett makes his version of a two-stage model very clear. And he defends it with six excellent reasons. His arguments are more persuasive than any other philosopher or scientist, including William James himself. Ironically, Dennett remains a firm believer in determinism and calls himself a compatibilist.

> "The model of decision making I am proposing has the following feature: when we are faced with an important decision, a consideration-generator whose output is to some degree undetermined produces a series of considerations, some of which may of course be immediately rejected as irrelevant by the agent (consciously or unconsciously). Those considerations that are selected by the agent as having a more than negligible bearing on the decision then figure in a reasoning process, and if the agent is in the main reasonable, those considerations ultimately serve as predictors and explicators of the agent's final decision."[16]

Dennett gives strong reasons why this is the kind of free will that libertarians say they want.

> 1. "First...The intelligent selection, rejection, and weighing of the considerations that do occur to the subject is a matter of intelligence making the difference."
>
> 2. "Second, I think it installs indeterminism in the right place for the libertarian, if there is a right place at all."
>
> 3. "Third...from the point of view of biological engineering, it is just more efficient and in the end more rational that decision making should occur in this way."

15 Dennett (1978) p. 293
16 Dennett (1978) p. 295

Chapter 12

4. "A fourth observation in favor of the model is that it permits moral education to make a difference, without making all of the difference."

5. "Fifth - and I think this is perhaps the most important thing to be said in favor of this model - it provides some account of our important intuition that we are the authors of our moral decisions."

6. "Finally, the model I propose points to the multiplicity of decisions that encircle our moral decisions and suggests that in many cases our ultimate decision as to which way to act is less important phenomenologically as a contributor to our sense of free will than the prior decisions affecting our deliberation process itself: the decision, for instance, not to consider any further, to terminate deliberation; or the decision to ignore certain lines of inquiry.

"These prior and subsidiary decisions contribute, I think, to our sense of ourselves as responsible free agents, roughly in the following way: I am faced with an important decision to make, and after a certain amount of deliberation, I say to myself: "That's enough. I've considered this matter enough and now I'm going to act," in the full knowledge that I could have considered further, in the full knowledge that the eventualities may prove that I decided in error, but with the acceptance of responsibility in any case." [17]

Robert Kane (1985)

In his 1985 book *Free Will and Values* Kane carefully considered the work of Compton, Popper, Eccles, and Dennett. He says he developed his own two-stage model before Dennett, but in the end he did not publish it or endorse Dennett because the two-stage model "did not go far enough."

Kane was actually quite bleak about the possibilities for a satisfactory libertarian model. He felt,

> "that any construction which escaped confusion and emptiness was likely to fall short of some libertarian aspirations - aspirations that I believe cannot ultimately be fulfilled." [18]

17 Dennett (1978) p. 295-7.

18 Kane (1985) p. 165.

His first model was a choice between "relativistic alternatives." The choice was in part rational and in part indeterministic. It could be explained by the agent giving his reasons. Even if the choice is by chance,

> "the agent has agreed beforehand to accept the chance selected outcome and to endorse reasons for it in a special way. That is, the selection is going to be 'willed to be so' on a provisional basis by the agent, whichever way it goes." [19]

Kane hoped to combine some rationality with some freedom in this model, so both determinists and libertarians would be happy. Unfortunately, neither was happy.

Although the two-stage model of earlier thinkers is an "essential and important part" of any adequate libertarian conception of free will, it does not go far enough for Kane because it does not fully capture the notion of ultimate responsibility (UR) during "self-forming actions" (SFAs) which depend on the agent's efforts. He has said that the two-stage model was merely a "significant piece in the overall puzzle of a libertarian freedom." [20]

> "The reason is that the chance ("free") part is not in the control of the agent and the "will" part is fully determined by a combination of the chance part and other determining factors, so the final choice is determined by factors, none of which the agent has control over at the time of choice. If all of our choices are determined at the time of choice that would not be libertarian freedom even if some chance events in the past were responsible for forming some of the determining factors that now determine our choice because however the determining factors were formed in the past, all of our choices would be determined when they are made." [21]

Kane agrees that these choices would not have been **predetermined** from before the chance events in the past (the generation of possibilities in the first stage), so are libertarian free.

Kane had previously accepted that the two-stage model could provide enough freedom for everyday practical decisions (vanilla or chocolate), but did not play a role in moral or prudential "torn"

19 Kane (1985) p. 96.
20 Kane (1985) p. 104.
21 Personal communication.

decisions between what the agent believes ought to be done and what the agent wants or desires to do.

Today Kane sees that two-stage models may generate the alternatives of his SFAs, based on character and motives. So they may explain the agent's conflicting motives in moral and prudential choices. and they even explain the (reasons for the) agent's efforts. Kane now agrees that the agent has libertarian freedom even when the two-stage model produces just one option and the agent can be described as "self-determined."

But when the two-stage model does not narrow down the alternatives to a single act of **self-determination**, and when the choice is moral or prudential, Kane says that his introduction of indeterminism into the decision itself provides "something more" than the two-stage model, and I now agree with him.

> "Now I believe these undetermined self-forming actions or SFAs occur at those difficult times of life when we are torn between competing visions of what we should do or become. Perhaps we are torn between doing the moral thing or acting from ambition, or between powerful present desires and long-term goals, or we are faced with difficult tasks for which we have aversions." [22]

> "In all such cases, we are faced with competing motivations and have to make an effort to overcome temptation to do something else we also strongly want. There is tension and uncertainty in our minds about what to do at such times, I suggest, that is reflected in appropriate regions of our brains by movement away from thermodynamic equilibrium — in short, a kind of "stirring up of chaos" in the brain that makes it sensitive to micro-indeterminacies at the neuronal level. The uncertainty and inner tension we feel at such soul-searching moments of self-formation is thus reflected in the indeterminacy of our neural processes themselves. What we experience internally as uncertainty about what to do on such occasions would then correspond physically to the opening of a window of opportunity that temporarily screens off complete determination by influences of the past. [23]

22 "Libertarianism," in Fischer (2007) p. 26.
23 *ibid.* p. 26.

Kane agrees that the ever-present noise in the brain is enough to provide the indeterminism. But he emphasizes that the agent's efforts are more the cause of the final decision than the indeterminism involved.

> "If indeterminism is involved in a process so that its outcome is undetermined, one might argue that the outcome must merely happen and therefore cannot be somebody's choice. But there is no reason to assume such a claim is true. A choice is the formation of an intention or purpose to do something. It resolves uncertainty and indecision in the mind about what to do. Nothing in such a description implies that there could not be some indeterminism in the deliberation and neural processes of an agent preceding choice corresponding to the agent's prior uncertainty about what to do. Recall from the preceding arguments that the presence of indeterminism does not mean the outcome happened merely by chance and not by the agent's effort. Self-forming choices are undetermined, but not uncaused. They are caused by the agent's efforts. [24]

To Kane's critics, the SFA's indeterminism raises the objection of loss of control, but Kane says the agent can decide to assume responsibility whichever way she chooses.

> "Suppose we were to say to such persons: 'But look, you didn't have sufficient or conclusive prior reasons for choosing as you did since you also had viable reasons for choosing the other way.' They might reply. 'True enough. But I did have good reasons for choosing as I did, which I'm willing to stand by and take responsibility for. If these reasons were not sufficient or conclusive reasons, that's because, like the heroine of the novel, I was not a fully formed person before I chose (and still am not, for that matter). Like the author of the novel, I am in the process of writing an unfinished story and forming an unfinished character who, in my case, is myself.'" [25]

Anthony Long and David Sedley (1987)

Anthony Long and David Sedley speculated in their masterwork *The Hellenistic Philosophers* that Epicurus' swerve of the

24 "Libertarianism," in Fischer (2007) p. 33
25 *ibid*, pp. 41-2.

atoms might be limited to providing undetermined **alternative possibilities** for action, from which the mind's power of volition could choose in a way that reflects character and values, desires and feelings.

> "Here at last a significant role for the swerve leaps to the eye. For it is to answer just this question, according to Cicero, that the swerve was introduced. The evident power of the self and its volitions to intervene in the physical processes of soul and body would be inexplicable if physical laws alone were sufficient to determine the precise trajectory of every atom. Therefore physical laws are not sufficient to determine the precise trajectory of every atom. There is a minimal degree of physical indeterminism — the swerve. An unimpeded atom may at any given moment continue its present trajectory, but equally may `swerve' into one of the adjacent parallel trajectories. [26]

Long and Sedley assume a non-physical (metaphysical) ability of the volition to affect the atoms, which is implausible. But the idea that a physical volition chooses - (consistent with and adequately determined by its character and values and its desires and feelings) from among alternative possibilities provided randomly by the atoms - is quite plausible.

> "It does so, we may speculate, not by overriding the laws of physics, but by choosing between the alternative possibilities which the laws of physics leave open. In this way a large group of soul atoms might simultaneously be diverted into a new pattern of motion, and thus radically redirect the motion of the body. Such an event, requiring as it does the coincidence of numerous swerves, would be statistically most improbable according to the laws of physics alone. But it is still, on the swerve theory, an intrinsically possible one, which volition might therefore be held to bring about..(It may be objected that swerves are meant to be entirely uncaused; but...that was only an inference by Epicurus' critics, made plausible by concentrating on the swerve's cosmogonic function...for there it must indeed occur at random and without the intervention of volition.)" [27]

---

26 Long and Sedley (1987) p. 110.
27 Long and Sedley (1987) p. 110.

Roger Penrose (1989)

In his 1989 book The Emperor's New Mind, Penrose suggests a two-stage process but is skeptical of the value of randomness in the first step. His thinking follows that of Jacques Hadamard and Henri Poincaré, who he has discussed in the previous pages.

> "In relation to this, the question of what constitutes genuine originality should be raised. It seems to me that there are two factors involved, namely a 'putting-up' and a 'shooting-down' process. I imagine that the putting-up could be largely unconscious and the shooting-down largely conscious. Without an effective putting-up process, one would have no new ideas at all. But, just by itself, this procedure would have little value. One needs an effective procedure for forming judgements, so that only those ideas with a reasonable chance of success will survive. In dreams, for example, unusual ideas may easily come to mind, but only very rarely do they survive the critical judgements of the wakeful consciousness. In my opinion, it is the conscious shooting-down (judgement) process that is central to the issue of originality, rather than the unconscious putting-up process; but I am aware that many others might hold to a contrary view." [28]

Chapter 12

Julia Annas (1992)

In her 1992 book, *The Hellenistic Philosophy of Mind*, Annas finds it hard to see how random swerves can help to explain free action. But she sees clearly that randomness can provide alternative possibilities for the will to choose from. She says, "there would be no point in having free will if there were no genuinely open possibilities between which to select," anticipating the two-stage model of free will.

Perhaps influenced by her classicist colleagues Sedley and Long, or maybe just coming to the same conclusions from reading the ancients, especially Epicurus and his swerve, Annas says.

> "...since swerves are random, it is hard to see how they help to explain free action. We can scarcely expect there to be a random swerve before every free action...random swerves would seem

28 Penrose (1989) p. 422.

to produce, if anything, random actions; we still lack any clue as to how they could produce actions which are free.

"An influential modern line of thought avoids these problems by arguing that our evidence does not demand that there be a swerve for each free action [Furley]. Rather, swerves explain the fact that people have characters capable of change and reaction that goes beyond mechanical response to stimuli. We act freely because we have characters that are flexible and spontaneous, and this is because we are composed of atoms which swerve occasionally. On this account, swerves do not have to be frequent, since they are not part of any mechanism of action; one swerve in your soul is enough for the kind of character flexibility that is required. Such an account avoids the problems attaching to any account that brings swerves into free action, but at the cost of not answering very closely to the evidence; the Lucretius passage certainly suggests that swerves are in some way relevant at the point of action.

"Another kind of suggestion is that swerves are not the causes of free actions at all. Rather, they come into the process whereby free actions are brought about. Swerves are supposed to explain something about the nature of free agency and how it works, but they do not cause free actions (by cutting across causal chains, for example). This suggestion can be developed in several ways...

"The role of swerves is to provide alternative possibilities for volitions to choose between, for there would be no point in having free will if there were no genuinely open possibilities between which to select." [29]

Albert Mele (1995)

In 1995 Alfred Mele, clearly influenced by Daniel Dennett and Robert Kane, proposed his "Modest Libertarianism," a two-stage process that combines an incompatibilist early phase followed by a compatibilist control phase.

"it might be worth exploring the possibility of combining a compatibilist conception of the later parts of a process issuing in full blown, deliberative, intentional action with an incom-

29 *The Hellenistic Philosophy of Mind*, pp. 184-88

> patibilist conception of the earlier parts. For example, it might be possible to gain "ultimate control" while preserving a considerable measure of nonultimate agential control by treating the process from proximal decisive better judgment through overt action in a compatibilist way and finding a theoretically useful place for indeterminacy in processes leading to proximal decisive better judgments."[30]

Mele sees that chance need not be the direct cause of action.

> "That a consideration is indeterministically caused to come to mind does not entail that the agent has no control over how he responds to it."[31]

Mele is very concerned about the location of any indeterminism, the problem of where and when indeterminism could occur in a way that helps and does not harm agent control.

The Problem of Luck

Mele has written extensively about the question whether chance events in our causal history mean that many of our actions are a matter of luck. Since chance is very real, many things are the result of good or bad luck. This is a not a problem for free will, but it is one for **moral responsibility**.

John Martin Fischer (1995)

Also in 1995, John Martin Fischer argued for a model based on Daniel Dennett's 1978 work. Fischer is best known for the idea of **semicompatibilism**, the idea that moral responsibility is compatible with determinism. Fischer is agnostic on whether free will itself is compatible or incompatible with determinism.

Fischer is most concerned to establish the control needed for responsibility, especially given Frankfurt-style examples challenging control. In any case, Fischer uses the Dennett idea - that the indeterminism comes at an early stage of the overall deliberation-decision process - to locate a Frankfurt-style "prior sign" needed by the hypothetical intervener at a place deterministically linked to the decision and subsequent action.

30 Mele (1995) p. 212.
31 Mele (2006) p. 10..

Fischer's main criticism of alternative possibilities for action is that it is implausible to suppose that one's **moral responsibility** is grounded on the possibility of forming a certain sort of judgment about what is best: a judgment on behalf of doing something there are no good reasons to do. The responsibility for doing good is not grounded in the possibility of doing bad. Note that free will is completely independent of, and merely a prerequisite to, **moral responsibility**. Otherwise it would be an ethical fallacy.

Fischer hopes to develop "another sort of libertarianism." He says he does not have the space to lay out his "second family of libertarian accounts," and gives us very little on how it differs from Dennett. He says "Dennett argues that it is the only sort of libertarianism that is plausible, and I believe that it is at least minimally plausible. I also believe that it is libertarianism." Fischer may be simply constructing a libertarianism with a built-in place for the Frankfurt intervener, in order to support the absence of **alternative possibilities** and his own **semicompatibilism**. Here is Fischer's sketch of his main idea.

> "I wish to develop (in an extremely sketchy way) another sort of libertarianism; on this kind of approach, the relationship between the relevant "sign" or "signal" and the subsequent choice is causally deterministic, but there is nevertheless a lack of causal determination along the sequence that issues in the decision (and action). And I shall point out that this approach also seems to lead to the view that an agent can be morally responsible for making a choice even though he could not have (at any relevant time) made a different choice.
>
> "I do not have the space here to lay out this second family of libertarian accounts fully or carefully. But I shall simply sketch the main ideas and hope that enough of the content of the approach will emerge to convince the reader that this family of views constitutes a minimally plausible, serious libertarian approach - worth further elaboration and evaluation in the context of the issues under discussion here. In his article, "On Giving Libertarians What They Say They Want," Daniel Dennett has presented this family of approaches; he does not necessarily

endorse the view, but presents it as the most plausible and appealing version of libertarianism.

"What is crucial to Dennett's view is that indeterminacy be installed at the appropriate place, and Dennett argues that this is not between the judgment that a particular act is the best among one's alternatives and the subsequent choice. He says, "Clearly, what the libertarian has in mind is indeterminism at some earlier point, prior to the ultimate decision or formation of intention...." Rather, Dennett argues that there can be lack of causal determinism (of a certain sort) within the process of deliberation that leads to the agent's judgment as to what is the best option (under the circumstances).

"So Dennett's picture suggested on behalf of the libertarian involves some lack of causal determination in the process of deliberation, but no such lack in the link between the judgment as to what is best and the formation of an intention (or the making of a decision). Let me emphasize that I am not in a position here fully to lay out this view (or set of views) or to defend it. Dennett argues that it is the only sort of libertarianism that is plausible, and I believe that it is at least minimally plausible. I also believe that it is libertarianism." [32]

Benjamin Libet and Stephen Kosslyn (2004)

In 2004, Stephen Kosslyn wrote a foreword to Benjamin Libet's book *Mind Time*. The book summarized Libet's famous experiments, in which he claimed a Readiness Potential (RP) *initiates* an action well before the conscious will is aware of the decision to act. See Chapter 17 for the details. At one point in the book, Libet suggests the RP might include multiple initiatives, implying multiple possible alternative actions. [33]

In a few brief paragraphs of the foreword, Kosslyn proposed a two-stage model of alternative choices that are constructed in part chaotically by nondeterministic processes, followed by decisions that are based on our character and values - "what one is." He sees a role for a *causa sui*.

32 Fischer (1995) p. 125
33 Libet (2004), p. 148.

> "The rationales and anticipated consequences — and even, depending on the situation, the alternative courses of action — are not simply "looked up" in memory, having been stashed away like notes in a file after previous encounters.

Here Kosslyn considers a first stage of free creation of alternative courses of action,

> "Rather, one constructs rationales and anticipated consequences, as appropriate for the specific situation at hand. This construction process may rely in part on chaotic processes. Such processes are not entirely determined by one's learning history (even as filtered by one's genes)... Depending on what one was just thinking about, the brain is in a different "start state" (i.e., different information is partially activated, different associations are primed) when one constructs rationales and anticipated consequences — which will affect how one decides. (Note that this idea does not simply move the problem back a step: What one was just thinking itself was in part a result of nondeterministic processes.) Our thoughts, feelings and behavior are not determined; we can have novel insights as well as "second thoughts."

> "Given the choices, rationales, and anticipated consequences, one decides what do on the basis of "what one is" (mentally speaking, to use [Galen] Strawson's term, which includes one's knowledge, goals, values, and beliefs)." [34]

Here Kosslyn considers a second stage of willed decisions that are determined by our goals, values, and beliefs -

> "What one is" consists in part of information in memory, which plays a key role in the processes that construct the alternatives, rationales, and anticipated consequences. In addition, "what one is" governs how one actually makes the decisions. And making that decision and experiencing the actual consequences in turn modifies "what one is," which then affects both how one constructs alternatives, rationales and anticipated consequences and how one makes decisions in the future. Thus, with time one's decisions construct what one is.

34 Kosslyn, in Libet (2005) p. xii-xii.

> "We are not simply accumulators of environmental events, filtered by our genetic make-ups. We bring something novel and unique to each situation — ourselves. Nietzsche (1886, as quoted in Strawson, 1994, p. 15) commented, "The causa sui is the best self-contradiction that has been conceived so far." Maybe not." [35]

John Searle (2007)

John Searle has written extensively on the problem of consciousness and almost always reflects on the problem of free will. His position rarely changed over the decades, but in his recent short book *Freedom and Neurobiology* he has tackled the problem more directly and for the first time embraced **indeterminism** as a positive factor. Indeed, he goes as far as to say that quantum indeterminism is a requirement for consciousness.

In a breakthrough of sorts, Searle admits that he could never see, until now, the point of introducing quantum mechanics into discussions of consciousness and free will. Now he says we know two things, which correspond to the two requirements for free will:

> First we know that our experiences of free action contain both indeterminism and rationality...Second we know that quantum indeterminacy is the only form of indeterminism that is indisputably established as a fact of nature...it follows that quantum mechanics must enter into the explanation of consciousness." [36]

Searle describes "open" alternative courses of action. It is very important to place the "gap" or *causa sui* before or during the generation of these alternative possibilities for deliberation to be followed by willed action. The result is a two-stage, temporal-sequence model.

Then in a 2007 lecture at Google (available on YouTube), Searle describes his "Hypothesis 2" for free will.

He says three things are necessary:

35 *ibid.*, p. xiii-xiv.
36 Searle (2007) p. 74-75

1. some quantum indeterminism must be involved, but at "a lower level,"

2. a quantum explanation of consciousness is needed,

3. the higher-level of consciousness must inherit the indeterminism, but without inheriting the randomness.

Compare Karl Popper above,

> "A choice process may be a selection process, and the selection may be from some repertoire of random events, *without being random in its turn*." [Popper's italics]

Martin Heisenberg (2009)

The most recent thinker to describe a two-stage model is Martin Heisenberg (son of physicist Werner), chair of the University of Würzburg's BioZentrum genetics and neurobiology section.

Since the indeterminacy principle was his father's work, Heisenberg's position that the physical universe is no longer determined and that nature is inherently unpredictable comes as no surprise. What is unusual is that Heisenberg finds evidence of free behavior in animals, including some very simple ones such as Drosophila, on which he is a world expert. Heisenberg argues for some randomness even in unicellular bacteria, followed by more lawful behaviors such as moving toward food.

> "Evidence of randomly generated action — action that is distinct from reaction because it does not depend upon external stimuli — can be found in unicellular organisms. Take the way the bacterium Escherichia coli moves. It has a flagellum that can rotate around its longitudinal axis in either direction: one way drives the bacterium forward, the other causes it to tumble at random so that it ends up facing in a new direction ready for the next phase of forward motion. This 'random walk' can be modulated by sensory receptors, enabling the bacterium to find food and the right temperature." [37]

37 Heisenberg (2009) p. 164

In higher organisms, the brain still may include elements that do a random walk creating options for action. The capability to generate new and unpredictable behaviors would have great survival value, and would likely be incorporated in higher organisms.

> "the activation of behavioural modules is based on the interplay between chance and lawfulness in the brain. Insufficiently equipped, insufficiently informed and short of time, animals have to find a module that is adaptive. Their brains, in a kind of random walk, continuously preactivate, discard and reconfigure their options, and evaluate their possible short-term and long-term consequences.
>
> "The physiology of how this happens has been little investigated. But there is plenty of evidence that an animal's behaviour cannot be reduced to responses. For example, my lab has demonstrated that fruit flies, in situations they have never encountered, can modify their expectations about the consequences of their actions. They can solve problems that no individual fly in the evolutionary history of the species has solved before. Our experiments show that they actively initiate behaviour." [38]

Heisenberg's combination of some randomness followed by some "lawful" behavior looks very much like WILLIAM JAMES' two-stage model, but now we have evidence for it in many animals. James would have been pleased.

In the next chapter, I will explain how my **Cogito** two-stage model solves some of the problems that have been raised about earlier two-stage models of free will.

I also show how the model can be extended to include **undetermined liberties** and the Self-Forming Actions of the libertarian ROBERT KANE.

38 Heisenberg (2009) p. 165.

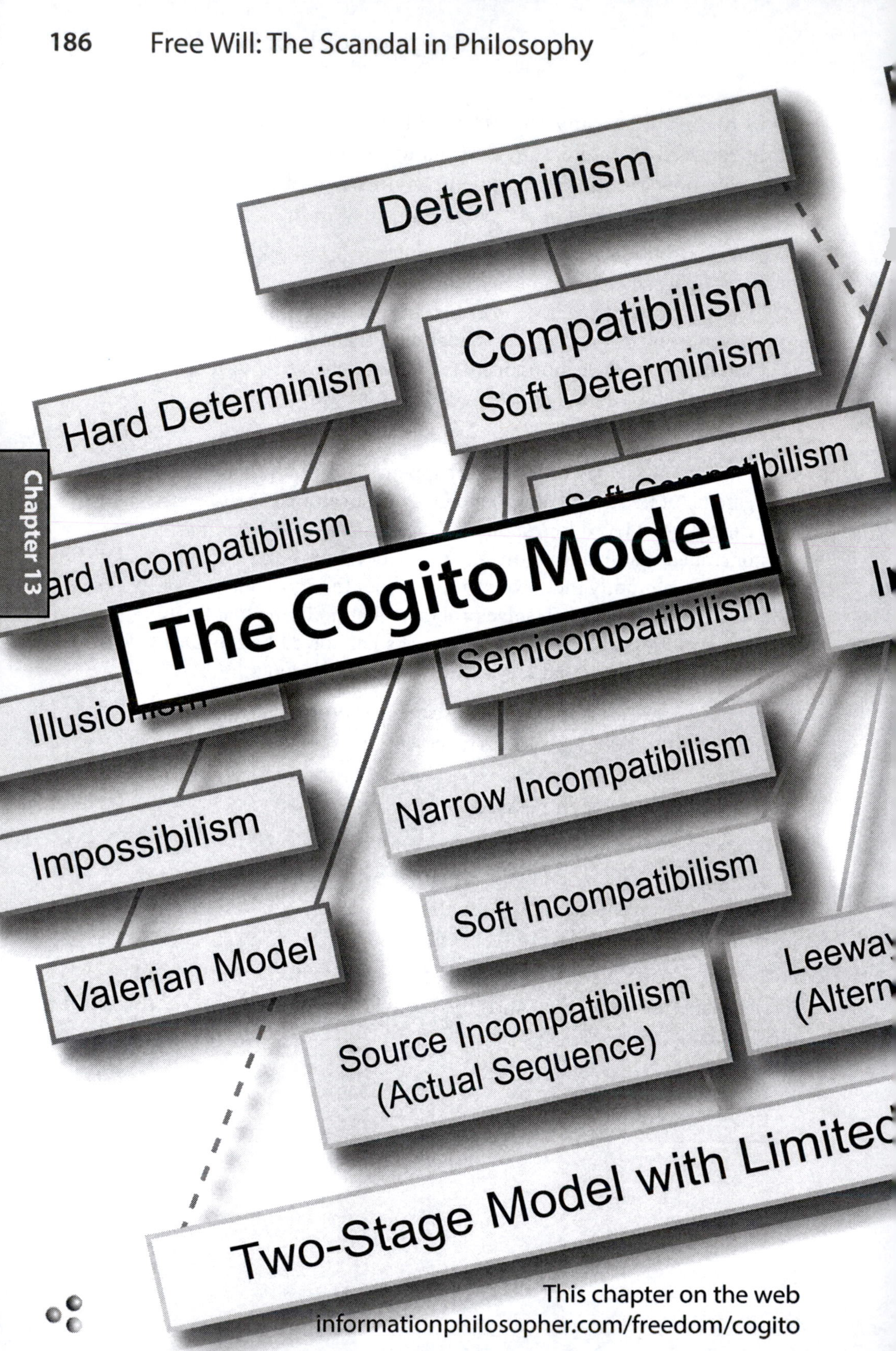

This chapter on the web
informationphilosopher.com/freedom/cogito

Indeterminism

The Cogito Model

The Cogito Model of human freedom locates randomness (either ancient **chance** or modern **quantum indeterminacy**) in the mind, in a way that breaks the causal chain of physical **determinism**, while doing no harm to **responsibility**.

The Cogito Model combines indeterminacy - first microscopic quantum randomness and unpredictability, then "adequate" determinism and macroscopic predictability, in a temporal sequence that creates new **information**.

Important elements of the model have been proposed by many philosophers since ARISTOTLE, the first indeterminist.

The insoluble problem for early attempts to incorporate indeterminism has been to explain how a random event in the brain can be timed and located - perfectly synchronized! - so as to be relevant to a specific decision. The answer is that it cannot be, for the simple reason that quantum events are totally unpredictable. Early attempts could not locate the randomness so as to make free will "intelligible," as libertarian ROBERT KANE puts it.

Two-stage models do not involve single random events, one per decision, but many random events in the brain that lead to **alternative possibilities** for the **adequately determined** will to evaluate and decide between.

As we saw in the last chapter, a number of modern philosophers and scientists, starting with WILLIAM JAMES, have proposed two-stage models of free will. So how is the Cogito model different? The Cogito model is the first to specify how it is that quantum indeterminacy creates the **alternative possibilities**.

I shall argue that **noise** generates new possibilities based on random variations of old experiences and knowledge.

The source of the randomness is the ever-present noise, both quantum and thermal noise, that is inherent in any information storage and communication system.

The mind, like all biological systems, has evolved in the presence of constant noise and is able to ignore that noise, unless the noise provides a significant competitive advantage, which it clearly can do as the basis for freedom and creativity.

Let's first see how randomness in the Cogito Model is never the direct cause of our decisions. Decisions themselves are normally **adequately determined**.

We assume that there are always many contributing causes for any event, and in particular for a mental decision. All the events in the past "light-cone" of special relativity can contribute causes.

In the ALLAN NEWELL - HERBERT SIMON "Blackboard" model and in BERNARD BAARS' "Theater of Consciousness" and "Global Workspace" models, there are many competing possibilities for our next thought or action.

Each of these possibilities is the result of a sequence of events that goes back in an assumed causal chain until its beginning in an uncaused event. ARISTOTLE called this original event an archē (ἀρχῆ), one whose major contributing cause (or causes) was itself uncaused. In modern terms, it involved quantum indeterminacy.

In Figure 13-1, we show many contributing causes as causal chains going back in time, in principle to the origin of the universe. None of them is completely controlling, but all make contributions to the decision process.

On the left, BERNARD BAARS' players in the Theater of Consciousness, or DANIEL DENNETT's functional homunculi, have causal chains that go back to Nature and Nurture – hereditary, environmental, and educational causes - and in principle beyond.

In the middle, the causes have chains that go back to ROBERT KANE's character development by Self-Forming Actions (SFAs).

On the right, my causes are brand new possibilities generated randomly *immediately after* being confronted by the circumstances from the "Fixed Past" and the "Laws of Nature." After evaluation of the alternatives, the new decision might be one of Kane's SFAs, contributing to our developing character.

Figure 13-1. Decisions have many contributing causes

Consider contributing causes of a decision on the left of the figure that go back before the birth of an agent, hereditary causes for example. To the extent that such causes **adequately determine** an action, we can understand why hard determinists think that the agent has no control over such actions.

But as long as we can opt out of those ancient causal chains at the last moment (RODERICK CHISHOLM points out that saying "no" is always an alternative possibility), and follow one of the new possibilities generated on the right, we retain enough control, and can properly take **responsibility** for our decisions.

Other contributing causes may be traceable back to environmental and developmental events, perhaps education, perhaps simply life experiences that were "character-forming" events. These and hereditary causes would be present in the mind of the agent as fixed habits, with a very high probability of "adequately determining" the agent's actions in many commonplace situations.

But other contributing causes of a specific action may have been undetermined up to the very near past, even fractions of a second before an important decision. The causal chains for these contributing causes originate in the noisy brain. They include the free generation of new **alternative possibilities** for thought or action during the agent's deliberations. They fit ARISTOTLE's criteria for causes that "depend on us" (ἐφ' ἡμῖν) and originate "within us" (ἐν ἡμῖν).

Causes with these most recent starting points are the fundamental reason why an agent can **do otherwise** in what are essentially (up to that starting point) the **same circumstances**. These alternatives are likely generated from our internal knowledge of practical possibilities based on our past experience.

Note that those possibilities that are handed up for consideration to Baars' "executive function" may be filtered to some extent by unconscious processes to be "within reason." They likely consist of random variations of past actions we have willed many times in the past.

Note that the evaluation and selection of one of these possibilities by the will is as deterministic and causal a process as anything that a determinist or compatibilist could ask for, consistent with our current knowledge of the physical world.

But instead of strict causal determinism, evaluation and selection involve only **adequate determinism**, and the indeterministic origins of alternative possibilities provides libertarian freedom of thought and action.

The Micro Mind

Imagine a Micro Mind with a randomly assembled "agenda" of possible things to say or to do. These are drawn from our memory of past thoughts and actions, but randomly varied by unpredictable negations, associations of a part of one idea with a part or all of another, and by substitutions of words, images, feelings, and actions drawn from our experience. In information communication terms, there is cross-talk and noise in our neural circuitry.

In a "content-addressable" information model, memories are stored based on their content - typically bundles of simultaneous images, sounds, smells, feelings, etc. So a new experience is likely to be stored in neural pathways alongside closely related past experiences. And a fresh experience, or active thinking about an experience that presents a decision problem, is likely to activate nearby brain circuits, ones that have strong associations with our current circumstances. These are likely to begin firing randomly, to provide unpredictable raw material for actionable possibilities.

The strong feeling that sometimes "we don't know what we think until we hear what we say" reflects our capability for original and creative thoughts, different from anything we have consciously learned. Something as simple as substituting a synonymous word, or more complex replacements with associated words (metonyms) or wild leaps of fancy (metaphor) are examples of building unpredictable thoughts. Picturing ourselves doing something we have seen others do, from "monkey see, monkey do" childhood mimicry to adult imitations, is a source for action items on the agenda, with the random element as simple as if and when we choose to do them.

The etymology of cogito is Latin co-agitare, to shake together. Why do we need quantum uncertainty involved in the shaking together of our agenda items? Will neuroscientists ever find information structures in the brain to generate our random agenda, structures small enough to be susceptible to microscopic quantum phenomena?

Speculations include the microtubules of the cellular cytoskeleton, tiny (25nm) structures that Roger Penrose and Stuart Hameroff believe may mediate consciousness. But will neuroscientists be able to distinguish random from non-random processes?

It is most unlikely that physically localized visually distinguishable random processes will be found. In the Cogito model, the randomness of the Micro Mind is simply the result of ever-present noise, both thermal and quantum noise, that is inherent in any information storage and communication system.

Constant, ever-present noise removes an important technical objection. Critics of the Epicurean swerve of the atoms asked when and where and how would a random event occur? The Cogito model randomly generates contextually appropriate alternative possibilities at all times.

The Cogito model is not a mechanism. It is a process, and information philosophy is a process philosophy.

Quantum uncertainty adds a "causa sui," an uncaused or self-caused cause, in the causal chain. But it need not directly determine the decision of the macroscopic will or the fully determined resulting action which is consistent with character and values.

Some argue that brain structures are too large to be affected at all by quantum events. But there is little doubt that the brain has evolved to the point where it can access quantum phenomena. The evolutionary advantage for the mind is freedom and creativity. Biophysics tells us that the eye can detect a single quantum of light (photon), and the nose can smell a single molecule.

The Macro Mind

If the Micro Mind is a random generator of frequently outlandish and absurd possibilities, the complementary Macro Mind is a macroscopic structure so large that quantum effects are negligible. It is the critical apparatus that makes decisions based on our character and values.

Information about our character and values is stored in the same noise-susceptible neural circuits of our brain, in our memory. So Macro Mind and Micro Mind are not necessarily in different locations in the brain. Instead, they are the consequence of different information processing methods.

The Macro Mind must suppress quantum noise when it makes an adequately determined decision.

The Macro Mind has very likely evolved to add enough redundancy, perhaps even the kind of error detection and correction we have in computers, to reduce the noise to levels required for an adequate determinism.

Our decisions are then in principle predictable, by a super-psychiatrist who was given knowledge of all our past experiences and given the randomly generated possibilities in the instant before a decision. However, only we know the contents of our minds. They exist only within our minds. Thus we can feel fully responsible for our choices, morally and legally.

The Cogito model accounts not just for freedom but for creativity, for original thoughts and ideas never before expressed. Unique and new information comes into the world with each new thought and action.

Biologists will note that the Micro Mind corresponds to random variation in the gene pool (often the direct result of quantum accidents). The Macro Mind corresponds to natural selection by highly determined organisms. See the biology discussion in Chapter 16 for other examples of random generation followed by adequately determined selection, like the immune system and protein/enzyme factories.

Psychologists will see the resemblance of Micro Mind and Macro Mind to the Freudian id and the super-ego (*das Ess und das Über-ich*).

The model accounts quantitatively for the concept of wisdom. The greater the amount of knowledge and experience, the more likely that the random agenda will contain more useful and "intelligent" thoughts and actions as alternative possibilities.

It also implies **degrees of freedom**. An educated mind is "more free" because it can generate a wider agenda and options for action. It suggests that "narrow" and "closed" minds may simply be lacking the capabilities of the Micro Mind. And if the Macro Mind were weak, it might point to the high correlation between creativity and madness suggested by a Micro Mind out of control.

Philosophers of Mind, whether hard determinist or compatibilist, should recognize this Macro Mind as everything they say is needed to make a carefully reasoned free choice.

But now choices include self-generated random possibilities for thought and action that no external agent can predict. Thus the choice of the will and the resulting willed action are unpredictable. The origin of the chosen causal chain is entirely within the agent, a condition noted first by ARISTOTLE for voluntary action, his ἐν ἡμῖν ("in us").

The combination of microscopic randomness and macroscopic determinism in our **Cogito** model for human freedom means it is both unpredictable and yet fully responsible for its willed actions. Chance in the first stage never leads directly to - never directly "causes" - an action.

Chance in the first stage provides the variety of **alternative possibilities**, each the possible start of a new causal chain, from which the deterministic judgment can choose an alternative that is consistent with its character and values. Our will is **adequately determined** and in control of our actions.

Note that the second stage may sometimes result in a willed decision to "flip a coin" and choose at random from the given alternatives. This is the ancient "**liberty of indifference**."

While it is chance that "determines" our action in this case, we are prepared to take responsibility, because we are choosing between alternatives that have all been adequately determined by good reasons. I call these "**undetermined liberties**." ROBERT KANE's Self-Forming Actions are a subset of undetermined liberties.

On the opposite page, I distinguish six increasingly sophisticated aspects on the role of chance and **indeterminism** in any **libertarian** model of free will.

Many libertarians have accepted the first two. Determinist and compatibilist critics of free will make the third their central attack on chance. It is the **randomness objection**.

But very few thinkers appear to have considered the last three essential requirements for chance to contribute to any model of **libertarian** free will, and especially the last two - that chance must be ever present, throughout the brain - but that it is always suppressible *at will*.

Six Critical Aspects of Chance

1. Chance exists in the universe. Quantum mechanics is correct. **Indeterminism** is true.

2. Chance is important for free will. It breaks the causal chain of **determinism**.

3. Chance cannot directly cause our actions. We cannot be responsible for random actions, unless we "deliberately" choose at random an **undetermined liberty**.

4. Chance can only generate random (unpredictable) **alternative possibilities** for action or thought. The choice or selection of one action must be **adequately determined**, so that we can take **responsibility**. And once we choose, the connection between mind/brain and motor control must be adequately determined to see that "our will be done."

5. Chance, in the form of **noise**, both quantum and thermal, must be ever present. The naive model of a single random microscopic event, amplified to affect the macroscopic brain, never made any sense. Under what *ad hoc* circumstances, at what time, at what place in the brain, would it occur to affect a decision?

6. Chance must be overcome or suppressed by the adequately determined will when it decides to act, de-liberating the prior free options that "one **could otherwise have done**."

In our Cogito model, "Free Will" combines two distinct concepts. "Free" is the chance and randomness of the Micro Mind. "Will" is the adequately determined choice of the Macro Mind. And these occur in a **temporal sequence**.

> Compatibilists and Determinists were right about Will,
> but wrong about Freedom.
> Libertarians were right about Freedom,
> but wrong about Will.

The Temporal Sequence of Free and Will

Free Will is best understood as a complex idea combining two antagonistic concepts - freedom and determination.

Many philosophers have called free will "unintelligible" because of this internal contradiction and the presumed simultaneity and identity of free and will.

Specifically, they mistakenly have assumed that "free" is a time-independent adjective modifying "will." And they have often taken "free" pejoratively to mean "random."

A careful examination of ordinary language usage shows that free will is actually a temporal sequence of two opposing concepts - first "free" and then "will."

First comes the consideration of alternative possibilities, which are generated unpredictably by acausal events (simply noise in neural network communications). This free creation of possible thoughts and actions allows one to feel "I can do otherwise."

Next comes de-liberation and determination by the will, the un-freeing of possibilities into actuality, the decision that directs the tongue or body to speak or act.

After the deliberation of the will, the true sentence "I can do otherwise" can be changed to the past tense and remain true as a "hard fact" in the "fixed past," and written "I could have done otherwise."

Thus we have the **temporal sequence** which William James saw so clearly over a century ago, with chance in a present time of random alternatives, leading to a choice which grants consent to one possibility and transforms an equivocal future into an unalterable and simple past.

Since the chance suggestions for alternative possibilities appear first in the theater of consciousness (though they are largely unconscious and competing for attention), the delay before a conscious choice could easily account for the results of Benjamin Libet's experiments. See the explanation of Libet's experiments as a predictable consequence of the two-stage model in Chapter 17 on neuroscience.

As John Locke knew more than three hundred years ago, "free" is an adjective that describes not the will, but the human mind.

Just as "free" needs to be separated from "will," we think "moral" should be separated from "responsibility." Furthermore "free will" should be separated from "moral responsibility" and "moral responsibility" should be separated from "retributive punishment" and vengeance. See Chapter 20 for more on the notion of separating these core concepts in the free will debates.

A Mind Model

Given the "laws of nature" and the "fixed past" just before a decision, philosophers wonder how a free agent can have any possible alternatives. This is partly because they imagine a timeline for the decision that shrinks the decision process to a single moment.

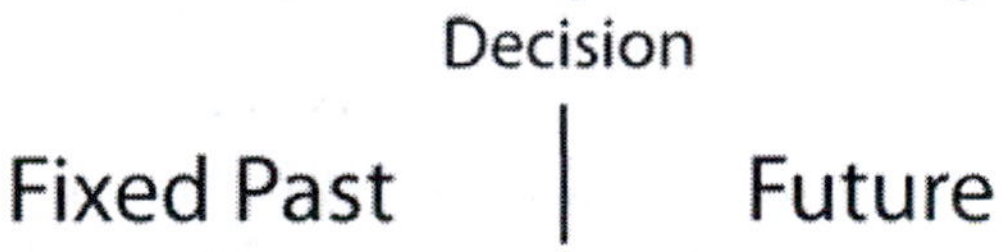

Decision

Fixed Past | Future

Figure 13-2. Decision as a single moment in time.

Collapsing the decision to a single moment between the closed fixed past and the open ambiguous future makes it difficult to see how free thoughts of the mind are followed by the willed and adequately determined action of the body in a **temporal sequence**, as shown in Figure 13-3.

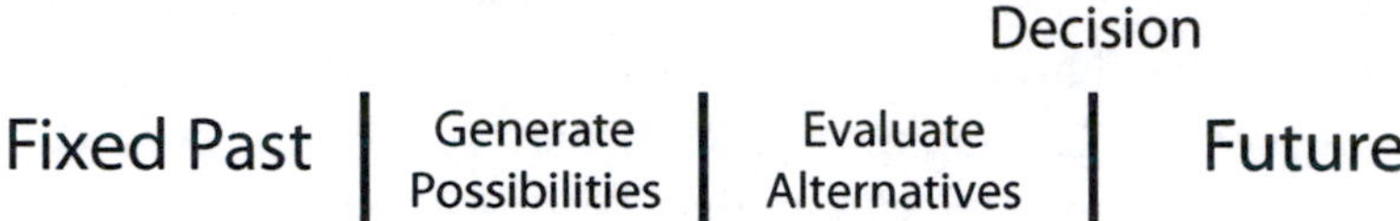

Figure 13-3. Decision as a two-stage temporal process

But the Cogito Mind Model is not limited to a single step of generating **alternative possibilities** followed by a single step of determination by the will. It is better understood as a continuous process of possibilities generation by the **Micro Mind** (parts of the brain that leave themselves open to noise) and **adequately determined** choices made from time to time by the Macro Mind (the same brain parts, perhaps, but now averaging over and filtering out the noise that might otherwise make the determination random).

Second Thoughts

In particular, note that a special kind of decision might occur when the Macro Mind finds that none of the current options are good enough for the agent's character and values to approve. The Macro Mind then might figuratively say to the Micro Mind, "Think again!"

Figure 13-4. Decisions are not determined as soon as alternatives are generated.

Critics of two-stage models often say that once the alternative possibilities are generated, the agent is "determined" to choose the best alternative, and thus they are not truly free.

First, we can see in Figure 13-4 that the agent is free to go back, time permitting, and generate more possibilities, until a really good alternative appears.

Second, because some of the alternatives generated may be truly new information that presented itself at random, there is no way that the agent's action was **pre-determined** by the laws of nature and the fixed past before the generation of **alternative possibilities** began. This is the core freedom of the Cogito model, even when the decision is adequately determined.

Doing Otherwise in the Same Circumstances

Many philosophers of mind and action have puzzled how an agent could do otherwise in exactly the **same circumstances**. Of course, since humans are intelligent organisms with memories, and given the myriad of possible circumstances, it is simply impossible that an agent is ever in exactly the same circumstances. The agent's memory (stored information) of earlier similar circumstances guarantees that.

So how can an agent do otherwise in exactly the **same circumstances**? First, we need to postulate that the agent can be in the very same circumstances. There are two ways we can do this.

One way is to imagine that the universe can be put back into the same circumstances, as William James first suggested,[1] and as Peter van Inwagen imagined God could do with his "instant replays." [2]

The second way is to relax the exactness required to merely very similar circumstances. It is enough that the agent simply believes the circumstances are the same, perhaps because they resemble a situation seen so many times before that the memory of earlier occasions is blurred.

The **Cogito** model can then explain how an agent can do otherwise in the same circumstances, given the "fixed past" and the "laws of nature," where the circumstances are defined as the moment before alternative possibilities begin to be generated. See figure 13-5 for the line that defines the moment of the starting circumstances that invoke possibilities generation. In our horizontal timeline view, we then have the following situation.

1 James (1956) p. 155.
2 Van Inwagen (2004) p. 227.

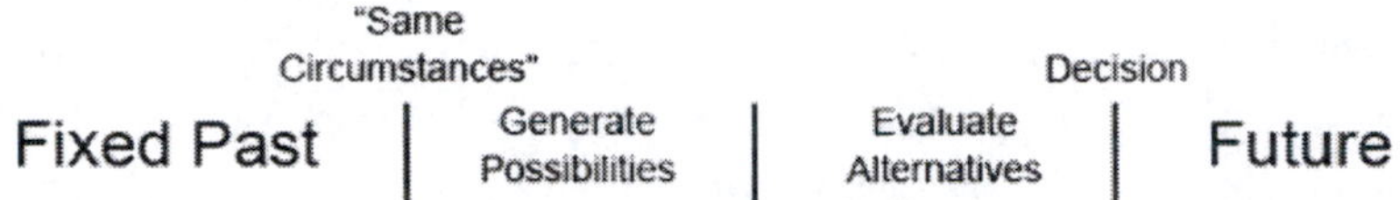

Figure 13-5. Doing otherwise in the same circumstances.

This view still makes an artificial separation between Micro Mind creative randomness and Macro Mind deliberative evaluation. These two capabilities of the mind can be going on at the same time. That can be visualized by the occasional decision to go back and think again, when the available alternatives are not good enough to satisfy the demands of the agent's character and values, or by noticing that the Micro Mind may still be generating possibilities while the Macro Mind is in the midst of evaluations.

Finally, not all decisions in the Cogito model end with an adequately determined **de-liberation** or **self-determination**. Many times the evaluation of the possibilities produces two or more alternatives that seem more or less of equal value.

Undetermined Liberties

In these cases, the agent may choose randomly among the alternatives, and yet have good reasons to take responsibility for whichever one is chosen. This is the **liberty of indifference**.

I call these **undetermined liberties**, because they remain undetermined until the moment of the decision. The choice is not completely determined by the deliberations, although we can still say that the agent "deliberately" chooses at random.

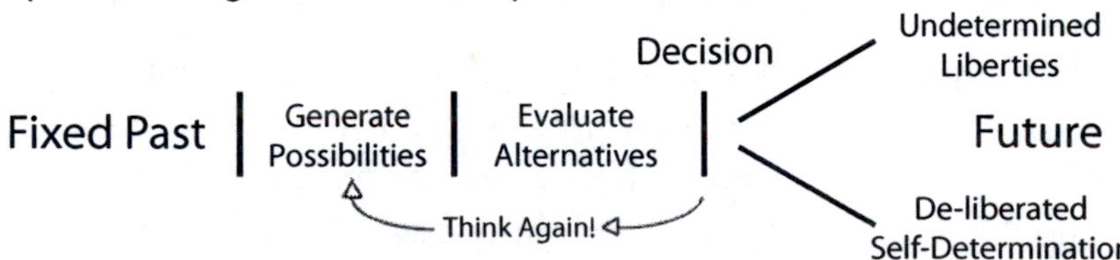

Figure 13-6. Undetermined Liberties and Self-Determination

The choice between undetermined liberties results in a kind of *arbitrary* self-determination that resembles the ancient *liberum arbitrium* notion of free will.

Free Thoughts, Willed Actions

Our thoughts are free and often appear simply to "come to us." Our actions are adequately determined for **moral responsibility** and appear, especially to others, to "come from us." They are "**up to us**" (Aristotle's ἐφ' ἡμῖν), our **self-determination**.

What then are the sources of alternative possibilities? To what extent are they our creations? We can distinguish three important sources, all of them capable of producing indeterministic options for thoughts and actions.

The first source is the external world that arrives through our perceptions. It is perhaps the major driving force in our lives, constantly requiring our conscious attention. Indeed, consciousness can be understood in large part as the exchange of actionable information between organism and environment. Although the indeterministic origin of such ideas is outside us, we can take full responsibility for them if they inspire our adequately determined willed actions.

The second source of options is other persons. The unique human ability to communicate information verbally means that alternative possibilities for our actions are being generated by our conversations, by reactions to the random thoughts of other minds. Peter Strawson's reactive attitudes come to mind.

Finally, and most importantly, our Micro Mind generates possibilities internally. These are the possibilities that truly originate within us (Aristotle's ἐν ἡμῖν).

Note that the sources of random options not only need not be internal, even internal random thoughts need not be contemporaneous with the current decision, as long as they "come to mind" as alternatives. They may have been originally generated at much earlier times in the agent's life, and only now get reconsidered and perhaps now get acted upon.

The Cogito Model Compared to Other Models

The **Cogito** Model can be seen as providing a purely physical explanation for **agent-causal libertarianism**.

"Agent-causal or "non-causal" views are thought to involve a form of "substance dualism" that makes the mind a different substance from the body, exempt from ordinary causality.

There is a sense in which the **Cogito** model shares aspects with the metaphysical idea of an immaterial substance dualism.

In so far as pure **information** is non-material, neither matter nor energy, more akin to spirit, genuinely new information entering the universe through the mind is a kind of "agent causality."

But the Cogito Model is primarily an "event-causal" view that locates breaks in the deterministic causal chain "in us," in our deliberations. These include the internal uncaused generation of new possibilities.

Indeterminism also arises from random sensory inputs from the environment and from communication with other persons.

And the Cogito Model now includes indeterminism in the final moment of choice, for those cases where the second stage has not narrowed down options to a single self-determined choice.

The Cogito Model is very similar to the two-stage models of Daniel Dennett and Alfred Mele. But unlike Dennett, the model needs quantum randomness and not simply computational "pseudo-randomness" to generate **alternative possibilities**. And unlike Mele, I believe that science has shown indeterminism to be the case and determinism to be "false." Mele remains an agnostic on these important questions, given the modern focus on **moral responsibility**.

Even if determinism were true, Mele says, we could nevertheless have moral responsibility. I agree that since we do have it, then if determinism were true, we would still have it.

Again, beyond the Dennett and Mele models, the Cogito Model proposes a specific process that avoids the single "quantum event in the brain" that gets amplified perfectly in time with our thought processes to help with free will. There are billions of quantum events in the brain every second. The miracle of the mind is that it can manage the resulting noise, averaging over these events when it needs to, yet utilizing them when it wants to.

Because the agent is actively controlling the process of deliberation up to the instant of the determining decision at the 'moment of choice,' the Cogito Model shares much with agent-causal views, without being metaphysical.

The "free" stage of the Cogito Model depends on thermal and quantal noise in the neural circuitry of the brain. This noise introduces errors in the storage and retrieval of information, noise that may be helpful in generating **alternative possibilities** for action.

The "will" stage of the Cogito Model suppresses this noise for the **adequately determined** process of evaluation and decision that normally terminates in an act of **self-determination**.

But there are times when more than one option remains at the end of the second stage. These **undetermined liberties** are then resolved in the moment of choice in an undetermined fashion, where the cause of the choice is attributed to the efforts of the agent, as described by Robert Kane in his "self-forming actions."

The Cogito Model is compatible with *both* indeterminism suitably located *and* determinism appropriately limited.

It is thus "doubly compatible" with a limited indeterminism and a limited but "adequate" determinism. This suggests what we call a "**comprehensive compatibilism**," one that might appeal to the many philosophers who prefer **compatibilism** to **libertarianism**.

The Cogito Model is also the only free-will model that is compatible with biological evolution. Chapter 16 will show how it evolved from "behavioral freedom" in lower animals.

This triply-compatible "**comprehensive compatibilism**" is developed in Chapter 28.

Next we turn to several objections that have been raised over the years against two-stage models.

Chapter 14

Objections to Two-Stage Models

Determinism

Hard Determinism

Compatibilism
Soft Determinism

Soft Compatibilism

ard Incompatibilism

Illusion

Impossibilism

Narrow Incompatibilism

Soft Incompatibilism

Valerian Model

Source Incompatibilism
(Actual Sequence)

Leewa
(Alter

Two-Stage Model with Limite

This chapter on the web
informationphilosopher.com/freedom/cogito/#objections

Objections to Two-Stage Models

The earliest objections were the concerns of some of the inventors of two-stage models themselves. Mostly they could not see how to reconcile the randomness of indeterminism with the determinism required for responsibility. They also tended to be metaphysical dualists, so they did not have a purely physical model for free will.

ARTHUR HOLLY COMPTON adhered to a view that human freedom might only be visible from the inside (subjectively), that from the outside a person would be seen (objectively) as deterministic. This was a variation on Bohr's dualist complementarity principle, which was popular among physicists at the time.

KARL POPPER, in his collaborations with the neurobiologist JOHN ECCLES, wanted the will to involve a metaphysical interaction between the mind (or soul) and the body. This was another form of dualism. Later (1977), Popper endorsed the idea of a two-stage model with quantum indeterminacy in the first stage, followed by a lawful determined selection process similar to Darwinian evolution.

HENRY MARGENAU wrestled with his mentor ERNST CASSIRER's views on determinism and indeterminism in physics. Cassirer also had strong Kantian dualism tendencies, but in the end he insisted that only determinism could provide the causality needed as a basis for science. Margenau nevertheless, and somewhat reluctantly, accepted indeterminism as the "first step" in an explanation of human freedom and possibly providing insight into ethical problems.

The Strongest Motive Objection

However many alternative possibilities are generated in the first stage of the model, some philosophers have argued that the agent has no really free choice, since he must always select the best option, the one with the strongest reasons or motives.

The ancients argued that to do anything other than the strongest option was evidence of **weakness of will (akrasia)**. This is a form of **ethical restrictivism**, the idea that only moral choices can be considered free choices.

Apart from the obvious ability of the agent to be contrary and act in a surprising, even irrational way occasionally, we must say the agents can choose to be irresponsible, or even act deliberately against community values. As the 19th-century philosopher SHADSWORTH HODGSON said,

> "A power to choose only the good is a contradiction in terms; and were such a power (*per impossibile*) to be attained, it would be at once the highest perfection of the character, and the *euthanasia* of Free-will." [1]

Daniel Dennett's Objections

In 1978, DANIEL DENNETT proposed a two-stage model that would "give the libertarians what they want." But he had serious reservations about his "Valerian" model, most important that he could find no place in it for quantum indeterminism.

Dennett's model for decision making started with elements from HENRI POINCARÉ random combinations model (via JACQUES HADAMARD and the poet Paul Valéry, at the 1936 Synthése conference in Paris exploring creativity). Dennett mentioned the amplification of a quantum event in the brain, which was first suggested by ARTHUR HOLLY COMPTON in 1931. Dennett had also read KARL POPPER, who had criticized Compton's "massive switch amplifier." He knew Popper's analogy of free will with natural selection as a two-stage process. Dennett's decision-making model was a variation of computer scientist HERBERT SIMON's "generate and test" two-stage model for computer problem solving. Dennett made an excellent case for his model as something that libertarians should want. Sadly, no libertarian saw the power in Dennett's two-stage model. [2]

Because Dennett saw clearly what was good about the model for Libertarians, he also could see what they might not accept.

---

1 Hodgson (1891) p. 180.

2 See Chapter 27 for what might have been if Kane accepted Dennett's model

Dennett knew that some libertarians insisted on indeterministic quantum events in the brain, but he could not understand the place for a quantum event, how exactly and when and where a quantum event in the brain could be amplified to help with decision making and not harm our control and responsibility for our actions.

As a determinist, Dennett said that a model with pseudo-random number generation in the first stage would be all that is needed. He found no value in adding true quantum randomness. I discuss my exchanges with Dennett in Chapter 25.

Robert Kane's Objections

Robert Kane independently developed the two-stage model before Dennett published *Brainstorms*. He had read the same sources (Compton and Popper), but he thought that "something more" was needed.

Basically, Kane felt that at the completion of the first stage in the model, when all the random considerations have been generated, there is a finite time, however small, during which the model assumes that the willed decision, the choice between alternative possibilities, is determined.

This is the most common objection to the two-stage model. But as we saw in Figure 13-6, the choice is not **pre-determined** from the time before deliberations began moments earlier. When viewed as an overall process, the self-determination of the two-stage model allows the agent to make a choice that is free from any deterministic chain of causation presumed to go back to the beginning of time.

Kane agrees that the decisions made in the two-stage model are not **pre-determined**. But his Self-Forming Actions require that the decision also not be determined by the agent's desires and beliefs, motives and feelings. These are just among the many causes that contribute to a decision. Kane says we should regard the agent's motives and desires as causes, but not determining causes, of the final decision.

And Kane has always wanted some decisions to remain undetermined up to and including the moment of choice. These must only be *determined by the choice*, Kane has said, and this is the case for his Self-forming Actions (SFAs), as we shall see.

Kane notes, as do Mele, Clarke, and other objectors, that the agent does not have complete control over the random considerations that get generated. Of course, complete control over randomness is an impossibility, but the agent can decide to stop generating new possibilities. Moreover, at any point that evaluation finds none satisfactory, the agent can go back and generate more.

But, says Kane, after the last new random option is generated, and during that time, however small, before the decision is made, Kane is concerned that the choice not be already determined by the agent's character, reasons, motives, and deliberations. When it is "adequately" determined, I say we should regard this as an act of de-liberated **self-determination**.

In my **Cogito** model, the decision could be reliably (though not perfectly) predicted by a super-psychiatrist who knew everything about the agent and was aware of all the **alternative possibilities** that were generated at any moment. This is because the second ("will") stage evaluation and decision process is indeed **adequately determined** by the deliberations and evaluations.

I agree with Kane that the second stage is determined, in this limited sense, but emphasize that it is in no way **pre-determined**.

And Kane agrees that, before the first stage of my two stage model, the decision is not determined. He agrees that it is at that time undetermined.

Kane says that he now endorses the two-stage model for practical deliberations, but still feels that "something more" is needed for prudential and moral decisions. Furthermore, he finds now that the two-stage model describes the deliberative processes that lead to the two or more conflicting choices that are involved in his Self-Forming Actions.

It is those cases where the two-stage model does not lead to self-determination narrowed down to a single choice that puts the agent in those situations that Kane describes as "torn" decisions.

Kane finds that in these cases, the agent's decision may not be determined by anything other than the agent's final choice, which can be rational (made for properly evaluated reasons), but nevertheless might (indeterministically) have been otherwise and yet be equally rational and voluntary.

He originally called this "dual (or plural) rational control." Today he calls it plural voluntary control.

I think that Kane's idea is an acceptable extension of my **Cogito** model, in that is does provide additional **libertarian** freedom. Let's see how it works.

Not all the second-stage decisions are **adequately determined**. Many times we do not have enough **information** to decide between the available options. To contrast them with self-determinations, I describe these cases as **undetermined liberties**. It is a subset of these undetermined liberties that Kane describes as his Self-Forming Actions.

In moral and prudential "torn" decisions, it is the agent's efforts that are the primary cause of the final choice of a Self-Forming Action. Indeterminism plays a secondary role in tipping the choice away from the options that fail, but the main cause of the option that succeeds is the efforts of the agent.

Kane thus deftly sidesteps the charge of critics who claim that an agent cannot be responsible for any decision involving indeterminism. In Kane's model, the agent can properly claim ultimate responsibility (UR), for good reasons, however the "torn" decision is made.

Richard Double's Objections to Kane's "Dual (or plural) rational control."

Kane's position has not been without its critics. Richard Double is one such critic. He finds many of Kane's views attractive, but has nonetheless developed objections that are mostly directed at Kane's efforts to establish **moral responsibility** for decisions that are **indeterministic**. Double develops challenges to three of Kane's requirements: the ability to have chosen otherwise, agent control, and rationality.

Double noted that Dennett's Valerian models introduce indeterminism in the early stages of deliberation, before the decision itself. He therefore calls Kane's views "Non-Valerian." These allow indeterminism in the decision process itself, which means that chance might be regarded as the direct cause of actions. Double argues (and this is the standard **randomness objection**) that Kane's approach jeopardizes agent control.

Double also develops his own theory, which he calls "Delay Libertarianism." The main idea is to recognize that free will is a process that takes place over a period of time, which is correct, of course. This gives Double the opportunity to locate the indeterminism in a delay between deliberations and resultant decisions.

Double notes that the deliberations "set the stage" for whatever decision will be made - if any decision is made. But he does not obviously show how delayed indeterminism can resolve the randomness objection.

Double recognizes that the act of the will might be simply to avoid a decision, and send the problem back for more deliberations, which could involve generating more alternative possibilities, as in our Cogito Model.

But in the end, says Double, delay libertarianism also fails, for the same reason - Kane's dual rational control condition.

Dual rational control is Kane's claim that the agent can do otherwise (indeterministically) with the alternative (dual) action just as rational and demonstrating just as much control as the original action. Double rejects this view, and winds up rejecting all libertarianism in his book *The Non-Reality of Free Will.*[3]

Alfred Mele's Doubts about His Own "Modest Libertarianism."

Mele's "Modest Libertarianism" is essentially the same as Dennett's "Valerian" model. But it has been attacked, by Mele.

> "Now, even if garden-variety compatibilists can be led to see that the problem of luck is surmountable by a libertarian, how

3 Double (1991)

> are theorists of other kinds likely to respond to the libertarian position that I have been sketching? There are, of course, philosophers who contend that moral responsibility and freedom are illusions and that we lack these properties whether our universe is deterministic or indeterministic — for example, Richard Double and Galen Strawson.
>
> "Modest libertarians can also anticipate trouble from traditional libertarians, who want more than the modest indeterminism that I have described can offer. Clarke, who has done as much as anyone to develop an agent-causal libertarian view, criticizes event-causal libertarianism on the grounds that it adds no "positive" power of control to compatibilist control but simply places compatibilist control in an indeterministic setting. Of course, given that combining compatibilist control with indeterminism in a certain psychological sphere was my explicit strategy in constructing a modest libertarian position, I do not see this as an objection. In any case, traditional libertarians need to show that what they want is coherent." [4]

Mele is probably right that his model will not satisfy Libertarians wanting more, whether "agent-causal" libertarians like Timothy O'Connor or "event-causal" libertarians like Robert Kane who wants indeterminism in the decisions.

Randolph Clarke's Objections to Dennett, Mele, Ekstrom, and Kane.

In his book *Libertarian Accounts of Free Will,* Clarke defines new technical terms for Double's "Valerian" and "Non-Valerian."

He calls Dennett's model "deliberative," since randomness internal to the mind is limited to the deliberations. And he calls Kane's model "centered," by which he means that Kane's (quantum) randomness is in the center of the decision itself.

Clarke accepts the Kane and Ekstrom views that if the agent's decision simply results from indeterministic events in the

4 Mele (2005) p. 9

deliberation phase that that could not be what he calls "directly free." Clarke thus calls this deliberative freedom "indirect."

"Indirectly free" is a reasonable description for our Cogito model, which limits indeterminism to the "free" deliberation stage and has a limited but "adequate" determinism in the "will" stage.

Although Clarke says that a "centered event-causal libertarian view provides a conceptually adequate account of free will," he doubts that it can provide for moral responsibility. He says that

> "An event-causal libertarian view secures ultimate control, which no compatibilist account provides. But the secured ultimacy is wholly negative: it is just (on a centered view) a matter of the absence of any determining cause of a directly free action. The active control that is exercised on such a view is just the same as that exercised on an event-causal compatibilist account." [5]

It is a bit puzzling to see how the active control of a libertarian decision based on quantum randomness is "just the same as that exercised" on a compatibilist account, unless it means, as Double argued, no control at all. So it may be worth quoting Clarke at some length.

> "Dennett requires only that the coming to mind of certain beliefs be undetermined; Mele maintains that (in combination with the satisfaction of compatibilist requirements) this would suffice, as would the undetermined coming to mind of certain desires.
>
> "[A] regress would result if Dennett or Mele required that the undetermined comings-to-mind, attendings, or makings of judgments that figure in their accounts had to either be or result from free actions.
>
> "Thus, given the basic features of these views, [they] must allow that an action can be free even if it is causally determined and none of its causes, direct or indirect, is a free action by that agent. Setting aside the authors currently under discussion, it appears that all libertarians disallow such a thing. What might be the basis for this virtual unanimity?

5 Clarke (2003) p. 220.

> "When an agent acts with direct freedom — freedom that is not derived from the freedom of any earlier action— she is able to do other than what she, in fact, does. Incompatibilists (libertarians included) maintain that, if events prior to one's birth (indirectly) causally determine all of one's actions, then one is never able to do other than perform the actions that one actually performs, for one is never able to prevent either those earlier events or the obtaining of the laws of nature." [6]

Clarke claims, as does Kane, that prior events thought up freely by the agent during deliberations will "determine" the agent's decision. This is roughly what the Cogito Model claims. After indeterminism in the "free" deliberation stage, we need "adequate" determinism in the "will" stage to insure that our actions are consistent with our character and values (including Kane's SFAs, which are a subset of our undetermined liberties), with our habits and (Ekstrom's) preferences, and with our current feelings and desires.

Clarke oddly attempts to equate events prior to our births with events that we indeterministically invent during our deliberations, claiming that they are equally deterministic.

Clarke thus says that a "deliberative" two-stage model, like my Cogito model, does not provide his "direct freedom."

> "If this is correct, then a time-indexed version of the same claim is correct, too. If events that have occurred by time *t* causally determine some subsequent action, then the agent is not able at *t* to do other than perform that action, for one is not able at *t* to prevent either events that have occurred by *t* or the obtaining of the laws of nature. An incompatibilist will judge, then, that, on Dennett's and Mele's views, it is allowed that once the agent has made an evaluative judgment, she is not able to do other than make the decision that she will, in fact, make...
>
> "If direct freedom requires that, until an action is performed, the agent be able to do otherwise, then these views do not secure the direct freedom of such decisions." [7]

The inadequacy that Clarke sees is that in the moment of choice things are becoming determined.

---

6 Clarke (2003) p. 62.

7 *ibid*. p. 63.

> "in acting freely, agents make a difference, by exercises of active control, to how things go. The difference is made, on this common conception, in the performance of a directly free action itself, not in the occurrence of some event prior to the action, even if that prior event is an agent-involving occurrence causation of the action by which importantly connects the agent, as a person, to her action. On a libertarian understanding of this difference-making, some things that happen had a chance of not happening, and some things that do not happen had a chance of happening, and in performing directly free actions, agents make the difference. If an agent is, in the very performance of a free action, to make a difference in this libertarian way, then that action itself must not be causally determined by its immediate antecedents. In order to secure this libertarian variety of difference-making, an account must locate openness and freedom-level active control in the same event — the free action itself — rather separate these two as do deliberative libertarian views.
>
> "On the views of Dennett, Ekstrom, and Mele, agents might be said to make a difference between what happens but might not have and what does not happen but might have, but such a difference is made in the occurrence of something nonactive or unfree prior to the action that is said to be free, not in the performance of the allegedly free action itself. Failure to secure for directly free actions this libertarian variety of difference-making constitutes a fundamental inadequacy of deliberative libertarian accounts of free action. [8]

Clarke is simply wrong in making the instant of the decision that he calls "t" one that still requires indeterminism, unless the agent must choose among multiple remaining options. These are my "**undetermined liberties**," a superset of Kane's SFAs, when the two-stage model has not narrowed options to one .

To see that the **Cogito** model allows the agent to make a real difference, we need only extend Clarke's instant "*t*" to include the process of decision from the start of free deliberations to the moment of willed choice, as in Figure 13-4. In many cases, this will be just the blink of an eye.

8 Clarke (2003) pp. 63-4

The agent will then be justified saying "I could have done otherwise," "This action was up to me," and "I am the originator of my actions and the author of my life."

Clarke goes on to consider the "centered" event-causal view, and initially claims that it provides an adequate account of free will, but his "adequate" is damning with faint praise.

> "If merely **narrow incompatibilism** is correct, then an unadorned, centered event-causal libertarian view provides a conceptually adequate account of free will. Such a view provides adequately for fully rational free action and for the rational explanation — simple, as well as contrastive — of free action. The indeterminism required by such a view does not diminish the active control that is exercised when one acts. Given incompatibilism of this variety, a libertarian account of this type secures both the openness of alternatives and the exercise of active control that are required for free will." [9]

Robert Kane has shown that "torn" decisions made indeterministically are under the voluntary control of the agent, because it is the agent's effort that is the main cause of such decisions. Kane says the agent has developed good reasons for going "either way," which is why such decisions should be considered Self-Forming Actions (SFAs) conferring ultimate responsibility (UR).

Having accepted such decisions with randomness "centered" in the decision, Clarke thinks random **alternative possibilities** are no longer needed. He then eliminates indeterminism in the prior "deliberative" stage, which is a great mistake

> "It is thus unnecessary to restrict indeterminism, as deliberative accounts do, to locations earlier in the processes leading to free actions. Indeed, so restricting indeterminism undermines the adequacy of an event-causal view. Any adequate libertarian account must locate the openness of alternatives and freedom-level active control in the same event — in a directly free action itself. For this reason, an adequate event-causal view must require that a directly free action be nondeterministically caused by its immediate causal antecedents.
>
> "If, on the other hand, broad incompatibilism is correct, then no event-causal account is adequate. An event-causal libertarian

9 Clarke (2003) p. 103.

> view secures ultimate control, which no compatibilist account provides. But the secured ultimacy is wholly negative: it is just (on a centered view) a matter of the absence of any determining cause of a directly free action. The active control that is exercised on such a view is just the same as that exercised on an event-causal compatibilist account." [10]

> "This sort of libertarian view fails to secure the agent's exercise of any further positive powers to causally influence which of the alternative courses of events that are open will become actual. For this reason, if moral responsibility is precluded by determinism, the freedom required for responsibility is not secured by any event-causal libertarian account. [11]

So for Clarke, all libertarian accounts fail if broad incompatibilism is true, i.e., if determinism is incompatible with moral responsibility. And his conclusion is that Kane's ultimate responsibility (UR) is empty, the absence of any determining cause for a free action. This, he says, offers no more control than compatibilism offers (viz., no control?).

The Luck Objections of Thomas Nagel, Bernard Williams, and Alfred Mele

In my view, luck is only a problem for **moral responsibility**. Some critics have mistakenly made it an objection to libertarian free will.

Since the world contains irreducible chance, it is a simple fact that many unintended consequences of our actions are out of our **control**.

Unfortunately, much of what happens in the real world contains a good deal of luck. Luck gives rise to many of the moral dilemmas that lead to moral skepticism.

Whether determinist, compatibilist, semicompatibilist, or libertarian, it seems unreasonable to hold persons responsible for

10 Clarke (2003) p. 105.
11 Clarke (2003) pp. 219-20.

the unintended and unforeseeable consequences of their actions, good or bad. In many moral and legal systems, it's the person's intentions that matter first and foremost.

Nevertheless, we are often held responsible for actions that were intended as good, but that had bad consequences. Similarly, we occasionally are praised for actions that were either neutral or possibly blameworthy, but which had good consequences.

Some thinkers are critical of any free will model that involves chance, because the apparent randomness of decisions would make such free will unintelligible. They say our actions would be a matter of luck.

This is the Luck Objection to free will, but it is properly only the problem of assigning moral responsibility when luck is involved.

Our three writers are concerned that if randomness is involved in a free decision, then perforce luck is involved, and this threatens moral responsibility.

Thomas Nagel

In his 1979 essay "Moral Luck," Nagel is pessimistic about finding morally responsible agents in a world that views agents externally, reducing them to happenings, to sequences of events, following natural laws, whether deterministic or indeterministic. Free will and moral responsibility seem to be mere illusions.

> "Moral judgment of a person is judgment not of what happens to him, but of him. It does not say merely that a certain event or state of affairs is fortunate or unfortunate or even terrible. It is not an evaluation of a state of the world, or of an individual as part of the world. We are not thinking just that it would be better if he were different, or did not exist, or had not done some of the things he has done. We are judging him, rather than his existence or characteristics. The effect of concentrating on the influence of what is not under his control is to make this responsible self seem to disappear, swallowed up by the order of mere events." [12]

This is truly the core of our scandal in philosophy. PETER F. STRAWSON said it arises when we treat human beings as objects

---

12 Nagel (1979)

governed by natural laws. This is the Naturalism view discussed in Chapter 21 Nagel says that our "selves" are disappearing.

> "We cannot simply take an external evaluative view of ourselves - of what we most essentially are and what we do. And this remains true even when we have seen that we are not responsible for our own existence, or our nature, or the choices we have to make, or the circumstances that give our acts the consequences they have. Those acts remain ours and we remain ourselves, despite the persuasiveness of the reasons that seem to argue us out of existence."[13]

Nagel can see no account of moral agency, nor an idea of how humans can be in control of their actions. He is a victim of the scandal in philosophy. The two-stage free will model of information philosophy restores human beings as authors of their lives and as co-creators of our world.

Bernard Williams

> "I entirely agree with [Nagel] that the involvement of morality with luck is not something that can simply be accepted without calling our moral conceptions into question. That was part of my original point; I have tried to state it more directly in the present version of this paper. A difference between Nagel and myself is that I am more sceptical about our moral conceptions than he is.
>
> "Scepticism about the freedom of morality from luck cannot leave the concept of morality where it was, any more than it can remain undisturbed by scepticism about the very closely related image we have of there being a moral order, within which our actions have a significance which may not be accorded to them by mere social recognition. These forms of scepticism will leave us with a concept of morality." [14]

Information philosophy has discovered an objective measure of **value** that is outside "mere social recognition." However, it offers no hope at all for eliminating the moral dilemmas that Williams says appear when luck is involved.

13 Moral Luck, reprinted in Nagel (1979) p. 37-38
14 Williams (1981)

Alfred Mele

Mele says there is a problem about luck for Libertarians.

> "Agents' control is the yardstick by which the bearing of luck on their freedom and moral responsibility is measured. When luck (good or bad) is problematic, that is because it seems significantly to impede agents' control over themselves or to highlight important gaps or shortcomings in such control. It may seem that to the extent that it is causally open whether or not, for example, an agent intends in accordance with his considered judgment about what it is best to do, he lacks some control over what he intends, and it may be claimed that a positive deterministic connection between considered best judgment and intention would be more conducive to freedom and moral responsibility.

Robust free will, with an intelligible explanation of the meaning of "could have done otherwise," is a prerequisite for responsibility.

Whether such free will exists is a scientific question. In particular, I try to show that science does not put any restrictions on human freedom, as most philosophers appear to believe. Whether a free action involves moral responsibility, however, is a question for the ethicists, not for science.

In any case, to the extent that luck is involved in an agent's free actions, that can and often does present problems for **moral responsibility**. But I believe that we can separate those consequential problems from the problem of free will. See Chapter 20 on the separability of free will from moral responsibility.

How the Cogito Model Meets the Objections

Since William James first suggested the two-stage model, a number of elements have been added to get to the current **Cogito** model. In the table at right, I try to identify the elements and give credit to those who saw the need for them.

Some philosophers and scientists may have thought of these details, but not made them explicit in their publications. Those fields are left blank.

All models use **chance** in the first stage. Some explicitly say the chance is quantum indeterminacy. Dennett alone denies this.

Doing otherwise means in exactly the same circumstances that obtain *before* the **alternative possibilities** are generated

Some models amplify a single quantum event to affect the decision. The idea of one quantum event per decision is called the Massive Switch Amplifier, or **MSA.**

Adequate determinism in the second stage is called various things, lawful, control etc. In the Cogito model it is explicitly only the statistical determinism consistent with quantum mechanics.

Three philosophers have written explicitly that random events in the first stage do not make the actions themselves random.

Second thoughts is the recognition that the decision process takes time, and, time permitting, the agent can go back and generate more alternative possibilities.

The analogy of free will to Darwin evolution was pointed out by James, the earliest thinker. It has appeared in a few later writers.

Undetermined liberties are cases where the agent in the second stage decides to choose an option at random, and is willing to take responsibility however and whatever is chosen.

Critics of Epicurus said that his choices were all undetermined. Robert Kane's SFAs were among the earliest examples of defending this view by selecting from options all of which have good reasons. Kane should note that this small number of options (dual or plural) is *as a group* as **adequately determined** as when there is only one option with good reasons. But his SFAs offer extra freedom.

	Quantum Chance	Can Do Otherwise	Adequate Determinism	Undetermined Liberties	MSA	Second thoughts	Actions not random	Darwin Analogy
James		Yes	Yes					Yes
Poincaré		Yes						
Compton	Yes				Yes			
Hadamard		Yes						
Adler		Yes						
Popper	Yes	Yes	Yes		Yes		Yes	Yes
Margenau	Yes	Yes	Yes					
Dennett	No	No	Yes		Yes	Yes		Yes
Kane	Yes	Yes		SFAs	No	Yes	Yes	Yes
Long/Sedley		Yes	Yes					
Penrose	Yes	Yes	Yes					
Annas		Yes	Yes					
Mele	Yes	Yes	Yes					
Kosslyn	Yes	Yes	Yes					
Searle	Yes	Yes	Yes				Yes	
Heisenberg	Yes	Yes	Yes					
Cogito	Yes	Yes	Yes	Yes	No	Yes	Yes	Yes

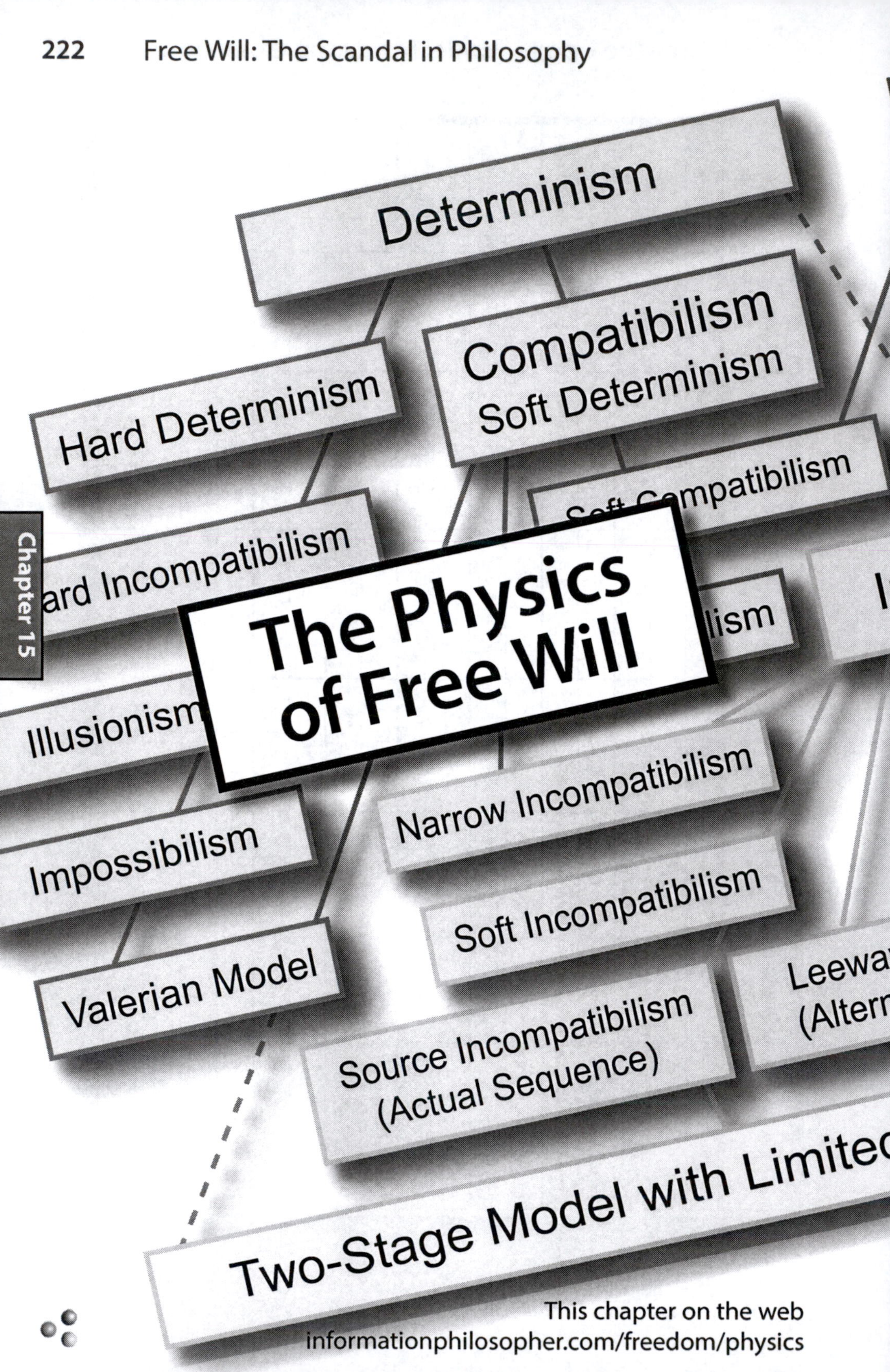

The Physics of Free Will

This chapter on the web
informationphilosopher.com/freedom/physics

The Physics of Free Will

Does physics, or more generally as philosophers describe the problem, do the causal "laws of nature" put limits on human freedom? The goal of information philosophy and information physics is to provide you with the current state of physical knowledge, to help you decide for yourself whether there are any such limits.

For information philosophy, the classical problem of reconciling free will with physical **determinism** (this reconciliation is accepted by all compatibilists) is now seen to have been the easier half of the free will problem. The more difficult half is reconciling free will with the physical **indeterminism** in the first stage of a **two-stage model**.

Modern physics sees the physical world as fundamentally undetermined. The universe began in a state of chaos and remains chaotic and random at the atomic scale (as well as some macroscopic regions of the cosmos). So the challenge presented by physics for free will is - how can anything at all be **adequately determined** with all this microscopic chaos and indeterminism?

We now know that even for very large objects, the laws of physics are only statistical laws. We have known this since Ludwig Boltzmann's work in 1877. Statistical physics was brilliantly confirmed at the level of atomic collisions by Max Born in 1926, and by Werner Heisenberg in 1927, with his quantum mechanical uncertainty principle. Unfortunately, "antipathy to chance"[1] has led many prominent physicists, then and even some now, to deny indeterminism and cling to a necessitarian deterministic physics.

Biologists knew about chance even earlier, from Charles Darwin's work in 1859. Chance is the driver for evolution and so chance must be a real part of the universe. Indeed, it is known that quantum collisions of high-energy cosmic rays with macromolecules carrying genetic information create the mutations that produce variation in the gene pool.

1 William James' characterization. James (1884) p. 153.

Charles Sanders Peirce, strongly influenced by Darwin, was the greatest philosopher to embrace chance, and he convinced his friend William James of it. James described the role of chance in free will in his essay, *The Dilemma of Determinism.*

Information philosophy has identified the cosmic creative processes (I call them "ergodic") that can overcome the chaotic tendency of indeterministic atomic collisions and create macroscopic, information-rich, structures. When these emergent structures are large enough, like the sun and planets, their motions become very well ordered and incredibly stable over time.

Even small macromolecular systems can have incredible stability, thanks to quantum mechanics. DNA has maintained its informational stability for nearly four billion years by adding error detection and correction processes ("proof reading" when replicating).

Early Greeks like Anaximander saw the universe as a "cosmos" and imagined laws of nature that would explain the cosmos. Later the Stoic physicists identified these laws of nature with laws of God, proclaimed nature to be God, and said both were completely determined.

For the Greeks, the heavens became the paradigm of perfection and orderly repetitive motions without change. The sublunary world was the realm of change and decay. When, two thousand years later, Isaac Newton discovered dynamical laws of motion for the planets that appeared to be perfectly accurate theories, he seemed to confirm a deterministic universe. But as Newton knew, and as Peirce and later Karl Popper were to argue, we never have observational evidence to support the presumed perfection. The physical laws had become a dogma of determinism.

This is epitomized in the super-intelligence of **Laplace's demon,** for whom the complete past and future are implicit in the current universe.

For most scientists, this determinism of classical physics has been invalidated by quantum mechanics. Statistical laws give us only **adequate determinism**. But some determinist philosophers doubt that current quantum theory is the last word. And others look to special relativitistic physics (also a classical theory) to prove determinism, as we will see below.

Quantum Physics

There is little doubt that there will be improvements in quantum theory in the future. Quantum mechanics has been made consistent with special relativity, but not yet with gravity and general relativity. The grand unification of the forces of nature may change something about the way we do quantum mechanics. But only if the predictions of the improved theory are as good or better than the current quantum theory, which is at this time the most accurate theory of physics, good to 15 significant figures or one part in 10^{15}.

The essential difference between classical physics and quantum physics is unlikely to change. Paul Dirac[2] identified the essential properties of quantum mechanics as **indeterminacy** and the *superposition* of quantum states.[3] The interference of probability-amplitude wave functions (shown in the two-slit experiment) is impossible for classical systems. Predictions of experimental outcomes are at best probabilistic and confirmable only statistically.

The decay of a radioactive particle is a good example. In a sample of radioactive material, it is impossible to predict when an electron will be ejected as one of the nuclei decay, but it is highly likely that after the "half-life" of the material, half of the radioactive nuclei will have decayed. In the language of the **Cogito model** of free will, the time to the next decay is **indeterminate**, but the number decayed after the half-life is **adequately determined**.

Special Relativity and the Block Universe

Einstein might have been surprised to find that several philosophers use his theory of special relativity to prove determinism, but he would not have been surprised to learn that they fail.

2 Dirac (2001), ch. 1.

3 See informationphilosopher.com/solutions/experiments/dirac_3-polarizers for a discussion.

Einstein was as strong a believer in determinism as any scientist. If he thought his special theory of relativity could be used to prove determinism, he surely would have done so.

Since the 1960's, several philosophers have thought that they could prove that determinism is true because of the special theory of relativity. They include J. J. C. Smart, C.W. Rietdijk, Hilary Putnam, Roger Penrose, Michael Lockwood, and Michael Levin. [4]

The basic idea behind using the special theory of relativity to prove determinism is that time can be treated mathematically as a fourth dimension. This gives us excellent results for experiments on moving objects. It predicts the strange Lorentz contraction of objects in space and dilations of clock speeds for observers in fast moving frames of reference (coordinate systems).

In Figure 15-1, observers A and B are moving toward one another at high speed. At the current time, they are at events A_0 and B_0. B_1 is an event that is in B's future. It is in a timelike separation from B_0. Special relativity says that A sees the event B_1 as happening "now" in A's fast-moving frame of reference. A_0 and B_1 are happening at the same time. But notice that, like the current events A_0 and B_0, the two events that A thinks are happening "now" are in a spacelike separation. There can be no causal connection from A_0 to B_1.

Similarly, B sees the event A_1 as synchronous with the event B_0 by his clocks. But any "influence" of B_0 on A_1 would have to move faster than the speed of light, which is impossible.

These philosophers jump to the unacceptable conclusion that the time dimension is like space and so the "future is already out there." Any event that is going to happen has already happened,.

This is a special relativistic version of Diodorus Cronus' ancient notion of actualism, only what actually will happen could ever happen.

---

4 See informationphilosopher.com/freedom/special_relativity.html

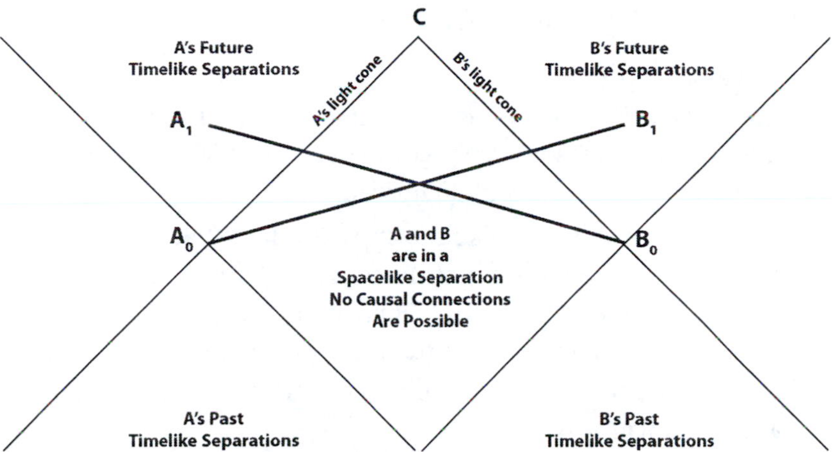

Figure 15-1. Space-time diagram for observers fast approaching one another.

But just because an event is placed on a space-time diagram, it is not made actual. It is still in the future.

Quantum mechanics has eliminated the kind of physical determinism that Laplace's demon might have used to connect present events causally with events in the future.

But despite quantum mechanics, ALBERT EINSTEIN remained a confirmed determinist. He might have been surprised to learn that so many philosophers have used his theory of special relativity in an attempt to prove determinism.

Einstein believed in determinism as much any scientist. He very likely did not develop this argument from his special theory of relativity because he knew it is absurd and knew it would fail.

But Einstein's special relativity has one more role to play in the free will problem. Nonlocality and entanglement are apparent violations of Einstein's limit on things traveling faster than the speed of light. Some philosophers and scientists think that the mysteries of nonlocality and entanglement can help solve the mysteries of consciousness and free will.[5]

5 E.g., Roger Penrose, John Conway, Simon Kocher, Nicolas Gisin, Antoine Suarez. See informationphilosopher.com/freedom/nonlocality.html

Nonlocality and Entanglement

Albert Einstein never liked Werner Heisenberg's indeterminacy principle in quantum mechanics, although it was the direct result of his own early confirmation of Max Planck's idea that nature is discrete and quantized.

Einstein also did not like the apparent fact that when the probability-amplitude wave function collapses, the values of the wave function change instantly over large distances, suggesting that the probability is traveling faster than the speed of light.[6] This violated Einstein's sense of "local" reality. He said that nature seemed to have non-local behaviors.

It is not clear which was worse for Einstein, the quantum **indeterminacy** that made physics indeterministic, or the faster-than-light implications of the Einstein-Podolsky-Rosen experiment and Bell's Theorem.

Einstein disliked indeterminism, famously saying that "The Lord God does not play dice." But he was also opposed to what he called the "spooky action at a distance" implied by the "nonlocal reality" of quantum mechanics.

Nonlocality shows up best in two-particle experiments like that proposed by Einstein and his Princeton colleagues, where measurements that detect a particle in one place instantly determine the properties (position, momentum, spin, etc.) of another "entangled" particle that can be at a very great distance from the first.[7]

Einstein might have been pleased to learn that many physicists and philosophers are still trying to confirm his notion of "local" reality. They use "hidden variable" theories to explain how a particle at point A can determine the properties of another particle far away at point B.

John Bell's famous theorem, if confirmed experimentally, could prove Einstein to be correct, restoring both determinism and local reality. Unfortunately, three decades of experiments continue to

6 See informationphilosopher.com/solutions/experiments/wave-function_collapse for an animated visualization

7 See informationphilosopher.com/solutions/experiments/EPR for an explanation and visualization of the Einstein-Podolsky-Rosen experiment.

show that Bell's theorem is violated and the nonlocality of quantum physics has been confirmed.

Information philosophy and physics can explain the mystery of "faster than light" effects in nonlocality and entanglement. The proper explanation is that only abstract information appears instantly over vast distances.

Information is neither matter nor energy. It needs matter for its embodiment and energy for its communication, but in its abstract form it can appear to travel at supraluminal speeds, even in non-quantum events. Consider a horse race.

Figure 15-2. Information about probabilities is instantaneous,

Moments before the winning horse's nose triggers the photo finish, there is still some probability that horses far behind might win the race. The other horses might collapse.

But at the instant the lead horse wins, the probability of horses at the rear winning falls to zero, faster than the speed of light. No signal travels faster than light. We can now see how this also explains nonlocality in the EPR experiment.

In figure 15-3, two electrons are entangled in the center with total spin equal zero. One electron must have spin up and the other spin down. But electrons are identical interchangeable particles. We cannot know which has which spin until we measure them. And until we measure them, we cannot label them either.

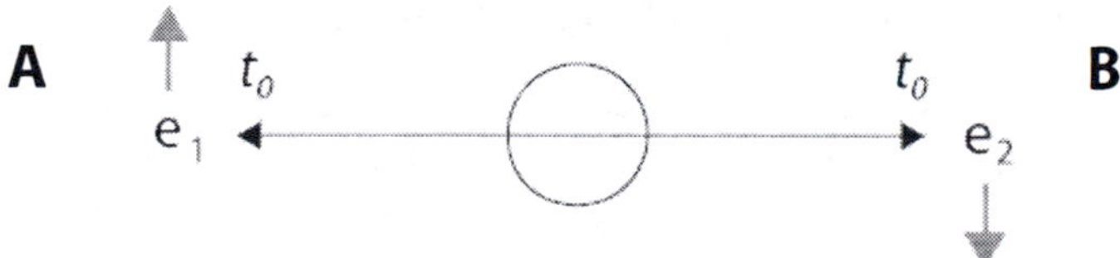

Figure 15-3. Electrons prepared with total spin = 0 at the center.

Let's now say that an observer A makes a measurement and finds an electron with spin up. We can now label that electron 1, and instantly we know that the other electron, now called 2, is an equal but opposite distance from the center and has been **determined** by A's measurement to have spin down.

But note that this was not **pre-determined** before A's measurement. This is the logical and physical mistake that you will find in most accounts of nonlocality. In the horse race, the horses are already numbered. But with quantum particles, we don't know their identity until we find them.

Note that because B and A have a spacelike separation, we know from the special relativity analysis above that observer B might have measured "first" at t_0 in his own frame of reference,

In the case of a single particle wave-function collapse, all the probability appears instantly at one point. In the two-particle case, the abstract probability information collapses instantly to two points, one for each particle. Those points are located so as to conserve the momentum, energy, and angular momentum (spin).

Despite exaggerated claims that nonlocality and entanglement introduce new quantum mysteries, there is actually nothing new beyond the fundamental mystery of wave-function collapses, except that we now have two particles.

These exaggerations have misled philosophers to make claims that nonlocality and entanglement can *explain* free will.

The Free Will Theorem

The mathematician JOHN CONWAY (well-known for his cellular automata and the Game of Life) and his Princeton colleague Simon Kochen use the EPR experiment[8] and tests of Bell's Inequality to show what some science writers have argued is "free will" for elementary particles.

Conway and Kochen's argument is that if

> "experimenters have sufficient free will to choose the settings of their apparatus in a way that is not determined by past history, then the particles' responses are also not determined by past history...
>
> "Since this property for experimenters is an instance of what is usually called "free will," we find it appropriate to use the same term also for particles." [9]

8 See informationphilosopher.com/freedom/free_will_theorem.html

9 Foundations of Physics 36 (10): 1441

What Conway and Kochen are really describing is the indeterminism that quantum mechanics has introduced into the world. While my **two-stage model** makes indeterminism a necessary precondition for human freedom, it is insufficient by itself to provide free will.

Another way of looking at their work is to say that if determinism is true, then all the experimental tests might have been predetermined (e.g., by a deceiving God) to convince us that quantum mechanics is correct and that indeterminism exists, but that the real underlying nature of the universe is deterministic. Even Einstein could not go this far.

The Free Will Axiom

Philosophers and scientists from René Descartes to those who today are leaders in experimental tests of Bell's Theorem have all assumed that free will is necessarily axiomatic.[10]

Descartes wrote in 1644, "The freedom of the will is self-evident." In his 1874 book *Principles of Science*, the great logician and economist William Stanley Jevons is unequivocal that scientists have a freedom to hypothesize. In a section entitled Freedom of Theorizing, he declares,

> "The truest theories involve suppositions which are most inconceivable, and no limit can really be placed to the freedom of framing hypotheses."

In 1880, the founder of two-stage models credited Jevons with explaining the **creativity** of the genius as dependent on random hypotheses. James said,

> "To Professor Jevons is due the great credit of having emphatically pointed out how the genius of discovery depends altogether on the number of these random notions and guesses which visit the investigator's mind. To be fertile in hypotheses is the first requisite, and to be willing to throw them away the moment experience contradicts them is the next." [11]

10 See informationphilosopher.com/freedom/free_will_axiom.html
11 James (2007)

John Searle said in 2005 that

> "The special problem of free will is that we cannot get on with our lives without presupposing free will. Whenever we are in a decision-making situation, or indeed, in any situation that calls for voluntary action, we have to presuppose our own freedom."[12]

The Swiss scientist Nicolas Gisin, winner of the first John Stewart Bell prize, who recently confirmed the violations of Bell's Inequality over a distance of 19km in Geneva, says:

> "I know that I enjoy free will much more than I know anything about physics. Hence, physics will never be able to convince me that free will is an illusion. Quite the contrary, any physical hypothesis incompatible with free will is falsified by the most profound experience I have about free will." [13]

The Contribution of Quantum Mechanics

Why is quantum indeterminacy involved in the shaking together (*co-agitare*) of our agenda items, the real **alternative possibilities** for thought or action that allow us to say we "could have **done otherwise**?" There are three important reasons:

- Before quantum indeterminacy, many philosophers, mathematicians, and statistical scientists argued that chance was just a name for our ignorance of underlying deterministic processes. They denied the existence of real, objective chance in the universe. They thought that chance was epistemic and subjective, a result of the ignorance of finite minds.
- As soon as quantum mechanics was established in the 1920's, first scientists and then philosophers began claiming that quantum indeterminism could explain free will. Chapter 12 looked at some of their ideas. After a few years thought, most scientists qualified their enthusiasm or reported admissions of failure. Only a few libertarian philosophers, mostly those following Robert Kane, have been reluctant to give up on quantum indeterminism. Among determinists, Ted

12 Searle (2007) p.11.
13 Gisin (2010) p.

HONDERICH has taken it very seriously, but DANIEL DENNETT has denied its significance, as we shall see. [14]

- Quantum uncertainty remains the best explanation for breaks in the causal chain of strict determinism. But attempts to use the strange non-intuitive aspects of quantum mechanics - such as unpredictable quantum jumps between energy levels, "collapse" of the wave function in physical measurements, non-local behavior of particles that have become "entangled," spontaneous decay of "metastable" states, etc. - as models for the decision process have been hopeless failures.

The **Cogito** model of Chapter 13 identified the critical aspect of quantum mechanical **indeterminacy** that makes an "intelligible" contribution to human freedom, while preserving **adequate determinism** and **moral responsibility**. It is simply noise.

As we will see in the next chapter, molecular biologists have doubted we could ever locate a randomness generator in the brain. Such a generator would need to be small enough to be susceptible to microscopic quantum phenomena, yet large enough to affect macromolecular structures like neurons, which may contain as many as 10^{20} atoms.

Proposed amplifier mechanisms have been bizarre failures.[15]

The Cogito model simply identifies the source of randomness as the inevitable **noise**, both thermal noise and quantum noise, that affects both proper storage of information and accurate retrieval of that information at later times.

These read/write errors are an appropriately random source of unpredictable new ideas and thoughts that provide **alternative possibilities** for action. Noise is ever present, yet suppressible by the macroscopic brain.

We need not look for tiny random-noise generators and amplifiers located in specific parts of the brain. They are no more necessary than the Cartesian Theater homunculi sometimes evoked by philosophers to parody a tiny internal free agent inside the mind.

14 Honderich in Chapter 23, Kane in 24, and Dennett in 25.

15 See informationphilosopher.com/freedom/free_will_mechanisms.html

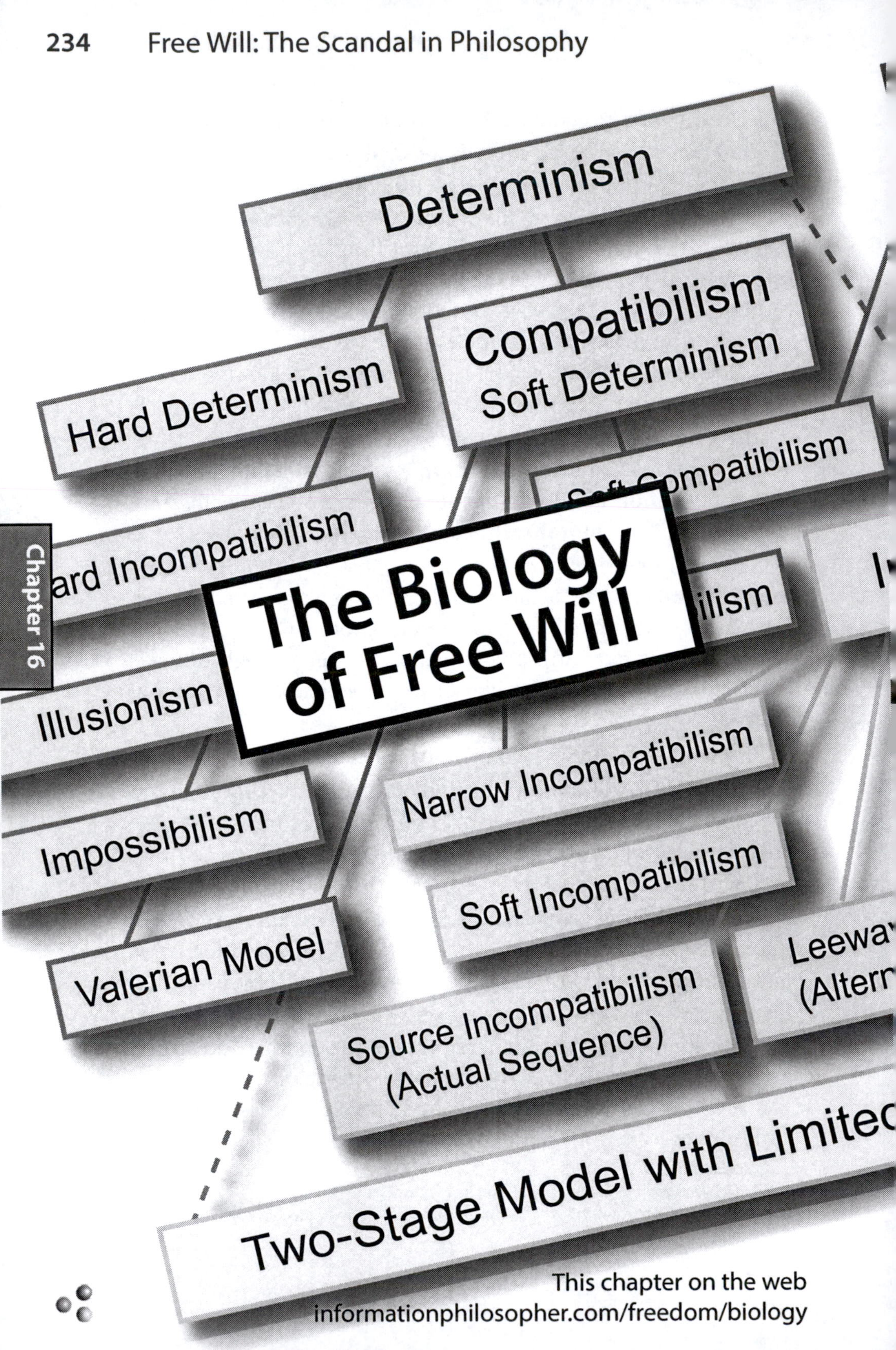

Chapter 16

The Biology of Free Will

This chapter on the web
informationphilosopher.com/freedom/biology

Indeterminism

The Biology of Free Will

Perhaps physics now puts no limits on human freedom, but what about biology? Each of us gets a significant amount of genetic information from our parents, which at least predisposes us to certain behaviors that have evolved to improve our reproductive success, sexual behavior, for example.

Are we completely "determined" by a combination of our biological nature and the social nurture of our environmental conditioning? Is biology itself all a causal process that is simply unfolding from a distant past that contained all the information about the one possible biological future?

Information biology says no. While the stability of biological systems is extraordinary, and while their error-free performance of vital functions over many-year lifetimes is astonishing, their dependence on randomness is clear. Biological laws, like physical laws, are only **adequately determined**, statistical laws.

At the atomic and molecular level, biological processes are stochastic, depending on thermal and quantal **noise** to deliver the "just-in-time" parts needed by assembly lines for the basic structural elements of life, such as the amino acids needed by the ribosome factories to assemble proteins.

So our question is how the typical structures of the brain have evolved to deal with microscopic, atomic level, noise. Do they simply ignore it because they are adequately determined large objects, or might they have remained sensitive to the noise because it provides some benefits?

We can expect that if quantum noise, or even ordinary thermal noise, offered benefits that contribute to reproductive success, there would have been evolutionary pressure to take advantage of the noise.

Many biologists argue that quantum-level processes are just too small to be important, too small for the relatively macroscopic biological apparatus to even notice. But consider this evidence to the contrary.

Proof that our sensory organs have evolved until they are working at or near quantum limits is evidenced by the eye's ability to detect a single photon (a quantum of light energy), and the nose's ability to smell a single molecule.

Biology provides many examples of ergodic creative processes following a trial-and-error model. They harness chance as a possibility generator, followed by an adequately determined selection mechanism with implicit information-value criteria.

Darwinian evolution was the first and greatest example of a two-stage creative process, random variation followed by critical selection. Darwin's example inspired William James to propose the original two-stage model of free will.

Here I will briefly consider some other such processes that are analogous to the two-stage **Cogito** model for the human mind.

Creativity in the Immune System

Consider the great problem faced by the immune system. It stands ready to develop antibodies to attack an invading antigen at any moment, with no advance knowledge of what the antigen may be. In information terms, it needs to discover some part of the antigen that is unique. Its method is not unlike Poincaré's two-stage method of solving a mathematical problem. First put together lots of random combinations, then subject them to tests.

Biological information is stored in the "genetic code," the sequence of genes along a chromosome in our DNA. "Sequencing" the DNA establishes the exact arrangement of nucleotides that code for specific proteins/enzymes. All the advances in molecular genetics are based on this sequencing ability.

The white blood cells have evolved a powerful strategy to discover unique information in the antigen. What they have done is evolve a "re-sequencing" capability. Using the same gene splicing techniques that biologists have now developed to insert characteristics from one organism into another, the white blood cells have a very-high-speed process that shuffles genes around at random. They cut genes out of one location and splice them in at random in

other locations. This combinatorial diversity provides a variation in the gene pool very much like the Darwinian mutations that drive species evolution.

But the marvelous immune system gets even more random. It has a lower-level diversity generator that randomly scrambles the individual nucleotides at the junctions between genes. The splicing of genes is randomly done with errors that add or subtract nucleotides, creating what is called junctional diversity.

Bacterial Chemotaxis

Some of the smallest organisms are equipped with sensors and motion capability that let them make two-stage decisions about which way to go. They must move in the direction of nutrients and away from toxic chemicals. Some bacteria do this with tiny flagella that rotate in two directions. Flagella rotating clockwise cause the bacterium to tumble and face random new directions. Rotation of the flagella counter-clockwise drives the bacterium straight ahead. As the bacterium moves, receptors on the bacterium surface detect gradients of chemicals. When the gradient indicates "food ahead" or "toxic behind," the bacterium keeps going. If the gradients are not promising, the bacterium reverses the flagella rotation direction, which makes it tumble again.

In Nature Magazine,[1] the German neurogeneticist MARTIN HEISENBERG challenged the idea, popular in the recent psychology and philosophy literature,[2] that human free will is an illusion. Heisenberg suggested that a lot could be learned by looking at lower animals. We can see that they do not merely respond to stimuli mechanically, but originate actions. He said,

> "when it comes to understanding how we initiate behaviour, we can learn a lot by looking at animals. Although we do not credit animals with anything like the consciousness in humans, researchers have found that animal behaviour is not as involuntary as it may appear. The idea that animals act only in response to external stimuli has long been abandoned, and it is

1 Nature, vol. 459, 2009, p. 164

2 Cf. especially Wegner (2002)

> well established that they initiate behaviour on the basis of their internal states, as we do."

One of Heisenberg's examples was bacterial chemotaxis.

> "Evidence of randomly generated action — action that is distinct from reaction because it does not depend upon external stimuli — can be found in unicellular organisms. Take the way the bacterium Escherichia coli moves. It has a flagellum that can rotate around its longitudinal axis in either direction: one way drives the bacterium forward, the other causes it to tumble at random so that it ends up facing in a new direction ready for the next phase of forward motion. This 'random walk' can be modulated by sensory receptors, enabling the bacterium to find food and the right temperature." [3]

An Error Detection and Correction System?

Errors in protein synthesis are arguably quantal. If errors prevent proper folding, the chaperone functions as an information error detection and correction system. If it succeeds in helping the protein to fold, the protein is released, otherwise the chaperone will digest and destroy the malformed protein.

Here the quantal noise will destroy the protein if the error cannot be corrected. It is of course not as if a new protein is being generated analogous to the accidental variations that genetic mutations introduce to the gene pool.

But it is instructive as an example of a two-stage process nonetheless, in that microscopic indeterministic errors are repaired by macroscopic, adequately determined, systems

Neurotransmitter Release as a Noise Source

Since information flows across the synapses, randomness of release times for transmitter quanta may be a source of information noise in memory storage and recall. Neurotransmitter "quanta" are of course huge compared to atomic-level quantum processes - containing thousands of molecules.

---

3 Nature, vol. 459, 2009, p. 165

John Eccles thought this to be a meaningful source of noise, that it could help the brain make undetermined decisions, but he did not have a coherent idea of the process, like the two-stage model of free will.

Four Levels of Selection

I propose that there have been four levels in the evolutionary development of free will. In all four levels, the source of the random generation of **alternative possibilities** in the first stage of my **two-stage model** is the same. It is the essential chaos and **noise** that is characteristic of information processes at the lower levels of any organism.

But in the second stage, I argue that new methods of selection of the best alternative possibility get added at the upper levels.

Instinctive Selection

At the lowest level, selection is instinctive. The selection criteria are transmitted genetically, shaped only by ancestral experiences.

Learned Selection

At the second level are animals whose past experiences guide their current choices. Selection criteria are acquired through experience, including instruction by parents and peers.

Predictive Selection

Third-level animals use their imagination and foresight to estimate the future consequences of their choices.

Reflective (Normative) Selection

At the highest level, selection is reflective and normative.[4] Conscious deliberation about community values influences the choice of behaviors.

4 Compare Christine Korsgaard's theory of normativity. Korsgaard (1996)

Chapter 17

The Neuroscience of Free Will

This chapter on the web
informationphilosopher.com/freedom/neuroscience

The Neuroscience of Free Will

Molecular biologists have assured neuroscientists for years that the molecular structures involved in neurons are too large to be affected significantly by quantum randomness.

Nevertheless, some neurobiologists looked for structures small enough to be affected. John Eccles identified what he called "critically poised neurons," whose synapses might discharge their vesicles with thousands of neurotransmitters as a result of "downward causation" from the mind. Roger Penrose and Stuart Hameroff see the microtubules in the cellular cytoskeleton as small enough to produce quantum coherence, perhaps some nonlocal entanglement.

As small as these structures are, they still contain many thousands of quantum level objects (atoms and molecules). How can any single quantum event in the brain get amplified to become macroscopically important? This is the question that has faced everyone who wants quantum randomness to be the basis for human freedom.

Will neuroscientists ever be able to look at a neuron and see exactly what it is thinking? Maybe not, but some have thought they can use brain activity measurements to prove that free will does not exist.

Libet's Experiment

Benjamin Libet's famous neuroscience experiments are widely regarded as having established that conscious will is an illusion, starting with Libet's own claim (mistaken, we shall argue below) that the readiness potential (RP) that he observed a few hundred milliseconds before the awareness of conscious will and the consequent muscle motion, "initiates" and is the **cause** of both the will and the action. [1]

As Alfred Mele has shown, the experimental data do not support a causal relationship. We can see this by interpreting the rise

1 Libet (2004) p. 136.

in the RP as the early stage in the two-stage model. The brain may only be considering its alternative possibilities!

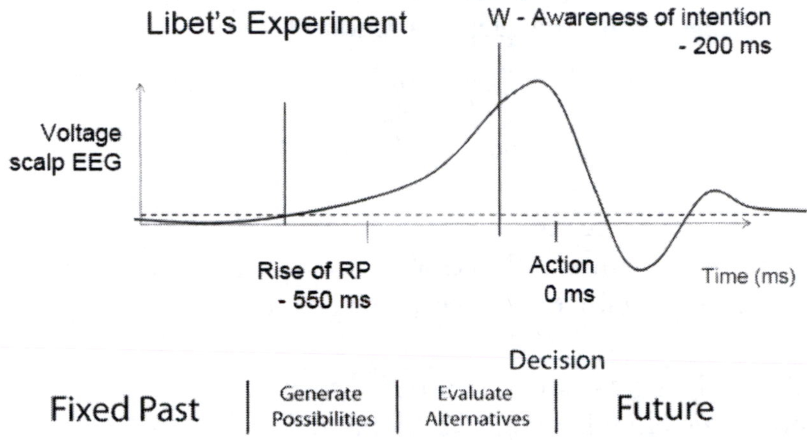

Figure 17-1. Early brain activity may only be considering possibilities.

Note that Libet proposed that the will could nevertheless be free, if there was time for it to "veto" its own prior decision, which had been caused by the early rise of the RP. But his main mistake was to conclude that the first sign of activity was causative, rather than merely enabling the later decision.

Although the abrupt and rapid decisions to flex a finger measured by Libet bear little resemblance to the kinds of two-stage deliberate decisions needed for responsibility, it seems reasonable to assume that neuronal activity might arise as the mind considers whether to flex or not to flex, when it forms the intention to flex. Roderick Chisholm argued that at least one alternative possibility always exists, we can always say no. So Libet's "veto" is already in the running as a possibility, and Libet need not have worried that there is too little time for it be effective, as his critics have maintained.

Libet, Patrick Haggard, Daniel Wegner, and the others who say the conscious will is not the cause of the action, because your neurons have already made the decision, cannot prove a causal relation between RP and action.

They are in fact begging the question of free will by assuming that a deterministic relation already exists between the early stage RP and the, action simply because it shows up earlier than the action (*post hoc, propter hoc*).

What if the early RP is just the first stage of developing options, followed by evaluating them, then deciding? In such an arbitrary choice - to flex or not flex, we should expect to see the readiness potential occasionally rise up, but then *not be followed by the W* point, and of course no muscle motion. The fact that Libet reports none of these may appear to lend weight to the idea that RP and muscle motion are indeed causally related. But this is a mistake, as pointed out by ALFRED MELE.[2]

All the Libet experiments work by permanently storing the last few seconds of data that have been collected, when triggered by detecting the wrist flex itself. If there is no wrist flex, there is no data collected. The equally likely (in my view) cases of a rise in RP followed by no wrist flex would have been systematically ignored by Libet's method of data collection.

Should new versions of the Libet experiments find this missing data, it would establish that there is no causal connection between RP and action, only between RP and considering alternative possibilities, to flex or not to flex, in the two-stage model of free will.

Libet and the Two-Stage Model

In his late work *Mind Time*, Libet surprisingly describes more than one "initiative," disconnecting the RP from the action.

> "We may view the unconscious initiatives for voluntary actions as "burbling up" unconsciously in the brain. The conscious will then selects which of these initiatives may go forward to an action, or which ones to veto and abort, so no action occurs." [3]

These initiatives are **alternative possibilities**, "burbling up" suggests they "present themselves" randomly, as WILLIAM JAMES says, and selection is clearly the **adequately determined** second stage of our two-stage model.

2 Mele (2010) p. 53.
3 Libet (2004) p. 148.

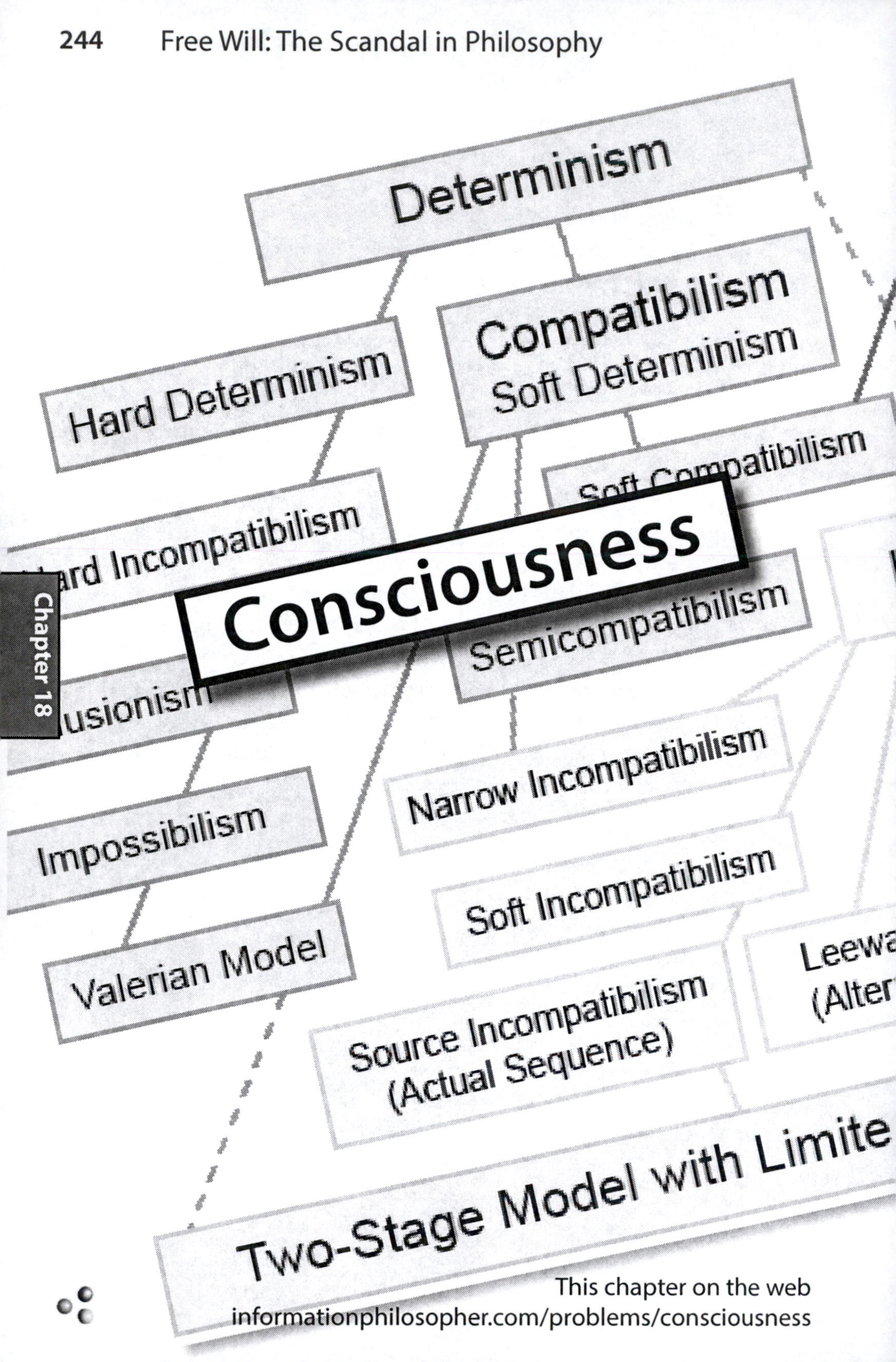

This chapter on the web
informationphilosopher.com/problems/consciousness

Consciousness

Consciousness can be defined in information terms as an entity (usually a living thing, but we can also include artificially conscious machines or computers) that reacts to the information (and particularly to changes in the information) in its environment.

In the context of information philosophy, we can define this as information consciousness.

Thus an animal in a deep sleep is not conscious because it ignores changes in its environment. And robots may be conscious in our sense. Even the lowliest control system using negative feedback (a thermostat, for example) is in a minimal sense conscious of changes in its environment.

The Experience Recorder Reproducer (ERR)

This definition of consciousness fits with our model of the mind as an experience recorder and reproducer (ERR). The ERR model stands in contrast to the popular cognitive science or "computational" model of a mind as a digital computer. No algorithms or stored programs are needed for the ERR model.

The physical metaphor is a non-linear random-access data recorder, where data is stored using content-addressable memory (the memory address is the data content itself). Simpler than a computer with stored algorithms, a better technological metaphor might be a video and sound recorder, enhanced with the ability to record smells, tastes, touches, and critically essential, feelings.

The biological model is neurons that wire together during an organism's experiences, in multiple sensory and limbic systems, such that later firing of even a part of the wired neurons can stimulate firing of all or part of the original complex.

Neuroscientists are investigating how diverse signals from multiple pathways can be unified in the brain. We offer no specific insight into these "binding" problems. Nor can we shed much light on the question of philosophical "meaning" of any given information structure, beyond the obvious relevance (survival value) for the organism of remembering past experiences.

A conscious being is constantly recording information about its perceptions of the external world, and most importantly for ERR, it is simultaneously recording its feelings. Sensory data such as sights, sounds, smells, tastes, and tactile sensations are recorded in a sequence along with pleasure and pain states, fear and comfort levels, etc.

All these experiential and emotional data are recorded in association with one another. This means that when the experiences are reproduced (played back in a temporal sequence), the accompanying emotions are once again felt, in synchronization.

The capability of reproducing experiences is critical to learning from past experiences, so as to make them guides for action in future experiences. The ERR model is the minimal mind model that provides for such learning by living organisms.

The ERR model does not need computer-like decision algorithms to reproduce past experiences. All that is required is that past experiences "play back" whenever they are stimulated by present experiences that resemble the past experiences in one or more ways. When the organism recreates experiences by acting them out, they can become "habitual" and "subconscious" information structures.

It is critical that the original emotions play back, along with any variations in current emotions. ERR might then become an explanatory basis for conditioning experiments, classical Pavlovian and operant, and in general a model for associative learning.

Bernard Baars' Global Workspace Theory uses the metaphor of a "Theater of Consciousness," in which there is an audience of purposeful agents calling for the attention of the executive on stage.

In the ERR model, vast numbers of past experiences clamor for the attention of the central executive at all times, whenever anything in current experience has some resemblance.

If we define "current experience" as all afferent perceptions and the current contents of consciousness itself, we get a dynamic self-referential system with plenty of opportunities for negative and positive feedback.

William James' description of a "stream of consciousness" together with a "blooming, buzzing confusion" of the unconscious appear to describe the ERR model very well.

In the "blackboard" model of Allan Newell and Herbert Simon, concepts written on the blackboard call up similar concepts by association from deep memory structures. The ERR model supports this view, and explains the mechanism by which concepts (past experiences) come to the blackboard.

In Daniel Dennett's consciousness model, the mind is made up of innumerable functional homunculi, each with its own goals and purposes.

Some of these homunculi are information structures formed genetically, which transmit "learning" or "knowledge" from generation to generation. Others are environmentally and socially conditioned, or consciously learned.

Four "Levels" of Consciousness

Instinctive Consciousness - by animals with little or no learning capability. Automatic reactions to environmental conditions are transmitted genetically. Information about past experiences (by prior generations of the organism) is only present implicitly in the inherited reactions

Learned Consciousness - for animals whose past experiences guide current choices. Conscious, but mostly habitual, reactions are developed through experience, including instruction by parents and peers.

Predictive Consciousness - The Sequencer in the ERR system can play back beyond the current situation, allowing the organism to use imagination and foresight to evaluate the future consequences of its choices.

Reflective (Normative) Consciousness– in which conscious deliberation about values influences the choice of behaviors.

Chapter 19

This chapter on the web
informationphilosopher.com/freedom/moral_responsibility.html

Moral Responsibility

Some philosophers deflect direct discussion of free will, primarily, no doubt, because of the scandal that the problem has resisted progress for so long. They study free will indirectly and only as the "control condition" for moral responsibility.

In his four-volume collection of articles on free will, JOHN MARTIN FISCHER made this observation.

> "Some philosophers do not distinguish between freedom and moral responsibility. Put a bit more carefully, they tend to begin with the notion of moral responsibility, and "work back" to a notion of freedom; this notion of freedom is not given independent content (separate from the analysis of moral responsibility). For such philosophers, "freedom" refers to whatever conditions are involved in choosing or acting in such a way as to be morally responsible.[1]

MANUEL VARGAS agrees:

> "It is not clear that there is any single thing that people have had in mind by the term "free will." Perhaps the dominant characterization in the history of philosophy is that it is something like the freedom condition on moral responsibility. Roughly, the idea is that to be morally responsible for something, you had to have some amount of freedom, at some suitable time prior to the action or outcome for which you are responsible. That sense of freedom — whatever it amounts to — is what we mean to get at by the phrase "free will." ... Although I think much of what I will say can be applied to other aspects of thinking about it, I will be primarily concerned with free will in its connection to moral responsibility, the sense in which people are appropriately praised or blamed.[2]

In the next chapter, I present arguments for *separating* free will from moral responsibility, just as my two-stage model of free will separates the "free" stage from the "will" stage.

---

1 Fischer (2005) v.I, p. xxiii
2 Fischer (2007) p. 128.

Indeed, I will go further and recommend that we separate "moral" from "responsibility." The latter is a scientific empirical problem. The former is an ethical problem to be settled by moral philosophers and social scientists in a cultural context.

The focus on **moral responsibility** had a very specific starting point in the history of the free will problem, as we noted in Chapter 7 (see p. 115).

Peter Strawson Changed the Subject

Peter Strawson argued in 1962 that whatever the deep metaphysical truth on the issues of determinism and free will, people would not give up talking about and feeling moral responsibility - praise and blame, guilt and pride, crime and punishment, gratitude, resentment, and forgiveness.

These "reactive attitudes" were for Strawson more real than whether they could be explained by fruitless disputes about free will, compatibilism, and determinism. They were natural "facts" of our human commitment to ordinary inter-personal attitudes. He said it was "a pity that talk of the moral sentiments has fallen out of favour," since such talk was "the only possibility of reconciling these disputants to each other and the facts."

Strawson himself was optimistic that compatibilism could reconcile determinism with moral obligation and responsibility. He accepted the facts of determinism. He felt that determinism was true. But he was concerned to salvage the reality of our attitudes even for libertarians, whom he described as pessimists about determinism.

> "What I have called the participant reactive attitudes are essentially natural human reactions to the good or ill will or indifference of others towards us, as displayed in their attitudes and actions. The question we have to ask is: What effect would, or should, the acceptance of the truth of a general thesis of determinism have upon these reactive attitudes? More specifically, would, or should, the acceptance of the truth of the thesis lead to the decay or the repudiation of all such attitudes? Would, or should, it mean the end of gratitude, resentment, and forgive-

ness; of all reciprocated adult loves; of all the essentially personal antagonisms?" [3]

Of course, from the earliest beginnings, the problem of "free will" has been intimately connected with the question of **moral responsibility**. Most of the ancient thinkers on the problem were trying to show that we humans have control over our decisions, that our actions "depend on us", and that they are not pre-determined by fate, by arbitrary gods, by logical necessity, or by a natural causal determinism.

But to say that today "free will is understood as the control condition for moral responsibility" is to make a serious blunder in conceptual analysis and clear thinking. Free will is clearly a prerequisite for responsibility. Whether the responsibility is a moral responsibility depends on our ideas of morality.

Are only Moral Decisions Free?

To say that a decision cannot be free unless it is a moral decision, I regard as an ethical fallacy, but it has a long tradition in the history of philosophy.

Some ancients and medieval thinkers argued that freedom could be equated with morality. Men were free to do good. If they did evil, it was the influence of some nefarious power preventing them from doing good.

ARISTOTLE, IMMANUEL KANT, and others often describe humans as free when we do good, otherwise as slaves to our ignorance. Aristotle's equation of "virtue as knowledge" claims that we do wrong only because we do not know the right.

Starting with his 1985 book, *Free Will and Values*, Robert Kane argued that important free choices (his Self-Forming Actions or SFAs) are those moral and prudential decisions that have not yet been narrowed down to an act of **self-determination**. He says that the agent does not have "all-things-considered" reasons to choose one rather than another.

But freedom is a physical question, insofar as it is based on arguments about determinism versus indeterminism. To be sure, the will is in part also a psychological/physiological question.

3 Strawson (1962) p. 10.

Responsibility is a causality question. Is the agent properly in the causal chain? Moral questions are not physical questions. To confound them is to connect ought with is.

Moral responsibility is a major field of ethics that can stand on its own without sophisticated attempts to deny the existence of free will. e.g., the sophistry of Frankfurt-type examples claiming to deny **alternative possibilities** and the ability to **do otherwise**.

Naturalism and Moral Responsibility

For some Naturalists, the equation of free will and moral responsibility is driven by their goal to eliminate what they see as unjust punishment, the result of a "culture of vengeance." Their specious reasoning goes something like this - "If free will is required for moral responsibility, we can deny moral responsibility by denying free will."

Equating free will with moral responsibility, then to use spurious arguments to deny free will, and thus to deny moral responsibility - in order to oppose punishment - is fine humanism but poor philosophy, and terrible science.

Naturalists seem to naively accept the ancient religious arguments that free will is an exclusive property of humans (some religions limit it to males, for example). One strand in the naturalist argument then is to say that humans are animals and so we lack free will.

It will be interesting to see naturalists react to the establishment of a biophysical basis for behavioral freedom in lower animals. This behavioral freedom is conserved and shows up in higher animals and humans as freedom of their wills, as we saw in Chapter 16.

So a refined view of naturalism would be to extend behavioral freedom to all animals. We no longer need defend an exceptional human nature.

Even If Determinism Were True

ALFRED MELE tells me that he and JOHN MARTIN FISCHER have agreed on the view that even if determinism were true, we would still have free will.[4]

This can be so for philosophers who have redefined free will as the control condition for **moral responsibility**. If the world is perfectly **pre-determined**, we might have no way to prove it, but we know that moral responsibility is a natural fact of life.

This hypothesis is just to agree with P. F. STRAWSON that even if determinism were true we would not give up the reactive attitudes of moral responsibility, so we can call it the Strawson/Fischer/Mele hypothesis.

In the next chapter, I argue strongly for the need to separate the free will problem from moral responsibility, in order to analyze it and understand it.

The Acquired Freedom of Self-Perfection

Mortimer Adler, in two-volume work, *The Idea of Freedom*, described three freedoms.[5]

One was his *Circumstantial* Freedom of *Self-Realization.*

This is voluntariness, Hobbes-Hume compatibilist **freedom of action**, Berlin's negative liberty.

Another was the *Natural* Freedom of *Self-Determination.*

This is Aristotle's "up to us," origination, alternative possibilities, the **libertarian** freedom of the will explained by my Cogito model.

The third was an *Acquired* Freedom of *Self-Perfection.*

This is becoming morally responsible. the acquired or learned knowledge needed to distinguish right from wrong, good from evil, true from false, etc.

This is the answer to MANUEL VARGAS' question "When do children acquire free will? See page 259 in the next chapter.

4 Personal communication

5 Adler (1958) pp. 127-135, and (1961) p. 225.

Chapter 19

The Separability of Free Will and Moral Responsibility

This chapter on the web
informationphilosopher.com/freedom/separability.html

The Separability of Free Will and Moral Responsibility

I propose four degrees of separation:

1. Separation of "Free" from "Will"
2. Separation of "Responsibility" from "Moral Responsibility"
3. Separation of "Free Will" from "Moral Responsibility"
4. Separation of "Free Will and Moral Responsibility" from "Punishment" - both Retributive and Consequentialist

The fundamental assumption of **two-stage models** for free will is that we can separate the concept "free" from the concept of "will" in order to better understand "free will," as John Locke recommended we do to avoid verbal confusion. He said,

> "I think the question is not proper, whether the will be free, but whether a man be free." [1]

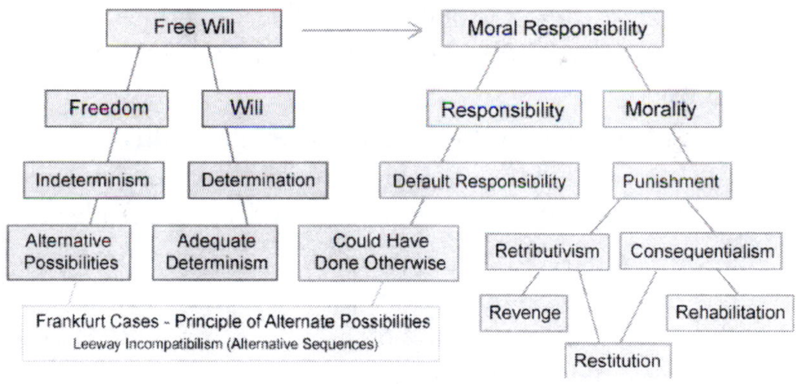

Figure 20-1. Separating Free Will from Moral Responsibility.

We must also separate "**moral responsibility**" from ordinary "responsibility" or simple accountability. If our intentions and decisions caused an action, we are responsible for it, but moral responsibility requires that the action has moral consequences. Immanuel Kant thought that only moral decisions can be free

1 Locke (1959) s. 21.

decisions. Mortimer Adler's *acquired* freedom of *self-perfection* is the idea from Plato to Kant that we are only free when our decisions are for reasons and we are not slaves to our passions (making moral choices rather than satisfying desires).[2] We think that is an "ethical fallacy."

We must go even further and clarify the relationship between free will and moral responsibility. Some philosophers (e.g., John Martin Fischer, Derk Pereboom, and Manuel Vargas) deflect direct discussion of free will and study it only as the "control condition for moral responsibility."

Finally, we should explore the connection between **moral responsibility** and punishment, both backward-looking retributive punishment (revenge or restitution) and forward-looking consequentialism (re-education and rehabilitation).

The Separation of "Free" from "Will"

"Free Will" - in scare quotes - refers to the common but mistaken notion that the adjective "free" modifies the concept "will." In particular, it indicates that the element of chance, one of the two requirements for free will is present in the determination of the will itself.

Critics of "libertarian free will" usually adopt this meaning in order to attack the idea of randomness in our decisions, which they think could not help to make us morally responsible.

But some indeterminism, centered in "torn" decisions between moral and self-interested choices, can be seen as an act "of one's own free will,. Indeterminism helps with a difficult decision, and the agent can take responsibility either way. This is the case of Robert Kane's Self-Forming Actions.

Despite the claim of some professional philosophers that they are better equipped than scientists to make conceptual distinctions and evaluate the cogency of arguments, in my view they have mistakenly conflated the concepts of "free" and "will." They (con)fuse them with the muddled term "free will," despite clear warnings from John Locke that this would lead to confusion.

2 Adler (1961) p. 225.

Locke said very clearly, as had ancients like Lucretius, it is not the will that is free (in the sense of undetermined), it is the mind.

Locke strongly endorsed the ideas of Freedom and Liberty, but he thought it was inappropriate to describe the Will itself as Free. The Will is a Determination. It is the Man who is Free. "I think the question is not proper, whether the will be free, but whether a man be free." "This way of talking, nevertheless, has prevailed, and, as I guess, produced great confusion," he said. It has and still does produce confusion

In chapter XXI, "Of Power," in his *Essay Concerning Human Understanding*, Locke calls the question of Freedom of the Will unintelligible. But for Locke, it is only because the adjective "free" applies to the agent, not to the will, which is determined by the mind, and determines the action.

> "Concerning a man's liberty, there yet, therefore, is raised this further question, Whether a man be free to will? which I think is what is meant, when it is disputed whether the will be free." [3]

> "This, then, is evident, That a man is not at liberty to will, or not to will, anything in his power." [4]

Freedom of the will requires the randomness of absolute chance to break the causal chain of determinism, yet the conscious knowledge that we are **adequately determined** to be responsible for our choices.

Freedom requires some events that are not causally determined by immediately preceding events, events that are unpredictable by any agency, events involving quantum uncertainty. These random events create alternative possibilities for action.

Randomness is the "free" in free will.

In short, there must be a Randomness Requirement, unpredictable chance events that break the causal chain of determinism. Without this chance, our actions are simply the consequences of events in the remote past. This randomness must be located in a place and time that enhances free will, one that does not reduce our will and our actions to pure chance.

3 Locke (1959) s. 22.

4 Locke (1959) s. 24.

(Determinists do not like this requirement.)

Freedom also requires an adequately determined will that chooses or selects from those alternative possibilities. There is effectively nothing uncertain about this choice.

Adequate determinism is the "will" in free will.

So there is also a Determinism Requirement - that our actions be adequately determined by our character and values. This requires that any randomness not be the direct cause of our actions.

(Libertarians do not like this requirement.)

Adequate determinism means that randomness in our thoughts about alternative possibilities does not directly cause our actions.

A random thought can lead to an adequately determined action, for which we can take full responsibility.

We must separate the "free" thoughts from the "willed" actions.

Our thoughts *come to us* freely.

Our actions *come from us* willfully.

The Separation of "Moral" from "Responsibility"

Responsibility for a willed action can be ascribed to an agent because the "adequately" determined will has started a new causal chain that includes the action and its foreseeable consequences.

But responsibility is not exactly the same as moral responsibility. It is merely a prerequisite for moral responsibility.

Responsibility is similar to accountability. Just as an action can said to be a cause of its consequences, so the agent can be held accountable for the action.

Different moral codes, which are the business of ethicists, may have different degrees of moral responsibility for the same actions and its consequences.

We must separate "moral" from "responsibility."

The Separation of "Free Will" from "Moral Responsibility"

From the earliest beginnings, the problem of "free will" has been intimately connected with the question of moral responsibility. Most of the ancient thinkers on the problem were trying to show that we humans have control over our decisions, that our actions "depend on us", and that they are not pre-determined by fate, by arbitrary gods,[5] by logical necessity, or by a natural causal determinism.

John Martin Fischer says that some philosophers want to relate these two very strongly:

> "Some philosophers do not distinguish between freedom and moral responsibility. Put a bit more carefully, they tend to begin with the notion of moral responsibility, and "work back" to a notion of freedom; this notion of freedom is not given independent content (separate from the analysis of moral responsibility). For such philosophers, 'freedom' refers to whatever conditions are involved in choosing or acting in such a way as to be morally responsible." [6]

The question of the existence of "free will" is an empirical and factual question about the nature of the mind. It does not depend in any way on the existence of "moral responsibility," which is a question for ethics.

Manuel Vargas' Question

Here is an example of the kind of problems caused by conflating free will with moral responsibility. Manuel Vargas follows John Martin Fischer in connecting free will to moral responsibility, then he wonders how and when children can suddenly acquire free will at a certain age. Vargas says:

> "Consider the question of how we go from being unfree agents to free agents. This is a puzzle faced by all accounts of responsibility, but there is something pressing about it in the case of

5 This was Democritus' reason for inventing determinism. See Chapter. 7.
6 Fischer (2005) p. xxiii

> libertarianism. As children we either had the indeterministic structures favored by your favorite version of libertarianism or we lacked them. If we lacked them as children, we might wonder how we came to get those structures. We might also wonder what the evidence is for thinking that we do develop said structures. Suppose the libertarian offers us an answer to these questions, and the other empirical challenges I raised in the prior section. We would still face another puzzle. What, exactly, does the indeterminism add? What follows in this section is not so much a metaphysical concern as it is a normative concern. It is a concern about what work the indeterminism does in libertarianism, apart from providing a way to preserve our default self-image as deliberators with genuine, metaphysically robust alternative possibilities." [7]

Children have free will from birth. It is part of their biological makeup. It is **moral responsibility** that they "come to get" at some age in their moral development as adults. [8]

We must separate "free will" from "moral responsibility."

The Separation of both "Free Will and Moral Responsibility" from Retributive Punishment and Consequentialist Punishment

Liberal humanitarian thinkers who see that retributive punishment is sometimes cruel and unproductive should not argue that punishment is not "deserved" *because* free will does not exist.

There are excellent stand-alone reasons for preferring rehabilitation and education to retributive vengeance.

Some philosophers and many scientists argue that humans are just a form of animal. They decry human *exceptionalism*.

They say that humans lack free will *because* animals lack it. The idea of no free will in animals, that they are completely determined, was the old religious argument that God had given man the special gift of free will.

7 Fischer (2007) p. 148.
8 See Chapter 19.

Some philosophers say that animals lack moral responsibility, but humans have it. This is now being questioned in many sociobiological studies of animal morality.

Whether man - and higher animals too - have free will is an empirical scientific question.[9] Whether they have moral responsibility is a social and cultural question.

The scientific question is being answered in the affirmative. Even the lowest forms of animal now are known to have *behavioral* freedom. That is to say, their actions are not **pre-determined**, not even **determined** reactions to external stimuli. They are stochastic beings that originate actions, as shown by MARTIN HEISENBERG. [10]

The social and cultural questions should not make free will depend on sensible arguments against vengeance and retributive punishment. This is to get the cart before the horse.

Equating free will with moral responsibility, then to use spurious arguments to deny free will, and thus to deny moral responsibility - in order to oppose punishment - is fine humanism but poor philosophy, and terrible science.

We must separate "free will and moral responsibility" from punishment, whether retributive or consequentialist.

Philosophers who call themselves "naturalist" especially like to make the argument that because humans are animals, and because animals are regarded as having no free will, that humans have no moral responsibility.

Naturalists do not separate free will and moral responsibility. Let's consider naturalism in the next chapter.

9 Balaguer (2009)

10 Heisenberg (2009) See Chapter 16.

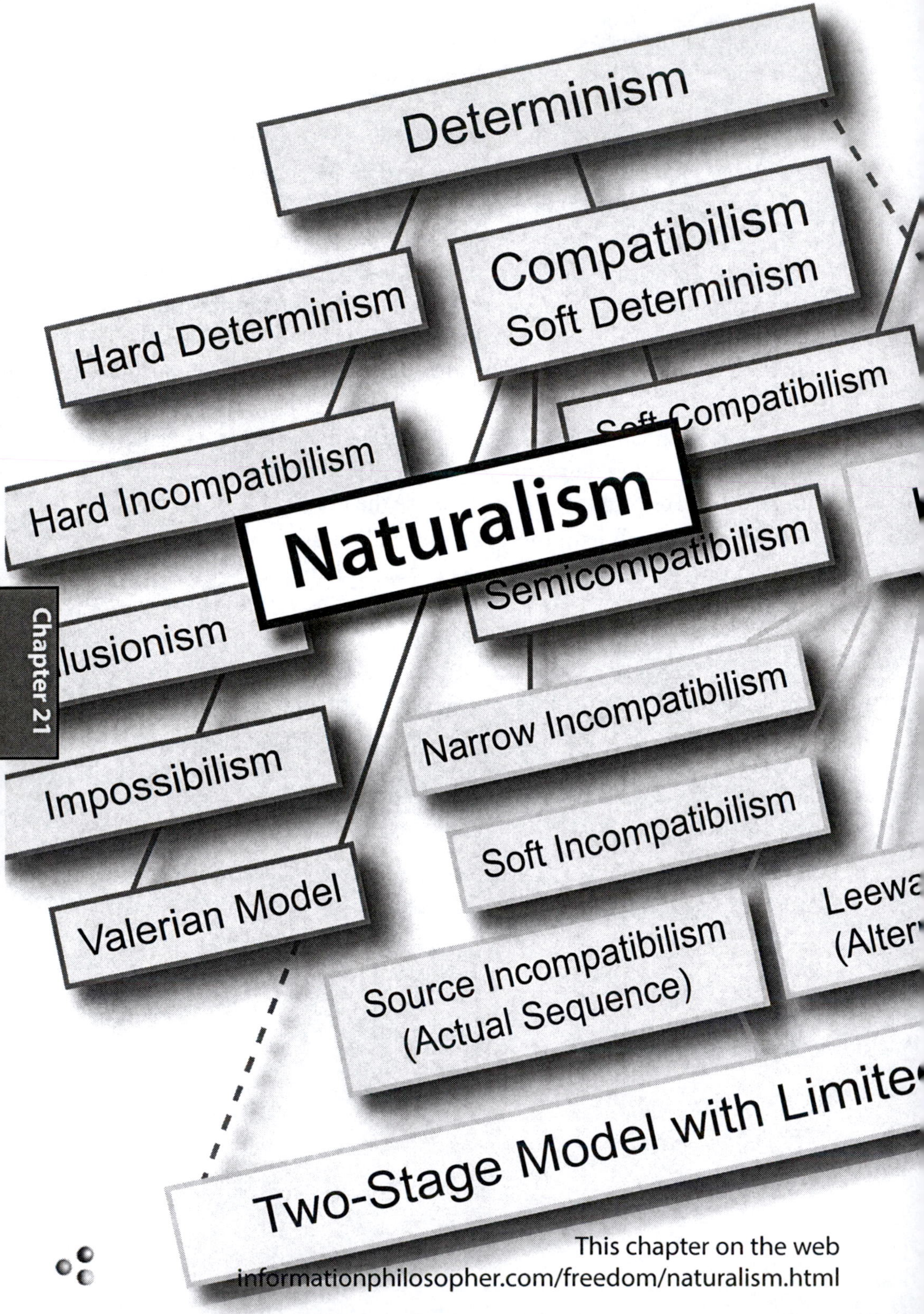

Determinism

Hard Determinism

Compatibilism
Soft Determinism

Soft Compatibilism

Hard Incompatibilism

Naturalism

Semicompatibilism

llusionism

Narrow Incompatibilism

Impossibilism

Soft Incompatibilism

Valerian Model

Leewa
(Alter

Source Incompatibilism
(Actual Sequence)

Two-Stage Model with Limite

Chapter 21

This chapter on the web
informationphilosopher.com/freedom/naturalism.html

Naturalism

Naturalism in philosophy, as it is in science, is the search for explanations that involve only Nature, ones that in particular do not involve supernatural ideas.

Metaphysical or ontological naturalism is the idea that there is nothing in the world but Nature. This leads to difficulties as to the existential status of ideas, abstract concepts like justice, and entities like numbers or a geometric circle.

Methodological naturalism accepts as explanations only arguments based on natural phenomena. If and when abstract ideas are properly understood, it will be because they have natural explanations.

Ethical naturalism moves the question of values and their origin outward from early humanist views, first to biological explanations (the evolution of ethics in higher organisms), but ultimately to the universe as a whole. Moral skeptics from Thomas Hobbes to Friedrich Nietzsche see ethics as invented for reasons of self-interest in a social contract.

Natural religion is an attempt to explain religious beliefs about the creation of the universe in wholly natural terms. Though some see this as a conflicted and futile attempt to naturalize supernaturalism, the philosophy of religion began in earnest with DAVID HUME's *Dialogues Concerning Natural Religion* and *The Natural History of Religion*.

Naturalism has a long history in the free will debates, beginning with Hume's arguments in the *Treatise on Human Nature* and the *Enquiries* that humans have "natural beliefs" that are prior to experience and shape our perceptions.

Anticipating IMMANUEL KANT's synthetic *a priori*, Hume argued that a skeptical view of empiricism prevented us from knowing basic things like causality and the external world, but that a "natural belief" in causality and the external world could not be negated by any skeptical arguments.

Hume the Skeptic vs. Hume the Naturalist

Hume hoped to build a science of Human Nature modeled on Isaac Newton's *Principia*, which had become the canonical model for all science. But Hume's reintroduction of mitigated academic skepticism made any science at all problematic. Hume's skepticism delivered a fatal blow to the quest for certainty.

Logical arguments can prove theorems in formal systems, but they cannot establish knowledge about the physical world, which requires empirical and contingent observations and experiments.

Epistemological theories that all knowledge was based on reasoning about sense data, perceived by a mind that began as a blank slate, run into the criticism that we can only know those sense data, and not the "things themselves" in the external world that are producing the perceptions.

For for the Scottish School of philosophy, which strongly influenced Hume, there are natural transcendental beliefs could trump reason. They are prior to reason. Hume argued that we could not reason without beliefs, desires, and passions. Indeed, he argued that an act of will was driven by beliefs and desires, never by reason, which was merely an instrument to evaluate various means to our ends. This was not unlike the position of Scholastic philosophers like Thomas Aquinas.

Natural beliefs that Hume felt could not be denied by the most clever reasoned arguments include ideas such as the principle of uniformity and the existence of the external world. These were incorporated by Kant into his transcendental theory that the mind imposed categories of understanding on the world. Kant's "synthetic *a priori*" claimed to establish certain truths about the world that could be known without empirical, *a posteriori*, studies of the world.

Among Kant's attempts at synthetic *a priori* truths were Euclidean geometry and determinism. The discovery of non-Euclidean geometries shows us that there is nothing that can be proved logically about the physical world.

Kant's argument that we must limit reason to make room for beliefs seems to me to be a simple extension of Hume's view that some beliefs necessarily precede any reason. Both the Humean and Kantian projects are best seen as trying to establish morality in an age of empirical and deterministic science, in short, to derive "ought" from "is."

PETER F. STRAWSON's influential argument that we would not give up our natural attitudes toward moral responsibility, even if we are presented with a powerful logical argument for the existence of determinism, is to me an example of applied Humean naturalism.

Freedom and Values

Today some of the most strongly held scientific beliefs are just assumptions or axioms that are tested by their explanatory power in empirical science.[1] But science and pure reason seem unable to deal with the fundamental questions of free will and moral responsibility, which for Hume and Kant (and later LUDWIG WITTGENSTEIN) were all-important.

Hume and Hobbes were the two leading compatibilists of their times, believing that free will was compatible with strict determinism. Hobbes categorically denied and Hume seriously questioned the reality of absolute **chance**. For them, chance was the result of human ignorance. Chance is an epistemic question, not an ontological problem.

But in contrast to Hobbes' moral skepticism and the supremacy of self-interest, Hume hoped to establish the foundations of a morality based on natural moral sentiments in *An Enquiry concerning the Principles of Morals*, Part II

> "Self-love is a principle in human nature of such extensive energy, and the interest of each individual is, in general, so closely connected with that of the community, that those philosophers were excusable, who fancied, that all our concern for the public might be resolved into a concern for our own happiness and preservation. They saw every moment, instances of

1 See the Free Will Axiom in Chapter 14.

approbation or blame, satisfaction or displeasure towards characters and actions; they denominated the objects of these sentiments, virtues, or vices; they observed, that the former had a tendency to encrease the happiness, and the latter the misery of mankind; they asked, whether it were possible that we could have any general concern for society, or any disinterested resentment of the welfare or injury of others; they found it simpler to consider all these sentiments as modifications of self-love; and they discovered a pretence, at least, for this unity of principle, in that close union of interest, which is so observable between the public and each individual.

"But notwithstanding this frequent confusion of interests, it is easy to attain what natural philosophers, after Lord Bacon, have affected to call the experimentum crucis, or that experiment, which points out the right way in any doubt or ambiguity. We have found instances, in which private interest was separate from public; in which it was even contrary; And yet we observed the moral sentiment to continue, notwithstanding this disjunction of interests. And wherever these distinct interests sensibly concurred, we always found a sensible encrease of the sentiment, and a more warm affection to virtue, and detestation of vice, or what we properly call, gratitude and revenge. Compelled by these instances, we must renounce the theory, which accounts for every moral sentiment by the principle of self-love. We must adopt a more public affection, and allow, that the interests of society are not, even on their own account, entirely indifferent to us. Usefulness is only a tendency to a certain end; and it is a contradiction in terms, that any thing pleases as means to an end, where the end itself no wise affects us. If usefulness, therefore, be a source of moral sentiment, and if this usefulness be not always considered with a reference to self; it follows, that every thing, which contributes to the happiness of society recommends itself directly to our approbation and good-will. Here is a principle, which accounts, in great part, for the origin of morality: And what need we seek for abstruse and remote systems, when there occurs one so obvious and natural?" [2]

2 Hume (1975)

Hume gives the argument for moral sentiment as superior to reason or judgment in Appendix I, *Concerning Moral Sentiment*, though reason helps with calculations of utility.

> "If the foregoing hypothesis be received, it will now be easy for us to determine the question first started, concerning the general principles of morals; and though we postponed the decision of that question, lest it should then involve us in intricate speculations, which are unfit for moral discourses, we may resume it at present, and examine how far either reason or sentiment enters into all decisions of praise or censure.
>
> "One principal foundation of moral praise being supposed to lie in the usefulness of any quality or action; it is evident, that reason must enter for a considerable share in all decisions of this kind; since nothing but that faculty can instruct us in the tendency of qualities and actions, and point out their beneficial consequences to society and to their possessors...And a very accurate reason or judgment is often requisite, to give the true determination, amidst such intricate doubts arising from obscure or opposite utilities.
>
> "But though reason, when fully assisted and improved, be sufficient to instruct us in the pernicious or useful tendency of qualities and actions; it is not alone sufficient to produce any moral blame or approbation. Utility is only a tendency to a certain end; and were the end totally indifferent to us, we should feel the same indifference towards the means. It is requisite a sentiment should here display itself, in order to give a preference to the useful above the pernicious tendencies. This sentiment can be no other than a feeling for the happiness of mankind, and a resentment of their misery; since these are the different ends which virtue and vice have a tendency to promote. Here, therefore, reason instructs us in the several tendencies of actions, and humanity makes a distinction in favour of those which are useful and beneficial." [3]

In the famous passage where Hume shows that "Ought" cannot be derived from "Is," he again makes the case for natural passions,

3 Hume (1975) Part II

motives, volitions, thoughts, and feelings as the source for sentiments of morality. There is no matter of fact discernible by reason alone.(Treatise, Book III, Sect I)

> "Nor does this reasoning only prove, that morality consists not in any relations, that are the objects of science; but if examin'd, will prove with equal certainty, that it consists not in any matter of fact, which can be discover'd by the understanding. This is the second part of our argument; and if it can be made evident, we may conclude, that morality is not an object of reason. But can there be any difficulty in proving, that vice and virtue are not matters of fact, whose existence we can infer by reason? Take any action allow'd to be vicious: Wilful murder, for instance. Examine it in all lights, and see if you can find that matter of fact, or real existence, which you call vice. In which-ever way you take it, you find only certain passions, motives, volitions and thoughts. There is no other matter of fact in the case. The vice entirely escapes you, as long as you consider the object. You never can find it, till you turn your reflection into your own breast, and find a sentiment of disapprobation, which arises in you, towards this action. Here is a matter of fact; but `tis the object of feeling, not of reason. It lies in yourself, not in the object. So that when you pronounce any action or character to be vicious, you mean nothing, but that from the constitution of your nature you have a feeling or sentiment of blame from the contemplation of it. Vice and virtue, therefore, may be compar'd to sounds, colours, heat and cold, which, according to modern philosophy, are not qualities in objects, but perceptions in the mind: And this discovery in morals, like that other in physics, is to be regarded as a considerable advancement of the speculative sciences; tho', like that too, it has little or no influence on practice. Nothing can be more real, or concern us more, than our own sentiments of pleasure and uneasiness; and if these be favourable to virtue, and unfavourable to vice, no more can be requisite to the regulation of our conduct and behaviour." [4]

Hume the Skeptic doubts "ought" can be derived from "is." Hume the Naturalist has no such problem. Here is the famous passage in which he criticizes previous philosophers.

4 Hume (1978) p. 468.

> "I cannot forbear adding to these reasonings an observation, which may, perhaps, be found of some importance. In every system of morality, which I have hitherto met with, I have always remark'd, that the author proceeds for some time in the ordinary way of reasoning, and establishes the being of a God, or makes observations concerning human affairs; when of a sudden I am surpriz'd to find, that instead of the usual copulations of propositions, is, and is not, I meet with no proposition that is not connected with an ought, or an ought not. This change is imperceptible; but is, however, of the last consequence. For as this ought, or ought not, expresses some new relation or affirmation, 'tis necessary that it shou'd be observ'd and explain'd; and at the same time that a reason should be given, for what seems altogether inconceivable, how this new relation can be a deduction from others, which are entirely different from it. But as authors do not commonly use this precaution, I shall presume to recommend it to the readers; and am persuaded, that this small attention wou'd subvert all the vulgar systems of morality, and let us see, that the distinction of vice and virtue is not founded merely on the relations of objects, nor is perceiv'd by reason." [5]

Long before Immanuel Kant, David Hume is putting limits on Reason to make room for natural Belief. Indeed, there seems to be very little in Kant in this regard that was not already present in some form in Hume.

Peter F. Strawson's Natural Moral Responsibility

Perhaps the most important recent discussion of naturalism and free will is P. F. Strawson's 1962 essay *Freedom and Resentment*, which changed the subject from the truth of determinism or free will to the Humean claim that moral attitudes exist quite independently of the reasoned "truth" of determinism or the free-will thesis.

This is of course also Hume's position, since no reasoned argument can cause us to abandon our natural beliefs that lead to sympathy with others and feelings of gratitude and resentment.

5 Hume (1978) p. 468.

Surprisingly, this famous Strawson essay has only a single reference to Hume, a footnote on Hume's denial of any "rational" justification of induction. So, says Strawson, there is no rational denial of moral responsibility, based on what he calls the reactive attitudes. This argument leads directly to JOHN MARTIN FISCHER's semi-compatibilism.

Strawson arrays "pessimists" - genuine moral skeptics - against "optimists" - apparently compatibilists - and hopes to reconcile them:

> "Some philosophers say they do not know what the thesis of determinism is. Others say, or imply, that they do know what it is. Of these, some — the pessimists perhaps — hold that if the thesis is true, then the concepts of moral obligation and responsibility really have no application, and the practices of punishing and blaming, of expressing moral condemnation and approval, are really unjustified. Others—the optimists perhaps—hold that these concepts and practices in no way lose their raison d'être if the thesis of determinism is true. Some hold even that the justification of these concepts and practices requires the truth of the thesis. There is another opinion which is less frequently voiced: the opinion, it might be said, of the genuine moral sceptic." [6]

Note Strawson uses the **standard argument** *against* free will

> "This is that the notions of moral guilt, of blame, of moral responsibility are inherently confused and that we can see this to be so if we consider the consequences either of the truth of determinism or of its falsity. The holders of this opinion agree with the pessimists that these notions lack application if determinism is true, and add simply that they also lack it if determinism is false. If I am asked which of these parties I belong to, I must say it is the first of all, the party of those who do not know what the thesis of determinism is. But this does not stop me from having some sympathy with the others, and a wish to reconcile them." [7]

In his 1985 book *Skepticism and Naturalism*, Strawson describes two naturalisms, a "reductive naturalism" (which he also

---

6 Strawson (1962) p. 1.
7 *ibid.*

calls strict or hard) and another naturalism, perhaps his own view (which he calls liberal, catholic, or soft).

He connects reductive naturalism to skepticism and scientism, which he feels denies some evident truths and realities (such as the existence of the world), but thinks the liberal naturalist might be accused of fostering illusions or propagating myths. He then applies these two approaches to his reactive moral attitudes.

> "The area I have in mind is that of those attitudes and feelings, or "sentiments," as we used to say, toward ourselves and others, in respect of our and their actions, which can be grouped together under the heads of moral attitudes and judgments and personal reactive attitudes and are indissolubly linked with that sense of agency or freedom or responsibility which we feel in ourselves and attribute to others.
>
> "The fundamental thought is that once we see people and their doings (including ourselves and our doings) objectively, as what they are, namely as natural objects and happenings, occurrences in the course of nature." [8]

Again, neither determinism nor chance can provide free will

> "— whether causally determined occurrences or chance occurrences — then the veil of illusion cast over them by moral attitudes and reactions must, or should, slip away. What simply happens in nature may be matter for rejoicing or regret, but not for gratitude or resentment, for moral approval or blame, or for moral self-approval or remorse.
>
> "Attempts to counter such reasoning by defending the reality of some special condition of freedom or spontaneity or self-determination which human beings enjoy and which supplies a justifying ground for our moral attitudes and judgments have not been notably successful; for no one has been able to state intelligibly what such a condition of freedom, supposed to be necessary to ground our moral attitudes and judgments, would actually consist in.

---

8 Strawson (1985) p. 31.

> "Such attempts at counter-argument are misguided; and not merely because they are unsuccessful or unintelligible. They are misguided also for the reasons for which counter-arguments to other forms of skepticism have been seen to be misguided; i.e. because the arguments they are directed against are totally inefficacious. We can no more be reasoned out of our proneness to personal and moral reactive attitudes in general than we can be reasoned out of our belief in the existence of body." [9]

A few years after Strawson's naturalistic arguments for the moral sentiments that he called the reactive attitudes, WILLARD VAN ORMAN QUINE argued that epistemology should be naturalized.

In his essay *Two Dogmas of Empiricism*, Quine argued that the distinction between analytic (*a priori*) and synthetic (*a posteriori*) knowledge was moot because ultimately the "truth" or validity of analytic statements depends on their applying in the world.

Naturalized epistemology has been called "scientism" because it makes science the last word on whether we know what we think we know. And Quine initially agreed with BERTRAND RUSSELL that "what science cannot discover, mankind cannot know."

Epistemological naturalism today assumes that science is the final arbiter of public knowledge arrived at by consensus of the community of inquirers. This was CHARLES SANDERS PEIRCE's idea of pragmatic knowledge. But it also admits some private knowledge that may be unsuitable for such public empirical verification.

9 Strawson (1985) p. 32.

The Center for Naturalism

We should mention here Tom Clark's Center for Naturalism,[10] most of whose members deny that individuals have ultimate responsibility for their actions (in the sense of origination, i.e., being the self-caused authors of their actions) and assert that free will is an illusion. Nevertheless, the Center believes that individuals should be held morally responsible for their actions, and should be given appropriate rewards or sanctions, to help control behavior. So their **moral responsibility** position is similar to that of David Hume, and perhaps to John Martin Fischer's **semicompatibilism**, although Fischer is agnostic on the free will question, and Hume's free will is compatible with determinism.

However, unlike Hume or Fischer, they take a strongly revisionist position with respect to our responsibility practices. They agree with philosophers such as Joshua Greene and Derk Pereboom that in light of determinism it's difficult to justify strong moral desert or retributive punishment, in which case our criminal justice system and our approach to behavioral health (e.g., to addiction, mental illness and obesity) should be premised on a humane consequentialism informed by a respect for human rights.

10 www.naturalism.org

This chapter on the web
informationphilosopher.com/freedom/creativity.html

Creativity

Creativity requires that new information come into the world. It must be information that was not implicit in earlier states of the world, determined by the "fixed past and the laws of nature."

Human creativity requires the same freedom of thought and action needed for free will in my **Cogito** Model.

If everything created was **pre-determined**, then all the works of Mozart would have been implicit in the first beat of an aboriginal drum. Einstein's $E=mc^2$ would have been already there at the time of the first Aristotle syllogism.

Cosmological systems are creative, because atoms and molecules did not exist in the first three minutes of the universe. And the great astrophysical structures made from atoms, like galaxies, stars, and planets, did not exist in the first million years.

Biological systems are creative. Darwinian evolution accounts for the creation of new species of organisms.

Many organisms create informational structures outside of themselves, in the world, like beehives, bird nests, and beaver dams.

Humans are the most conspicuous creators and consumers of new informational structures, altering the face of planet Earth. And they create the constructed ideal world of thought, of intellect, of spirit, including the laws of nature, in which we humans play a role as co-creator.

All creative processes have the same underlying physics as the cosmic creative process.

Biological processes add the element of natural selection. This is accomplished by something Jacques Monod called the teleonomic information, the purposive element in all life.

> "This allows us to put forward at least the principle of a definition of a species' "teleonomic level." All teleonomic structures and performances can be regarded as corresponding to a certain quantity of information which must be transmitted for these

> structures to be realized and these performances accomplished. Let us call this quantity "teleonomic information." A given species' "teleonomic level" may then be said to correspond to the quantity of information which, on the average and per individual, must be transferred to assure the generation-to-generation transmission of the specific content of reproductive invariance." [1]

Blind Variation and Selective Retention

The best known theory of **creativity** is the two-stage model proposed by DONALD CAMPBELL, who investigated creative thought and described it as a process involving the generation of "blind" variations of ideas, followed by a selective retention of good ideas.

Campbell proposed that his Blind Variation and Selective Retention (BVSR) could also explain the development of human knowledge, including inventions and the increase in scientific knowledge. I agree that all human knowledge creation is the same two-stage process that explains human freedom.

Creativity and Free Will are two sides of the same coin.

BVSR is itself a variation on common-sense and ancient notions of trial-and-error, and, like my free will model, it seems directly inspired by the two-step process of biological evolution, but Campbell sees it as more general than these. He says BVSR is applicable to organic evolution, the learning process in individual organisms, and the social construction of knowledge.

BVSR clearly describes my two-stage **Cogito** model for free will. Other biological examples include the immune system and quality control in protein/enzyme factories.

But DEAN KEITH SIMONTON, a social psychologist who has investigated the origins of and evolution of genius, creativity, and leadership., is wary of identifying "blind" with the chance of two-stage models for free will. [2]

1 Monod (1971), Chance and Necessity, p. 14.
2 Simonton (2004)

Simonton has researched the personal, social, cultural, developmental, and cognitive factors that contribute to greatness in the arts, the humanities, and especially the sciences.

He uses the tools of historiometrics, a combination of personal histories, biographies, and psychometrics, to build theories and principles of human behavior that might account for the development of pre-eminent individuals.

But Simonton is cautious about identifying the variation principle with irreducible ontological chance, because that concept is still controversial in the social sciences. Recall that the founders of "social physics," who produced the rise of statistical thinking in the nineteenth century, did not believe that chance was real. It is merely epistemic, they maintained. [3]

Simonton hopes to establish "blindness" as the main requirement, viz., that the creative process cannot see ahead - sightedness is antithetical to creativity, he says. [4]

Then, because randomness is inherently blind, there should be no problem incorporating chance once blindness is established.

In biological evolution, the original blind variation is preserved by genetic inheritance. In learning, random variations are preserved by individual organisms memories. In social knowledge, chance variation of ideas get preserved as new inventions, new works of art, and new scientific theories. Whether any of these get selected and retained depends on their pragmatic usefulness to the species, the individual and the society.

The idea that units of cultural knowledge undergo variation and then are selected for is perhaps better known from the recent work of RICHARD DAWKINS, who named the self-replicating unit of cultural evolution the "meme" in his 1976 book *The Selfish Gene*.

BVSR is widely used in cybernetics. For example, the "general problem solver" programs of ALLAN NEWELL and HERBERT SIMON involve two stages, first the blind generation of theorems and then testing of the theorems for validity.

3 See Quételet and Buckle in Chapter 7, p. 91.
4 personal communication.

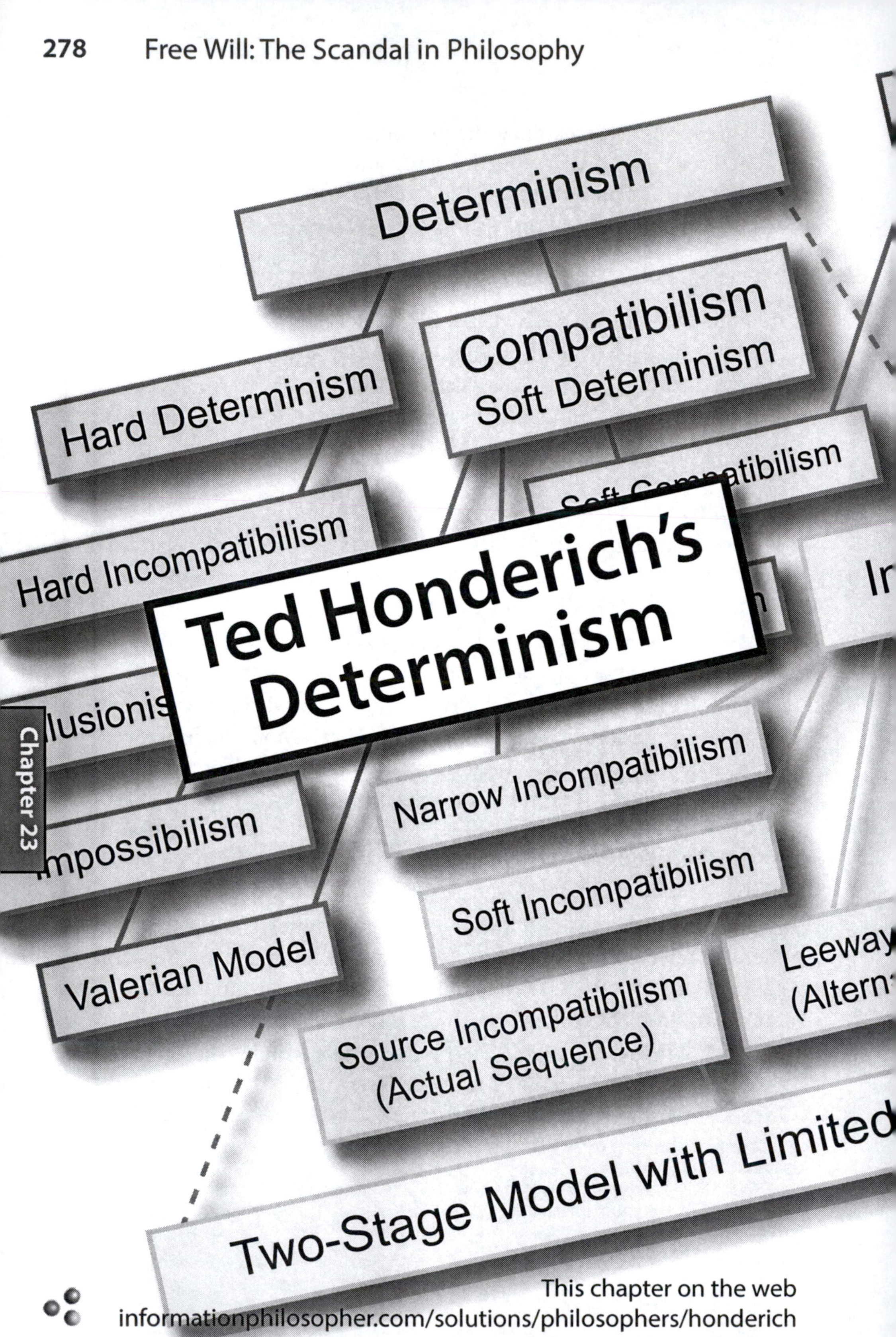

Ted Honderich's Determinism

This chapter on the web
informationphilosopher.com/solutions/philosophers/honderich

Ted Honderich's Determinism

TED HONDERICH is the principal spokesman for strict physical **causality** and "**hard determinism**."

He has written more widely (with excursions into quantum mechanics, neuroscience, and consciousness), more deeply, and certainly more extensively than most of his colleagues on the problem of **free will**.

Unlike most of his determinist colleagues specializing in free will, Honderich has not succumbed to the easy path of **compatibilism** by simply declaring that the free will we have (and should want, says DANIEL DENNETT) is completely consistent with **determinism**, namely a Humean "voluntarism" or "**freedom of action**" in which our will is completely caused by prior events.

Nor does Honderich go down the path of **incompatibilism**, looking for non-physical substances, dualist forms of agency, or gifts of God. He does not simply identify freedom with Epicurean **chance**, as have many scientists with ideas of brain mechanisms amplifying quantum mechanical indeterminism to help with the uncaused "origination" of actions and decisions. [1]

Honderich does not claim to have found a solution to the problem of free will or determinism, but he does claim to have confronted the *consequences of determinism*.[2] He is "dismayed" because the truth of determinism requires that we give up "origination" with its promise of an open future, restricting - though not eliminating - our "life hopes."

Unlike many of his hard determinist colleagues, who appear to welcome determinism and enjoy describing belief in free will as an **illusion**, Honderich is unique in his passionate sense of real loss. We might have been the author of our own actions, he says, we could have **done otherwise**, and thus be held accountable and **morally responsible** in a way more acceptable to common sense.

1 informationphilosopher.com/freedom/free_will_mechanisms.html
2 Honderich (1990)

Honderich describes the main life hope that is lost as a future we can make for ourselves.

> "We have a kind of life-hope which is incompatible with a belief in determinism. An open future, a future we can make for ourselves, is one of which determinism isn't true.
>
> "Suppose you become convinced of the truth of our theory of determinism. Becoming really convinced will not be easy, for several reasons. But try now to imagine a day when you do come to believe determinism fully. What would the upshot be? It would almost certainly be dismay. Your response to determinism in connection with the hope would be dismay. If you really were persuaded of determinism, the hope would collapse.
>
> "This is so because such a hope has a necessary part or condition on which the rest of it depends. This is the image of origination. There can be no such hope if all the future is just effects of effects. It is for this reason, I think, that many people have found determinism to be a black thing. JOHN STUART MILL felt it as an incubus, and, to speak for myself, it has certainly got me down in the past." [3]

Though he is its foremost champion, I find it most extraordinary that Honderich characterizes determinism as a "black thing" and as what JOHN STUART MILL called an "incubus." Determinism gives him "dismay." he says.

In my readings of hundreds of philosophers and scientists on the problem of free will, I have found none with such deep heartfelt feelings and frank openness about the implications of their work for the state of humanity.

The Failure of Compatibilism and Incompatibilism

In Honderich's article for Kane's *Oxford Handbook of Free Will*, he says "Determinism is True, Compatibilism and Incompatibilism are False."

3 Honderich (2002) p. 94.

Honderich faults both the Compatibilists and Incompatibilists on three counts.

First, he says that **moral responsibility** is not all that is at stake, there are personal feelings, reactive attitudes, problems of knowledge, and rationalizing punishment with ideas of limited responsibility.

Second, these problems can not be resolved by logical "proofs" nor by linguistic analyses of propositions designed to show "free" and "determined" are logically compatible.

And third, he faults their simplistic idea that one or the other of them must be right.

Furthermore, unlike some of his colleagues, Honderich does not completely dismiss **indeterminism** and considers the suggestion of "near-determinism." He says,

> "Maybe it should have been called determinism-where-it-matters. It allows that there is or may be some indeterminism but only at what is called the micro-level of our existence, the level of the small particles of our bodies." [4]

Despite this openness to indeterminism, in his book *On Determinism and Freedom*, Honderich has an extensive discussion of Quantum Theory in which he says

> "Does Quantum Theory as interpreted have some clause, hitherto unheard of, that its random events occur only in such places as to make us morally responsible in a certain sense? This objection of inconsistency, perhaps, is less effective with some uncommitted philosophers because they do not really take the philosophers of origination seriously. If it really were accepted as true that a random event could get in between the question and the intention, with great effect, then it would have to be accepted that one could get in between the intention and the lie, with as much effect. Any attempt to exclude the possibility is bound to be fatally ad hoc." [5]

---

4 Honderich (2003) p. 5.
5 Honderich (2005) p. 125.

Here Honderich puts his finger on the stumbling block that has prevented philosophers and scientists from accepting an amplified quantum event as the source of indeterminism in a decision.

It is highly unlikely that individual quantum events could be synchronized and located precisely, near or inside the right neurons for example. The "master switch amplifier" concept of Arthur Holly Compton seems only to have been offered as a source of randomness centered in the second stage of the decisions themselves.

Robert Kane recognized this problem in his early work, when he thought he needed a random event precisely at the moment of his Self-Forming Actions (SFAs). Today he sees ever-present noise in the brain as providing the required indeterminism.

Kane described the problem,

> "We do not know if something similar goes on in the brain of cortically developed creatures like ourselves, but I suspect it must if libertarian theories are to succeed. The main problem is the one addressed by Eccles of locating the master switch and the mechanisms of amplification. We have no substantial empirical evidence on these matters (especially regarding the master switch), merely speculation, and libertarian theories may fail dismally at this juncture. But there is much to be learned yet about the brain; and research exists...suggesting that master switch plus amplifier processes play more roles in the functioning of organisms than was previously supposed." [6]

Honderich is right that quantum events do not "occur only in such places as to make us morally responsible," as various free will mechanisms have proposed.[7] But the "inconsistency" is not with the quantum mechanics, just its misapplication by philosophers.

In my Cogito model, I depend on the fact that quantum noise is ever present. It just normally averages out in macroscopic situations. Microscopic situations, like the storage and retrieval of information in the neurons of the mind/brain, are much more susceptible to noise. Information structures in computers, and in

6 Kane (1985) p. 168.
7 informationphilosopher.com/freedom/free_will_mechanisms.html

modern digital media devices like CDs and DVDs, are also susceptible to random noise. Media devices, and perhaps the brain, have elaborate error detection and suppression capabilities.

On Determinism

Honderich has long defended what he calls the "truth" of determinism. I agree that there must be "**adequate determinism**" in our choices and actions for us to take **moral responsibility**. I have tried to convince Honderich that all we lose with my "adequate determinism" is the truly grand, but unsupportable, idea of **pre-determinism**, namely that every event and all prior events form a causal chain back to the origin of the universe. Indeed, in *On Determinism and Freedom* (p. 6), Honderich calls for "the truth of a conceptually adequate determinism." [8]

In some of his earliest thoughts, Honderich wrote in 1973, in his essay "One Determinism," that determinism may preclude responsibility (as David Hume also had feared) ..

> "States of the brain are, in the first place, effects, the effects of other physical states. Many states of the brain, secondly, are correlates. A particular state accompanied my experience the other moment of thinking about having walked a lot on Hampstead Heath, and a like state accompanies each like experience: each of my experiences of thinking of having walked a lot on Hampstead Heath. Given our present concern, it is traditional that the most important experiences are decidings and choosings. Some states of the brain, thirdly, are causes, both of other states of the brain and also of certain movements of one's body. The latter are actions. Some are relatively simple while others, such as speech acts and bits of ritual, depend on settings of convention and have complex histories. Simple or complex, however, all actions are movements, or of course stillnesses, caused by states of the brain. It follows from these three premisses, about states of the brain as effects, as correlates and as causes, that on every occasion when we act, we can only act as in fact we do. It follows too that we are not responsible for our actions, and, what is most fundamental, that we do not possess selves of a certain character." [9]

8 Honderich (2005) p. 6.
9 Honderich (1973) p. 187.

Most compatibilists and determinists since Hobbes and Hume never mention the fact that a causal chain of events going back before our birth would not provide the kind of liberty that common sense expects But Hume, like Honderich, frankly admits (in a passage rarely quoted by compatibilist philosophers) that such a causal chain would be a serious objection to his theory.

> "I pretend not to have obviated or removed all objections to this theory, with regard to necessity and liberty. I can foresee other objections, derived from topics which have not here been treated of. It may be said, for instance, that, if voluntary actions be subjected to the same laws of necessity with the operations of matter, there is a continued chain of necessary causes, pre-ordained and pre-determined, reaching from the original cause of all to every single volition, of every human creature. No contingency anywhere in the universe; no indifference; no liberty. While we act, we are, at the same time, acted upon." [10]

To escape this objection, we might imagine that Hume wanted some kind of agent-causal freedom in voluntarist acts?

The Consequences of Determinism

Honderich's great work is the 750-page *The Theory of Determinism*, Oxford, 1988, later broken into two volumes, of which one is *The Consequences of Determinism*. Honderich claims to have solved the "problem of the consequences of determinism."

Note that this is not the problem of free will and determinism. Honderich believes determinism is true.

Rather than discuss the problem of free will directly, or even indirectly via the familiar though muddled terms determinism, compatibilism, incompatibilism, and libertarianism, Honderich introduces new concepts and still more new terminology.

In the style of Peter F. Strawson, Honderich's interest is in our feelings and attitudes toward the truth of determinism, as what he calls our "life-hopes" are altered by belief in determinism.

One hope is that we should be able to originate the actions affecting our future life. The truth of determinism, which denies

10 Hume (1975) p. 99.

the freedom to originate actions, might give rise to a "sad" attitude of "dismay." In this respect, Honderich regards determinism as a "black thing." He calls *dismay* the "sad" attitude toward determinism.

But we can have another "tough" attitude, that of *intransigence*, in that our hope involving belief in "voluntariness" is consistent with determinism. This kind of voluntarism goes back to THOMAS HOBBES and **freedom of action.**[11] With his term intransigence, Honderich wants us to resist compromise with ideas like origination. But he seems to imply that moral responsibility can be reconciled with determinism.

Finally, Honderich argues that we can choose the attitude of *affirmation* rather than *intransigence* or *dismay.*

It might appear that Honderich's terms dismay and intransigence roughly correlate with the ideas of

- incompatibilist libertarian free will (involving randomness), which is denied by determinism, leading to his attitude of dismay
- compatibilism which is reconciled to determinism, leading to the attitude of intransigence, (irreconcilable with the "fiction" of origination)

But Honderich says he avoids the mistakes of Incompatibilism and Compatibilism. His point of their mistakes is subtle. It depends on his introduction of the two kinds of "life hopes," the one voluntariness alone, the other voluntariness plus origination. He says:

> "Let us finish here by having clear the relation of affirmation to Compatibilism and Incompatibilism. Affirmation differs wholly from both in that it recognizes the existence of two attitudes where Compatibilism and Incompatibilism assert a single conception and a single connection with moral responsibility and the like. Affirmation does involve reliance on a single attitude, having to do only with voluntariness, which of course is related to the single conception of initiation which Compatibilists assign to us. Affirmation also has to do with the other attitude, pertaining also to origination, related to the single conception

11 informationphilosopher.com/freedom/freedom_of_action.html

> which Incompatibilists assign to us. It is not much more like Compatibilism than Incompatibilism." [12]

The mistake of Incompatibilism appears to be that it assumes that determinism destroys moral approval and disapproval. This, Honderich says, ignores the tough attitude of *intransigence*.

The mistake of Compatibilism, is to assert that nothing changes as a consequence of determinism, when clearly we have lost the life-hope of origination. This ignores the sad attitude of *dismay*.

Honderich recapitulates his lengthy argument.

> "The argument about the consequences of determinism has been a long one, and can usefully be brought into a succinct form.
>
> "*1.2* All our life-hopes involve thoughts to the effect that we somehow initiate our future actions. Some involve not only beliefs as to voluntariness or willingness but also an idea, or what is more an image, of our originating our future actions. To think of life-hopes of this kind, and their manifest inconsistency with determinism, and to accept the likely truth of determinism, is to fall into dismay. We are deprived of the hopes." [13]

In my **Cogito** model, our life-hopes are *thoughts*. They present themselves freely to us in the undetermined first stage of the two-stage model. This gives us Honderich's "origination."

But Honderich makes it clear, and I agree, that some determinism is needed in, is consistent with, our voluntary *actions*,

> "*1.3* We also have life-hopes involving only beliefs as to voluntariness — that we will act not from reluctant desires and intentions, but from embraced desires and intentions, that we will act in enabling circumstances rather than frustrating ones. These circumstances have to do with at least the way of my world, the absence of self-frustration, independence of others, and absence of bodily constraint. Thinking of hopes of this kind, and noting the clear consistency of a determinism with them, may issue in intransigence. These life-hopes are not at all significantly threatened by determinism."

12 Honderich (1990b) p. 149.
13 Honderich (1990b) p. 169.

In my view, all the determinism that Honderich needs is R. E. Hobart's determination (See p. 23).

P. F. Strawson distinguished treating some persons as autonomous participants in our moral universe, from others who are treated "objectively," as ruled by deterministic forces. Honderich feels dismay about the latter, intransigence about the former.

> "*1.4* We have appreciative and also resentful feelings about others, owed to their actions deriving from good or bad feelings and judgements about us. Both sorts of personal feelings involve assumptions somehow to the effect that others could do otherwise than they do. It is natural in one way of thinking and feeling to take the assumptions to amount to this: others act with knowledge, without internal constraint, in character, and in line with personality, not out of abnormality, not because of constraint by others. This second one of a set of fundamentally like conceptions of voluntary action, wholly consistent with determinism, may lead us to make the response of intransigence with respect to personal feelings. However, we also have other personal feelings, having a certain person-directed character and including an assumption as to a power or control of their actions by others. The assumption is inconsistent with determinism and may lead to dismay." [14]

Honderich recognizes that in a deterministic universe our knowledge claims are suspect. Information philosophy puts the basis of knowledge on the sounder foundation of information, in the universe outside us, and isomorphic information in our brains. But that is the subject of another book.

Honderich thinks (correctly) that origination is needed to ground knowledge claims. (See the Free Will Axiom on page 231.)

> "*1.5* We accept that our claims to knowledge derive in part from beliefs and assumptions to our mental acts and our ordinary actions, by which we come to have evidence and the like. We may take it that originated acts and actions are necessary, and, taking them as ruled out by a determinism, suffer a want of confidence in our beliefs, a dismay having to do with the possibility of a further reality. Inevitably, however, we can have a

14 Honderich (1990b) p. 169.

> different kind of confidence, owed only to an assumption as to voluntariness, the possibility of our satisfying our desires for information. Hence intransigence about knowledge. These are facts which the Epicurean tradition of objection to determinism has greatly misconstrued." [15]

On Consciousness and *Radical Externalism*

Honderich's study of *Mind and Brain*, originally the first two parts of *Theory of Determinism*, informs Honderich's later works *On Consciousness* and *Radical Externalism.*

How do these works reveal Honderich's perception of the problem of the originator, the kind of free will that libertarians are looking for?

A careful reading of *Mind and Brain* tells us that Honderich is concerned about micro-indeterministic chance being the direct cause of action. He calls this the "Postulate of Neural Indeterminacy," and generally opposes the idea.

> "How could an unnecessitated or chance event be something for which the person in question could be censured in the given way?"

(p. 184)

He finds

> "strong and clear support for the proposition that neural sequences are somehow or in some way causal sequences."

(p. 266)

Neurobiologists, and cell biologists before them, have long shown that the size of cellular structures is macroscopic enough for quantum micro-indeterminism to be irrelevant in the normal operations of a cell. We grant this, and it seems as if this is the basic evidence for Honderich's claim of determinism and causality in the "Psychoneural Intimacy" of the mind/brain.

But there is another level of operations in the mind, the one computer scientists and cognitive scientists use to defend the "mind as computer" or "machine." That is the famous analogy of the relationship of software to the hardware.

15 Honderich (1990b) p. 169-170.

The identity theory of mind says that mind and brain are one thing. Philosophers of mind take a more nuanced view and say that mind events "supervene" on brain events. There is a one-to-one correspondence that sounds like Gottfried Leibniz and Immanuel Kant's ideas of a parallel noumenal or mental world in "pre-established harmony" with the physical noumenal world.

My **Cogito** model is a purely physical model. But like the cognitive scientists, I see an important distinction between the software, considered as "pure" information, and the hardware, considered as embodied information structures.

The macroscopic neurological brain is storing and retrieving pure information to serve the mind's consciousness of its surroundings, to inform its actions and interactions with the world.

Now we know that there is no such thing as an information system that can communicate without noise in the system, both quantum noise and the more common thermal noise. Such noise is the informational equivalent of those chance microscopic events in Honderich's "Postulate of Neural Indeterminacy," but now the emphasis must be on the psyche side of Psychoneural intimacy. It is indeterminacy of *thought*, not of *action*.

Indeterminacy of thought, while not directly causing action, can influence our choices for action, not by causing them, and not by changing their **probabilities**, but simply by becoming **alternative possibilities** for action by the **adequately determined** will, which also includes determination of our muscular motions to implement the action.

We may occasionally exhibit spastic behaviors, but there is absolutely no evidence, and no need, for actions that are affected randomly by microscopic quantum uncertainty, despite the fears of many philosophers of the consequences of admitting some indeterminism.

Determinists have been right about the Will, but wrong about Freedom (or origination).

Libertarians have been right about Freedom, but wrong about the Will, which must be as **adequately determined** as the rest of our physical selves.

Consciousness as Existence

What does this information in the mind/brain have to do with Honderich's theory of "Consciousness as Existence" or more recently "Radical Externalism?" Consciousness is quintessentially ideas, including of course our feelings about those ideas, which as associationists from Hume's time thought, are recollections of sense experiences.

Now small errors or "noise" in our recollections are the stuff of "new ideas," such as we experience when dreaming or half-dreaming, musing about possibilities.

Radical Externalism says that:

> "Consciousness is perceptual, reflective or affective — in brief it has to do with seeing, thinking and wanting. We are as good as never engaged in only one of the sorts of things. There are large problems here. One is the understanding of the mixing and melding of the three parts, kinds, sides or whatever of consciousness, of how one contributes to another, even in ordinary seeing and acting." [16]

Honderich wants his "perceptual consciousness" to encompass not merely the representation of the world in the mind but a commitment to the existence of the perceived world. In informational terms we say that there is at least a partial isomorphism, a "mapping" of the information stored in our neural systems onto the information in the external world that I am seeing.

> "You are seeing this page. What does that fact come to? What is that state of affairs? The natural answer has a lot in it, about the page as a physical thing, whatever one of those is, and about your retinas and your visual cortex. It also has in it philosophy and science about the relation between a neural process and your consciousness.
>
> "So there is more to your seeing the page than your consciousness of it." [17]

16 Freeman (2006) p. 6.
17 Freeman (2006) p. 3.

Honderich seems to agree with the partial isomorphism in his description of reflective and affective consciousness, which can have thoughts that correspond not to the real world, but to a modified world of the imagination, including states of affairs that the agent has the power to originate, to bring about in an open future.

> "Now a few words about reflective consciousness, say thinking of home, and affective consciousness, say wanting to be there or intending to get there.
>
> "Very briefly, what it seems to be to think of home now is for something to exist that has some of the properties of home. That is what a representation essentially is — something that shares some effects with what is represented.
>
> "As for wanting to be at home or intending to get there, and affective consciousness generally, one essential point is that this too is to be understood in terms of the characters of anyone's perceptual and also reflective consciousness." [18]

Can Honderich see that our affective consciousness is so much more powerful if it can imagine, if it can freely create, ways of wanting the world (for example, wanting to be home) that are not already **pre-determined** in the one possible future of his *intransigence* attitude toward the meagre "life-hope" he accepts in voluntarism with no origination?

We can originate, we can create, in the abstract world of **information**, thoughts in our minds about how we want the world to be. These thoughts can then activate our reflective consciousness, and stimulate our affective consciousness, helping our deliberations and evaluations of those thoughts, before we act on one of them.

In his latest work for the second edition of the *Oxford Handbook of Free Will*, Honderich takes a stand opposing Peter F. Strawson, who said that he did not understand the problem of determinism and free will.[19] Honderich says,

> "Determinism is not one of those theories filling up the world whose truth you cannot be sure about because you cannot be sure what the theory is, or what it really comes to. You know

18 Freeman (2006) pp. 8-9.
19 Strawson (1962) p. 1.

> what determinism is. It is even plainer in its essentials than the lovely theory of evolution... So much for the essential content of determinism. Come round as quickly to the question of the truth of the theory—the truth of the proposition that every event, each thing that happens, is a standard effect." [20]

But Honderich is unhappy with our current understanding of quantum mechanics, that some events are merely probable, not **necessitated**. I call it "soft" causality. It is not that the causative event does not exist, but that it itself was only probable. Honderich remarks...

> "about probabilism. It is argued that interpretations of quantum mechanics establish, about events of which we are sure that they cause cancer, that these events are undetermined or unnecessitated. So, unless we take causation to be probabilistic, we will have to be agnostic about well-supported or even best supported causal claims. A reply is that there is a less confusing and maybe less confused response. If later unnecessitated events are said to be explained by prior events only in some unnecessitating way, then the prior events are not causes and the later events not effects, whatever else is to be said of them in terms of some kind of explanation.
>
> "Probabilism, it seems, despite the great interest, history, and technical competence of work on probability, is the intrusion of a specialism into a subject not explained by it and not in need of it."

Sadly, Honderich is no scientist, not even a philosopher of science. He says he must "navigate around" what he does "not understand and cannot judge." But judge he does,

"It is my own judgment that modern physics at least does not give consistent support to a denial of general determinism.... No doubt a little intemperately, I have in the past spoken of the interpretations of quantum mechanics, and in particular those taken to show that the world is indeterministic, as a mess." [21]

20 Kane (2011) p. 442.
21 Kane (2011) p. 447.

Honderich, as always, is keeping up with events in physics. He mentions Bell's theorem, and the recent experimental tests (which confirm quantum mechanics). He says he polled a number of his colleague philosophers, and found only hesitation on whether the experiments establish indeterminism.[22]

But these philosophers (of science mostly) are still clinging to the hope (shared originally by JOHN BELL) that Einstein was right, that quantum reality might be shown to be "local" and that determinism would be restored.

I have presented the latest evidence on **nonlocality** and entanglement in several web pages.[23] I hope that Honderich and his colleagues will study them closely. I have edited a video presentation by JOHN BELL, shortly before his death in 1990, in which he confirms that the experimental tests of his theorem show Einstein to have been quite wrong about his idea of "local" reality. [24]

Honderich himself maintains a website on Determinism and Freedom, with a selection of important pieces by various thinkers, and a companion guide to the terminology.[25] His website was an inspiration for my own.

---

22 Kane (2011) p. 456.

23 See informationphilosopher.com/solutions/experiments/Bells_Theorem/

24 See youtube.com/watch?v=V8CCfOD1iu8 or search YouTube for John Bell

25 http://www.ucl.ac.uk/~uctytho/dfwTerminology.html

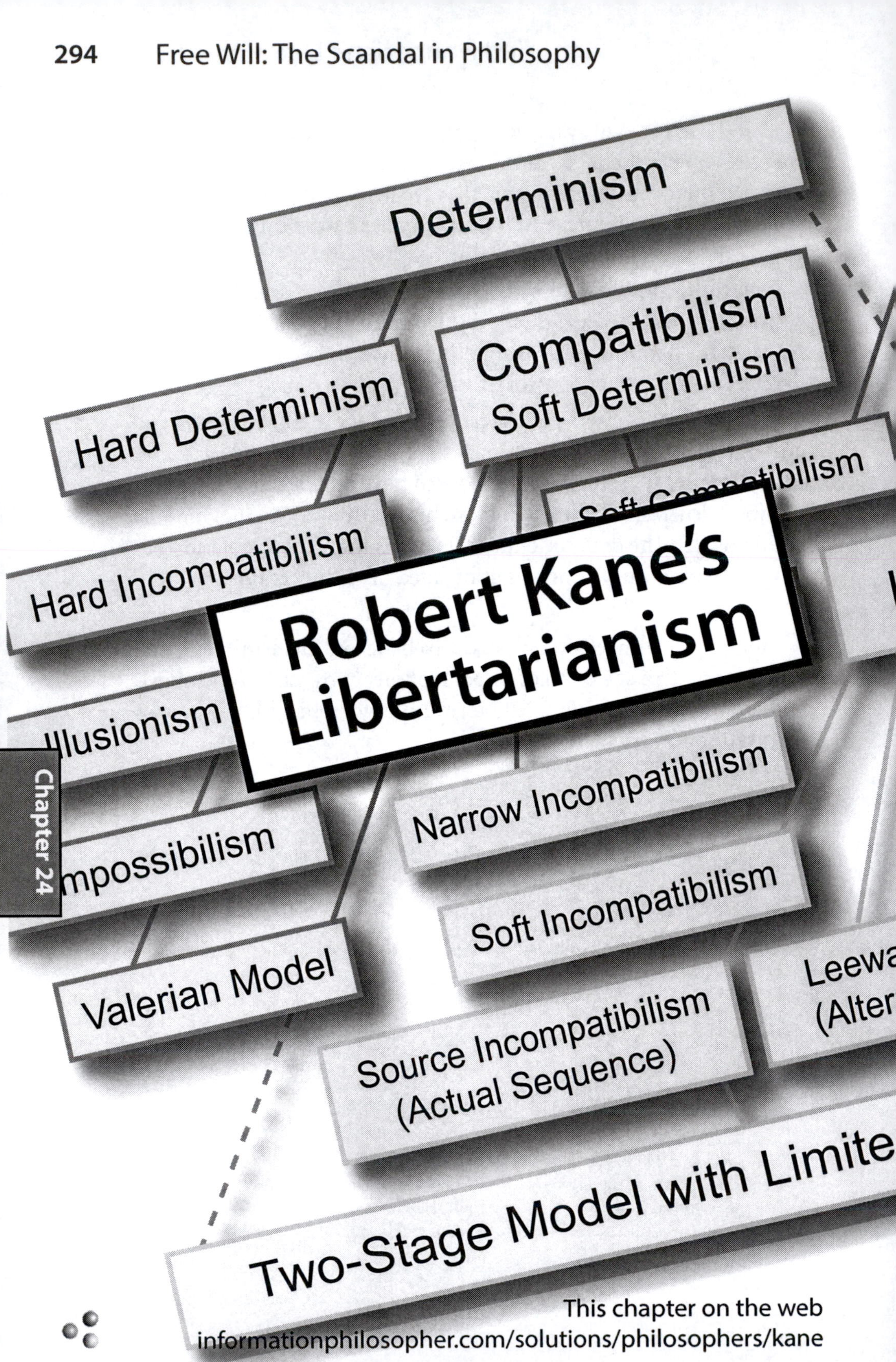

This chapter on the web
informationphilosopher.com/solutions/philosophers/kane

Indeterminism

Robert Kane's Libertarianism

ROBERT KANE is the acknowledged dean of the **libertarian** philosophers actively writing on the free will problem. In the first half of the twentieth century, many Anglo-American philosophers had largely dismissed libertarian free will as a "pseudo-problem."

In addition, when Kane began work in the 1960's, most philosophers and scientists thought free will was compatible with determinism, or perhaps impossible because of determinism.

Kane developed the Aristotelian view that even if most of our actions are **determined** entirely by our character, these actions can be free if we at times in the past freely created our own character (and if we remain free to change it) with what he calls "Self-Forming Actions" (SFAs).

Kane's model for free will is designed to provide an agent with what he calls Ultimate Responsibility (UR), based on his idea of the Self-Forming Action.

Kane's importance in the history of the free will problem is fourfold. First, his **event-causal** free will model has in recent years been the libertarian model most often discussed, and the one against which other models are compared. Second, his prolific writing has produced several important books on free will and ethics. His editing has given us a free will anthology and the massive *Oxford Handbook of Free Will*. Thirdly, he has mentored many of the current participants in the free will debates.

But for me, the fourth reason that Kane is critically important is because he is one of the very few thinkers to find a place for **quantum indeterminacy** in a free-will model. Most all other thinkers can see no way that quantum events can make a coherent and intelligible contribution to human freedom. Kane continues to look for ways that quantum randomness contributes. Today he does not look to individual quantum events affecting individual decisions, but the general quantum and thermal noise in the brain as providing the needed indeterminacy at all times.

I want to look closely in this chapter at Kane's work over the years, to see how his idea of Self-Forming Action (SFAs) and Ultimate Responsibility (UR) has evolved and how I believe that SFAs can now be integrated into my two-stage model of free will.

Kane has always maintained that two-stage models of the kind proposed by Karl Popper and Daniel Dennett were an important "part of the puzzle" of free will. For me, two-stage models are the central element. In my view, Kane's Self-Forming Actions add another"free" element to human decisions, and I will try below to show how I understand the way in which they are involved in the formation of one's character.

As we shall see, Kane regards my **two-stage Cogito model** of free will as "determined," because once the last of the **alternative possibilities** is generated, the agent's choice is, and Kane and I agree on this, **adequately determined**, by the agent's character and values, beliefs and desires, etc. See Chapter 13 for details on my **Cogito model,** especially Figure 13-6.

Kane now agrees that decisions in my model are not **pre-determined** by the laws of nature or the fixed past before deliberations begin. So, looking at the overall decision process, which involves some time between the starting circumstances and the final action resulting from a decision, Kane and I agree that my two-stage model is as free from the many forms of determinism as any model of libertarian free will needs to be.

And I argue that my two-stage decisions are as good a candidate for assigning responsibility as Kane's Ultimate Responsibility (UR), which he traces back in time to the remote past when one of his free Self-Forming Actions added to an agent's character.

To be sure, many of our decisions that are not adequately determined by character and value, by motives and reasons, may well be decided indeterministically. These are related to decisions that the ancients described as the "liberty of indifference" (*liberum arbitrium indifferentiae*). But Kane's SFAs are not "arbitrary" in the sense that there are no good reasons to choose. Unlike the liberty of indifference, there are equally good and important reasons on both (or all) sides. I call them **undetermined liberties**.

In a Self-Forming Action, an agent chooses between two (or more) equally justifiable actions, each with excellent reasons, so that the agent can take responsibility for either choice.

In this kind of choice, Kane has cleverly defeated the common objection made against indeterministic libertarian free will, that if chance is involved, the agent has no control and thus cannot be responsible for the action. I agree that Kane's agent can claim ultimate responsibility either way in an SFA, and the reduction in control is more than offset by the gain in freedom, as we shall see.

In his book *Libertarian Accounts of Free Will*, RANDOLPH CLARKE criticized Kane's ultimacy as

> "wholly negative: it is just a matter of the absence of any determining cause of a directly free action. The active control that is exercised on such a view is just the same as that exercised on an event-causal compatibilist account." [1]

Clarke says that Kane's model provides no more control than the compatibilist view, that is to say, no control at all. This is wrong. The agent has control over which actions are considered in an SFA.

Kane's Libertarian Free Will Model

Perhaps Kane's most original contribution to the free-will debates are his examples of decisions that are indeterministic, but for which the agent can properly claim moral responsibility.

Chance as the *direct* cause of an action compromises agent control and therefore any responsibility. But in the case of what Kane calls a "torn decision," the agent may have excellent reasons for choosing "either way." In such a case, the agent can choose indeterministically, yet properly take responsibility for either option. Kane calls this "dual (or plural) rational control."

In the normal case of self-determination in the two-stage model, the second ("will") stage arrives at the best choice based on the complex set of the agent's character and values, reasons and motives, feelings and desires.

1 Clarke (2003) p. 220.

But there are times when the two-stage model does not narrow down the alternatives to a single choice. In such cases, and especially where the decisions are "torn" and involve moral or prudential considerations, Kane says that in these cases the agent must exert an effort to make a decision, indeed must make dual or plural efforts in defense of each option.

The role of indeterminacy is to reduce the likelihood of some options, making them fail, but for the option that does succeed, it is not the indeterminism that deserves credit as the cause of success, but the efforts of the agent.

This type of torn decision is made in the Self-Forming Actions (SFAs) that form the basis for an agent's "ultimate responsibility" (UR). By ultimate responsibility Kane means that the sources or origins of our actions lie "in us" rather than in something else (such as decrees of fate, foreordained acts of God, or antecedent causes and laws of nature) which are outside us and beyond our control.

Aristotle and Epicurus said that decisions "in us" or that "depend on us" are a **tertium quid**, or third thing, that is neither chance nor necessity.

Kane at first argued that having **alternative possibilities** for action (he calls them AP) is not enough to establish free will. It is ultimate responsibility (UR), he says, that is required for free will. Ultimate responsibility requires that some of our actions are self-forming actions (SFAs). In turn, our self-forming actions require plural rational control in our decisions. And it is the plural rational control that requires alternative possibilities (AP).

Much of Kane's work has been to establish the role of quantum indeterminacy in making at least some of our actions undetermined. Let's look at Kane's major works over the past four decades to understand the development of his free will model.

Free Will and Values

In his 1985 book *Free Will and Values*, Kane considered the **two-stage models** of Karl Popper (as described by Popper in his 1965 Arthur Holly Compton memorial lecture, "Of Clouds and Clocks"), and Daniel Dennett (as presented in Dennett's 1978 book *Brainstorms,* especially the chapter, "On Giving Libertarians What They Say They Want").

To produce quantum indeterminacy, Kane initially proposed an ambitious amplifier model for a quantum randomizer in the brain - a spinning wheel of fortune with probability bubbles corresponding to **alternative possibilities**, in the massive switch amplifier (MSA) tradition of Compton.

Kane imagines a specific mechanism for incorporating the indeterminacy. This work is squarely in the tradition of several other brain mechanisms proposed to underlie freedom of the will (these all are described in detail on the I-Phi website).[2]

- James Clerk Maxwell's "Singularities" (1856)
- Arthur Stanley Eddington's "Free Electrons" (1928)
- Arthur Holly Compton's Photocell Amplifier (1931)
- John Eccles' "Critically Poised Neurons" (1953)
- A. O. Gomes' Quantum Composer (1964)

Kane says:

> "What I would like to do then, is to show how an MSA [massive switch amplifier] model, using Eccles' notion of critically poised neurons as a working hypothesis, might be adapted to the theory of practical, moral and prudential decision making.
>
> "Keeping these points in mind, let us now suppose that there are neurons in the brain "critically poised" in Eccles' sense, whose probability of firing within a small interval of time is .5. (We shall tamper with this simplifying assumption in a moment.) For every n such neurons, there are 2^n possible ordered combinations of firings and non-firings, which may be represented by sequences, such as (101...), (01101...), where the "1" 's indicate firings, the "0" 's non-firings, and the dots indicate that the sequences are continued with "0" 's up to n figures. A reasonably small number of such neurons, say a dozen, would yield ordered combinations, in the thousands, enough for the

2 informationphilosopher.com/freedom/mechanisms.html

purposes of the theory. As indicated in 8.4, the exact number of possible alternatives or partitionings does not matter so long as it is large; it would likely depend on the exigencies of neurological programming rather than the demands of the theory.

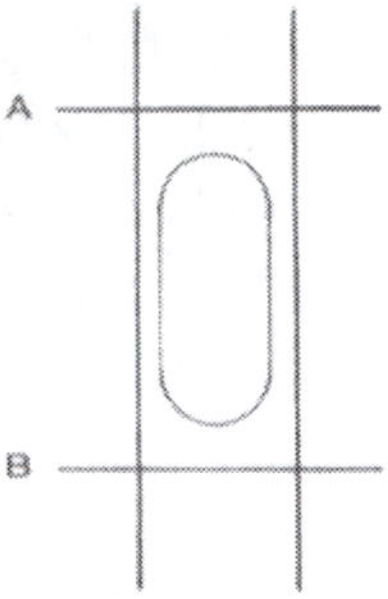

“For practical choice, these ordered combinations of firings and non-firings of critically poised neurons would correspond to places on a spinning wheel, most of which would give rise to chance selected considerations, opening doors to consciousness of possibly relevant memories, triggering associations of ideas and/or images, focussing attention in various ways, etc. Some combinations of firings and non-firings might draw a blank. But the wheel would keep spinning until it hit something worth considering, so long as the practical reasoner or creative thinker were in a receptive, yet reflective, state of mind. Then the relevance of the consideration to deliberation would have to be assessed and the consideration either accepted or rejected.” [3]

A

B

Kane introduces his mechanism as a probability bubble.

“One might think of this as a picture of an air bubble in a glass tube filled with a liquid, with the lines A and B marked on the outside of the glass as on an ordinary carpenter’s level. But this description is merely an aid to the imagination. We are going to give the bubble some extraordinary properties. The bubble may represent either the desire to choose to act from duty (out of equal respect) or the effort made to realize this desire in choice. The respective desire and effort are conceptually related because the desire is defined as the disposition to make the effort; and the intensity of the desire is measured by the intensity of the effort. The lines A and B in the figure represent choice thresholds. If the bubble passes above the line A, the choice is made to act from duty; if it passes below B, the choice is made to act on self interested motives. When the bubble is between the lines, as in the figure, no choice has yet been made. A downward pull of gravity in the figure may be thought to represent the natural pull of one’s self interested motives, which must be counteracted by an effort to resist temptation.”

3 Kane (1985) p. 169

Kane's example of SFAs involves moral choices between a Kantian deontological duty and motives of self interest.

> "There is an ambiguity, essential to our problem, about what it means to say that the bubble "passes above" the line A, or "below" the line B. If the bubble passes above A, or below B, then the choice is made to act from duty, or from self interest, respectively.
>
> "To complicate matters further, we want to assume that the bubble or probability space does not have an exact position vis a vis the thresholds at any given time and that this inexactness of position is also due to the undetermined movement of the point particle in the regions. There are a number of ways to represent this in the diagram, but the simplest way is the following. Imagine, as in the following figure, that the choice thresholds A and B have indeterminate position so that they can be anywhere between (or on) the extremes A'-A" and B'-B" respectively:

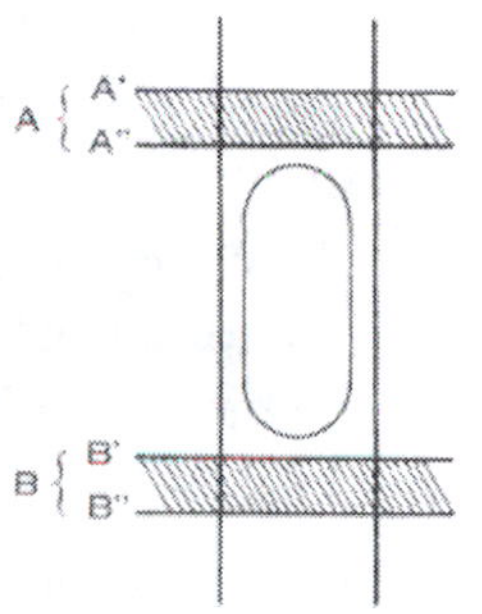

> "The distances between any two possible threshold positions for A (or any two for B) are equal and each possible threshold position corresponds to a region in the bubble such that, if the point particle is in that region, the threshold is at the corresponding position. But adjacent regions in the bubble need not correspond to adjacent positions of the thresholds and higher or lower regions of the bubble need not correspond to higher and lower threshold positions respectively.
>
> "What all this means is that the intensity of the effort to overcome temptation at any given time, which is measure of the intensity of the desire to act from duty (represented by the position of the bubble vis a vis the thresholds and the position of the point particle within the bubble) is indeterminate. And, as a consequence, the outcome of the choice situation at a given time is undetermined and unpredictable as long as the bubble is not wholly above A' or wholly below B". [4]

4 Kane (1985) pp. 144-146.

To summarize his 1985 book, *Free Will and Values*, Kane described two-stage models as a "significant piece in the overall puzzle of a libertarian freedom." [5] But he thought them limited to practical decision making, and not suitable for moral decision making, which require his dual rational control and chance in the decision itself to provide "ultimate responsibility" (UR).

Given the random **alternative possibilities** in the first stage of the model, Kane thought that an agent would be **determined** in the second stage to choose the best available option.

But I have pointed out to Kane, and he agrees, that the agent would not be **pre-determined**, even from moments just before deliberations began. As John Locke noted, the will itself can be determined, it need not itself be free in the sense of random. It is the man that is free, not the will, said Locke. [6]

Kane's model is also "restrictive," a term coined by John Martin Fischer to describe Peter van Inwagen's claim that only a tiny fraction of our decisions and actions can properly be called free actions. For van Inwagen, it is those which have closely balanced alternatives (the ancient problem of the **liberty of indifference**).

Kane disagreed with van Inwagen on the frequency of free decisions. For Kane, they are not rare but quite common. They include not only the "torn" moral and prudential decisions but many everyday practical decisions.

In this early work, Kane was not completely satisfied with his solution. He explained that the main reason for failure is

> "locating the master switch and the mechanism of amplification...We do not know if something similar goes on in the brains of cortically developed creatures like ourselves, but I suspect it must if libertarian theories are to succeed." [7]

We shall see that in later work, Kane sees the source of indeterminism as the general noise that is ever-present in the brain, as in any information processing system.

---

5 *ibid.*, p. 104.
6 Locke (1959) p. 323.
7 Kane (1985) p. 168.

Doing Otherwise in the Same Circumstances

Kane claims he needs **quantum indeterminacy** because the major criticism of all libertarian models is how they explain the power to choose or **do otherwise** in "exactly the same conditions." He calls this "dual rational (or voluntary) self-control." Given that A was the rational choice, how can one defend doing B under exactly the same circumstances?" [8] Kane himself was concerned that such a "dual power" could be seen as arbitrary, capricious, and irrational. Critics of Kane's theory, Randolph Clarke and Richard Double, for example, focus on this concern.

Apart from the fact that information-rich systems with a history are never in the exact same conditions, and ignoring the fact that random **alternative possibilities** are unlikely to repeat, an **adequately determined** will would indeed very likely make the same choice, for the same reasons, from the same set of alternative possibilities. It might even exercise its irrational prerogative! We humans are unpredictable, which makes us occasionally capricious and arbitrary. While this is possible, and amounts to a kind of freedom, Kane wants the freedom without the irrationality.

The Significance of Free Will

In his 1995 book *The Significance of Free Will,* Kane again invokes quantum events in the brain at the moment of decision:

> "We now turn to the second part of an answer to the question of how prior reasons or motives can explain the effort to resist temptation without also explaining the choice that terminates the effort. We must now look at this "effort of will" (to resist moral or prudential temptation) that intervenes between prior reasons or motives, on the one hand, and the resulting choice, on the other.
>
> "T24 (on FW): Let its suppose that the effort of will (to resist temptation) in moral and prudential choice situations of T22 and T23 is (an) indeterminate (event or process), thereby making the choice that terminates it undetermined.

8 Kane (1985) p. 59.

> "Consider a quantum analogue. Imagine an isolated particle, such as an electron, moving toward a thin atomic barrier. Whether or not the particle will penetrate the barrier is undetermined. There is a probability that it will penetrate, but not a certainty, because its position and momentum are not both determinate as it moves toward the barrier. Imagine that the choice (to overcome temptation) is like the penetration event. The choice one way or the other is undetermined because the process preceding it and potentially terminating in it (i.e., the effort of will to overcome temptation) is indeterminate." [9]

Kane's approach here was similar to Arthur Stanley Eddington's in 1928 - making an analogy between human freedom and "free" electrons. Kane did not think that was enough and then added chaos to amplify the microscopic quantum indeterminacy up to the macroscopic neurons.

> "But this quantum analogy is merely that — an analogy. Our efforts of will most likely correspond to complex processes in our brains that are macro processes involving many neuron firings and connections. Since we know that the effects of quantum level fluctuations are usually negligible at the macro level, how can these efforts be indeterminate? One way to begin thinking about this issue is to imagine that the neural processes occurring when the efforts are being made are chaotic processes, in the sense of what is nowadays called "chaos theory." In chaotic systems, very minute changes in initial conditions grow exponentially into large differences in final outcome, a phenomenon called "sensitivity to initial conditions."
>
> "But chaotic behavior, though unpredictable, is not necessarily indeterministic. In fact, chaos theory has shown that one can have determinism without predictability. Yet chaos theory may nonetheless be significant for discussions of human freedom, if quantum indeterminacy is also brought into the picture." [10]

Kane described the tension during "torn" decisions as stirring up deterministic chaos. He makes the deterministic chaos sensitive to quantum indeterminacy at the neuronal level (in a way resembling JOHN ECCLES' ideas about "critically poised neurons.").

9 Kane (1995) p. 128.
10 Kane (1995) p. 129.

"T25 (on FW): Imagine that the indeterminate efforts of will of T24 are complex chaotic processes in the brain, involving neural networks that are globally sensitive to quantum indeterminacies at the neuronal level. Persons experience these complex processes phenomenologically as "efforts of will" they are making to resist temptation in moral and prudential situations. The efforts are provoked by the competing motives and conflicts within the wills of the persons described in T22 and T23. These conflicts create tensions that are reflected in appropriate regions of the brain by movement further from thermodynamic equilibrium, which increases the sensitivity to micro indeterminacies at the neuronal level and magnifies the indeterminacies throughout the complex macro process which, taken as a whole, is the agent's effort of will.

"T26 (on FW): In effect, conflicts of will of the kinds described in T22 and 23 stir up chaos in the brain and make the agents' thought processes more sensitive to undetermined influences. The result is that, in soul-searching moments moral and prudential struggle, when agents are torn between conflicting visions of what they should become (that is, on the occasions of self-forming willings, or SFWs), the outcomes are influenced by, but not determined by, past motives and character. The uncertainty and inner tension that agents feel at such moments are reflected in the indeterminacy of their neural processes." [11]

A Contemporary Introduction to Free Will

In 2005, Kane wrote a perceptive analysis of a two-stage solution for free will like our **Cogito** mind model and the suggestions of Arthur Holly Compton, Karl Popper, Daniel Dennett, and Alfred Mele.

"The final libertarian theory I want to consider in this chapter takes a very different approach to explaining libertarian free choices. This view rejects both simple indeterminism and agent-causation. Instead it focuses on the process of deliberation. When we deliberate, for example, about where to vacation or which law firm to join, many different thoughts,

11 Kane (1995) p. 130.

images, feelings, memories, imagined scenarios, and other considerations pass through our minds. Deliberation can be quite a complex process. When Mike thinks about Hawaii, he pictures himself surfing, walking on sunny beaches, eating in his favorite Hawaiian restaurants; and these various thoughts incline him to choose Hawaii. But he also thinks about skiing, sitting by a fireplace after a long day on the slopes, and visiting with friends he knows in Colorado; and he leans toward Colorado. Back and forth he goes, until after a period of time considerations on one side outweigh the others and he finally chooses one option. (Unless, of course he is one of those indecisive types who finds it hard to make up his mind.)" [12]

Note that in Kane's first stage he describes our free thoughts as 'coming to mind,' like William James' "present themselves."

"In the course of such deliberations — which may sometimes take hours or days and may be interrupted by daily activities — new thoughts, memories or images can often come to mind that influence our deliberations. Mike may suddenly remember a lively nightclub he visited in Honolulu when he was last there — great music, great girls — and the idea of going back to this place gives him an added reason to favor Hawaii, a reason that hadn't previously entered his deliberation. Other images that flit through his mind may turn him against Hawaii. Imagining himself out on the beach all day, suddenly he remembers his doctor's warning about not getting too much sun if he wants to avoid skin cancer.

"Now one could imagine that some of these various thoughts, memories, and imagined scenarios that come to mind during our deliberations are undetermined and arise by chance and that some of these 'chance selected considerations' might make a difference in how we decide. If this were to happen in Mike's case, the course of his deliberation, hence his choice, would be undetermined and unpredictable. A Laplacian demon could not know in advance which way Mike would go, even if the demon knew all the facts about the universe prior to Mike's deliberation, for these facts would not determine the outcome." [13]

12 Kane (2005) p. 64.
13 Kane (2005) p. 64.

In Kane's second stage, choices result from rational evaluations of the alternative possibilities that have come in part by chance

> "Yet Mike would still have control over his choice in a certain sense. He could not control all the thoughts and imagined scenarios that come to mind by chance. But he would be in control of how he reacted to those thoughts and imaginings once they did occur. And his choice of Hawaii in the end would be perfectly rational, not arbitrary, if the weight of all the considerations that did come to mind (some of them by chance) weighed in favor of Hawaii. In this way, choices could thus be controlled and rational even though indeterminism was involved in the deliberations leading up to them." [14]

Kane calls this "causal indeterminism" or "event-causal libertarianism." It is, like my **Cogito**, a two-stage model, first "free" thoughts, then "willed" actions. But, like DANIEL DENNETT and ALFRED MELE, Kane did not at that time endorse this view.

> "A view of this kind is called causal indeterminism or event–causal libertarianism, for it allows that our thoughts, images, memories, beliefs, desires, and other reasons may be causes of our choices or actions without necessarily determining choices and actions; and yet this view does not postulate any extra kind of agent-causation either. Two philosophers who have suggested causal indeterminist views of this kind (without endorsing them), Daniel Dennett and Alfred Mele, argue that a view of this kind would give libertarians at least some of the important things they demand about free will. Such a view, for example, provides for an "open future," such as we think we have when we exercise free will. We would not have to think that our choices and the future direction of our lives had somehow been decided long before we were born. Nor would it be possible for behavioral engineers to completely control our behavior as in Walden Two or for Laplacian demons to know what we were going to do, if chance considerations might enter our deliberations." [15]

It is unfortunate that Kane did not accept Dennett's 1978 ideas for "giving libertarians what they want." [16] He might have reconciled many libertarians and compatibilists.

14 Kane (2005) pp. 64-5.
15 Kane (2005) p. 65.
16 See Chapter 27, What If - Kane had accepted Dennett's ideas?

Instead, Kane focused on the "something more" - **indeterminism** in the decision itself - so that our actions are not determined by our prior deliberations and **alternative possibilities**, however much these are our own creations, and our own reasons.

> "Yet, as Dennett and Mele also admit, a causal indeterminist view of this deliberative kind does not give us everything libertarians have wanted from free will. For Mike does not have complete control over what chance images and other thoughts enter his mind or influence his deliberation. They simply come as they please. Mike *does* have some control *after* the chance considerations have occurred." [17]

The evaluation of **alternative possibilities** is of course only **adequately determined**, but this is real **control**, and Kane was still concerned that control in the second stage implied an unacceptable determinism.

> "But then there is no more chance involved. What happens from then on, how he reacts, is *determined* by desires and beliefs he already has. So it appears that he does not have control in the libertarian sense of what happens after the chance considerations occur as well. Libertarians require more than this for full responsibility and free will. What they would need for free will is for the agent to be able to control which of the chance events occur rather than merely reacting to them in a determined way once they have occurred.
>
> "Yet, as Mele points out, while this causal indeterminist view does not give us all the control and responsibility that libertarians have wanted, it does give us many of the things they crave about free will (an open future, a break in the causal order, etc.). And it is clearly a possible view. Perhaps it could be further developed to give us more; or perhaps this is as much as libertarians can hope for." [18]

Kane seems to want his freedom both ways. He wants the agent to "control which of the chance events occur" and he also wants chance to be involved at the later decision stage to prevent its be-

17 Kane (2005) p. 65.
18 Kane (2005) p. 65.

ing controlled by the agent or "determined by desires and beliefs he already has."

In my two-stage **Cogito** model, the main place for chance is in the first stage, where **alternative possibilities** are generated. And control is only needed in the second stage, where decisions and choices are **adequately determined** by the agent's character and values, beliefs and desires.

Kane gets his "something more" by adding indeterminism to "torn" decisions, to produce what he calls "dual (or plural) rational control" over our actions, allowing us to choose different options, while still taking responsibility for the indeterministic choice.

> "When we wonder about whether agents have freedom of will (rather than merely freedom of action), what interests us is not merely whether they could have done otherwise, even if the doing otherwise is undetermined, but whether they could have done otherwise voluntarily (or willingly), intentionally, and rationally. Or, more generally, we are interested in whether they could have acted in more than one way voluntarily, intentionally, and rationally, rather than only in one way voluntarily, and so on, and in other ways merely by accident or mistake, unintentionally or irrationally. [19]

Kane appreciates that our thoughts "come to us" unbidden, we cannot control them, at least sometimes. We do have control, in the second stage, which insures that our actions "come from us." Our willed actions "depend on us," as Aristotle required.

Kane offers an illustrated version of the **standard argument** against free will. He describes the usual determinism and randomness objections (the two horns of the Libertarian Dilemma) as the ascent and descent of what he calls "Incompatibilism Mountain." [20]

The ascent problem is to show free will is incompatible with determinism. The descent problem is to show that free will is compatible with indeterminism. In earlier works Kane described ascent as "the compatibility question" and descent as "the intelligibility problem."

---

19 Kane (2005) p. 128.

20 See the discussion of Incompatibilist Mountain in Chapter 4, p. 44.

This is similar to what I do in a critical analysis of the **standard argument** against free will, in my **two-stage model** for free will, and in the two-fold **requirements** for free will.

Free will is incompatible with strict causal determinism, but it actually requires an **adequate determinism** for **moral responsibility**. And free will is compatible with an **indeterminism** that generates **alternative possibilities** without making chance the direct cause of actions. Finally, I agree that indeterminism can play a positive role in Kane's "torn" decisions.

Four Views on Free Will

In a recent work (*Four Views on Free Will*, 2007), Kane defends his libertarian free-will model and again suggests that his Self-Forming Actions might involve a tension and uncertainty in our minds that stirs up a deterministic "chaos" which is sensitive to micro-indeterminacies at the neuronal level.

> "All free acts do not have to be undetermined on the libertarian view, but only those acts by which we made ourselves into the kinds of persons we are, namely the "will-setting" or "self-forming actions" (SFAs) that are required for ultimate responsibility." [21]

> "Now I believe these undetermined self-forming actions or SFAs occur at those difficult times of life when we are torn between competing visions of what we should do or become. Perhaps we are torn between doing the moral thing or acting from ambition, or between powerful present desires and long-term goals, or we are faced with difficult tasks for which we have aversions."

Note that SFAs are similar in some respects to cases of the classical "**liberty of indifference**," where the choice can go either way. I call these **undetermined liberties**.

> "In all such cases, we are faced with competing motivations and have to make an effort to overcome temptation to do something else we also strongly want. There is tension and uncertainty

21 Kane (2007) p. 26.

in our minds about what to do at such times, I suggest, that is reflected in appropriate regions of our brains by movement away from thermodynamic equilibrium — in short, a kind of 'stirring up of chaos' in the brain that makes it sensitive to micro-indeterminacies at the neuronal level. The uncertainty and inner tension we feel at such soul-searching moments of self-formation is thus reflected in the indeterminacy of our neural processes themselves. What we experience internally as uncertainty about what to do on such occasions would then correspond physically to the opening of a window of opportunity that temporarily screens off complete determination by influences of the past." [22]

"When we do decide under such conditions of uncertainty, the outcome would not be determined because of the preceding indeterminacy — and yet the outcome can be willed (and hence rational and voluntary) either way owing to the fact that in such self-formation, the agents' prior wills are divided by conflicting motives." [23]

"Now let us add a further piece to the puzzle. Just as indeterminism need not undermine rationality and voluntariness of choices, so indeterminism in and of itself need not undermine control and responsibility. Suppose you are trying to think through a difficult problem, say a mathematical problem, and there is some indeterminacy in your neural processes complicating the task — a kind of chaotic background." [24]

Henri Poincaré said chance led to **alternative possibilities** for the solutions of mathematical problems..

"It would be like trying to concentrate and solve a problem, say a mathematical problem, with background noise or distraction. Whether you are going to succeed in solving the problem is uncertain and undetermined because of the distracting neural noise. Yet, if you concentrate and solve the problem nonetheless, we have reason to say you did it and are responsible for it, even though it was undetermined whether you would succeed. The indeterministic noise would have been an obstacle that you overcame by your effort." [25]

---

22 *ibid.*
23 Kane (2007) p. 26.
24 *ibid.* p. 27.
25 *ibid.*

Kane says that the indeterminism arising from a tension-creating conflict in the will

> "would be reflected in appropriate regions of the brain by movement away from thermodynamic equilibrium. The result would be a stirring up of chaos in the neural networks involved. Chaos in physical systems is a phenomenon in which very small changes in initial conditions are magnified so that they lead to large and unpredictable changes in the subsequent behavior of a system." [26]
>
> "Now determinists are quick to point out that chaos, or chaotic behavior, in physical systems, though unpredictable, is usually deterministic and does not itself imply genuine indeterminism in nature. But some scientists have suggested that a combination of chaos and quantum physics might provide the genuine indeterminism one needs. If the processing of the brain does 'make chaos in order to make sense of the world' (as one recent research paper puts it), then the resulting chaos might magnify quantum indeterminacies in the firings of individual neurons so that they would have large-scale indeterministic effects on the activity of neural networks in the brain as a whole. If chaotic behavior were thus enhanced in these neural networks by tension-creating conflict in the will, the result would be some significant indeterminism in the cognitive processing of each of the competing neural networks." [27]
>
> "'indeterminism' is a technical term that merely rules out deterministic causation, though not causation altogether. Indeterminism is consistent with nondeterministic or probabilistic causation, where the outcome is not inevitable. It is therefore a mistake (in fact, one of the most common in debates about free will) to assume that 'undetermined' means 'uncaused' or 'merely a matter of chance.'" [28]

I agree with Kane that something that is probabilistically caused is still caused, but it is not a mistake to say that is a 'matter of chance." It is an **undetermined liberty**.

Chapter 24

26 *ibid.*
27 Kane (2007) p. 28.
28 *ibid.* p. 31.

Kane wants to reconcile the role of chance in his Self-Forming Actions, by emphasizing the fact is that it is not mere chance that gets credit for the final choice between **alternative possibilities**.

> "If indeterminism is involved in a process so that its outcome is undetermined, one might argue that the outcome must merely happen and therefore cannot be somebody's choice. But there is no reason to assume such a claim is true. A choice is the formation of an intention or purpose to do something. It resolves uncertainty and indecision in the mind about what to do. Nothing in such a description implies that there could not be some indeterminism in the deliberation and neural processes of an agent preceding choice corresponding to the agent's prior uncertainty about what to do. Recall from the preceding arguments that the presence of indeterminism does not mean the outcome happened merely by chance and not by the agent's effort. Self-forming choices are undetermined, but not uncaused. They are caused by the agent's efforts." [29]
>
> "In a similar fashion, the idea is not to think of the indeterminism involved in free choices as a cause acting on its own, but as an ingredient in a larger goal-directed or teleological process or activity." [30]
>
> "What we need when we perform purposive activities, mental or physical, is rather macro-control of processes involving many neurons — complex processes that may succeed in achieving their goals despite the interfering effects of some recalcitrant neurons. We don't micro-manage our actions by controlling each individual neuron or muscle that might be involved. We don't know enough about neurology or physiology to do that; and it would be counterproductive to try. But that does not prevent us from macro-managing our purposive activities (whether they be mental activities such as practical reasoning, or physical activities, such as arm-swingings) and being responsible when those purposive activities attain their goals.
>
> "In summary, I think the key to understanding the role of chance in free will is not to think of chance as a causal factor by

Chapter 24

29 Kane (2007) p. 33..
30 *ibid.* p. 35.

> itself, but rather to think of chance as an interfering ingredient in larger goal-directed processes. Viewing chance in this way is related to a peculiarly modern scientific way of understanding human agency that also his its roots in the ancient view of Aristotle. Agents, according to this modern conception with ancient roots, are to be conceived as information-responsive complex dynamical systems." [31]

Here Kane insightfully suggests that information theory may help understanding the problem of will. He proposes that indeterminism is a limited ingredient in the teleological process of will. But it should not be seen as the main "cause" of a decision. That causal credit goes to the agent's efforts on behalf of each of the possible choices.

> "We should concede that indeterminism, wherever it occurs, does diminish control over what we are trying to do and is a hindrance or obstacle to the realization of our purposes." [32]

But all the options are hindered by the introduction of indeterminism, so the agent's efforts to make them all succeed will be affected slightly differently by indeterminism. Some will fail, partly as a result of chance, but the one that succeeds should not be credited to mere chance, but rather to the effort of the agent.

Kane addresses the implications of adding chance "centered" in the decision itself, which threatens to make chance the direct cause of our actions.

> "Let me conclude with one final objection to the account of free will presented here, which is perhaps the most telling and has not yet been discussed. Even if one granted that persons, such as the businesswoman, could make genuine self-forming choices that were undetermined, isn't there something to the charge that such choices would be arbitrary? A residual arbitrariness seems to remain in all self-forming choices since the agents cannot in principle have sufficient or conclusive prior reasons for making one option and one set of reasons prevail over the other.

31 *ibid.* p. 40.

32 Kane (2007) p. 39.

"There is some truth to this objection also, but again I think it is a truth that tells us something important about free will.

"Suppose we were to say to such persons: 'But look, you didn't have sufficient or conclusive prior reasons for choosing as you did since you also had viable reasons for choosing the other way.' They might reply. 'True enough. But I did have good reasons for choosing as I did, which I'm willing to stand by and take responsibility for. If these reasons were not sufficient or conclusive reasons, that's because, like the heroine of the novel, I was not a fully formed person before I chose (and still am not, for that matter). Like the author of the novel, I am in the process of writing an unfinished story and forming an unfinished character who, in my case, is myself.' "[33]

The Cogito Model

ROBERT KANE independently developed a two-stage model before DANIEL DENNETT published his 1978 book *Brainstorms*. He had read the same sources (Compton and Popper), but he thought that "something more" was needed.

Kane had always felt that at the completion of the first stage in my **Cogito** model, when all the random considerations have been generated, there is a finite time, however small, during which the model assumes that the willed decision, the choice between **alternative possibilities**, is determined.

Kane feels that the two-stage model is adequate for practical everyday decisions, and that it may play a role in moral and prudential choices by providing the considerations for different choices. Where the two-stage deliberative process does not result in a single choice, we can say that the options that remain were *as a group* **self-determined**, namely, consistent with the agent's character and values, reasons and motives, desires and feelings.

Kane says that libertarian free will requires that the decision not be completely determined by the agents desires and beliefs, which are among the causal factors, but not determining factors. In the case of his SFAs, decisions remain undetermined up to the moment of choice. It is *determined by the choice*, says Kane.

33 Kane (2007) pp. 41-42.

Just as Kane accepts the loss of some control in SFAs, the agent does not have complete control over the random considerations that get generated in my two-stage model. Of course, the agent can decide when to stop generating new possibilities. And if evaluation finds none satisfactory, can go back and generate more. Kane agrees with the importance of these "second thoughts." But after the last new random option is generated, and during that time, however small, before the decision is made, Kane is right that the choice at that point is already **adequately determined** by the agent's character, reasons, motives, etc. - unless, of course more than one option remains.

In my **Cogito** model, I admit that the decision could be reliably (though not perfectly) predicted by a super-psychiatrist who knew everything about the agent and was aware of all the alternative possibilities. This is because the second ("will") stage evaluation and decision process is indeed **adequately determined**.

I therefore agree with Kane that the second stage is normally "determined," in the sense of **adequately determined**, but note that it is in no way **pre-determined** before deliberations began.

Kane agrees with me that, before the first stage of the two-stage model, the decision has not yet been determined. It is at that time undetermined. So our decisions are not **pre-determined** back to the Big Bang.

Kane agrees that my two-stage **Cogito** model, with indeterminism in the first stage, is libertarian free.

But in Kane's Self-Forming Actions, indeterminism remains up to and including the moment of choice.

Kane's Self-Forming Actions

Kane has found a way to avoid any "determinism" at all in these cases, not even the **determination** by character and values, reasons and motives, feelings and desires, that compatibilists properly think is needed for **moral responsibility**. For Kane, reasons and motives are only partial causes of the decisions.

These are Kane's Self-Forming Actions (SFAs). He says the agent's decision may not be "determined" by anything other than the agent's choice, which can be rational (made for properly evaluated reasons), but nevertheless might have been **otherwise** and yet be equally rational and voluntary.

As we have seen, Kane calls this "dual (or plural) control." I now see that this is an acceptable extension of my **Cogito** model, one that adds still more libertarian freedom. Let's see how it works.

To find a way around the "determinism" of my second stage, without invoking metaphysical agent-causality, Kane adds event-causal randomness in the decision itself. RANDOLPH CLARKE calls such randomness "centered" in the decision,[34] as opposed to chance located earlier in the "deliberative" stage (my "free" stage).

There are times when the deliberation and evaluation process of the two-stage process may not narrow down to a single self-determined option. In such cases, the agent has developed reasons for more than one option. None of these options should be seen as random, in the sense that *as a group* they have been **adequately determined** by the deliberations of the second stage.

For everyday practical decisions, the agent may essentially "flip a coin" to make the decision between equally attractive options, and take responsibility for the outcome.

However, in difficult moral or prudential decisions, the agent may be seriously conflicted about the remaining options. This conflict requires extra effort on the part of the agent to make the decision, which Kane says may generate noise in the brain's neural circuitry. This noise may make the specific decision indeterminate, although it selects from among options that are all defended by reasons.

Although the actual decision is indeterminate, and chance has played a role in the decision, Kane rejects the view that chance is the "cause" of the decision. The role of chance has increased the probability that the agent's efforts for some of the options will fail, but for the option that succeeds, says Kane, it is the agent's effort that deserves the major credit. Effort is the cause of the choice.

34 See page 211.

I agree with Kane that it is inappropriate to make chance the "cause" of the decision.

My two-stage Cogito model accepts decisions that are made at random, when the reason (the non-reason?) is that the agent has no good reasons to prefer one option over others, and thus "deliberately" chooses at random.

I call these **undetermined liberties**, to distinguish them from the de-liberated **self-determination** of my second stage.

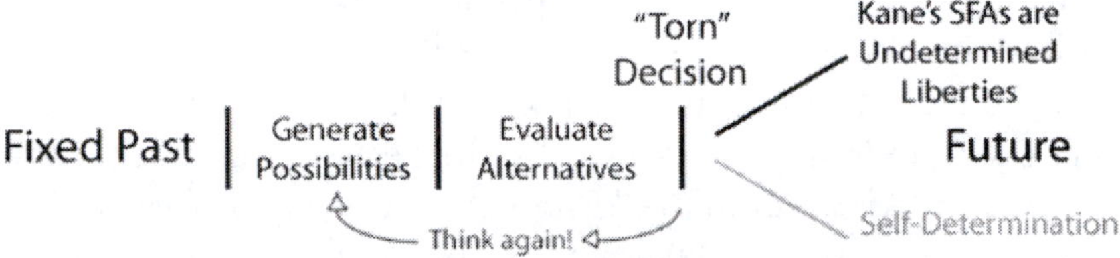

Figure 24-1. Kane's Self-Forming Actions are Undetermined Liberties.

As I see it, the second stage has left the agent with a group of options that are equally attractive. The final choice seems to me arbitrary, any one of them will have adequate reasons for agent responsibility. This, in my view, is related to the ancient *liberum arbitrium* and the **liberty of indifference**.

But for many years, Kane has vigorously denied that his Self-Forming Actions are arbitrary and the random result of chance. To make chance a contributing cause devalues the effort of the agent that deserves the credit for the decision. Negative words like random and chance mislead many thinkers. Kane accepts indeterminism (his noise results from quantum indeterminacy), but rejects random chance.

I agree with Kane that it is inappropriate to say that chance is the cause of the action. I have been mistaken to say so in the past.

But I must go farther to defend the positive role for chance in the universe as a critical part of the **cosmic creation process**. I trace negative attitudes about chance to the ancient idea that chance explains nothing so cannot be a cause (the Greek word for cause, ἀιτία, means explanation) or even stronger, that chance is unintelligible and perhaps atheistic.

Kane's critics, and perhaps even Kane to some degree, share what WILLIAM JAMES called "antipathy to chance."

> "The stronghold of the deterministic sentiment is the antipathy to the idea of chance. As soon as we begin to talk indeterminism to our friends, we find a number of them shaking their heads. This notion of alternative possibilities, they say, this admission that any one of several things may come to pass, is, after all, only a roundabout name for chance; and chance is something the notion of which no sane mind can for an instant tolerate in the world...many persons talk as if the minutest dose of disconnectedness of one part with another, the smallest modicum of independence, the faintest tremor of ambiguity about the future, for example, would ruin everything, and turn this goodly universe into a sort of insane sand-heap or nulliverse, no universe at all.
>
> "In every outwardly verifiable and practical respect, a world in which the alternatives that now actually distract your choice were decided by pure chance would be by me absolutely undistinguished from the world in which I now live. I am, therefore, entirely willing to call it, so far as your choices go, a world of chance for me.
>
> "Determinism denies the ambiguity of future volitions, because it affirms that nothing future can be ambiguous. Indeterminate future volitions do mean chance. Let us not fear to shout it from the house-tops if need be; for we now know that the idea of chance is, at bottom, exactly the same thing as the idea of gift,--the one simply being a disparaging, and the other a eulogistic, name for anything on which we have no effective claim.
>
> "We have seen what determinism means: we have seen that indeterminism is rightly described as meaning chance; and we have seen that chance, the very name of which we are urged to shrink from as from a metaphysical pestilence, means only the negative fact that no part of the world, however big, can claim to control absolutely the destinies of the whole." [35]

More than perhaps any other philosopher, Kane has accepted the reality and importance of quantum indeterminism. In my

35 James (1956) pp. 153-159.

view, he should not shy away from recognizing indeterminism as pure chance just because the current philosophical community has a strong bias against randomness and chance.

Kane's Businesswoman Example

Kane's best-known case of an SFA is the businesswoman on the way to an important meeting when she witnesses an attack on a victim in an alley. She has to decide whether to stop and aid the victim (deontological moral choice) or continue on to her meeting (self-interest).

But now consider what my Cogito model offers her. Rather than stop with these two options, she could go back and generate more **alternative possibilities** in the first stage of my model.

She might get out her cell phone and call 911 for an ambulance to help the victim (giving more real assistance than she would be able provide herself).

Or a random event might occur. Another passerby might appear that she can ask to aid the victim.

I don't mean to dismiss Kane's example, which he restricts to the "torn" moral decisions he claims are the only truly free SFAs. But my variation on his example nicely puts the emphasis on the origination and **creativity** in my model of free will.

Kane's SFAs as Adequately Determined

Kane has long held that his last-possible-second indeterministic decisions at the moment of choice provide the long-held libertarian dream of some sort of absolute freedom at that moment.

Kane is not thinking metaphysically, of course, but before that "libertarian free" moment there is an element of "self-determination" by motives and reasons, by character and values, that Kane recognizes always come just before examples of dual (or plural) rational control..

In my two-stage model, the agent may generate a great many **alternative possibilities**, as we saw in my extended version of Kane's businesswoman. Evaluation of those possibilities normally

reduces the possibilities to the one chosen, but it may only narrow them down to two or more equally attractive options, which gives us **undetermined liberties** like Kane's cases.

The possibilities in a Kane "torn decision" have *as a group* been "**adequately determined**" by the second stage of my model, though not as much as if they had been reduced to only one.

Kane in Barcelona

Kane and I were invited in October 2010 to an "Experts Meeting" in Barcelona, Spain at the Social Trends Institute (STI). The question debated was "Is Science Compatible with Our Desire for Freedom?" The meeting was organized by Antoine Suarez of The Center for Quantum Philosophy in Geneva.

Also invited was Alfred Mele, who directs the *Big Questions in Free Will* project at Florida State University, and Martin Heisenberg, the neurogeneticist and son of Werner Heisenberg, the founder of quantum mechanics.

There were animated exchanges between all of us. The proceedings were videotaped and are available on the STI website.[36] I edited the discussion between Mele, Kane, myself, and remarks by Heisenberg.[37]

In Kane's presentation, he said of the current situation,

> "As Bob Doyle also notes in his conference paper, my own first efforts at dealing with this problem in the 1970's was to formulate a two-stage model very much like the one he nicely presents in his paper. I thought from the beginning that a two-stage model must be a part of the solution to the free will problem. But I also believed that it could not be the complete solution. Hence I did not publish anything about it in the 1970's and was surprised to see that Daniel Dennett had come up with a similar idea in a 1978 paper. He also believed a two-stage model was not all that libertarians wanted, but thought it at least provided some of what they wanted, as did Al Mele who also later formulated such a view. I believe Dennett and Mele were correct in thinking the two-stage model could not be all of what libertar-

36 www.socialtrendsinstitute.org/Activities/Bioethics/Is-Science-Compatible-with-Our-Desire-for-Freedom/Free-Will-debate-on-YouTube.axd

37 youtube.com/watch?v=iwDZUXr6dIc

ians wanted; and hence, while I made the two-stage model part of my own theory in my first book on free will in 1985, it was only a part of the theory and I also tried to go beyond it.

> "I am even more convinced today through the work of Martin Heisenberg as well as these others just mentioned and at this conference that not only is the two-stage model an important part of any adequate theory of free will, but that it is also an important, indeed a crucial, step in the evolution of human free will. The ability to randomize in lower organisms affords them flexibility and creativity as it does for humans. But I believe, as I did in the 70's, that a number of other steps are needed to get from this first crucial evolutionary step to the full evolution of free will in human beings, and that the two-stage model must be folded into a larger picture." [38]

Since William James in the 1880's, more than a dozen philosophers and scientists, including Heisenberg and myself have called for indeterminism in the first stage of our model. Since the 1980's, Robert Kane has called for indeterminism when second-stage deliberations do not result in a single act of **self-determination**. These are two places in what Kane calls a "larger picture" of free will where indeterminism can break the causal chain of determinism without reducing agent control or responsibility for decisions and actions.

Kane at Harvard

I had the privilege in 2009 of hosting Kane at the Harvard Faculty Club and recording an 82-minute video on his life's work.

Entitled *Free Will: Some New Perspectives on an Ancient Problem*, the Information Philosopher published it as a DVD, and Kane recently agreed to make it available on YouTube,[39] in the hope that it will be widely seen by philosophy students.

The above-mentioned YouTube videos can be found without typing in complex URLs, by searching in my YouTube channel called "infophilosopher."

38 Presentation at STI "Experts Meeting," October 30, 2010

39 youtube.com/watch?v=A61X-5b847U

Kane's Oxford Handbook of Free Will

In addition to his own work to find some pathway through what he calls the "free will labyrinth" to an intelligible account of freedom, Kane has assembled in his massive sourcebook *The Oxford Handbook of Free Will* perhaps the best survey of modern positions on free will, from theology and fatalism to metaphysical libertarian perspectives.

The Handbook, now in its second (2011) edition, has contributions from over two dozen contemporary philosophers with strong ideas about free will. Sadly, most continue to be inconclusive debates and attempts to logically refute one another's positions. Daniel Dennett calls this "philosophical judo."

The articles reflect the fact that Peter F. Strawson changed the subject of the discussions from free will to **moral responsibility**, Harry Frankfurt changed the debate from free will to the existence of **alternative possibilities**, and Peter van Inwagen changed the problem from showing **indeterminism** to be true to showing **incompatibilism** to be true.

They ask convoluted questions like "Is Incompatibilism Intuitive?" and describe freedom as Nondeterministic Incompatibilism.

Many of the writers tend to conflate free will and **moral responsibility**. They describe free will as the "control condition" of **moral responsibility**. Free will is indeed a prerequisite for responsibility. But whether an action is moral is a question for ethicists, not for psychologists and neuroscientists who study the nature of the mind and its capacity for free actions.

While no reflection on the editorial quality, that there is little new, and that it is sometimes dismissive of freedom as unintelligible, makes the Oxford Handbook an accurate reflection of the current state of the free will problem.

Kane insightfully remarks "One may legitimately wonder why worries about determinism persist at all in the twenty-first century, when the physical sciences - once the stronghold of determinist thinking - seem to have turned away from determinism." [40] Amen.

40 Kane (2011) p. 5.

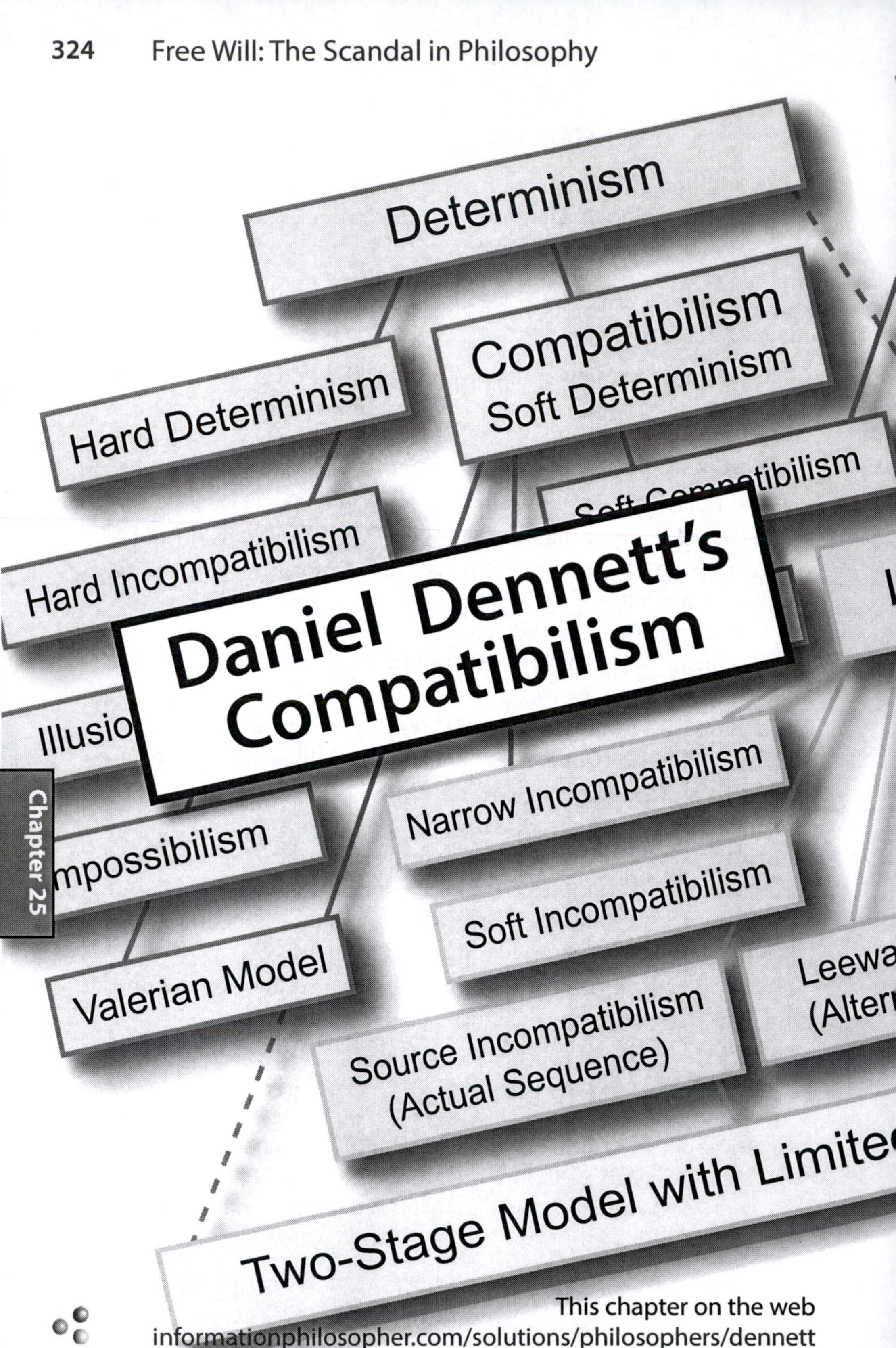

Daniel Dennett's Compatibilism

Chapter 25

This chapter on the web
informationphilosopher.com/solutions/philosophers/dennett

Indeterminism

Daniel Dennett's Compatibilism

While he himself is a confirmed compatibilist, even a determinist, in "On Giving Libertarians What They Say They Want," Chapter 15 of his 1978 book Brainstorms, DANIEL DENNETT articulated the case for a two-stage model of free will better than any libertarian had done at the time.

His "Valerian" model of decision making, named after the poet Paul Valéry, combines **indeterminism** to generate **alternative possibilities,** with (in my view, adequate) determinism to choose among the possibilities.

> "The model of decision making I am proposing, has the following feature: when we are faced with an important decision, a consideration-generator whose output is to some degree undetermined produces a series of considerations, some of which may of course be immediately rejected as irrelevant by the agent (consciously or unconsciously). Those considerations that are selected by the agent as having a more than negligible bearing on the decision then figure in a reasoning process, and if the agent is in the main reasonable, those considerations ultimately serve as predictors and explicators of the agent's final decision."[1]

Dennett gives six excellent reasons why this is the kind of free will that libertarians say they want. He says,

1. "First...The intelligent selection, rejection, and weighing of the considerations that do occur to the subject is a matter of intelligence making the difference."

2. "Second, I think it installs indeterminism in the right place for the libertarian, if there is a right place at all."

3. "Third...from the point of view of biological engineering, it

1 Dennett (1978) p. 295. Dennett studied in Oxford under Gilbert Ryle, whose "Concept of Mind" (1949) revolutionized the approach to philosophical psychology within analytic philosophy, eliminating mind as a "ghost in the machine.".

is just more efficient and in the end more rational that decision making should occur in this way."

4. "A fourth observation in favor of the model is that it permits moral education to make a difference, without making all of the difference."

5. "Fifth - and I think this is perhaps the most important thing to be said in favor of this model - it provides some account of our important intuition that we are the authors of our moral decisions."

6. "Finally, the model I propose points to the multiplicity of decisions that encircle our moral decisions and suggests that in many cases our ultimate decision as to which way to act is less important phenomenologically as a contributor to our sense of free will than the prior decisions affecting our deliberation process itself: the decision, for instance, not to consider any further, to terminate deliberation; or the decision to ignore certain lines of inquiry." [2]

I might add a seventh reason to Dennett's otherwise comprehensive list, that this kind of free will is a process that could have evolved naturally from the lower animals.

"These prior and subsidiary decisions contribute, I think, to our sense of ourselves as responsible free agents, roughly in the following way: I am faced with an important decision to make, and after a certain amount of deliberation, I say to myself: "That's enough. I've considered this matter enough and now I'm going to act," in the full knowledge that I could have considered further, in the full knowledge that the eventualities may prove that I decided in error, but with the acceptance of responsibility in any case." [3]

At times, Dennett seems pleased with his result.

"This result is not just what the libertarian is looking for, but it is a useful result nevertheless. It shows that we can indeed install indeterminism in the internal causal chains affecting human behavior at the macroscopic level while preserving the intelligibility of practical deliberation that the libertarian requires. We may have good reasons from other quarters for embracing determinism, but we need not fear that macroscopic indeter-

2 Dennett (1978) pp. 295-207.

3 *ibid.*

minism in human behavior would of necessity rob our lives of intelligibility by producing chaos." [4]

"we need not fear that causal indeterminism would make our lives unintelligible." [5]

He realizes that his model is still at its base deterministic.

"Even if one embraces the sort of view I have outlined, the deterministic view of the unbranching and inexorable history of the universe can inspire terror or despair, and perhaps the libertarian is right that there is no way to allay these feelings short of a brute denial of determinism. Perhaps such a denial, and only such a denial, would permit us to make sense of the notion that our actual lives are created by us over time out of possibilities that exist in virtue of our earlier decisions; that we trace a path through a branching maze that both defines who we are, and why, to some extent (if we are fortunate enough to maintain against all vicissitudes the integrity of our deliberational machinery) we are responsible for being who we are." [6]

At other times, Dennett is skeptical. His model, he says,

"installs indeterminism in the right place for the libertarian, if there is a right place at all." and "it seems that all we have done is install indeterminism in a harmless place by installing it in an irrelevant place." [7]

Dennett seems to be soliciting interest in the model - from libertarian quarters? It is too bad that libertarians did not accept and improve Dennett's two-stage model. See What if Libertarians Had Accepted What Dan Dennett Gave Them in 1978? in Chapter 27.

If they had, the history of the free will problem would have been markedly different for the last thirty years, perhaps reconciling indeterminism with free will, as the best two-stage models now do, just as Hume reconciled freedom with determinism.

"There may not be compelling grounds from this quarter for favoring an indeterministic vision of the springs of our action, but if considerations from other quarters favor indeterminism, we can at least be fairly sanguine about the prospects of incor-

4 Dennett (1978) p. 292.
5 *ibid*. p. 298.
6 *ibid*. p. 299.
7 *ibid*. p. 295.

> porating indeterminism into our picture of deliberation, even if we cannot yet see what point such an incorporation would have." [8]

The point of incorporating indeterminism is of course first to break the causal chain of pre-determinism, and second to provide a source for novel ideas that were not already implicit in past events, thus explaining not only free will but **creativity**. This requires irreducible and ontological quantum **indeterminacy**.

But Dennett does not think that irreducible quantum randomness provides anything essential beyond the deterministic pseudo-random number generation of computer science.

> "Isn't it the case that the new improved proposed model for human deliberation can do as well with a random-but-deterministic generation process as with a causally undetermined process? Suppose that to the extent that the considerations that occur to me are unpredictable, they are unpredictable simply because they are fortuitously determined by some arbitrary and irrelevant factors, such as the location of the planets or what I had for breakfast." [9]

With his strong background in computer science and artificial intelligence, it is no surprise that Dennett continues to seek a "computational" model of the mind.

But man is not a machine and the mind is not a computer.

Dennett accepts the results of modern physics and does not deny the existence of quantum randomness. He calls himself a "naturalist" who wants to reconcile free will with natural science.

But what is "natural" about a computer-generated pseudo-random number sequence? The algorithm that generates it is quintessentially artificial. In the course of evolution, quantum mechanical randomness (along with the quantum stability of information structures, without which no structures at all would exist) is naturally available to generate **alternative possibilities**.

Why would evolution need to create an algorithmic computational capability to generate those possibilities, when genuine and irreducible quantum randomness already provides them?

---

8 *ibid*. p. 299.
9 ibid. p. 298.

And who, before human computer designers, would be the author or artificer of the algorithm? Gregory Chaitin tells us that the information in a random-number sequence is only as much as is in the algorithm that created the sequence. And note that the artificial algorithm author implicitly has the kind of knowledge attributed to **Laplace's Demon**.

Since Dennett is a confirmed atheist, it seems odd that he has the "antipathy to chance" described by WILLIAM JAMES that is characteristic of religious believers. Quantum randomness is far more atheistic than Dennett's pseudo-randomness, with the latter's implicit author or artificer still conceivable.

Despite his qualms, Dennett seems to have located randomness in exactly the right place, in the first stage of a two-stage model. His model randomly generates alternative considerations for his adequately determined selection process. He is not concerned that random possibilities make the decisions themselves random.

Evolution as an Algorithmic Process

Dennett maintains that biological evolution does not need quantum randomness, and says he was shocked by JACQUES MONOD's claim that random quantum processes are "essential" to evolution. Monod defines the importance of chance, or what he calls "absolute coincidence" as something like the intersection of causal chains that ARISTOTLE calls an "accident." But, says Dennett, in his 1984 book *Elbow Room*,

> "when Monod comes to define the conditions under which such coincidences can occur, he apparently falls into the actualist trap. Accidents must happen if evolution is to take place, Monod says, and accidents can happen — "Unless of course we go back to Laplace's world, from which chance is excluded by definition and where Dr. Brown has been fated to die under Jones' hammer ever since the beginning of time." (*Chance and Necessity*, p. 115)
>
> "If "Laplace's world" means just a deterministic world, then Monod is wrong. Natural selection does not need "absolute"

Chapter 25

coincidence. It does not need "essential" randomness or perfect independence; it needs practical independence — of the sort exhibited by Brown and Jones, and Jules and Jim, each on his own trajectory but "just happening" to intersect, like the cards being deterministically shuffled in a deck and just happening to fall into sequence. Would evolution occur in a deterministic world, a Laplacean world where mutation was caused by a non-random process? Yes, for what evolution requires is an unpatterned generator of raw material, not an uncaused generator of raw material. Quantum-level effects may indeed play a role in the generation of mutations, but such a role is not required by theory." [10]

Where Quantum Indeterminism Might Matter?

Dennett graciously invited me to participate in his graduate seminar on free will at Tufts in the Fall of 2010.[11] He challenged me to provide cases where quantum indeterminism would make a substantive improvement over the pseudo-randomness that he thinks is enough for both biological evolution and free will. Dennett does not deny **quantum indeterminacy**. He just doubts that quantum randomness is necessary for free will. Information philosophy suggests that the primary importance of quantum indeterminacy is that it breaks the causal chain of **pre-determinism**.

See the I-Phi page *Where, and When, is Randomness Located?* for more details on where indeterminism is located in the two-stage models of Bob Doyle, Robert Kane, Alfred Mele, and Dennett's Valerian Model of free will. [12]

Quantum randomness has been available to evolving species for billions of years before pseudo-randomness emerges with humans. But Dennett does not think, as does Jacques Monod, for example, that quantum indeterminacy is necessary for biological evolution. The evolved virtual creatures of artificial life programs demonstrate for Dennett that biological evolution is an algorithmic process.

10 Dennett (1985) p. 150.
11 See informationphilosopher.com/solutions/philosophers/dennett/seminar
12 informationphilosopher.com/freedom/location.html

Below are five cases where quantum chance is critically important and better than pseudo-randomness. They all share a basic insight from information physics. Whenever a stable new information structure is created, two things must happen. The first is a collapse of the quantum wave function that allows one or more particles to combine in the new structure. The second is the transfer away from the structure to the cosmic background of the entropy required by the second law of thermodynamics to balance the local increase in negative entropy (information).

Laplace's Demon

Indeterministic events are unpredictable. Consequently, if any such probabilistic events occur, as Dennett admits, Laplace's demon cannot predict the future. Information cosmology provides a second reason why such a demon is impossible. There was little or no information at the start of the universe. (See the Layzer diagram on page 11.) There is a great deal of information today, and more being created every day. There is not enough information in the past to determine the present, let alone completely determine the future. Creating future information requires quantum events, which are inherently indeterministic. The future is only probable, though it may be "adequately determined." Since there is not enough information available at any moment to comprehend all the information that will exist in the future, Laplace demons are impossible.

Intelligent Designers

Suppose that determinism is true, and that the chance driving spontaneous variation of the gene pool is merely epistemic (human ignorance), so that a deterministic algorithmic process is driving evolution. Gregory Chaitin has shown that the amount of information (and thus the true randomness) in a sequence of random numbers is no more than that in the algorithm that generates them.

This makes the process more comprehensible for a supernatural intelligent designer. And it makes the idea of an intelligent designer, deterministically controlling evolution with complete foreknowledge, more plausible. This is unfortunate.

An intelligent designer with a big enough computer could reverse engineer and alter the algorithm behind the pseudo-randomness driving evolution. This is just what genetic engineers do.

But cosmic rays, which are inherently indeterministic quantum events, damage the DNA to produce mutations, variations in the gene pool. No intelligent designer can control such evolution.

So genetic engineers are intelligent designers, but they cannot control the whole of evolution.

Frankfurt Controllers

For almost fifty years, compatibilists have used Frankfurt-style Cases to show that alternative possibilities are not required for freedom of action and moral responsibility.

Robert Kane showed in 1985[13] that, if a choice is undetermined, the Frankfurt controller cannot tell until the choice is made whether the agent will do A or do otherwise. Compatibilists were begging the question by assuming a deterministic connection between a "prior sign" of a decision and the decision itself.

More fundamentally, information philosophy tells us that because chance (quantum randomness) helps generate the alternative possibilities, information about the choice does not come into the universe until the choice has been made.

Either way, the controller would have to intervene before the choice, in which case it is the controller that is responsible for the decision. Frankfurt controllers do not exist.

Dennett's Eavesdropper

We can call this Dennett's Eavesdropper because, in a discussion of quantum cryptography, Dennett agrees there is a strong reason to prefer quantum randomness to pseudo-randomness for encrypting secure messages. He sees that if a pseudo-random number sequence were used, a clever eavesdropper might discover the algorithm behind it and thus be able to decode the message.

13 David Widerker independently showed this in the 1990's.

Quantum cryptography and quantum computing use the non-local properties of entangled quantum particles. Non-locality shows up when the wave-function of a two-particle system collapses and new information comes into the universe. See the Einstein-Podolsky-Rosen experiment.[14]

Creating New Memes

Richard Dawkins' unit of cultural information has the same limits as purely physical information. CLAUDE SHANNON's mathematical theory of the communication of information says that information is not new without probabilistic surprises. Quantum physics is the ultimate source of that probability and the possibilities that surprise us. If the result were not truly unpredictable, it would be implicitly present in the information we already have. A new meme, like Dennett's intuition pumps, skyhooks, and cranes, would have been already predictable there in the past and not his very original creations.

The Valerian Model

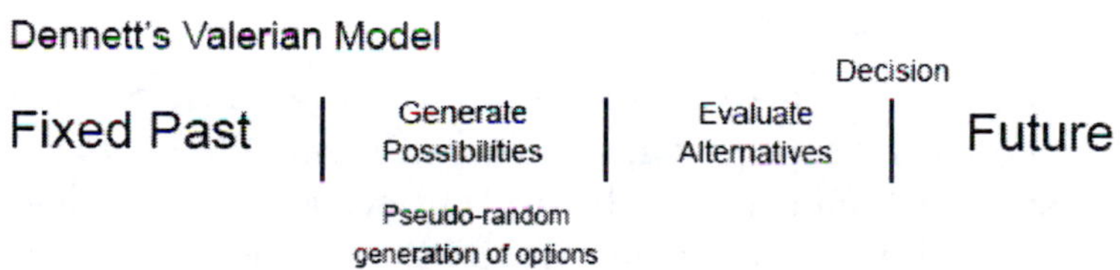

Figure 25-1. Dennett's Valerian Model.

Dennett's Valerian Model of decision making adds randomness in the first-stage generation of considerations, but he believes that pseudo-randomness (the kind generated by computer algorithms) is random enough.

Dennett sees no need for genuine irreducible quantum randomness in the mind, although he does not deny that the world contains genuine quantum indeterminacy. He also does not think, as does Jacques Monod, for example, that quantum indeterminacy is necessary for biological evolution. The evolved virtual creatures

14 informationphilosopher.com/solutions/experiments/EPR/

of artificial life programs demonstrate for Dennett that biological evolution is an algorithmic process.

Dennett says of the second stage that "after a certain amount of deliberation, I say to myself: 'That's enough. I've considered this matter enough and now I'm going to act,' in the full knowledge that I could have considered further, in the full knowledge that the eventualities may prove that I decided in error, but with the acceptance of responsibility in any case."

He says that "this model...provides some account of our important intuition that we are the authors of our moral decisions."

Who's Afraid of Indeterminism?

Dennett and his colleague Christopher Taylor wrote an article for the *Oxford Handbook of Free Will* entitled "Who's Afraid of Determinism." They say that "introducing indeterminism adds nothing in the way of worthwhile possibilities, opportunities, or competences to universe... Though pseudo-random generators may not produce genuinely random output, they come so close that no ordinary mortals can tell the difference."

Taylor and Dennett liken a deterministic universe to a computer playing games of chess.

> "Computers are marvels of determinism. Even their so-called random number generators only execute pseudo-random functions, which produce exactly the same sequence of "random" digits each time the computer reboots. That means that computer programs that avail themselves of randomness at various "choice" points will nevertheless spin out exactly the same sequence of states if run over and over again from a cold start... If you turned off the computer and then restarted it, running the same program, exactly the same variegated series of games would spin out." [15]

The purpose of the Taylor and Dennett article is "to untangle the complexity of the underlying concepts" in two "deeply confused theses concerning possibility and causation: (1) In a deterministic

15 Kane (2002) p. 257.

universe, one can never truthfully utter the sentence 'I could have done otherwise,' and (2) In such universes, one can never really take credit for having caused an event, since in fact all events have been predetermined by conditions during the universe's birth."

We agree that these two theses are confusing, but the confusion seems not that deep.

To clarify the first, (1) In a deterministic universe, the meaning of the true statement "I could have done otherwise" is "I could have done otherwise, if the past had been slightly different and I had chosen to do otherwise."

To clarify the second, (2) In such universes, one can take credit for having caused an event, since in fact the event and one's taking credit for it both would have been predetermined by conditions during the universe's birth."

Even if indeterminism were true, Taylor and Dennett say, the theses would be unaltered. But is this the case? At a minimum, some important points in their article would be altered.

Most important, the "fact"of predeterminism in thesis 2 would not be a fact. Indeed, they note the discovery of indeterminacy in modern quantum mechanics (p.259) and go on to observe (in footnote 22) that randomness could result from the presence or absence of a pulse from a Geiger counter. This would produce what they refer to as "genuine" randomness. (p.270)

It would then follow that a chess computer equipped with access to "genuine" quantum randomness would not "spin out exactly the same sequence of states if run over and over again from a cold start." But more significantly, there is no way for an indeterministic universe at its birth to know the future. There is simply not enough information present at the origin, or any other time, to describe perfectly and completely the present and future.

Determinism

Hard Determinism

Compatibilism
Soft Determinism

Soft Compatibilism

Hard Incompatibilism

Illusionis

mpossibi

Narrow Incompatibilism

Soft Incompatibilism

Valerian Model

Source Incompatibilism
(Actual Sequence)

Leewa
(Alter

Two-Stage Model with Limite

Alfred Mele's Modest Libertarianism

This chapter on the web
informationphilosopher.com/solutions/philosophers/mele/

Alfred Mele's Modest Libertarianism

Alfred Mele has developed the idea of autonomous agents, who among other things exercise a kind of self-control that is related to metaphysical freedom terms like "free will" and "free action." He has also developed a number of models for free will, most notably his 1995 two-stage model called "Modest Libertarianism. Others include Soft Compatibilism, Soft Libertarianism, and Daring Soft Libertarianism

Without committing himself to the idea that human autonomy is compatible with determinism or incompatible (the position of the libertarians), Mele provides arguments in support of autonomous agents for both positions. He is, as he says, "officially agnostic about the truth of compatibilism" and describes his position as "agnostic autonomism."

Mele's opponents are those who believe there are no free and morally responsible human beings. They are philosophers who deny both compatibilism and libertarianism - Richard Double and Ted Honderich, for example, "Impossibilists" like Galen Strawson, "Hard Incompatibilists" like Derk Pereboom and "Illusionists" Saul Smilansky. Mele has debated the psychologist Daniel Wegner, whose position is that the conscious will is an illusion, based primarily on the Libet experiments.

Note that Randolph Clarke's "narrow incompatibilism" denies the compatibilism of free will and determinism, but accepts the compatibilism of **moral responsibility** and determinism. John Martin Fischer's "semicompatibilism" similarly accepts the compatibilism of **moral responsibility**, while remaining agnostic about free will and the truth of determinism. Clarke's and Fischer's morally responsible agents presumably would be Mele "autonomous agents."

Agnostic Autonomous Agents

Most libertarians, Mele thinks, both agent-causalists like TIMOTHY O'CONNOR and event-causalists, like ROBERT KANE, might subscribe to his "autonomous agent" idea.

> "My plan in Mele [Autonomous Agents] 1995 was to use the resources both of libertarianism and of compatibilism in defending agnostic autonomism and to do that partly by developing the best compatibilist and libertarian positions I could develop. Part of my strategy was to construct an account of an ideally self-controlled agent (where self-control is understood as the contrary of akrasia: [a Greek term, meaning] roughly, weakness of will), to argue that even such an agent may fall short of autonomy (or free agency), and to ask what may be added to ideal self-control to yield autonomy (or free agency). I offered two answers, one for compatibilists and another for libertarians. I then argued that a disjunctive thesis associated with both answers—agnostic autonomism - is more credible than [believing there are no free and moral human beings] NFM." [1]

Modest Libertarianism

Mele in his 1995 book *Autonomous Agents*, had proposed a "Modest Libertarianism" for consideration by libertarians.[2] He himself did not endorse the idea. But he is concerned about the proper place to locate the indeterminism. His soft libertarians locate it somewhere in the chain of events leading up to the formation of intentions, the evaluation of options, the decision and ultimate action. His "daring soft libertarians" move the indeterminism up into the "time of action," where indeterministic alternative possibilities for actions may (or may not) exist.

He made it clear, following DANIEL DENNETT's "Valerian" model in *Brainstorms*, 1978, that any **indeterminism** should come early in the overall process. He even describes the latter - decision - stage of the process as **compatibilist** (effectively **determinist**). This of course could only be **adequate determinism**. Mele

1 Mele (2006) p. 5.
2 Mele (1995) p. 211.

proposes a "soft compatibilism" that sees some value for indeterminism in the early stages. This will be the basis for our "**Comprehensive Compatibilism**" proposal in Chapter 28.

> "These observations indicate that it might be worth exploring the possibility of combining a compatibilist conception of the later parts of a process issuing in full blown, deliberative, intentional action with an incompatibilist conception of the earlier parts. For example, it might be possible to gain "ultimate control" while preserving a considerable measure of nonultimate agential control by treating the process from proximal decisive better judgment through overt action in a compatibilist way and finding a theoretically useful place for indeterminacy in processes leading to proximal decisive better judgments." [3]

For Mele and most other modern compatibilists, quantum physics has shown that determinism is not true.

> "Recall that compatibilism does not include a commitment to determinism. The thesis is that determinism does not preclude autonomy. Treating the process from proximal decisive better judgment through overt action in a compatibilist way does not require treating it in a determinist way. Compatibilists may, in principle be willing to accept an account of causation that accommodates both deterministic and probabilistic instances, and they are not committed to holding that probabilistic causation in the process just mentioned precludes the freedom of its product. In the same vein, advocates of autonomy who seek a "theoretical useful place" for indeterminism in the springs of action need not insist that indeterminism does not appear at other places, as well, in internal processes issuing in autonomous action. Their claim on that matter may merely be that indeterminism at these other junctures is of no use to them.
>
> "External indeterminism, as I have already explained, does not give libertarians what they want. That leaves internal indeterminism. Assume, for the sake of argument, that human beings sometimes act autonomously, that acting autonomously requires "ultimate control," and that the latter requires internal indeterminism. Then, with a view to combining ultimate control

3 Mele (1995) p. 212.

> with robust nonultimate control, we can ask what location(s) for internal indeterminism would do us the most good." [4]

A Problem about Luck for Libertarians

Mele's plan in his book *Free Will and Luck* is to pay more attention to Frankfurt-style examples and to "agential luck."

> "Agents' control is the yardstick by which the bearing of luck on their freedom and moral responsibility is measured. When luck (good or bad) is problematic, that is because it seems significantly to impede agents' control over themselves or to highlight important gaps or shortcomings in such control. It may seem that to the extent that it is causally open whether or not, for example, an agent intends in accordance with his considered judgment about what it is best to do, he lacks some control over what he intends, and it may be claimed that a positive deterministic connection between considered best judgment and intention would be more conducive to freedom and moral responsibility.
>
> "This last claim will be regarded as a nonstarter by anyone who holds that freedom and moral responsibility require agential control and that determinism is incompatible with such control. Sometimes it is claimed that agents do not control anything at all if determinism is true. That claim is false.
>
> "As soon as any agent...judges it best to A, objective probabilities for the various decisions open to the agent are set, and the probability of a decision to A is very high. Larger probabilities get a correspondingly larger segment of a tiny indeterministic neural roulette wheel in the agent's head than do smaller probabilities. A tiny neural ball bounces along the wheel; its landing in a particular segment is the agent's making the corresponding decision. When the ball lands in the segment for a decision to A, its doing so is not just a matter of luck. After all, the design is such that the probability of that happening is very high. But the ball's landing there is partly a matter of luck.

4 Mele (1995) p. 213.

> "All libertarians who hold that A's being a free action depends on its being the case that, at the time, the agent was able to do otherwise freely then should tell us what it could possibly be about an agent who freely A-ed at t in virtue of which it is true that, in another world with the same past and laws of nature, he freely does something else at t. Of course, they can say that the answer is "free will." But what they need to explain then is how free will, as they understand it, can be a feature of agents — or, more fully, how this can be so where free will, on their account of it, really does answer the question. To do this, of course, they must provide an account of free will — one that can be tested for adequacy in this connection." [5]

Mele proposes his "modest libertarianism" to satisfy these needs. It includes a two-stage process that first generates random alternative possibilities, which is then followed by a determination stage. When he first mentioned his idea in 1995, Mele cited the similar "Valerian" example DANIEL DENNETT had proposed in 1978 as something libertarians should want.

Note that both Dennett and Mele are skeptical that any such process exists, but note that Mele's model does indeed satisfy most of the **requirements** for libertarian free will. [6]

A Modest Libertarian Proposal (redux)

> "According to typical event-causal libertarian views, the proximate causes of free actions indeterministically cause them. This is a consequence of the typical event-causal libertarian ideas that free actions have proximate causes and that if an agent freely A-s at t in world W, he does not A at t in some other possible world with the same laws of nature and the same past up to t. Now, approximate causes of actions, including actions that are decisions, are internal to agents." [7]

> "In light of the general point about the proximate causation of actions, typical event-causal libertarianism encompasses a commitment to what may be termed agent-internal indeterminism.

5 Mele (2006) p. 7.
6 See Chapter 5.
7 Mele (2006) p. 9.

"What I call modest libertarianism (see Mele 1995, pp. 211-21) embraces that commitment, too, even though it rejects the idea that the proximate causes of free actions indeterministically cause the actions. Indeterministic worlds in which every instance of causation within any agent is deterministic are hostile environments for libertarian freedom. What libertarians want that determinism precludes is not merely that agents have open to them more than one future that is compatible with the combination of the past and the laws of nature, but that, on some occasions, which possible future becomes actual is in some sense and to some degree up to the agents. The want something that seemingly requires that agents themselves be indeterministic in some suitable way - that some relevant things that happen under the skin are indeterministically caused by other such things. The focus is on psychological events, of course (as opposed, for example, to indeterministically caused muscle spasms), and, more specifically, on psychological events that have a significant bearing on action.

"Requiring internal indeterminism for free action and moral responsibility is risky. To be sure, quantum mechanics, according to leading interpretations, is indeterministic. But indeterminism at that level does not ensure that any human brains themselves sometimes operate indeterministically, much less that they sometimes operate indeterministically in ways appropriate for free action and moral responsibility. One possibility, as David Hodgson reports, is that "in systems as hot, wet, and massive as neurons of the brain, quantum mechanical indeterminacies quickly cancel out, so that for all practical purposes determinism rules in the brain" (2002, p. 86). Another is that any indeterminism in the human brain is simply irrelevant to free action and moral responsibility. Modest libertarians join other event-causal libertarians in taking this risk." [8]

"In principle, an agent-internal indeterminism may provide for indeterministic agency while blocking or limiting our proximal control over what happens only at junctures at which we have no greater proximal control on the hypothesis that our universe is deterministic. Obviously, in those cases in which

8 Mele (2006) p. 10.

we act on the basis of careful, rational deliberation, what we do is influenced by at least some of the considerations that "come to mind" — that is, become salient in consciousness — during deliberation and by our assessments of considerations. Now, even if determinism is true, it is false that, with respect to every consideration — every belief, desire, hypothesis, and so on — that comes to mind during our deliberation, we are in control of its coming to mind, and some considerations that come to mind without our being in control of their so doing may influence the outcome of our deliberation. Furthermore, a kind of internal indeterminism is imaginable that limits our control only in a way that gives us no less proximal control than we would have on the assumption that determinism is true, while opening up alternative deliberative outcomes. (Although, in a deterministic world, it would never be a matter of genuine chance that a certain consideration came to mind during deliberation, it may still be a matter of luck relative to the agent's sphere of control.) As I put it in Mele 1995, "Where compatibilists have no good reason to insist on determinism in the deliberative process as a requirement for autonomy, where internal indeterminism is, for all we know, a reality, and where such indeterminism would not diminish the nonultimate control that real agents exert over their deliberation even on the assumption that real agents are internally deterministic — that is, at the intersection of these three locations — libertarians may plump for ultimacy-promoting indeterminism (p. 235). Modest libertarians try to stake out their view at this intersection." [9]

"One kind of possible deliberator may be so constituted that no beliefs and desires of his that are directly relevant to the topic of his current deliberation have a chance of not coming to mind during his deliberation, whereas it is causally open whether some of his indirectly relevant beliefs and desires will come to mind. The causally open possibilities of this kind do not need to be extensive to secure the possibility of more than one deliberative outcome. Modest libertarians both need and fear internal indeterminism, and they are disposed to constrain it when engaged in the project of inventing indeterministic agents who can act freely and morally responsibly." [10]

9 Mele (2006) pp. 11-12.
10 *ibid.*

Alfred Mele here comes as close as any philosopher to my Cogito model of free will.

> "The modest indeterminism at issue allows agents ample control over their deliberation. Suppose a belief, hypothesis, or desire that is indirectly relevant to a deliberator's present practical question comes to mind during deliberation but was not deterministically caused to do so. Presumably, a normal agent would be able to assess this consideration. And upon reflection might rationally reject the belief as unwarranted, rationally judge that the hypothesis does not merit investigation, or rationally decide that the desire should be given little or no weight in his deliberation. Alternatively reflection might rationally lead him to retain the belief, to pursue the hypothesis to give the desire significant weight. That a consideration is indeterministically caused to come to mind does not entail that the agent has no control over how he responds to it. Considerations that are indeterministically caused to come to mind (like considerations that are deterministically caused to come to mind) are nothing more than input to deliberation. Their coming to mind has at most an indirect effect on what the agent decides, an effect that is mediated by the agent's assessment of them. They do not settle matters. Moreover, not only do agents have the opportunity to assess these considerations, but they also have the opportunity to search for additional relevant considerations before they decide, thereby increasing the probability that other relevant considerations will be indeterministically caused to come to mind. They have, then, at least sometimes, the opportunity to counteract instances of bad luck — for example, an indeterministically caused coming to mind of a misleading consideration or, a chance failure to notice a relevant consideration. And given a suitable indeterminism regarding what comes to mind in an assessment process, there are causally open alternative possibilities for the conclusion or outcome of that process." [11]

"Compatibilists who hold that we act freely even when we are not in control of what happens at certain specific junctures in the process leading to action are in no position to hold that an indeterministic agent's lacking control at the same junctures

11 Mele (2006) p. 12.

precludes free action. And, again, real human beings are not in control of the coming to mind of everything that comes to mind during typical processes of deliberation. If this lack of perfect proximal control does not preclude its being the case that free actions sometimes issue from typical deliberation on the assumption that we are deterministic agents, it also does not preclude this on the assumption that we are *indeterministic* agents.

"Now, even if garden-variety compatibilists can be led to see that the problem of luck is surmountable by a libertarian, how are theorists of other kinds likely to respond to the libertarian position that I have been sketching? There are, of course, philosophers who contend that moral responsibility and freedom are illusions and that we lack these properties whether our universe is deterministic or indeterministic — for example, Richard Double (1991) and Galen Strawson (1986)." [12]

"Modest libertarians can also anticipate trouble from traditional libertarians, who want more than the modest indeterminism that I have described can offer. Clarke, who has done as much as anyone to develop an agent-causal libertarian view, criticizes event-causal libertarianism on the grounds that it adds no "positive" power of control to compatibilist control but simply places compatibilist control in an indeterministic setting. Of course, given that combining compatibilist control with indeterminism in a certain psychological sphere was my explicit strategy in constructing a modest libertarian position (Mele 1995, pp. 212-13, 217), I do not see this as an objection. In any case, traditional libertarians need to show that what they want is coherent." [13]

In my view, there is no avoiding luck in general, but keeping randomness out of the decision and action prevents it from undermining control and responsibility

"That requires showing that what they want does not entail or presuppose a kind of luck that would itself undermine moral responsibility. The typical libertarian wants both indeterminism and significant control at the moment of decision. That is

12 Mele (2006) pp. 13-14.
13 Mele (2006) p. 14.

> the desire that prompts a serious version of the worry about luck I sketched earlier. In the absence of a plausible resolution of the worry, it is epistemically open that a modest libertarian proposal of the sort I sketched is the best a libertarian can do. Of course, even if I happen to hit on the best libertarian option, it does not follow that I have hit on the best option for believers in free action and moral responsibility — as long as compatibilism is still in the running."[14]

But true compatibilism, which assumes determinism is true, is not in the running. Mele and his colleagues have long ago given up hope for determinism being true. See the Strawson/Fischer/Mele hypothesis below.

The Modest Libertarianism Process

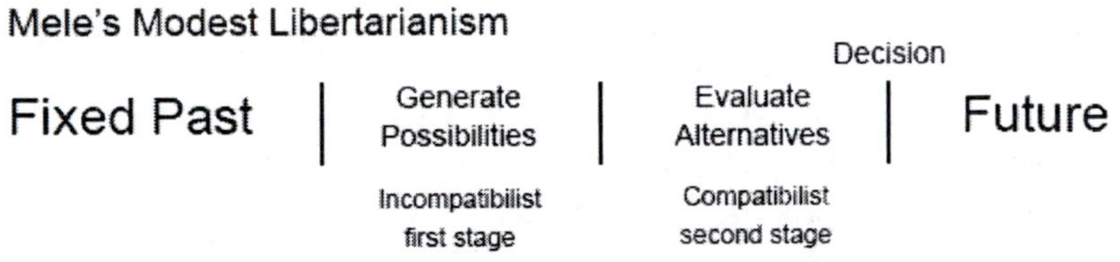

Mele's Modest Libertarianism

Decision

Fixed Past | Generate Possibilities | Evaluate Alternatives | Future

Incompatibilist first stage

Compatibilist second stage

Figure 26-1. Mele's Modest Libertarianism.

Al Mele's **modest libertarianism** provides what he calls an "incompatibilist" first stage (he means **indeterminist**) and a compatibilist second stage (he means **determinist**).

Mele does not (as do many philosophers since a mistaken reading of R. E. Hobart's 1934 *Mind* article) think this **determination** of the will would imply **pre-determinism**.

Mele locates the randomness in the incompatibilist first stage of his two-stage model, where **alternative possibilities** are generated.

Mele's model is similar to Dennett's, but he does not argue for Dennett's pseudo-random (deterministic) randomness. However, because Mele is agnostic about the truth of determinism and indeterminism, he does not discuss the importance of quantum randomness explicitly.

14 Mele (2006) p. 14.

Mele's Other Models for Free Will

Being a self-proclaimed "agnostic" on these questions, Mele has developed both compatibilist and libertarian positions. His position on compatibilism needs some explaining. He says that because contemporary compatibilists (he mentions especially John Martin Fischer) attend to what modern quantum physics tell us, the overwhelming majority do not believe that determinism is true.

One might then ask what they think free will is compatible with, if not determinism. The answer is that they believe that even if determinism were true, it would leave it open that people sometimes act freely. "Freely" here is in the compatibilist sense of free will that Immanuel Kant called a "wretched subterfuge and William James called a "quagmire of evasion." I call their idea the Strawson/Fischer/Mele Hypothesis.

Mele says this is the traditional framing of the problem of whether "free action" (to be distinguished from free will") is precluded by determinism. Ever since Hume, as long as an agent is not coerced physically, her/his actions could be judged to be free, even if they are part of a deterministic causal chain. But "freedom of action" (Isaiah Berlin's negative liberty) is distinctly not freedom of the will. See Chapter 3.

Mele's 1995 Modest Libertarianism discussed above is Mele's strongest two-stage model. In 1996 he developed a related position called "Soft Libertarianism," useful in the context of Frankfurt-style cases. Then in his 2006 work he developed a variation called "Daring Soft Libertarianism."

Soft Libertarianism

Soft libertarians find determinism unacceptable because it claims that for all their intentions, evaluations, decisions, and subsequent actions, events were in progress before they were born that cause all those intentions and actions. This is the core concern of Peter van Inwagen's **Consequence Argument**. Soft libertarians are not primarily motivated because indeterminism may provide the alternative possibilities that are denied by Frankfurt cases, but simply that the causal chain of determinism might be broken, allowing them to make a causal contribution. He says,

> "Unlike hard libertarians, soft libertarians leave it open that determinism is compatible with our actions' being up to us in a way conducive to freedom and moral responsibility [presumably in the second stage of a two-stage model?]. However, they believe that a more desirable freedom and moral responsibility require that our actions not be parts of the unfolding of deterministic chains of events that were in progress even before we were born. If soft libertarians can view themselves as making some choices or decisions that are not deterministically caused or that are deterministically caused by, for example, something that includes deliberative judgments that are not themselves deterministically caused, then they can view themselves as initiating some causal processes that are not intermediate links in a long deterministic causal chain extending back near the big bang." [15]

Soft libertarianism differs from modest libertarianism in that it does not require robust alternative possibilities. But, somewhat inconsistently?, Mele says (p.113) that soft libertarians do not assert that free action and moral responsibility require the falsity of determinism. Mele briefly mentions a "soft compatibilism," but does not develop it beyond saying that "soft compatibilism leaves soft libertarianism open but is not committed to it."

Daring Soft Libertarianism

In his 2006 book Free Will and Luck, Mele extended his soft libertarian idea to "Daring Soft Libertarianism." Mele reaches out to Robert Kane's idea of Ultimate Responsibility, in which we can be responsible for current actions, ones that are essentially determined by our character and values, as long as we formed

15 Mele (2006) p. 97.

that character ourselves by earlier free actions that he calls Self-Forming Actions (SFAs). SFAs in turn require brains that are not deterministically caused by anything outside the agent.

Some may argue that a modest libertarianism gives libertarians all the openness they can get without introducing into an agent a kind of openness that entails freedom-precluding and responsibility-precluding luck. But libertarians like Kane will not settle for such modest libertarianism. For them, Mele developed a more daring soft libertarian view, DSL.

Daring soft libertarians, he says, especially value a power to make decisions that are not deterministically caused - a certain initiatory power. They opt for event-causal soft libertarianism (p. 113). They do not like decisions made indeterministically or at random, what Mele calls basically free action. But they accept what Mele calls basically* free action (note the asterisk), whose requirement for alternative possibilities at the time of action are reduced, but whose requirement for indeterministic free actions some time in the past (Kane's SFAs?) is intact (p. 115).

They can then replace the indeterministic connection between judgments and actions with a deterministic one (p. 117). (Note this can only be the adequate determinism of the two-stage models like Mele's modest libertarianism.)

Mele says that,

> "Part of what DSLs are driving at in their claims about influence is that probabilities of actions — practical probabilities — for agents are not always imposed on agents. Through their past behavior, agents shape present practical probabilities, and in their present behavior they shape future practical probabilities. The relationship between agents and the probabilities of their actions is very different from the relationship between dice and the probabilities of outcomes of tosses. In the case of dice, of course, the probabilities of future tosses are independent of the outcomes of past tosses. However, the probabilities of agents' future actions are influenced by their present and past actions."[16]

16 Mele (2006) p. 122.

> "DSLs maintain that in the vast majority of cases of basically* free actions and actions for which agents are basically* morally responsible, agents have some responsibility for the relevant practical probabilities... These chances are not dictated by external forces, and they are influenced by basically* free and morally responsible actions the agents performed in the past." [17]

The Strawson/Fischer/Mele Hypothesis

Mele tells me that he and John Martin Fischer subscribe to the view that "even if determinism were true, we would still have free will." [18] This can only be what Immanuel Kant calls the "wretched subterfuge" of "compatibilist free will." As I see it, this hypothesis derives from two sources. First, there is P. F. Strawson's view that whether determinism or indeterminism is true, we would not be willing to give up moral responsibility. Second, there is Fischer's view that free will is only the "control condition" for moral responsibility.

So we can restate the hypothesis as "even if determinism were true, we would still have moral responsibility." Determinism is not "true," but with this hypothesis I can completely agree.

And I can go farther and formulate what might be called the Strawson/Doyle hypothesis - "even if indeterminism is true, we still have free will and moral responsibility." In my two-stage model, indeterminism in the first stage does not prevent our will and our actions from being **adequately determined** by reasons, motives, feelings, etc., as compatibilists have always wanted. But the existence of indeterminism in the first stage means that our actions were not **pre-determined** from the moment just before we began to generate **alternative possibilities** for our actions, let alone from before we were born or from the origin of the universe.

Thoughts *come to us* freely. Actions *go from us* willfully.

First chance, then choice. First "free," then "will."

---

17 *ibid.* p. 123.

18 Personal communication.

Mele and the Libet Experiments

Mele has lectured and written extensively on interpretations of the Libet experiments.[19] (See Chapter 17.) He has debated Daniel Wegner, the Harvard psychologist and author of *The Illusion of Conscious Will*, who claims that the experiments deny free will.

Mele's main criticism is what he sees as a systematic bias in data collection. All the Libet experiments work by permanently storing the last few seconds of data that have been collected, when triggered by detecting the wrist flex itself.

If there is no wrist flex, there is no data collected. The equally likely (in my view) cases of a rise in the readiness potential (RP) followed by no wrist flex would have been systematically ignored by Libet's method of data collection.

It seems to imply a one-to-one relationship between initial rise in RP and the flex, which is misinterpreted as a causal relationship.

I explain the initial rise in the readiness potential as the first stage in my Cogito model, where alternative possibilities for action are being considered, including to flex or not to flex. See pages 241-3 for more details.

Big Questions in Free Will

Mele directs a four-year project at Florida State funded with $4.4 million from the Templeton Foundation. He will be offering multiple $40,000/year post-doc positions. We can expect some significant new research on the free-will problem over the next four years. My hope is that the post-docs will read this book.

Mele in Barcelona

You can see a discussion between Mele, Robert Kane, and myself on YouTube debating whether two-stage models should be called "determined," because the word implies **pre-determinism** to so many philosophers, and our two-stage models are distinctly not pre-determined.[20]

19 Mele (2010)

20 www.youtube.com/watch?v=iwDZUXr6dIc

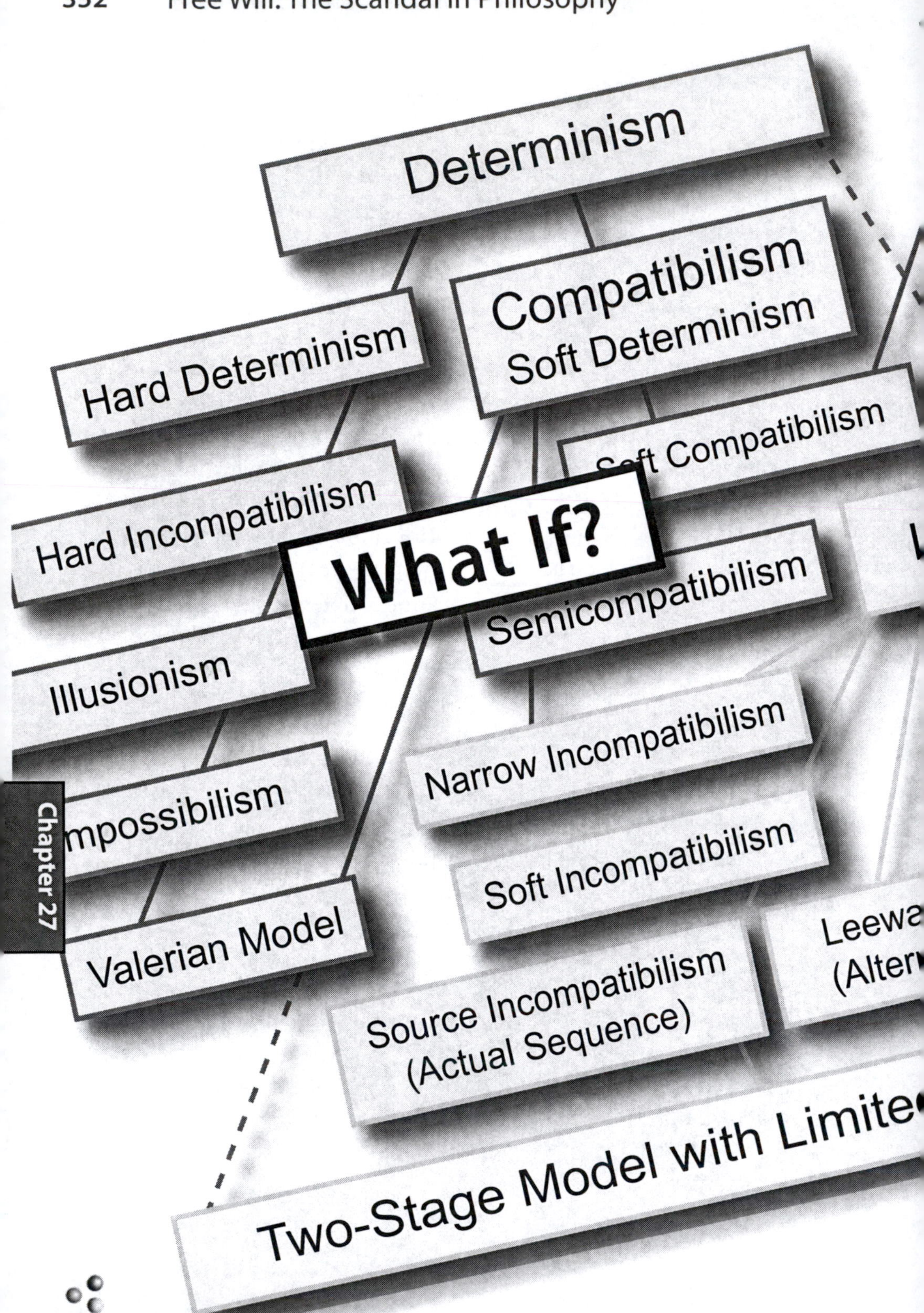
Determinism
Hard Determinism
Compatibilism
Soft Determinism
Soft Compatibilism
Hard Incompatibilism
What If?
Semicompatibilism
Illusionism
Narrow Incompatibilism
mpossibilism
Soft Incompatibilism
Valerian Model
Source Incompatibilism
(Actual Sequence)
Two-Stage Model with Limite

What If?

What if Libertarians Had Accepted What Dan Dennett Gave To Them In 1978?

Over thirty years ago, DANIEL DENNETT proposed a decision-making model that he thought would appeal to libertarians. Unfortunately, libertarians largely ignored Dennett's proposal.

The history of the free-will problem would have been quite different if libertarians had accepted and credited what I might call "Dennett's Dangerous Idea." I imagine the difference below.

In chapter 15 of his 1978 book *Brainstorms*, entitled "On Giving Libertarians What They Say They Want," Dennett articulated the case for a two-stage model of free will better than most libertarians had done before.[1]

Dennett concluded his essay optimistically, but he sounds very much like TED HONDERICH in the concern that his determinism inspires despair (Honderich calls it dismay. See Chapter 23).

> "Even if one embraces the sort of view I have outlined, the deterministic view of the unbranching and inexorable history of the universe can inspire terror or despair, and perhaps the libertarian is right that there is no way to allay these feelings short of a brute denial of determinism. Perhaps such a denial, and only such a denial, would permit us to make sense of the notion that our actual lives are created by us over time out of possibilities that exist in virtue of our earlier decisions; that we trace a path through a branching maze that both defines who we are, and why, to some extent (if we are fortunate enough to maintain against all vicissitudes the integrity of our deliberational machinery) we are responsible for being who we are. That prospect deserves an investigation of its own. All I hope to have shown here is that it is a prospect we can and should take seriously." [2]

1 Dennett (1978), p. 293. See Chapter 25 for more on Dennett's Valerian model.
2 Dennett (1978), p. 299

I, for one, took Dennett very seriously. When I read this passage, my immediate reaction was that Dennett had invented the two-stage model that was my **Cogito** model[3] from the early 1970's, with the exception of my basing the random generation of alternative possibilities on true quantum randomness.

I was convinced that other scientists and philosophers would add quantum randomness to Dennett's model and soon publish the equivalent of my **Cogito** model. I set my philosophy aside and continued to entrepreneur and develop productivity tools.

At the Barcelona "Experts Meeting" on Free Will in October 2010, Robert Kane says that he also had independently thought of Dennett's two-stage model but did not publish it. He says he wanted "something more," because once the alternatives are spelled out in the first stage, the second-stage decision is "determined" by the agent's character and values.

I agree with Kane that decisions are **adequately determined**, given the agent's character, values, etc., but that they are not **predetermined** from before the first considerations are generated and deliberations began.

The "something more" that Kane wants is some randomness in the decision itself, something he calls "plural rationality." This allows the agent to flip a coin as long as she has good reasons for whatever she chooses randomly. Kane gives an example of a businesswoman on the way to a meeting who witnesses an assault and must decide between aiding the victim and continuing to her work. Note that Dennett had already described a similar case in *Brainstorms* - a new Ph.D. who could choose randomly between assistant professorships at Chicago and Swarthmore. She could have an "intelligible rationale" and feel responsible whichever way she decided, because both ways had good reasons. [4]

And note that Kane, like me, specifically is trying to use quantum randomness as the basis for a free-will model, where Dennett thinks some computer pseudo-randomness might be enough to

3 See Chapter 13

4 Dennett (1978), p. 294

generate alternatives. Neither of them could see where such randomness would be located in the brain, without making everything random. Kane and I differ primarily in the timing of the quantum randomness, I put it in the first stage, he in the second.

Neither Kane nor Dennett see the randomness located throughout the brain, like my model.

It takes two - Cogito and Intelligo

In chapter 5 of Brainstorms, Dennett described the work of the poet Paul Valéry, who took part in a 1936 Synthése conference in Paris with Jacques Hadamard. The conference focused on Henri Poincare's two-stage approach to problem solving, in which the unconscious generates random combinations. In his book, *The Psychology of Invention in the Mathematical Mind*, Hadamard quoted Valéry (as did Dennett later), summarizing the conference opinion,

> "It takes two to invent anything. The one makes up combinations; the other one chooses, recognizes what is important to him in the mass of things which the former has imparted to him." [5]

The Valéry reference has led to Dennett's model (and similar ones from Alfred Mele, for example) being called "Valerian." At the end of chapter 5, Dennett finds names for the generator and tester phases in St. Augustine's note that the Latin *cogito* means to "shake together" and *intelligo* means to "select among."

"The Romans, it seems, knew what they were talking about," Dennett comments.

Actually, most Romans were Stoics. And they violently opposed Epicureans like Lucretius, who argued for some chance (the swerve) to break the chain of determinism. For the Stoics, and for modern determinists who crave strong natural causal laws, **chance** is anathema and atheistic. For them, Nature was synonymous with God and Reason.

5 Hadamard (1949), p.30, cited by Dennett (1978), p.293.

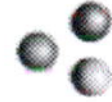

What If Kane and Dennett Had Done Otherwise?

Dan Dennett's phone rings a short time after publication of his 1978 book, *Brainstorms*.

Kane: Hi, Dan. This is Bob Kane. I've just been reading your essay "On Giving Libertarians What They Say They Want" and see a lot to like in it. You know that WILFRID SELLARS challenged me some years ago to reconcile his Manifest Image, in which we all feel we have free will, with his Scientific Image, in which physics either makes everything determined, in which case we are not free, or if modern quantum mechanics is right, everything is undetermined and we can't have responsibility for our actions.

Dennett: Good to hear from you, Bob. You know, I am a naturalist and think the will is a natural product of physical laws and biological evolution, so Sellars' Scientific Image should be good enough. And Sellars is a Compatibilist, like me.

Kane: I know, but I feel we need something more than your decision-making model with its intelligent selection from what may be a partially arbitrary or chaotic or random production of options. Don't you see that the agent would be determined to select the best option from those which were randomly generated, consistent with the agent's reasons, motives, feelings, etc.? Libertarians want something more, some freedom in the decision itself.

Dennett: What's wrong with our actions being determined by our reasons and motives? R. E. Hobart said in 1934 that free will requires some determination, otherwise, our actions would be random and we wouldn't be responsible.

Kane: Right, but I think I can show that randomness does not always eliminate responsibility. I have this idea that a businesswoman could be torn between helping a victim and going on to her business meeting. She has good reasons for doing either one and she could feel responsible even if she acted indeterministically. What do you think?

Dennett: I agree. I showed the same thing, with my example of a new Ph.D. choosing between the University of Chicago and

Swarthmore. Her choice would depend on what considerations happened to come to her before her decision. But luck is real. I think we need to keep randomness out of the decision and limit it to generating options, what you libertarians call the alternative possibilities.

Kane: Well, having alternative possibilities (I call them AP) is not enough. I want what I call Ultimate Responsibility (or UR). That needs what I call a self-forming action (an SFA) in which the choice is a torn decision like that of the businesswoman.

Dennett: But if that torn decision is ultimately based on a coin flip, or a quantum event in your brain amplified to the neuron level, as Compton suggested, it would be random actions that form your self. Is that intelligible?

Kane: I'm not happy with it. I concede that indeterminism, wherever it occurs, diminishes control over what we try to do.

Dennett: I think that my model installs indeterminism in the right place for a libertarian, if there is a right place at all.

Kane: I haven't figured out the location and the mechanism of amplification, but something like quantum randomness must be going on in our brains if we are free.

Dennett: Isn't it the case that my proposed model for human deliberation can do as well with a random-but-deterministic generation process as with a causally undetermined process?

Kane: Don't pseudo-random number generators always have an algorithm that determines them? Wouldn't the author of that algorithm determine your life, like Laplace's demon? And aren't computer algorithms quintessentially artificial and not natural?

Dennett: You have a point. Quantum randomness is no doubt more natural than the pseudo-random number generators we cognitive scientists are using in artificial intelligence and computational models of the mind.

Kane: I could perhaps agree that randomness should be limited to generating ideas for your intelligent selection process, if you would agree that the randomness could be quantum randomness.

Dennett: I never denied the existence of quantum randomness. I'm just not convinced it is necessary for free will.

Kane: It seems to be necessary, if we want to break the causal chain that pre-determines every event since the beginning of the universe. The cosmic-rays that cause genetic variations are irreducibly random quantum events. Otherwise, every new biological species would have been pre-determined at the universe creation. That would satisfy the intelligent design crowd. Do we want to do that?

Dennett: Absolutely not. Did you see that Karl Popper recently gave a lecture at Darwin College, Cambridge, and he likened free will to genetic evolution? He said that the selection of a kind of behavior out of a randomly offered repertoire may be an act of free will.

I can quote him. He said

> "I am an indeterminist; and in discussing indeterminism I have often regretfully pointed out that quantum indeterminacy does not seem to help us; for the amplification of something like, say, radioactive disintegration processes would not lead to human action or even animal action, but only to random movements.
>
> "I have changed my mind on this issue. A choice process may be a selection process, and the selection may be from some repertoire of random events, without being random in its turn. This seems to me to offer a promising solution to one of our most vexing problems, and one by downward causation."

Popper says he changed his mind! Not usual for a philosopher. He compared free will to natural selection. Again I quote him:

> "New ideas have a striking similarity to genetic mutations. Now, let us look for a moment at genetic mutations. Mutations are, it seems, brought about by quantum theoretical indeterminacy (including radiation effects). Accordingly, they are also probabilistic and not in themselves originally selected or adequate, but on them there subsequently operates natural selection which eliminates inappropriate mutations. Now we could conceive of a similar process with respect to new ideas and to free-will decisions, and similar things."

Dennett: What do you think, Bob? Could libertarians accept this as the most plausible and practical model for free will? It has your quantum randomness but also my limiting randomness to the consideration-generator in my decision-making model.

Kane: Perhaps I should accept your point (and Hobart's) that our willed decisions need to be determinations. Ever since Hume, you Compatibilists have insisted that free will can be reconciled with some determinism. I guess I should go along.

Dennett: And I can accept quantum indeterminism as a natural part of the free-will process. If Hume reconciled free will with determinism, perhaps we can say that we reconciled it with indeterminism?

Kane: Sounds good to me. My Libertarian friends, most of whom had little appetite for my idea that genuine quantum randomness helps with the free will problem, might be pleased with your two-part Valerian idea, if quantum indeterminism in the right place does no harm to the will.

Dennett: Compatibilists, and most of my friends are compatibilists, will be delighted that they were right all along insisting on compatibility with some determinism, to make their actions reasons responsive. What should we call our compromises?

Kane: Maybe a "corrected" or more comprehensive compatibilism? Since you compatibilists are in the majority, I think you should keep the naming rights. And "Libertarian" is too easily confused with the politicians anyway.

Dennett: That sounds good to me. Comprehensive compatibilism makes free will compatible with *both* some determinism and some indeterminism, both in the right places at last. [6]

6 If Dennett and Kane could have seen this compromise, today I would just be writing the history of philosophy, instead of helping to make the history of philosophy with the two-stage model for comprehensive compatibilism. See the next chapter.

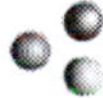

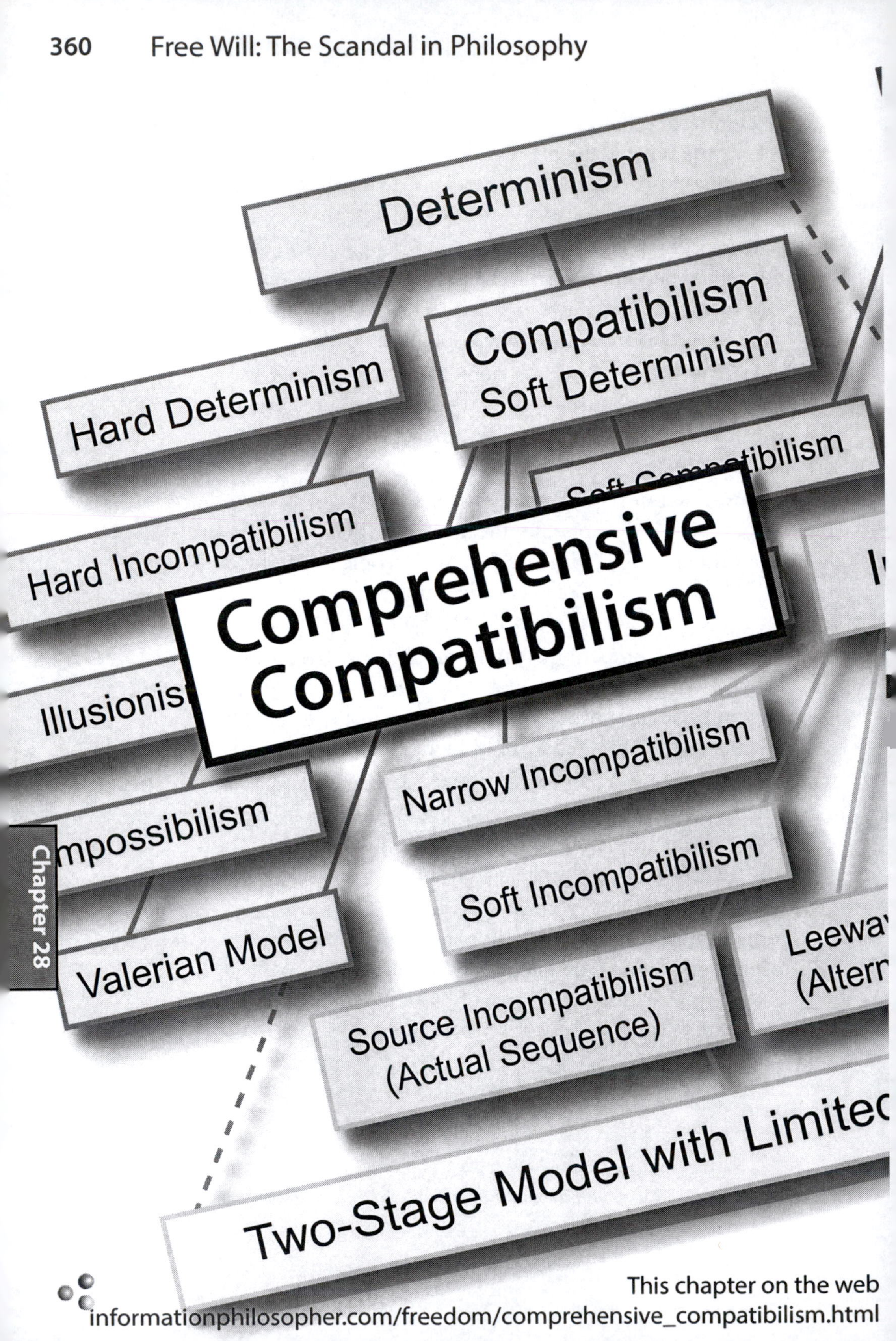

This chapter on the web
informationphilosopher.com/freedom/comprehensive_compatibilism.html

Comprehensive Compatibilism

Comprehensive compatibilists believe that Free Will can be *reconciled* both with **adequate determinism** (as David Hume and R.E. Hobart believed) and with **indeterminism** (as many thinkers since William James and I believe).

Comprehensive compatibilists also believe in a free will model that is compatible with biological evolution, a human free will that could have evolved naturally from "behavioral freedom" in lower animals. The two-stage model is thus *triply* compatible.

Free will is not a metaphysical mystery or gift of God. It evolved from a natural biophysical property of all organisms

Comprehensive compatibilists believe that normally actions are **adequately determined** by deliberations prior to a decision, including one's character and values, one's feelings and desires, in short, one's reasons and motives. They believe that free will is "**reasons responsive**." This is traditional **self-determination**.

Comprehensive compatibilists put limits on both **determinism** and **indeterminism**. Pure **chance**, irreducible randomness, or **quantum indeterminacy** in the two-stage model of free will is limited in the first stage to generating **alternative possibilities**.

But also note that sometimes we can "deliberately" choose to act randomly, when there is no obvious reason to do one thing rather than another. This resembles the ancient "**liberty of indifference**," which I call **undetermined liberty**.

Comprehensive compatibilists believe that humans are free from strict physical determinism - or **pre-determinism**, and all the other diverse forms of determinism.[1]

They accept the existence of ontological chance, but believe that when chance is the *direct and primary* cause of actions, it precludes agent control and **moral responsibility**.

1 See Chapter 9.

Note that for information philosophy and its theory of values, there is a critical **separation** of the question of free will from questions about moral responsibility.[2]

The existence of **free will** is a scientific question for physics, biology, psychology, and neuroscience.

Moral responsibility, on the other hand, is a cultural question for ethicists and sociologists. Information philosophy also separates responsibility from the ideas of retributive punishment, which is still another social and cultural question.

Libertarians believe that determinism and freedom are incompatible. Freedom requires some form of **indeterminism**.

But the two-stage models of free will favored by **comprehensive compatibilists** also require **adequate determination** of an action by the agent's motives and reasons, following deliberation and evaluation of the **alternative possibilities** for action generated by that indeterminism. This we call **self-determination**.

Critics of libertarianism (both determinists and compatibilists) attack the view of some extreme libertarians that chance is the direct cause of actions or even that actions are not caused at all. If an agent's decisions are not connected in any way with character and other personal properties, they rightly claim that the agent can hardly be held responsible for them.

Robert Kane's "torn decisions" and Self-Forming Actions are an exception to this criticism, because the agent has excellent reasons and has put in great efforts for acting whichever way the ultimate decision goes. Kane's SFAs are special cases of our **undetermined liberties.**[3]

Many determinists and perhaps most compatibilists now accept the idea that quantum physics requires real indeterminism in the universe. Comprehensive compatibilists can agree with them that if indeterministic chance were the direct and primary cause of our actions, that would not be freedom with responsibility.

Although any quantum event is probabilistic, quantum processes in macroscopic objects like biological organisms are highly regular, because of the statistical law of large numbers. Even in

2 See Chapter 20.
3 See Chapter 24. and page 365.

microscopic structures like atoms and molecules, it is quantum mechanics that provides the phenomenal stability of such structures over cosmic lifetimes.

I hope that determinists and compatibilists might also agree that if chance is not a direct and primary cause of our actions, such chance would do no harm to responsibility. In this case, **comprehensive compatibilists** should be able to convince some **hard determinists** of their position.

In a personal communication, Galen Strawson agrees that comprehensive compatibilism offers a "kind of freedom that is available" to us. If chance is limited to providing real **alternative possibilities** to be considered by the **adequately determined** will, it provides an intelligible freedom and can explain both freedom and **creativity**.

Comprehensive compatibilists can give the determinists, at least the compatibilists, the kind of freedom they say they want, one that provides an **adequately determined** will and actions for which we can take responsibility.

As to the indeterminists, they should know that the model of comprehensive compatibilism uses indeterminism in two places, first in the generation of alternative possibilities in the first stage of the two-stage model, and then, when the two-stage model does not result in a single act of **self-determination**, in Robert Kane's cases of the "torn" decisions of Self-Forming Actions.

I should note that Kane is concerned that my attempt to change the terminology of the free will debates will only confuse issues further. I am sensitive to that criticism. But in my opinion, the emphasis on Peter van Inwagen's "incompatibilism" (discussed in Chapter 6) has set back understanding. In any case, my goal is only to restore the traditional terminology, to *reconcile* liberty not with necessity, but with **self-determination**.

What could be simpler than a return to the traditional categories of the free will debates, with the new insight that my two-stage model can reconcile free will with *both* adequate determinism *and* indeterministic libertarianism?

A Taxonomy for Comprehensive Compatibilism

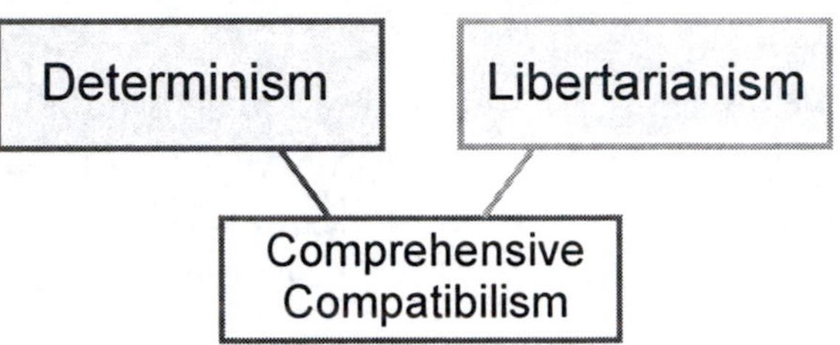

Figure 28-1. A simplified taxonomy of free will categories

You will recognize the traditional taxonomy of Chapter 6, but instead of the compatibilists being determinists who euphemistically call their position "free will," they now have an element of genuine, but limited, **indeterminism**, to provide them with origination, creativity, and to make them the authors of their lives.

How Comprehensive Compatibilism Does Otherwise in the Same Circumstances

The physical location of indeterminacy in the brain[4] and the timing of chance mental events relative to the decision are the two most critical problems for any model of libertarian free will.

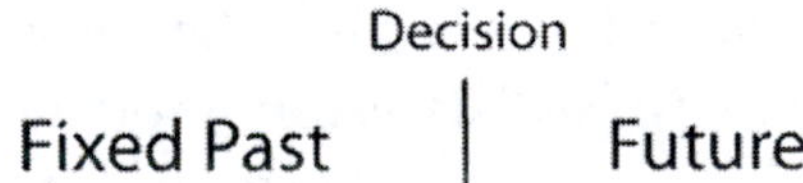

Figure 28-2. Decisions considered as a point in time.

My two-stage **Cogito** model of free will expands the decision from a single point in time between the "fixed past" and the future.

It becomes a two-stage process, first a "free" stage, then a "will" stage." Each of these takes some time.

Note that the two-stage model explains how an agent can be in exactly the "same circumstances," and given the fixed past and the laws of nature, the agent can nevertheless act differently, that is to say, choose to **do otherwise.** [5]

4 See informationphilosopher.com.freedom/location.html

5 See Chapter 13, p. 199 for more details.

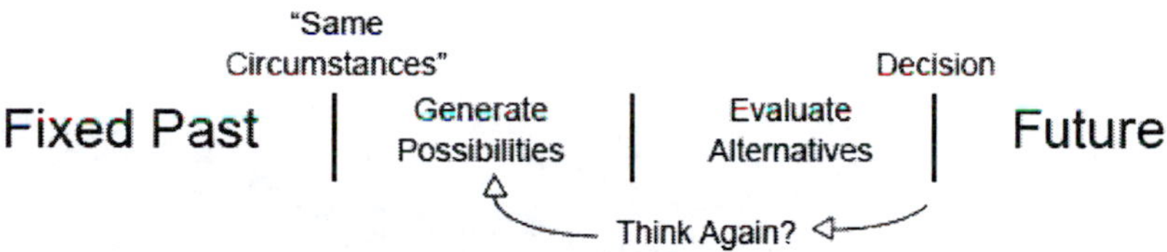

Figure 28-3. Doing otherwise in the "same circumstances."

This is because the decision is at the end point of a temporal process that begins with those "same" circumstances. The decision-making process is not an instant in time.

Note also that the decision is not determined as soon as possibilities are generated and the alternatives evaluated. The agent may decide that none of the options is good enough and, time permitting, go back to "think again," to generate more possibilities.

The decision is **adequately determined**, but it is not **pre-determined** from the "fixed past" just before the circumstances.

We can now integrate ROBERT KANE's Self-Forming Actions (SFAs) into **comprehensive compatibilism**. My Two-Stage Model and Kane's Self-Forming Actions are connected seamlessly in a temporal sequence. The sequence uses indeterminism at the start, to generate **alternative possibilities** for action that could not have been pre-determined, and it again uses indeterminism at the end, in those cases where the second-stage of the two-stage model can not narrow down the possibilities to a single self-determined action.

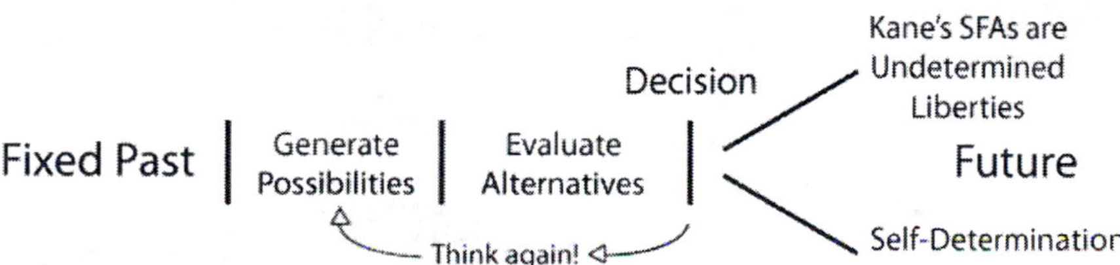

Figure 28-4. Undetermined liberties and self-determination.

Undetermined liberties include Kane's SFAs, which are "torn" decisions that require effort to resolve conflicts between moral and prudential choices. See Chapter 24.

Chapter 29

Ending The Scandal

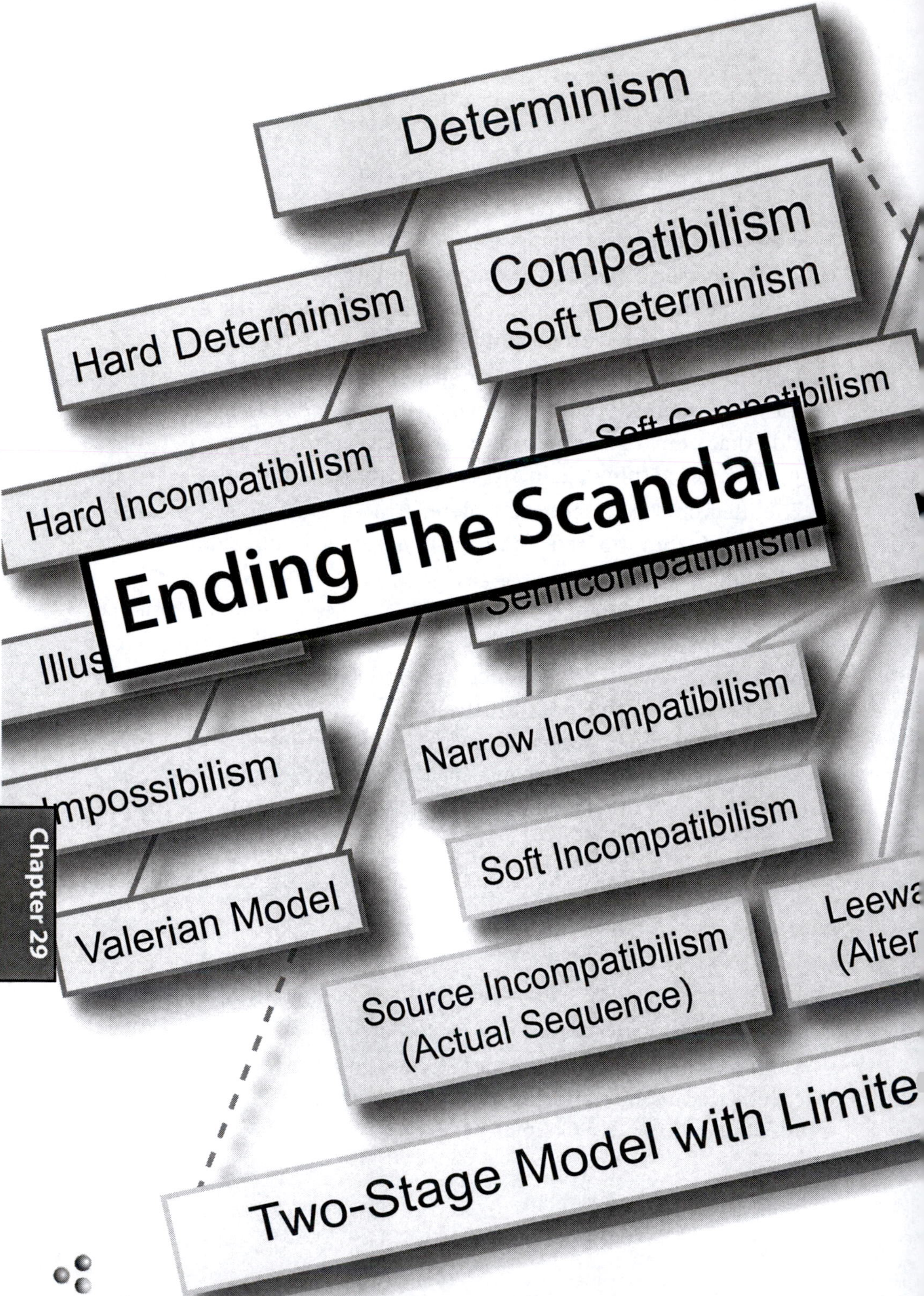
Determinism
Hard Determinism
Compatibilism
Soft Determinism
Hard Incompatibilism
Impossibilism
Valerian Model
Narrow Incompatibilism
Soft Incompatibilism
Source Incompatibilism
(Actual Sequence)
Two-Stage Model with Limite

Ending The Scandal

The main goal of the INFORMATION PHILOSOPHER website has been to provide students everywhere with the resources they need to be more knowledgeable than their professors on some classical problems of philosophy that remain unsolved today. Free will is the most important of these problems.

I hope also that professors can find some new information they need to improve on things they learned from their teachers.

Our goal is to break the great causal chain of sophisticated but unproductive arguments, sophistical and paradoxical dialogues, logical puzzles and language games that are still worth teaching *as history of philosophy*, but are hopelessly inadequate as philosophical principles for the free and creative young minds we are preparing for an open future in which they author their own lives.

We cannot solve the problem of free will with logical paradoxes, despite centuries of clever determinisms designed to limit the freedom of our "finite" minds by comparison with the "infinite" power of the laws of Nature and of Nature's God.

And we cannot *dis*-solve the pseudo-problem of free will with language games that dress old concepts in new jargon, that change the subject from free will to **moral responsibility**, that change the debate from **determinism** to the impossibility of **alternative possibilities**, and that change the momentous contest between free will and determinism to juggling words like **compatibilism** and **incompatibilism**.

Compatibilism is a "quagmire of evasion," said WILLIAM JAMES. PETER VAN INWAGEN's reframing the problem as "incompatibilism" is a "tarpit of confusion," I say, because it puts libertarians and hard determinists in the same category.

One way to look at the moral scandal that concerns me is to focus on the **actualism** of compatibilist and determinist philosophers. They believe that there is but one possible actual future.

This is not the message that academic philosophers should be delivering to students, especially because determinism cannot be proved, and current scientific evidence is to the contrary.

Aristotle made clear the essential difference between the actual and the possible. Something was actual for Aristotle when it happened, when it realized its end or purpose. Otherwise it had the power or potential to be **otherwise.** [1]

The last thing we want to tell young people is that they have no potential, that their future is already determined. It's not only poor philosophy and bad psychology, it's terrible science.

Men are not machines, and minds are not computers.

As Martin Heisenberg has shown us, even the lowest organisms are autonomous and have the behavioral freedom to realize their goals, to go from the possible to the actual.

> "A hallmark of biological organisms is their autonomy. In evolutionary terms, their autonomy allowed them to invent active locomotion (automobility = locomotion not caused from the outside) and to explore space. For going multicellular, cells had to give up behavioral autonomy and those new creatures had to reinvent automobility via the nervous system and eventually the brain. Self-ness turned animals with brains into subjects. In my view the Self is a decisive feature in the evolution of freedom. This allows for strong ownership. Behavior has to be our own to be well adaptive." [2]

How can determinist and compatibilist philosophers convince themselves that the causal laws of nature imply just one actual future, when causality is not provable and the laws only statistical? We must go back to David Hume to understand this.

Our Natural Belief in Free Will

David Hume's skepticism showed the inability of logic to "prove" facts in the physical world. No number of regular successions of event A followed by event B can prove that A *causes* B.

Hume the Skeptic thus denied causality. But Hume the Naturalist said that we have a *natural belief* in causality. Similarly, we have a natural belief in the uniformity of nature. The sun will rise tomorrow. The laws of nature are not changing, so the past is a reliable guide to the future. None of these beliefs is *logically* true. But they all are plausible and have significant practical value.

1 actual = entelechy (ἐν + τέλος + ἔχειν), possible = dynamis (δύναμις)

2 Personal communication (2011).

Hume was an empiricist. He based his ideas on observed experience. But he had a theoretical model for human nature. He based it on ISAAC NEWTON's equations of motion that describe the physical world. At that time, it appeared that Newton's laws were so perfect at explaining phenomena that they must be *necessary*. Hume equated physical necessity with logical necessity, and even with moral necessity, in which human volitions are *caused* by motives, and motives are caused by prior events.

The debates today as between free will and determinism were then debates between "liberty" and "necessity." Liberty was thought to involve chance events or mental events (the "will") not caused by prior events. Hume denied the existence of chance and any other uncaused events. Following Hobbes, he defined freedom as *freedom from* external coercion, e.g., being in chains or in jail.

Hume's model of the mind as governed by physical laws "reduced" the mind, and indeed all living things, to material physical systems. But as ARISTOTLE first noted, biological systems are different. They have a purpose or goal. Aristotle called it *telos*.

The simplest molecules that were precursors of life "learned" to replicate themselves, at which point their elemental goal was to maintain themselves (preserve their information, using negative entropy from the sun) and replicate themselves. Chance errors in the replication created different molecules, some of which were better replicators, and the rest is biological history.

Even very young children intuitively know ARISTOTLE's essential difference between inanimate physical objects, which follow natural laws, and living things, which can originate actions, can behave differently in the same circumstances, and which can make choices.

To choose is to decide between **alternative possibilities**. That these are real and not apparent is because **chance**, which Hume and his contemporaries denied as absurd and atheistical, is the source of novelty, creativity, and new information in the universe.

Hume's dream of a classical mechanical Newtonian Mind as his explanation for human nature, following the same deterministic

causal physical laws as freely falling apples and the orbiting planets, is a philosophical failure. It fails for the same reason that Einstein's dream of a deterministic and causal explanation for the merely statistical laws of quantum mechanics has failed. Nature does play dice.

And until the die is cast, until the mind decides, until the information about the decision is recorded, our choices are free.

Remember that the causal explanations that Hume and Einstein wanted are not provable logically or by sophisticated language claims. Causality is a natural belief, beyond logic and language.

But there is a competing and more vital natural belief, also unprovable, namely that we have free will and can take responsibility for our choices.

Without chances and possibilities, choices are not real. Without an initial chance stage, the choice stage would be **pre-determined**.

My two-stage model is not a monolithic "free will." It is a process, first chance, then choice, first "free," then "will."

Our thoughts are free. Our actions are willed.

Most actions are "determined" by the "de-liberations" that we call **self-determination.** But these were not **pre-determined** from the "fixed past" just before our deliberations began.

Others of our actions are **undetermined liberties**. When our deliberations do not produce a single possible action, we can choose any of the equally attractive options remaining, and take full responsibility for whichever one we finally choose. Closely related to the ancient *liberum arbitrium*, these undetermined liberties only become self-determined in the moment of choice.

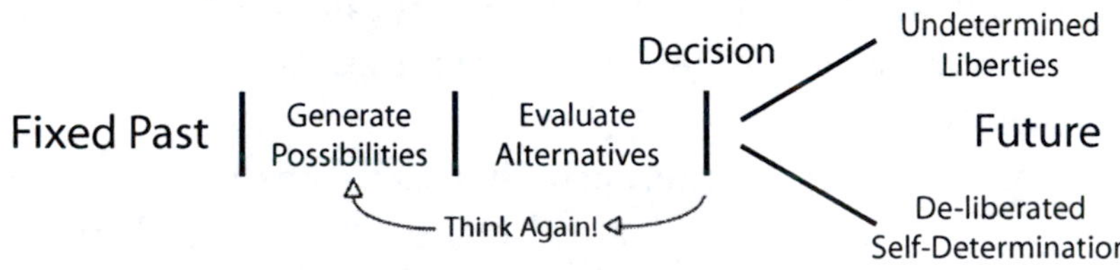

Figure 29-1. The Two-Stage Cogito Model of Free Will.

Two-Step Processes

Why two steps, two-stages, two parts? You will need to know a bit more about information philosophy than there was room for in the introduction to this book on free will. I hope those of you with a serious interest in philosophy will *become* information philosophers and help me with I-PHI.

For now, it's enough to know three important two-step processes.

1) The cosmic creation process requires two steps.[3] The first is a microscopic quantum (hence **indeterministic**) event that forms an information structure. The second is a macroscopic thermodynamic event, in which the entropy and energy that would destroy a new information structure, if it stayed around, is carried away to a dark corner of the universe.

2) Biological evolution is a two-step process. The first is a microscopic change in the genetic code of an organism, its central information structure. The change is usually the result of a quantum event, like a cosmic-ray collision with the DNA. The second step is the natural selection of some changes because they are reproductively successful and propagate.

3) The third two-step process to create information is free will.

The Two-Stage Cogito Model of Free Will

The first step is random thoughts about **alternative possibilities** for action that are generated in the mind, generated in part because of quantum-level noise in the brain's information structure as it recalls past experiences to help with its deliberations.

The second step is normally an **adequately determined** decision following an adequately determined evaluation of the options. It includes the ability to "think again," to go back and generate more options as needed. And we can always "flip a coin" when there is no clear best option.

In such cases, the final decision itself can be undetermined. The brain has access to quantum level events. It can see a single photon and smell a single molecule. So when it makes an undetermined

3 See the next chapter.

decision, it may access quantum level indeterminacy. But a random decision does not necessarily imply lack of responsibility. [4]

The two-stage model for free will explains how we "can **do otherwise** in exactly the **same circumstances**." [5] And it shows how our decisions are not **pre-determined**, not even **determined** by the **fixed past** and the **laws of nature** at the moment the generation of **alternative possibilities** begins.

If you agree that this two-stage model deserves to be considered in philosophy classes today, I believe we need to formulate some brief ways for you to frame the problem historically in the context of past proposed solutions. And then some very simple explanations of the proposed new solution.

How You Can Make the Best Case for Free Will

If you have read a significant part of this book, then you are well-equipped to discuss the two-stage model in depth. But can you explain it in a few lines to your friends and even to scholars like philosophy professors who may have fixed views on the subject?

I suggest that one way to start is to situate the problem and the solution historically as follows, in three parts.

Part 1 - Reconciling Free Will with Adequate Determinism

David Hume, in his "Of Liberty and Necessity," section VII of the 1748 *Enquiries concerning Human Understanding*, famously *reconciled* freedom with determinism.

> "For what is meant by liberty, when applied to voluntary actions? We cannot surely mean that actions have so little connexion with motives, inclinations, and circumstances, that one does not follow with a certain degree of uniformity from the other"

> "By liberty, then, we can only mean a power of acting or not acting, according to the determinations of the will" [6]

R. E. Hobart in 1934 clarified the fact that a free will involves **determination** of the will by reasons and motives. It requires neither logical necessity nor strict physical determinism.

Chapter 29

4 Dennett and Kane have shown this. See p. 356-357

5 See p. 199 for details.

6 Hume (1975) p. 95.

Hume, as moderated by Hobart, provided the second, **adequately determined** stage of the **Cogito** model, which we now give the traditional name of de-liberated **self-determination**.

Part 2 - Reconciling Free Will with Indeterminism

WILLIAM JAMES, in 1884, provided the critical first stage, by *reconciling* free will with objective **chance**.

My own work has refined James' explanation, to make it consistent with quantum indeterminism.

So you can say that Hume and Hobart provided half the answer to the problem of free will. Their adequate determination *reconciled* a compatibilist free will with the laws of classical physics.

James and the others in Chapter 12 who proposed two-stage models found the second half of the answer. In particular, I hope to be remembered as the INFORMATION PHILOSOPHER who *reconciled* libertarian free will with the probabilistic laws of quantum physics.

Part 3 - Will Compatibilists Accept This Improvement and Call Themselves *Comprehensive* Compatibilists?

Compatibilists were right all these centuries to reject the radical idea that freedom means an **extreme libertarianism** that denies reasonable causes for human actions. Can we convince them that our two-stage model simply adds creative and free elements to their current thinking on **self-determination**?

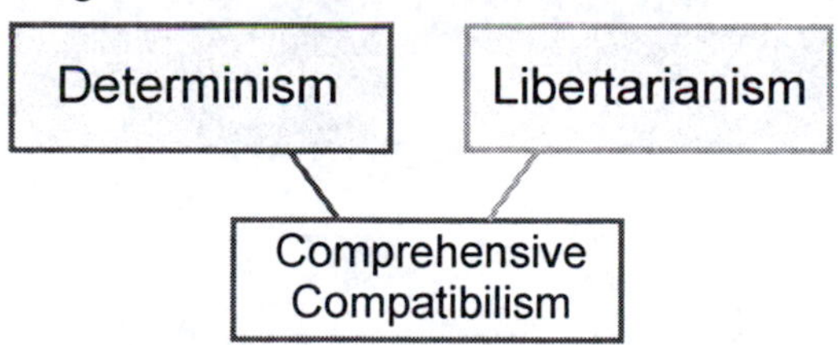

Figure 29-2. A comprehensive compatibilist taxonomy.

Since most modern compatibilists are agnostics on the truth of determinism (or indeterminism), we hope they will accept a free will model that is *triply* compatible - with Hume's definition, with James' definition, and with MARTIN HEISENBERG's evolution of human free will from the behavioral freedom of lower animals.

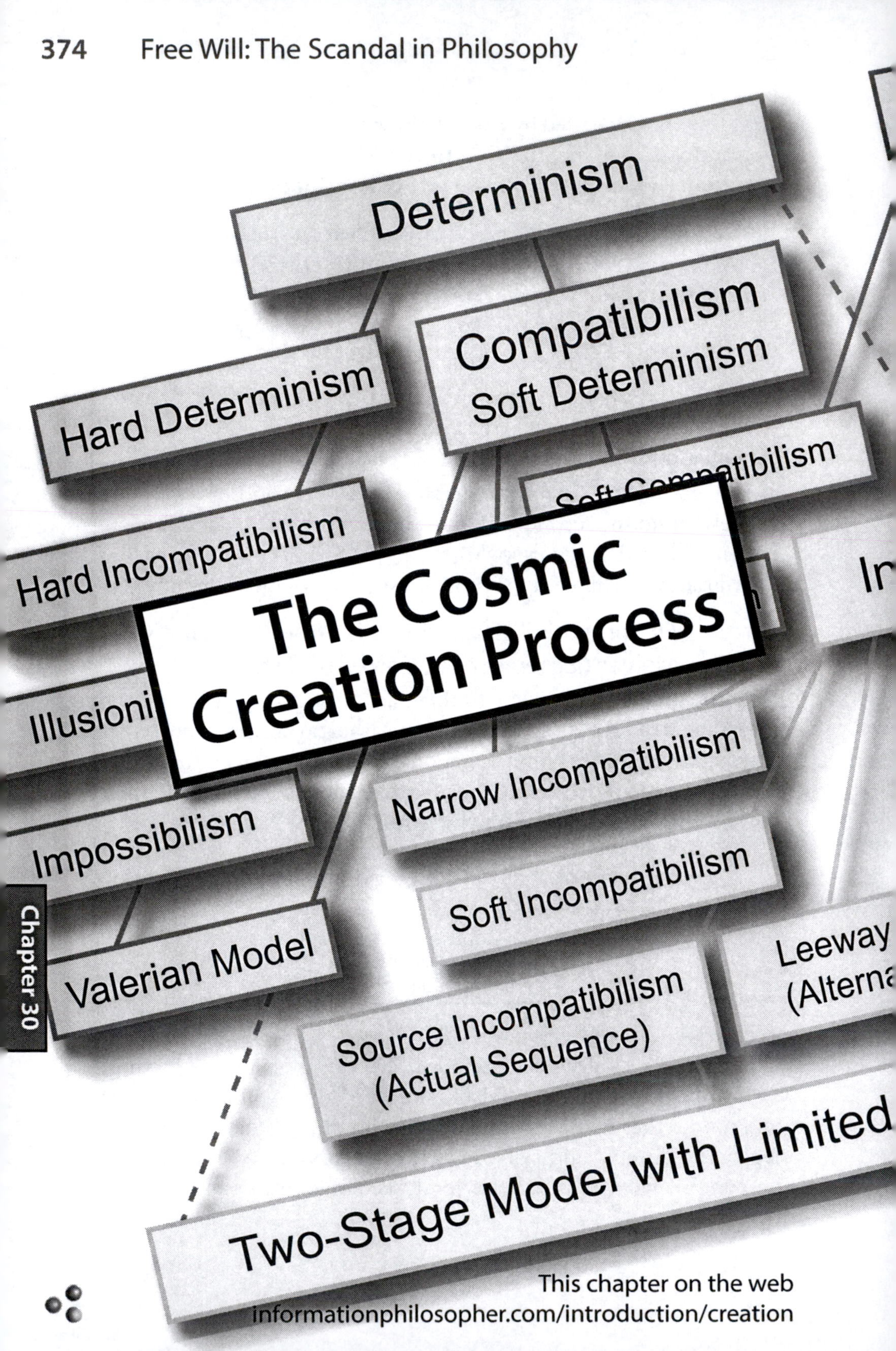

This chapter on the web
informationphilosopher.com/introduction/creation

Indeterminism

The Cosmic Creation Process

Cosmic creation is horrendously wasteful. In the existential balance between the forces of destruction and the forces of construction, there is no contest. The dark side is overwhelming. By quantitative physical measures of matter and energy content, there is far more chaos than cosmos in our universe. But it is the cosmos that we prize.

As we saw in the introduction, my philosophy focuses on the qualitatively valuable **information** structures in the universe. The destructive forces are entropic, they increase the entropy and disorder. The constructive forces are anti-entropic. They increase the order and information.

The fundamental question of information philosophy is therefore cosmological and ultimately metaphysical.

What creates the information structures in the universe?

At the starting point, the archē (ἡ ἀρχή), the origin of the universe, all was light - pure radiation, at an extraordinarily high temperature. As the universe expanded, the temperature of the radiation fell. When the first material particles formed, they were quickly destroyed by energetic photons of light. But at low enough temperatures, the quantum cooperative constructive forces were able to overcome the destructive non-material particles of light energy, the radiation field of photons.

The great stability of the material world is thus the result of quantum mechanics, which most philosophers and even scientists normally view as disruptive and uncertain. Quantum **indeterminacy** is involved in everything new, including our creativity and free will. Let's see how.

As the universe expands (see Figure 1-3), negative entropy is generated. Most of this degrades to normal thermodynamic entropy, which is known as the Boltzmann Entropy. But some survives as what is often called the Shannon Entropy, a measure of the information content in the evolving universe.

David Layzer showed how entropy and information can increase at the same time in the expanding universe.[1] There are two information/entropy flows. In any process, the positive entropy increase is always at least equal to, and generally orders of magnitude larger than, the negative entropy in any created information structures, to satisfy the second law of thermodynamics.

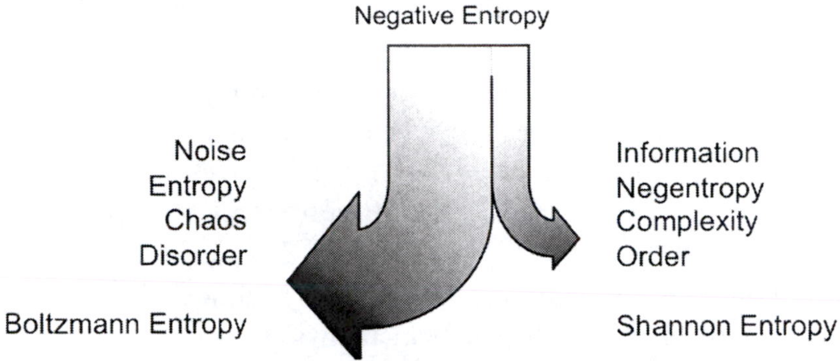

Figure 30-1. Information flows into Boltzmann and Shannon Entropy.

Material particles are the first information structures to form in the universe. They are quarks, baryons, and atomic nuclei, which combine with electrons to form atoms and eventually molecules, when the temperature is low enough. These particles are attracted by the force of universal gravitation to form the gigantic information structures of the galaxies, stars, and planets.

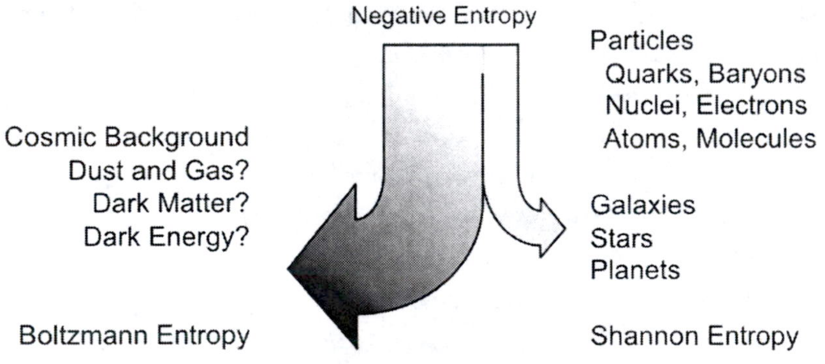

Figure 30-2. Cosmological information flows.

Microscopic quantum mechanical particles and huge self-gravitating systems are stable and have extremely long lifetimes, thanks in large part to quantum stability.

1 See page 10 in the Introduction.

Stars are another source of radiation, after the original Big Bang cosmic source, which has cooled down to 3 degrees Kelvin (3K) and shines as the cosmic microwave background radiation.

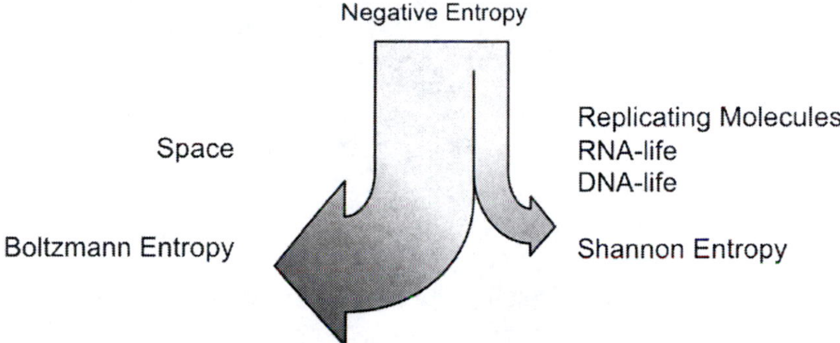

Figure 30-3. Sun to Earth information flow.

Our solar radiation has a high color temperature (5000K) and a low energy-content temperature (273K). It is out of equilibrium and it is the source of all the information-generating negative entropy that drives biological evolution on the Earth. Note that the fraction of the light falling on Earth is less than a billionth of that which passes by and is lost in space.

A tiny fraction of the solar energy falling on the earth gets converted into the information structures of plants and animals. Most of it gets converted to heat and is radiated away as waste energy to the night sky.

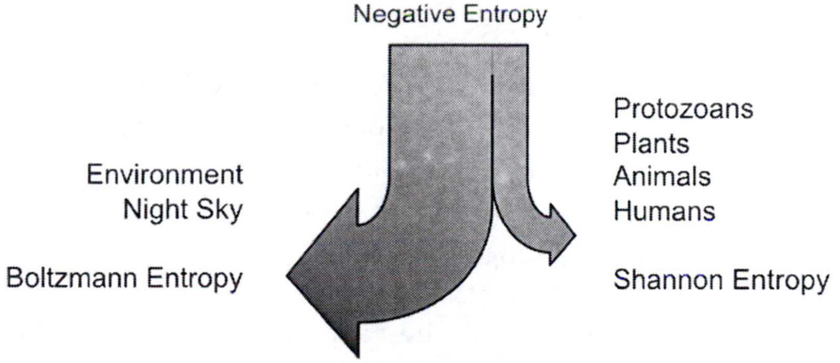

Figure 30-4. Information flows into life.

Every biological structure is a quantum mechanical structure. DNA has maintained its stable information structure over billions of years in the constant presence of chaos and noise.

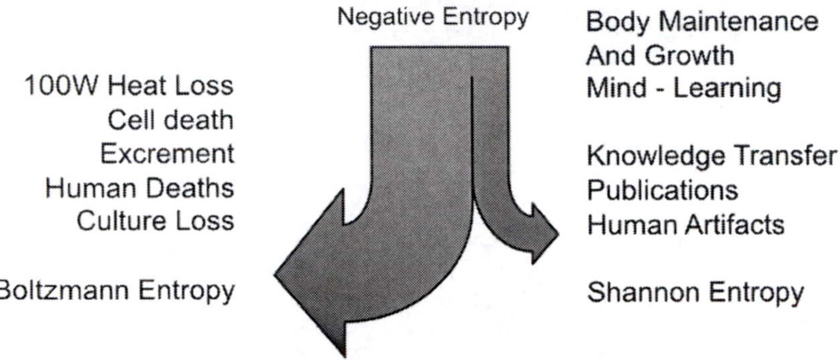

Figure 30-5. Information flows in a human being.

The stable information content of a human being survives many changes in the material content of the body during a person's lifetime. Only with death does the mental information (spirit, soul) dissipate - unless it is saved somewhere.

The total mental information in a living human is orders of magnitude less than the information content and information processing rate of the body. But the information structures created by humans outside the body, in the form of external knowledge like this book, and the enormous collection of human artifacts, rival the total biological information content.

Man Is Not a Machine

And the mind is not a computer, running evolved computer programs. The proper way to view man, indeed any organism, is as an incredible information processing system.

A biological information processor is vastly more powerful and efficient than any computing machine. We can divide the human body into layers, with the mind at the top. The amount of information processing going on in the lower layers is, like the other entropy/information flow diagrams above, vastly greater than the mental stream of consciousness.

We philosophers like to think that the mental activity is somehow most important, perhaps even prior in some essential sense.

Plato thought the ideas come first, the instances later, as did the neo-Platonists and the Christian tradition. In the beginning, was the logos. Έν ἀρχή, ἐν ό λόγος. But we shall see that the logos is the end result of a vast layering of biological processes.

From Aristotle to the Existentialists, some philosophers knew that existence precedes essence. And if bare existence were not organized into information structures, there would be no intelligence to contemplate their essences.

The information processing going on in a human body is over a billion times the amount processed in the mind. To appreciate this, let's consider just one maintenance function. Every second a significant fraction of our red blood cells die and must be replaced.

100 million red blood cells die each second
x
300 million hemoglobin proteins in each RBC
x
100s of amino acids in each hemoglobin
=
100,000 terabytes of information per second

Hemoglobin protein

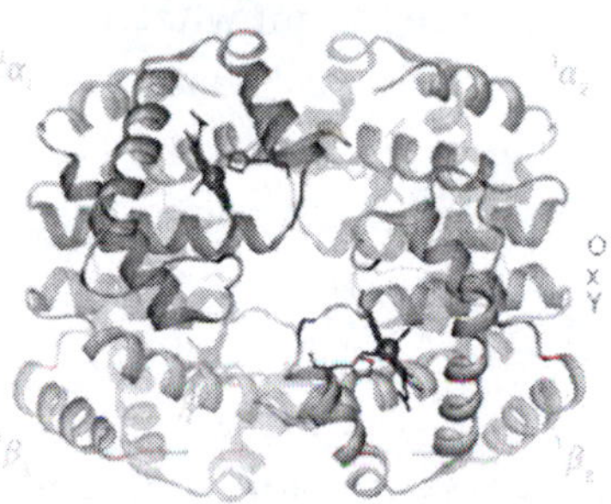

Every time a tRNA adds a new amino acid to the growing polypeptide chain it is a *quantum event*!

Figure 30-6. Information processing to maintain our red blood cells.

Chromosomal information is being processed from our DNA to messenger RNA to transfer DNA to the ribosome factories where a chaotic soup of randomly moving amino acids are sorted out to select exactly the right one to add to the rapidly growing polypeptide chain of a new protein.

Quantum cooperative phenomena account for the phenomenal speed and accuracy of creating new macromolecules.

It is helpful to distinguish at least four levels of information processing, from the bottom physical layer of bodily maintenance to the top layer in the thinking mind.

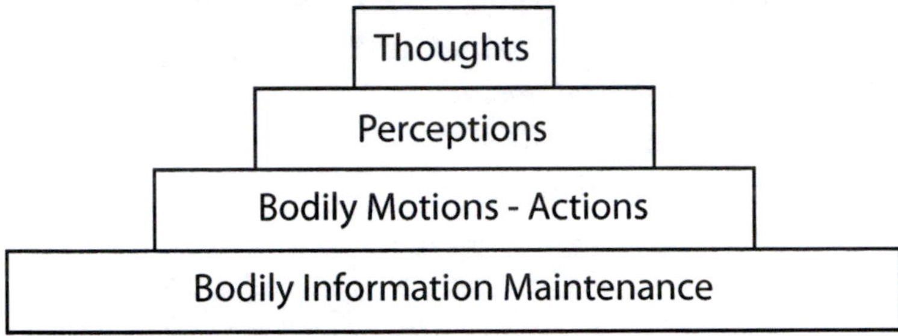

Figure 30-7. Four levels of information processing.

Bodily motions consume a great deal of information processing. Perceptions somewhat less, but they are the subject of a great deal of psychological and philosophical speculation. There is little room in a work on free will to go into detail, but note that WILLIAM JAMES' notion of focusing attention is easy to understand in information terms.

Consider a hawk flying over a field of waving grass, who can instantly pick out a field mouse by its unique pattern of motion. Consider our ability to distinguish the recognizable voice of a friend in a noisy party. Our brain can separate that voice from nine others of equal volume (a 10 decibel ratio of signal to noise). If we can see the lips, we can go down 20db, to understand sounds that are 1/100 of the crowd noise.

In BERNARD BAARS' Theater of Consciousness, there are untold numbers of perceptions and conceptions that are vying for the attention of the decision-making executive function. Baars and Dennett picture these as individual agents or homunculi with special knowledge who are processing the information in parallel. The information data rate of this unconscious parallel perceptual level is thus orders of magnitude higher than the serial processing rate of the conscious mind.

James called the lower level a "blooming, buzzing, confusion" and the upper level a "stream of consciousness." Thus our conscious ability to communicate information, with others in speech, with ourselves in thoughts, is practically restricted to a small amount of information per second, compared to the bodily information at the lower levels being processed at rates comparable to today's best computers and communication systems.

Cosmic Creation and Free Will

How does this picture of information processing levels relate to the **two-stage model** of free will? The lower levels, driven in large part by chaotic processes and always involving quantum cooperative phenomena to create information, are the biological source for the first stage that generates **alternative possibilities.**

It was convenient to introduce the two-stage model as a temporal sequence. And it is easy to teach it this way, drawing heuristic diagrams on the white board to illustrate it for students.

But as was mentioned in Chapter 13,[2] the random generation stage is going on constantly, driven by internal proprioceptions and external environmental perceptions.

Visualizing the information processing in layers provides a deeper understanding of how behavioral freedom in lower animals has evolved to become free will in higher animals and humans.

Recall from Chapter 12 that Martin Heisenberg has found evidence that the lowest animals and even bacteria have a kind of behavioral freedom.[3] They can originate stochastic actions and are not simple Cartesian stimulus-response reactive machines.

I propose that there are four levels in the evolutionary development of free will. In all four levels, the source of the random generation of alternative possibilities in the first stage of my two-stage model is the same. It is the essential chaos and noise that is characteristic of information processes at the lower levels of the organism as shown in Figure 30-7.

But in the second stage, I argue that new methods of selecting the best possibility are added in the upper levels.

2 p. 201.
3 p. 184.

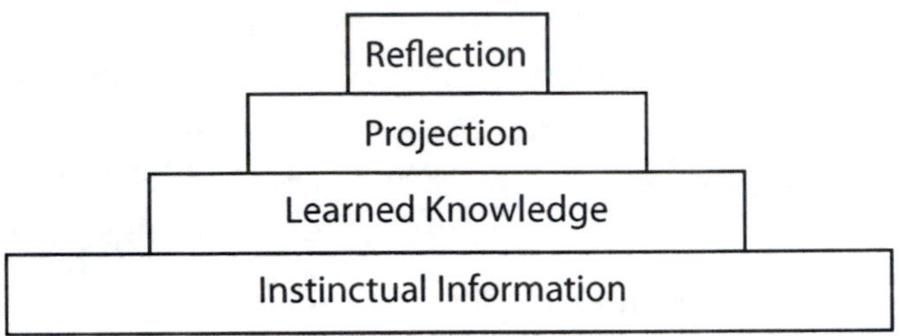

Figure 30-8. The evolution of behavioral freedom to become free will.

At the lowest level, selection is instinctive. The selection criteria are transmitted genetically, shaped only by ancestral experiences.

At the second level are animals whose past experiences guide their current choices. Selection criteria are acquired through experience, including instruction by parents and peers.

Third-level animals use their imagination and foresight to estimate the future consequences of their choices.

At the highest level, selection is reflective and normative[4] Conscious deliberation about community values influences the choice of behaviors.

If we go back and compare the information-processing levels of Figure 30-8, we see that bodily maintenance uses only the lowest level of instinctual information to operate. Everything the cells know comes to them via DNA and inherited cell processes.

Bodily motions at the next level can be learned, muscle memory for example. The parallels break down for the upper two levels.

But the highest level of information processing in humans helps us to see the essential difference between humans and other animals. Many animals have evolved mirror neurons that allow them to feel what other animals are feeling. And altruistic genes in many organisms may explain why some animals sacrifice themselves for their communities.

But the ability to translate our thoughts into language and communicate that information to others is unique. We may not be the only species that has thoughts, but we are the only ones that can share our thoughts.

4 Compare Christine Korsgaard's theory of normativity. Korsgaard (1996)

Information and Love

We began Chapter 1 asking what is information?

We have seen that the creation of information involves quantum mechanics to form structures, followed by the transfer away of entropy to allow those structures to be stable against the second law of thermodynamics.

We found that the un-pre-determined information created in a decision is the basis of human freedom.

We saw that information is immaterial and likened it to spirit, the soul in the body, the ghost in the machine.

We showed that information is the stuff of thought, and that it is our thoughts that are the origin of human freedom and creativity.

We found that humans are unique in that they can share their thoughts with other human beings.

I want to end by arguing that sharing information has an astonishing resemblance to another human characteristic.

Like love, information is not consumed when we give it to others, but increased. Both love and information do not follow the usual economic laws of scarcity.

Charles Sanders Peirce made evolutionary love, his agapē, the third and ultimate step in his philosophy. For Peirce, it was *sharing* information with other thinkers in an open community of inquirers that assured the advance of knowledge.

For me, it is *caring* for the work of others that matters even more for that advance of knowledge. I want to provide my forebears with the maximum measure of information immortality.

If we don't remember the work of our colleagues in the past, we don't deserve to be remembered by future colleagues.

Forgetting is entropic. The moral foundation of information philosophy is very simple. All things being equal, choose the option that preserves the most information.

Other Problems in Philosophy and Physics

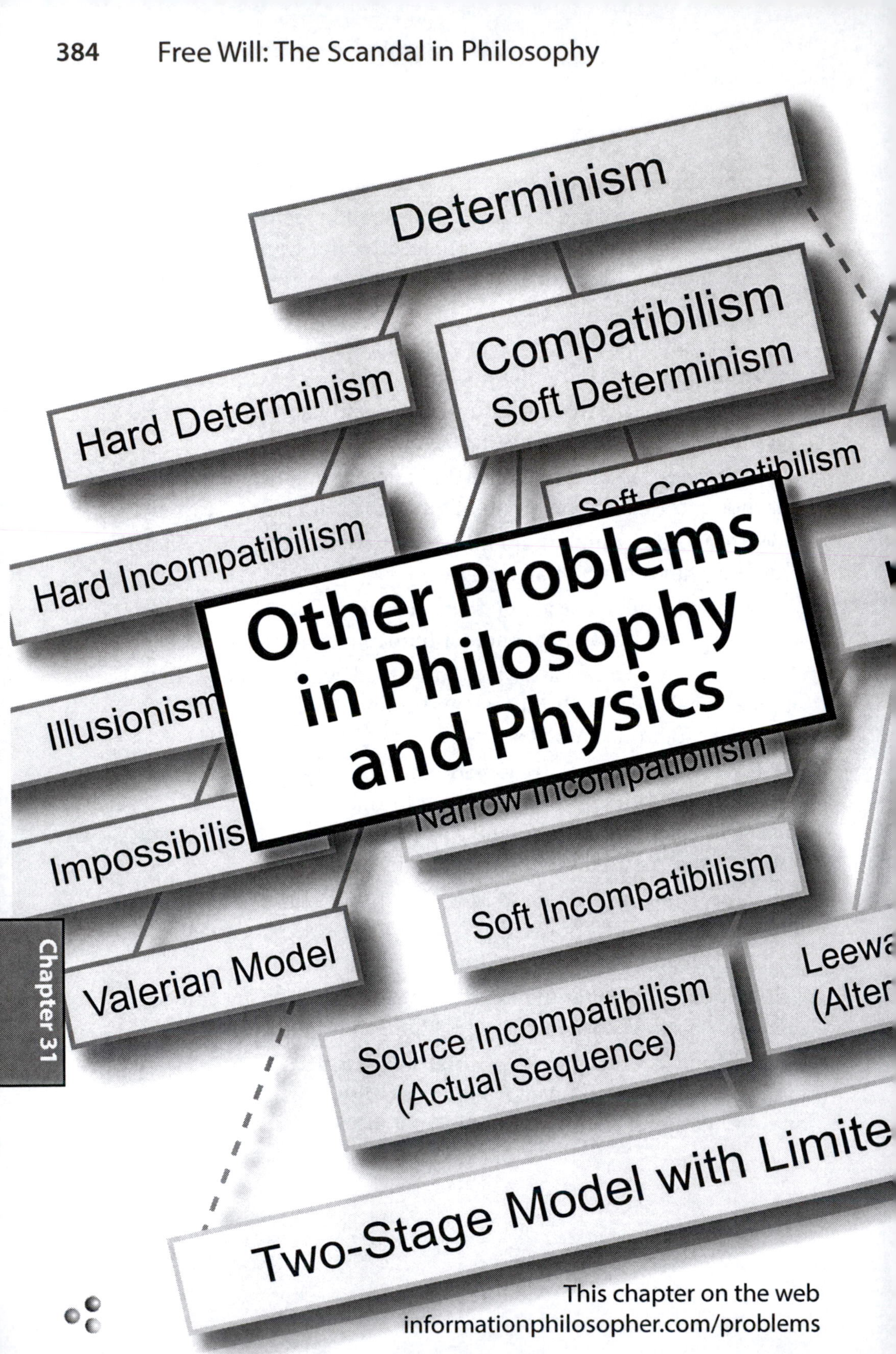

This chapter on the web
informationphilosopher.com/problems

I-Phi Philosophical Problems

The fundamental question of information philosophy is cosmological and ultimately metaphysical.

> *What is the process that creates information structures in the universe?*

Given the second law of thermodynamics, which says that any system will over time approach a thermodynamic equilibrium of maximum disorder or entropy, in which all information is lost, and given the best current model for the origin of the universe, which says everything began in a state of equilibrium some 13.75 billion years ago, how can it be that living beings are creating and communicating new information every day? Why are we not still in that state of equilibrium?

The elucidation by information philosophy of a two-part **cosmic creation process** casts light on some classical problems in philosophy and in physics, because it is the same process that creates new biological species and explains the freedom and creativity of the human mind.

Some Other Philosophical Problems

The Problem of Knowledge

Epistemology is the problem of *certain* knowledge, when our means of perception is limited and fallible. Instead of logical language debates about "justified true belief," information philosophy looks to information structures in the brain that correspond to structures in the world and in other minds.

The Problem of Value[1]

Information philosophy moves the source of ultimate value beyond man and our created Gods, beyond Life and the Earth, to its origins in a Cosmic Providence, which creates stable information structures we call Ergo. Note that quantum mechanics, though normally thought of as adding only indeterminacy, is the source of the stability in most information structures.

1 informationphilosopher.com/value

Note that the problem of freedom (in this book) and the problem of value are tightly linked.

Values without Freedom are Useless.

Freedom without Value is Absurd.

The first of these views was the position of the John Stuart Mill utilitarians and the early twentieth-century Anglo-American philosophers, who argued for utilitarian value but accepted determinism.

The second view was that of the Continental Existentialists, from Nietzsche to Heidegger to Sartre, that we have freedom, but because God is dead there are no absolute values.

The Problem of Free Will[2]

A dozen thinkers since William James in 1884 have proposed "two-stage" models of free will - first "free," then will," - first chance, then choice, - first alternative possibilities, then one actuality. The most plausible and practical solution to the 2400-year old problem of free will is our **Cogito** model. The critical random component of the first stage is provided by noise in the brain's information processing. The second stage is determined, but not pre-determined.

Consciousness[3]

Consciousness can be defined as the capacity of an entity, usually a living thing but we can also include artificially conscious machines or computers, to react to the information, and particularly to changes in the information, in its environment. We call it information consciousness.

The Problem of Evil[4]

Theodicy - "If God is Good He is not God. If God is God He is not Good." (from J.B., by Archibald MacLeish) The question is not "Does God exist?" The question is "Does Goodness exist?" The

2 informationphilosopher.com/freedom
3 informationphilosopher.com/problems/consciousness
4 informationphilosopher.com/problems/evil

solution lies in a dualist world with both bad and good. If ergodic information is an objective good, then entropic destruction of information is "the devil incarnate," as Norbert Wiener put it.

Immortality[5]

Information philosophy implies two kinds of immortality, the material survival of genetic information and the survival of ideas in the Sum of all knowledge and human artifacts. The survival of parts of the genetic code in DNA is the longest approximation to immortality known in living things. The "immortals" among us are those whose life's work is remembered.

The Mind-Body Problem[6]

Solved in part by our Sum model, which explains how abstract information, an idea, or knowledge is incorporated into a human mind, and how pure ideas act on the physical world. Information is neither energy nor matter. But it needs matter for its embodiment and energy for its communication.

Information is the mind in the body, the ghost in the machine, as close to a spirit or soul as science can get. When we die, it is our information that is lost.

Our ERR (experience recorder and reproducer) model for the mind is simpler than, but superior to, cognitive science computational models of the mind.

Man is not a machine. And the mind is not a computer.

5 informationphilosopher.com/problems/immortality
6 informationphilosopher.com/problems/mind_body

Some Other Physics Problems

It is of the deepest philosophical significance that information is based on the mathematics of probability. If all outcomes were certain, there would be no "surprises" in the universe. Information would be conserved and a universal constant, as some mathematicians mistakenly believe it is.

Information philosophy requires the ontological uncertainty and probabilistic outcomes of modern quantum physics to produce new information. But at the same time, without the extraordinary stability of quantized information structures over cosmological time scales, life and the universe we know would not be possible.

Quantum mechanics reveals the architecture of the universe to be discrete rather than continuous, to be digital rather than analog.

Moreover, the "correspondence principle" of quantum mechanics and the "law of large numbers" of statistics ensures that macroscopic objects can normally average out microscopic uncertainties and probabilities to provide the "**adequate determinism**" that shows up in all our Laws of Nature.

The Arrow of Time[7]

Arthur Stanley Eddington connected "Time's Arrow" with the direction of increasing entropy and the second law of thermodynamics. We now show that it is also the direction of increasing information.

Entanglement/Nonlocality[8]

This is a mysterious phenomenon that seems capable of "transmitting" information over vast distances faster than the speed of light. Information physics shows that measurements change probabilities everywhere, faster than the speed of light, although no signaling is possible, since no matter or energy is transmitted.

Macroscopic Recurrence[9]

Ernst Zermelo argued against Ludwig Boltzmann's H-Theorem (his derivation of the second law of thermodynamics),

7 informationphilosopher.com/problems/arrow_of_time
8 informationphilosopher.com/solutions/experiments/EPR
9 informationphilosopher.com/problems/recurrence

on the grounds that given enough time, any system would return to the same starting conditions and thus entropy must decrease as well as increase. Information physics shows that exactly the same circumstances can never recur. Friedrich Nietzsche's "Eternal Return of the Same" is a physical impossibility, because of the increasing information in the universe.

Microscopic Reversibility[10]

Joseph Loschmidt also argued against Ludwig Boltzmann on the grounds that if time were reversed the entropy would decrease. Boltzmann agreed that it would, according to his initial version of the H-Theorem which was derived from classical dynamical physics. He then defended his case for entropy increase on the basis of probabilities and an assumption of "molecular disorder." A quantum-mechanical treatment of binary (two-particle) collisions validates Boltzmann's "molecular disorder" assumption.

The Problem of Measurement[11]

We explain how our measuring instruments, which are usually macroscopic objects and treatable with classical physics, can give us information about the microscopic world of atoms and subatomic particles like electrons and photons, which are described with quantum physics. The so-called "cut" (John Bell called it the "shifty split") between the classical and quantum worlds occurs at the moment that stable observable information enters the world. It does not require the consciousness of an observer.

Schrödinger's Cat[12]

Erwin Schrödinger's paradox of simultaneous live and dead cats is solved by noting that the wave function probabilities refer to the proportions of live and dead cats that would be found in many identical experiments. In every particular case, the wave functions collapse at the instant the random quantum event produces stable information in the world. No "conscious observer" is needed. The cat is its own observer.

10 informationphilosopher.com/problems/reversibility
11 informationphilosopher.com/problems/measurement
12 informationphilosopher.com/solutions/experiments/schrodingerscat

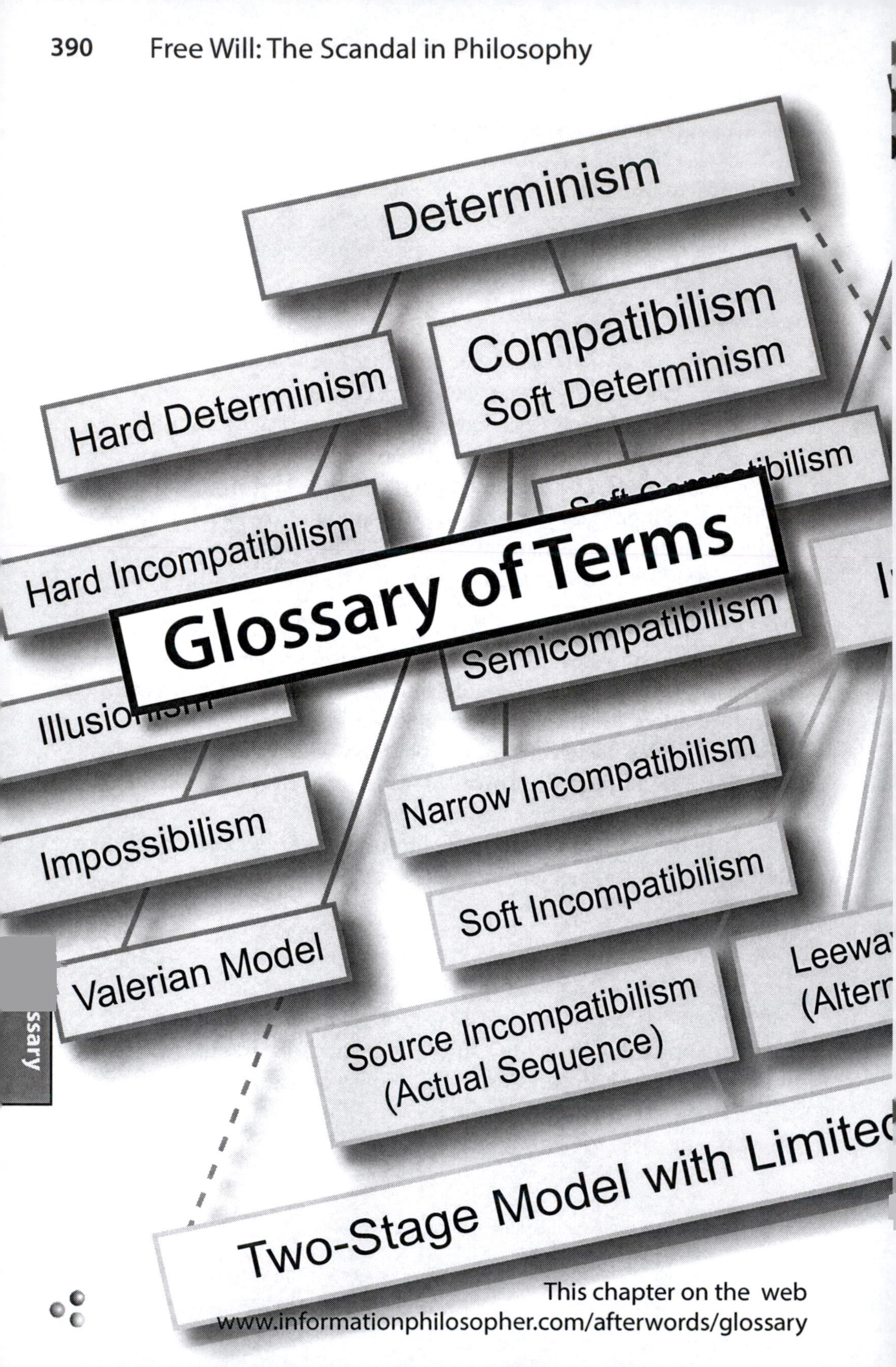

This chapter on the web
www.informationphilosopher.com/afterwords/glossary

Glossary of Terms

On the Information Philosopher website, our glossary of terms uses hyperlinks (with blue underlines) to provide recursive definitions from within each entry. We cannot do this in print, of course.

Hyperlinks go to other pages in the I-Phi website and to external sites such as the Stanford Encyclopedia of Philosophy and Wikipedia, where available.

The web version also offers "Search I-Phi" links to find all the pages on the I-Phi website that refer to the given term. In this print version we provide an index. Some glosses also offer a click on "I-Phi Page" to get a much more detailed description of the term in the Core Concepts sections of the website.

The website also links to other online glossaries of relevant philosophical terms, such as:

- Ted Honderich's Determinism and Freedom Terminology
- Alfred Mele's Lexicon for the *Big Questions in Free Will* Project

A

Actualism

Actualism is the idea that the events that do happen are the only possible events that could possibly have happened. Actualism denies the existence of alternative possibilities.

Other glosses - Alternative Possibilities, Alternative Sequences, Consequence Argument, Direct Argument, Frankfurt-style cases, Indirect Argument, Standard Argument

Actual Sequence

The Actual Sequence is the sequence of events in the past that lead up to the current moment of deliberation and decision. The term is used in Direct Arguments, such as Peter van Inwagen's Consequence Argument, Frankfurt-style cases and John Martin Fischer's Semicompatibilism.

It is contrasted with the Alternative Sequences that result from Alternative Possibilities. Arguments for incompatibilism that consider alternative possibilities are called Indirect Arguments.

Other glosses - Alternative Possibilities, Alternative Sequences, Consequence Argument, Direct Argument, Frankfurt-style cases, Indirect Argument, Standard Argument, Tracing, Transfer Principle

Adequate Determinism

Adequate Determinism is the kind of determinism we have in the world. It is also called "near determinism" (Ted Honderich), "almost causal determinism" (John Fischer), and "micro-indeterminism" (John Searle). Macroscopic objects are adequately determined in their motions, giving rise to the appearance of strict causal determinism.

Microscopic objects, on the other hand, show the probabilistic consequences of indeterminism, due to quantum mechanics. These probabilistic effects usually average out in large objects, leading to the illusion of strict causal physical determinism, including the powerful and very productive idea of deterministic laws of nature.

Other glosses -- Determination, Determinism, Indeterminism, Laws of Nature, Quantum Mechanics

Agent Causal

Agent-causal libertarianism is the idea that an agent can originate new causal chains, actions that are not predetermined to happen by events prior to the agent's deliberation (between alternative possibilities perhaps) and decision. Some agent-causal theories are metaphysical, assuming that the agent's mind is not bound by the physical laws that govern the body. Some philosophers claim mental events are "non-causal."

Other glosses - Alternative Possibilities, Causality, Causa Sui, Event Causal, Indeterminism, Origination

Agnostic

Most modern philosophers claim to be agnostic on the "truth" of determinism or indeterminism. For example, Alfred Mele claims his arguments for "Agnostic Autonomy" are valid whether or not determinism is true. John Fischer says semicompatibilists are agnostic. And Derk Pereboom has renamed "hard determinism" to "hard incompatibilism" to remain agnostic.

Agnosticism ignores the great asymmetry between determinism and indeterminism. Determinism is congenial to claims that freedom consists of following the laws of nature and that God has foreknowledge of our actions. Indeterminism is much more difficult to reconcile with a

responsible freedom, since it has such negative implications - randomness, chance, uncertainty, and contingency - leading to the randomness objection to free will.

Other glosses - Determinism, Foreknowledge, Indeterminism, Standard Argument

Akrasia

Akrasia, from the Greek a-kratos (no power), describes "weak-willed" actions taken against one's better judgment. Rationalism assumes there is always a single best way to evaluate an agent's options or alternative possibilities, so that weakness of will is fundamentally irrational.

Other glosses - Strongest Motive, Weakness of Will

Alternative Possibilities

Alternative Possibilities for thought and action were thought to be a requirement for free will and moral responsibility until Harry Frankfurt extended John Locke's "locked room" example of a person who freely chose to stay in a room, unaware that the doors had been locked, so that alternative possibilities did not exist for him.

Note that alternative possibilities should not be interpreted as probabilities for actions. This is a mistake made by many prominent philosophers who assume that indeterminism makes chance the direct cause of action.

Other glosses - Determination, Direct Argument, Frankfurt Examples, Indeterminism, Indirect Argument, Undetermined Liberty

Alternative Sequences

Alternative Sequences are hypothetical counterfactual sequences of events in the past that lead up to the current moment of deliberation and decision. They result from Alternative Possibilities. Arguments for incompatibilism that consider alternative possibilities are called Indirect Arguments.

Alternative Sequences are contrasted with the Actual Sequence that leads up to the current moment of deliberation and decision. The term is used in Frankfurt-style cases and John Fischer's Semicompatibilism.

Other glosses - Alternative Possibilities, Frankfurt-style cases, Indirect Argument

Asymmetry

There are two important uses of this term in free will and moral responsibility.

The first is the great asymmetry between determinism and indeterminism in the standard argument against free will. Determinism is much easier to reconcile with the will than is indeterminism (pure chance).

Susan Wolf has pointed out the strange asymmetry between praise and blame. Those opposed to punishment for retributive reasons (as opposed to practical consequentialist reasons) are often in favor of praise for good deeds. This reflects the ancient Platonic view that we are responsible only for the good we do. Our errors we blame on our ignorance, which is, unfortunately, no excuse before the law.

Other glosses - Illusion, Consequentialism, Determinism, Indeterminism, Moral Responsibility, Revisionism, Retributivism

Authenticity

Authenticity (from Greek authentes, author) suggests that we are the author of our actions, that we originate actions which are "up to us." But various forms of determinism claim other authors for many or all actions.

Other glosses - Autonomy, Control, Determinism, Origination, Up To Us

Autonomy

Autonomy, (from auto + nomos) is literally self-lawful, self-governing, or self-rule, is often used in the free will debates as an alternative to free will, freedom of choice, freedom of action, etc.

Like the term authentic, autonomy suggests that we are the author of our actions, that our actions are "up to us."

Other glosses - Authenticity, Control, Freedom, Free Will, Origination, Up To Us

Avoidability

Avoidability is a synonym for "could have done otherwise."

It is the libertarian condition that the agent has alternative possibilities for action. Daniel Dennett defends avoidability as an evolved freedom even in a deterministic universe.

Other glosses - Alternative Possibilities, Done Otherwise, Yes-No Objection

B

Basic Argument

Galen Strawson developed a Basic Argument that denies the existence of free will and moral responsibility. It is based on an infinite regress and denial of any causa sui or uncaused cause. Briefly stated, the regress says that you do what you do because of your character. To be responsible for your character, you must have done something to form that character. But that something was done by your character at an earlier time, and so on ad infinitum, or at least to when you were too young to be responsible.

Although Strawson is agnostic and says his argument works whether determinism or indeterminism is true, his denial of any causa sui effectively cancels indeterminism and the Basic Argument resembles the Consequence Argument.

Other glosses - Agnostic, Consequence Argument, Direct Argument, Moral Responsibility, Standard Argument, Ultimacy

Broad Incompatibilism

Broad Incompatibilism is Randolph Clarke's synonym for traditional compatibilism. Clarke distinguishes it from his Narrow Incompatibilism, which is a synonym for John Martin Fischer's concept of Semicompatibilism.

Broad Incompatibilism is incompatible with both free will and moral responsibility.

Other glosses - Compatibilism, Incompatibilism, Moral Responsibility, Narrow Incompatibilism, Semicompatibilism

C

Causality

Causality is the basic idea that all events have causes. When every event is caused completely by prior events and their causes, it leads to the idea of determinism. A causal chain links all events to earlier events in a limitless sequence. Theologians inconsistently imagine the chain to break with an uncaused cause (causa sui) which they identify with God and miracles.

Quantum indeterminacy produces uncaused causes. There is still a causal chain, but it no longer permits complete predictability. Events are now merely probable, no longer certain, though the probability can be arbitrarily close to certainty. Most macroscopic events are, for practical purposes, as predictable as perfect determinism would have allowed. Nevertheless, a break in the causal chain is a requirement for free will.

Other glosses - Adequate Determinism, Causa Sui, Determinism, Indeterminism

Causa Sui

Causa Sui describes an event that is self-caused or uncaused. The event might be the product of an agent with metaphysical power. It might be a random accident with only probabilistic outcomes. Theologians identify the *causa sui* with miracles, saying that only God is a causa sui. Friedrich Nietzsche famously called it "the best self-contradiction that has been conceived so far, it is a sort of rape and perversion of logic "

Other glosses - Agent Causation, Causality, Indeterminism

Chance

Chance has been called an illusion by philosophers who argued that probability is only the result of human ignorance. William James saw an "antipathy to chance" in most philosophers.

Chance has historically been seen as a negative idea, associated with gambling, for example. Chance has been regarded as atheistic, since it appears to deny Foreknowledge.

Other glosses - *Causa Sui,* Randomness Objection, Undetermined Liberty

CNC

CNC is Robert Kane's term for the Covert and Non-constraining Control of the kind in Frankfurt-style cases and manipulation of agents.

Other glosses - Frankfurt-style cases, Manipulation Argument

Compatibilism

Classical compatibilism is the idea that free will exists in a world that is deterministic. It was invented by the Stoic Chrysippus and developed by Thomas Hobbes and David Hume.

Classical compatibilists are determinists. Immanuel Kant called compatibilism a "wretched subterfuge." William James called compatibilism

a "quagmire of evasion." He called compatibilists "soft determinists," who evade the fact of their "antipathy to chance."

Most modern compatibilists, aware of modern quantum physics, avoid the determinist label, claiming to be agnostic about the "truth" of determinism or indeterminism. Alfred Mele defines "soft compatibilism" as admitting that some indeterminism might be useful, since it breaks the causal chain beck to the Big Bang.

After P. F. Strawson, philosophers have changed the debate from free will to moral responsibility. Many now conflate free will and moral responsibility.

Semicompatibilists, following John Martin Fischer, argue for the compatibilism of moral responsibility and determinism (or indeterminism). Like Strawson, they say that even if determinism were true, we would not surrender the idea of moral responsibility implicit in our natural attitudes toward blame and praise, punishment and reward.

Other glosses - Agnostic, Determinism, Incompatibilism, Indeterminism, Semicompatibilism

Consequence Argument

If our current actions are caused directly by and traceable to events long before our birth, we can not be morally responsible for them. Peter van Inwagen coined this term for his argument, which is simply a variation on the standard Determinism Objection to free will. He developed this argument as an improvement on the Traditional Argument that had depended on avoidability or the ability to do otherwise, which implied the agent had alternative possibilities for action. Van Inwagen accepted the idea that Frankfurt-style cases had called alternative possibilities into question.

Other glosses - Alternative Possibilities,, Causality, Direct Argument, Frankfurt Examples, Moral Responsibility, Tracing, Traditional Argument

Consequentialism

Consequentialism is a theory of moral responsibility that makes moral judgments based on the consequences of an action. Moritz Schlick argued that it is acceptable to punish agents despite their lack of free will because of the beneficial effects on behavior that result.

Consequentialism also describes theories of punishment that are justified because of the consequences, e.g., the deterrence of a certain

crime, as opposed to a retributivist theory, that punishes because the agent simply deserves the blame.

Other glosses - Consequence Argument, Moral Luck, Moral Responsibility, Retributivism

Control

Control is what is needed for an agent to feel an action originates with and is "up to her."

Some (e.g, Harry Frankfurt) say control is found in a hierarchy of desires. Some (e.g, John Fischer) say control is being "responsive to reasons." Fischer divides control into "guidance control" and "regulative control," the latter involving alternative possibilities.

Determinism undermines control, as do various manipulation schemes including behavioral conditioning, hypnosis, brainwashing, and the like, as well as physiological problems like addictions, obsessions, and other mental disorders. External coercion denies even the freedom claimed by classical compatibilism.

In Frankfurt-style cases, hypothetical interveners exert control over decisions if and only if the actions appear to be ones the intervener does not want.

Other glosses - Agent Causation, Alternative Possibilities, Compatibilism, Determinism, Frankfurt Examples, Guidance Control, Hierarchy Of Desires, Origination, Reasons-Responsive, Up To Us

D

Degrees of Freedom

Degrees of Freedom is the idea that freedom is not an all-or-nothing true/false question. Freedom is always limited by constraints on action, whether simply physical constraints, external coercion, or internal disabilities. Fewer constraints mean more degrees of freedom.

When freedom depends on the existence of viable alternative possibilities, an agent with greater intelligence, education, or experience is qualitatively more free because she is more likely to generate workable options, more ways to do otherwise. More alternatives mean more freedom.

Other glosses - Alternative Possibilities, Done Otherwise

Deliberation

Deliberation is the consideration of alternative possibilities and their evaluation according to the agent's character, values, desires, and beliefs, with the aim of choosing one of the alternatives as a course of action.

Note that even determinists appear to believe they have alternative courses of action when they deliberate. That is, they must practically consider that their alternatives are undetermined before their choice is made, and that they are free to choose any of them. If the agent knew with certainty that only one alternative existed, she could no longer deliberate.

Randolph Clarke uses "deliberative" to describe two-stage models of free will, which locate indeterminism in the first stage, to distinguish them from "centered" free will models like that of Robert Kane, that locate indeterminism in the decision stage. Clarke also calls deliberative freedom "indirect" freedom.

Other glosses - Alternative Possibilities, Determinism, Determined Deliberation, Indeterminism

Determination

Determination is the act of deciding, ending a process of deliberation and evaluation. It can include undetermined liberties, in which there is chance "centered" in the decision itself and determined deliberations, in which there is no chance in the decision.

Other glosses - Deliberation, Determined Deliberation, Determinism, Self-Determination

Determined Deliberation

A decision that is adequately determined by the available alternative possibilities. There is no randomness in the decision itself. These are examples of Hobart determination. But they are not necessarily predetermined before the generation of alternative possibilities began.

Other glosses - Deliberation, Determinism, Self-Determination, Undetermined Liberty

Determinism

Determinism is the idea that there is but one possible future, and that it is determined by the "fixed" past and the (mistakenly presumed deterministic) Laws of Nature.

There are many kinds of determinism. None of them are based on sufficient evidence. Most have become mere dogmatic truths. Determinism remains a hypothesis that is very popular among philosophers, but it is entirely unjustified. Determinism is an illusion.

Aware of modern quantum physics, most philosophers admit the world is indeterministic, but they say that free will would be compatible with determinism, if determinism were true.

Other glosses - Causality, Compatibilism, Determination, Indeterminism, Pre-Determinism

Determinism Objection

The Determinism Objection is the first horn in the traditional dilemma of free will. Either determinism is true or indeterminism is true. In neither case can there be any moral responsibility. Note that the great asymmetry between determinism and indeterminism has led philosophers to favor the kind of deterministic or causal explanations that are the apparent basis for laws of nature. But determinism is an illusion. Many philosophers declare themselves agnostic on this objection to free will. The determinism objection is the core idea behind Peter van Inwagen's Consequence Argument.

Other glosses - Agnostic, Consequence Argument, Determinism, Luck Objection, Illusion, Standard Argument, Randomness Objection

Direct Argument

The Direct Argument for the incompatibility of determinism and moral responsibility does not depend on avoidability or the ability to do otherwise. John Fischer developed it as an improvement on Peter van Inwagen's Consequence Argument, using a Transfer Principle of Non-Responsibility which traces the causes of current decisions and actions back in the causal chain of the "actual sequence."

Other glosses - Actual Sequence, Alternative Possibilities, Consequence Argument, Indirect Argument, Done Otherwise, Standard Argument, Tracing, Transfer Principle

Do Otherwise

The idea that an agent could have done otherwise was historically seen as a requirement for free will. This idea is in clear conflict with the deterministic idea that the past allows but one possible future.

G. E. Moore and others say that "could have done otherwise" simply means "if the agent had chosen to, he could have done otherwise." This obviously requires a different past (which implies past alternative possibilities). Some philosophers call this the "if-then" hypothetical or conditional analysis.

Harry Frankfurt developed sophisticated arguments to show that alternative possibilities need not exist to claim that an agent is free.

Nevertheless, if in the present an agent has alternative possibilities, she can say "I can do otherwise." Change that to the past tense once the agent has chosen and she can say "I could have done otherwise."

Other glosses - Alternative Possibilities, Fixed Past, Frankfurt Examples

Downward Causation

Downward Causation is the idea that higher-level processes can exert a "downward" influence on lower levels. Examples include the dualist immaterial mind influencing the body, and macroscopic systems, such as the brain, influencing quantum-mechanical wave functions at the level of the atoms. Where reductionism assumes all causation is from the bottom up., downward causation works from the top down.

Other glosses - Quantum Mechanics

Dual Control

Dual Control is the power of an agent to act or not to act, in exactly the same circumstances. That is given the Fixed Past and the Laws of Nature just before the action (or the lack thereof), the agent can either act or avoid performing the act.

Robert Kane and Richard Double call this "dual (or plural) rational control." Double suggests that it may be impossible to act rationally in two different ways, given the same reasons to act. Kane also called it the "plurality condition" when there are many alternative possibilities for action, each of which has comparable good reasons.

Actions that have dual or plural rational control are Undetermined Liberties.

Other glosses - Alternative Possibilities, Compatibilism, Control, Determinism, Done Otherwise, Laws of Nature, Undetermined Liberty, Yes-No Objection

E

Epistemic Freedom

Epistemic Freedom is the idea that since we cannot know the future, we have a kind of freedom even in a deterministic world.

It is closely related to epistemic probability, which says there is no real (or ontological) chance. There is only human ignorance about the complete details that would allow us to predict the future exactly. Religious thinkers credit this to our finite minds, whereas the infinite mind of God has complete Foreknowledge.

Other glosses - Foreknowledge, Ontological, Probability

Event Causal

Event-causal libertarianism denies strict causality, the idea that every event has antecedent physical causes which completely determine all subsequent events. Some causes must be uncaused to break the causal chain of determinism. Uncaused causes include quantum events, whose outcomes are only probable. Event-causal theories raise the randomness objection in the standard argument against free will.

Other glosses - Agent Causal, Causality, Determinism, Indeterminism, Standard Argument

F

Fixed Past

The Fixed Past refers primarily to the obvious fact that past events are not changeable. But it appears often in determinist/compatibilist accounts of whether an agent could have done otherwise. "One could only have done otherwise if either the Fixed Past or the Laws of Nature had been different," goes the argument.

The conclusion is "There is but one possible future, and it is determined at each moment by the Fixed Past and the (deterministic) Laws of Nature."

G. E. Moore and others say that "could have done otherwise" simply means "if the agent had chosen to, he could have done otherwise." This obviously would have been a different past, one of the alternative possibilities. Some philosophers call this the "if-then" hypothetical or conditional analysis.

Other glosses - Alternative Possibilities, Compatibilism, Determinism, Do Otherwise, Laws of Nature

Foreknowledge

Foreknowledge is the idea that the future is already known, usually to a supernatural being.

In classical Newtonian physics, a Laplacian super intelligence could in principle predict the future from the classical laws of physics, given knowledge of the positions and velocities of all the atoms in the universe.

Other glosses - Determinism, Free Will, Laws of Nature

Frankfurt Cases

Frankfurt-style case or examples claim that an agent can be responsible, can be said to act freely, even though no alternative possibilities exist. Harry Frankfurt attacked what he called the Principle of Alternate Possibilities (PAP). Alternative possibilities for thought and action were considered to be a requirement for free will and moral responsibility until Frankfurt extended John Locke's "locked room" example of a person who freely chose to stay in a room, unaware that the doors had been locked, so that an alternative possibility did not exist. In Frankfurt-style thought experiments a hypothetical demon blocks all possibilities except the one that he wants the agent to choose.

Note that Frankfurt assumes that alternative possibilities do in fact exist, or there would be nothing for his hypothetical intervening demon to block. Since information about the agent's decision does not exist until she makes her decision, Frankfurt's hypothetical intervening demon (much like the similar Laplacian demon or God's Foreknowledge) does not exist. This is the Information Objection to Frankfurt-style examples.

Other glosses - Alternative Possibilities, Indirect Argument, Information Objection, Kane-Widerker Objection, Leeway Incompatibilism

Freedom of Action

Freedom of Action must be carefully distinguished from Freedom of the Will.

An action is said to be free by classical compatibilists like Thomas Hobbes and David Hume if the agent is not coerced by external forces.

The action may be completely determined by causal chains going back in time before the agent's birth, but they are nevertheless free in the compatibilist sense.

In his essay, Two Concepts of Liberty, Isaiah Berlin defined freedom of action as "negative freedom," and free will as "positive freedom." It is also known as Voluntarism, in contrast to Origination. And it is the Liberty of Spontaneity rather than Liberty of Indifference.

Other glosses - Causality, Compatibilism, Determinism, Free Will, Liberty of Indifference, Liberty of Spontaneity, Origination, Voluntarism

Free Will

Free Will is sometimes called Freedom of Action. Libertarian Free Will includes the availability of Alternative Possibilities and the ability to Done Otherwise.

John Locke encouraged the separation of the adjective free, which describes deliberation, from the (adequate) determination of the will.

Other glosses - Adequate Determinism, Alternative Possibilities, Deliberation, Done Otherwise

Future Contingency

The most famous Future Contingent is Aristotle's Sea Battle (De interpretatione 9). The Principle of Bivalence says that the statement "There will be a sea battle tomorrow" is either true or false. And either way necessarily binds the truth of the future contingent event.

Diodorus Cronus' "Master Argument" denied any future contingency.

Aristotle, ever sensible, decided that there was no present truth or falsity to a future contingent statement. He denied that the truth of a proposition is a necessary truth, and thus denied Logical Determinism. Indeed, contingency means that the event depends on the future, and so does its truth.

Many Stoics appear to have regarded the truth of future contingent statements as predetermining all future events. But Chrysippus denied necessity even as he affirmed fate and physical causal determinism.

Modern philosophers (especially J. Łukasiewicz) have developed a three-valued logic to handle such statements, but not with complete success.

Other glosses - Determinism, Principle of Bivalence, Master Argument, Standard Argument

G

Guidance Control

John Martin Fischer separates an agent's control into two kinds. The first he calls "guidance control" - the kind of control needed to initiate or originate an action, by being "reasons-responsive" and taking ownership of the action, meaning the agent can say the action was "up to me." For Fischer, this includes steering a vehicle which is on a fixed track and actually can only make determined turns.

Another kind of control is "regulative control" - the kind needed to choose between "alternative possibilities." Fischer describes guidance control as happening in the "actual sequence," where regulative control refers to "alternative sequences" of events. Derk Pereboom uses the related terms source and leeway incompatibilism.

Other glosses - Actual Sequence, Alternative Possibilities, Alternative Sequences, Control, Direct Argument, Leeway Incompatibilism, Origination, Reasons-Responsive, Source Incompatibilism

H

Hard Determinism

Hard Determinism was coined by William James to describe determinists who fully accept the negative implications of determinism. They reject any free will. They deny the voluntarism of Thomas Hobbes, the negative "freedom from" external constraints on our actions. They also deny any positive "freedom to" originate our actions, to be the authors of our lives, the claim that things "depend on us" (in Greek ἐφ ἡμῖν).

Other glosses - Compatibilism, Determinism, Hard Incompatibilism, Origination, Up To Us, Voluntarism

Hard Incompatibilism

Hard incompatibilists deny any indeterminism in the "actual sequence" of events. No event "originates" in the agent. Since nothing is "up to us," they argue for the incompatibility of determinism and moral responsibility.

Hard incompatibilists deny both free will and moral responsibility. They call free will an "illusion" and some call for revisionism. William James called such thinkers "hard determinists." Derk Pereboom coined the new term for those who are agnostic on indeterminism and deny free will and moral responsibility, whether determinism is true or not.

Other glosses - Actual Sequence, Agnostic, Illusion, Indeterminism, Origination, Revisionism, Source Incompatibilism, Up To Us

Hierarchy Of Desires

Harry Frankfurt formulated the idea of a Hierarchy Of Desires. First-order desires or volitions are desires to act. Second-order desires are desires to desire, for example, to want to act. The theory invites a regress of willings, and recalls the comments of John Locke and Arthur Schopenhauer. "We are free to will, but can we will what we will?"

Frankfurt says moral responsibility requires a first-order desire with which the agent "identifies," which means she has a second-order desire that is consistent with the first-order desire that moves her to action.

Other glosses - Moral Responsibility

I

Illusion

It is now common among hard incompatibilists to call free will an illusion. this may be because of Frankfurt Examples that claim to prove that Alternative Possibilities do not exist. Or it may be because of the standard argument against free will. In any case, the real illusion is determinism, in its many forms.

Illusionists are often revisionists calling for an end to retributive punishment.

Other glosses - Alternative Possibilities, Frankfurt Examples, Hard Incompatibilism, Standard Argument, Retributivism, Revisionism

Incompatibilism

Incompatibilists come in two kinds. Both claim that determinism is incompatible with free will. One kind were called "hard determinists" by William James. They deny free will. The other are libertarians. They deny determinism.

Today many incompatibilists declare themselves agnostic about the "truth" of determinism and say the incompatibilities extend to indeterminism as well.

Derk Pereboom coined "hard incompatibilism" to describe agnostics on determinism who deny both free will and moral responsibility. They call free will an "illusion" and some call for revisionism.

The traditional argument for incompatibilism assumes alternative possibilities and the ability to do otherwise. The Consequence Argument and Direct Argument do not.

Other glosses - Agnostic, Alternative Possibilities, Broad Incompatibilism, Consequence Argument, Determinism, Done Otherwise, Direct Argument, Hard Incompatibilism, Indeterminism, Illusion, Indeterminism, Illusion, Leeway Incompatibilism, Semicompatibilism, Source Incompatibilism, Traditional Argument

Indeterminism

Indeterminism is the idea that some events are uncaused, specifically that they are random accidents with only probabilistic outcomes. In ancient times, Epicurus proposed that atoms occasionally swerve at random, breaking the causal chain of determinism and allowing for moral responsibility. In modern physics, we now know that atoms constantly swerve, or move indeterministically, whenever they are in the presence of other atoms. The universe is irreducibly random on the atomic scale. Laws of Nature are therefore probabilistic or statistical. Although for large objects, the departure from classical laws of motion is usually entirely insignificant, indeterministic quantum noise plays a role in the two-stage model of free will.

Other glosses - Causality, Causa Sui, Determinism, Laws of Nature, Moral Responsibility, Probability

Indirect Argument

The Indirect Argument for the incompatibility of determinism and moral responsibility depends on avoidability or the ability to do otherwise. If the agent does not have alternative possibilities, she cannot do otherwise, and she cannot be morally responsible.

Other glosses - Alternative Possibilities, Basic Argument, Consequence Argument, Direct Argument, Standard Argument

Information Objection

The Information Objection claims that Frankfurt examples can not prove that Alternative Possibilities do not exist, because the information needed by an intervener to block alternatives does not exist until the moment of an agent's decision.

Other glosses - Alternative Possibilities, Frankfurt Examples, Kane-Widerker Objection, Standard Argument, Yes-No Objection

Intellect

Intellect is often contrasted with Will, when the latter is identified with the desires and passions and the former identified with reason. From Aquinas to Hume, some philosophers argued that acts of will are always based on emotions and desires, not the pure intellect that generates, evaluates, and deliberates the alternative possibilities.

Other glosses - Alternative Possibilities, Deliberation, Evaluation, Reasons-Responsive

K

Kane-Widerker Objection

Robert Kane and later David Widerker objected to Frankfurt-style examples that posit a demon or intervener who allows the agent to do "freely" whatever the intervener wants her to do. The objection notes that the intervener can not know what an agent is going to do without assuming the agent is determined and the intervener has Foreknowledge. This is an epistemic objection.

The intervener needs a "prior sign" of the causal chain. Such a sign is an event that leads causally to the decision, and thus Frankfurt examples "beg the question" by assuming determinism. Information about the agent's decision does not exist until she makes her decision (the ontological Information Objection), so Frankfurt's hypothetical intervening demon (much like the similar Laplacian demon or God's Foreknowledge) can not exist.

Other glosses - Alternative Possibilities, Frankfurt Examples, Information Objection, Yes-No Objection

L

Laws of Nature

The "Laws of Nature" are often cited in compatibilist arguments as controlling events, together with the "Fixed Past."

The idea appears often in determinist/compatibilist accounts of whether an agent could have done otherwise. "One could only have

done otherwise if either the Fixed Past or the Laws of Nature had been different," goes the argument. The Fixed Past refers primarily to the obvious fact that past events are not changeable.

The usual conclusion is "There is but one possible future, and it is determined at each moment by the Fixed Past and the (deterministic) Laws of Nature."

However, the real Laws of Nature, beginning with the most fundamental laws of physics, are indeterministic and probabilistic, reflecting the availability of alternative possibilities..

Other glosses - Alternative Possibilities, Compatibilism, Determinism, Done Otherwise, Fixed Past

Leeway Incompatibilism

Leeway Incompatibilism requires indeterminism in the "alternative sequences" provided by alternative possibilities, to establish incompatibility of determinism and moral responsibility. By contrast, Source Incompatibilism depends on actions that originate within the agent in the "actual sequence." Derk Pereboom coined this term, which is a variation on the Principle of Alternative Possibilities (PAP).

Other glosses - Alternative Possibilities, Source Incompatibilism

Liberty of Indifference

Liberty of Indifference (liberum arbitrium indifferentiae) is an ancient case of two options so similar that only a miniscule effort is needed to choose one over the other. This seemed to be a case where even an immaterial mind might move a material body. It was also argued that where options are identical, randomness would suffice to choose one. Some philosophers argued that this randomness was at the heart of free will, showing its absurdity and unintelligibility. In a famous example typical of philosophical test cases, the scholastic teacher Jean Buridan placed an ass equidistant between identical bales of hay. Since animals lack our God-given liberty, Buridan argued, the ass would starve to death.

Other glosses - Alternative Possibilities,

Liberty of Spontaneity

Liberty of Spontaneity was Descartes' (and the Scholastics') term for what Thomas Hobbes called Voluntarism. Spontaneity translates the Greek automaton (αὐτόματον).

Descartes contrasted it with Liberty of Indifference, but they are not proper opposites. It is more properly contrasted with Libertarian "Free Will" and with Berlin's Positive Freedom, which is the "freedom to" choose or act that comes with genuine Alternative Possibilities and results in actions that are "up to us.,"that we originate.

Other glosses - Alternative Possibilities, Liberty of Indifference, Self-Realization, Voluntarism

Logical Fallacy

The Logical Fallacy is to assume that purely logical (and linguistic) analysis can yield "truths" about the world. Logical positivism was in practical terms a logical fallacy. The hundreds of papers published on Harry Frankfurt's attacks on the idea of alternative possibilities are a prime example. Nothing is logically true of the physical world. Modal analyses using the idea of possible worlds shows that anything that is not internally contradictory can be postulated of some possible world.

Other glosses - Alternative Possibilities, Frankfurt-style Examples,

Luck Objection

The Luck Objection to free will and moral responsibility arises because the world contains irreducible indeterminism and chance. As a result, many unintended consequences of our actions are out of our control.

We are often held responsible for actions that were intended as good, but that had bad consequences. Similarly, we occasionally are praised for actions that were either neutral or possibly blameworthy, but which had good consequences.

In a deterministic world, it is hard to see how we can be held responsible for any of our actions. Counterintuitively, semicompatibilist philosophers hold that whether determinism or indeterminism is true, we can still have moral responsibility.

At the other end of the spectrum, some libertarians are critical of any free will model that involves chance, because the apparent randomness of outcomes would make such free will unintelligible, because it would be a matter of luck.

Unfortunately, much of what happens in the real world contains a good deal of luck, giving rise to many of the moral dilemmas that lead to moral skepticism.

Whether determinist, compatibilist, semicompatibilist, or libertarian, it seems unreasonable to hold persons responsible for the unin-

tended consequences of their actions, good or bad. In many moral and legal systems, it the person's intentions that matter first and foremost.

And in any case, actions need not have moral consequences to be free, that would commit the moral restrictivism of restricting free decisions to moral decisions.

Other glosses - Agnostic, Consequentialism, Control, Determinism Objection, Moral restrictivism, Indeterminism, Mind Argument, Moral Luck, Standard Argument, Randomness Objection

M

Manipulation Argument

The Manipulation Argument grows out of the accepted loss of control and moral responsibility for agents who are addicted or induced to act by hypnosis and the like. As with the hypothetical interveners in Frankfurt-style cases, these arguments often postulate counterfactual manipulators - such as evil neuroscientists who control the development of persons from the egg (as in Brave New World) or condition them in their formative years (like a "Skinner box" reinforcing selected behaviors). The argument says that if we deny responsibility when such manipulators have control, why not deny it when causal determinism (or random indeterminism) is in control?

The Manipulation Argument is only meant to enhance the intuition of lost control, in order to support the Consequence Argument and similar Determinism Objections in the standard argument against free will. Derk Pereboom's Four-Case Argument is a well-known example of a Manipulation Argument.

Other glosses - Consequence Argument, Control, Moral Responsibility, Standard Argument

Master Argument

The Master Argument was first formulated by Diodorus Cronus, a late 4th-century philosopher of the Megarian School, who argued that the actual is the only possible and that some true statements about the future imply that the future is already determined. He formulated a "Master Argument" to show that if something in the future is not going to happen, it was true in the past that it would not happen.

This is related to the problem of future contingency, made famous in the example of Aristotle's Sea-Battle in *De Interpretatione 9.* Aristotle thought statements about the future lacked any truth value.

Note that the truth value of a statement made in the past can "actually" be changed if an event does or does not happen, showing that the "fixed past" has some changeability.

Other glosses - Actualism, Basic Argument, Consequence Argument, Future Contingency, Principle of Bivalence, Standard Argument

Mind Argument

The Mind Argument is Peter van Inwagen's name for the Randomness Objection in the standard argument against free will. Alfred Mele calls it the "Luck Objection."

Van Inwagen named the Mind Argument for the journal Mind, where most of the randomness objections were published, especially R. E. Hobart's 1934 classic "Free Will As Involving Determination And Inconceivable Without It."

Other glosses - Luck Objection, Randomness Objection, Standard Argument

Modal Fallacy

The Modal Fallacy usually involves possible or contingent statements that are falsely claimed to be necessary. For example:

This proposition is true. (contingent)

If it is true, it cannot be false. (contingent)

If it cannot be false, then it is true and necessarily true (modal fallacy).

Ted Warfield clams that his colleague Peter van Inwagen's Consequence Argument contains contingent premises that make it a modal fallacy. Warfield has reformulated a purely necessary form of the argument. Unfortunately, necessary arguments do not apply to the world.

Other glosses - Consequence Argument

Modest Libertarianism

Modest Libertarianism is a concept proposed by Alfred Mele for consideration by Libertarians. It is a two-stage model of free will in which indeterminism is limited to the early stages of the deliberation process which consider alternative possibilities that may or may not "come to mind." Modest libertarianism is a variation of Daniel Dennett's 1978 two-stage "Valerian" decision model, in his provocative essay "Giving Libertarians What They Say They Want."

Mele feels that randomness anywhere in the causal chain leads to his Luck Objection, a variation on the standard Randomness Objection.

Other glosses - Alternative Possibilities, Indeterminism, Luck Objection, Randomness Objection

Moral Luck

Moral Luck is Thomas Nagel's notion that since an action's consequences are beyond the agent's control, randomness makes moral responsibility a matter of chance. This is often framed as the Luck Objection, a variation on the randomness objection Since there is irreducible randomness in the universe, there are no doubt many cases where luck enters into moral situations, but not universally. Many actions are adequately determined and have reliable and predictable consequences, enough to establish the general concept of moral responsibility.

Other glosses - Adequate Determinism, Consequentialism, Control, Luck Objection, Moral Responsibility, Standard Argument, Randomness Objection

Moral Restrictivism

Moral Restrictivism is to assume that free choices are restricted to moral decisions. Robert Kane does this, as did Plato and the Scholastics. This is not to deny that moral responsibility is historically intimately connected with free will and even dependent on the existence of free will (for libertarians and broad compatibilists). Any decision can be free. Our freedom to act also includes merely practical, financial, and fiduciary judgments, as well as occasional non-rational flip-of-the-coin decisions and even misjudgments.

Other glosses - Moral Responsibility, Restrictivism

Moral Responsibility

Moral Responsibility is historically tightly connected to the problem of free will, but it is an moral restrictivism to require that free choices be moral decisions.

Other glosses - Moral Restrictivism

Moral Sentiments

Moral Sentiments arguably would exist whether or not determinism is "true." David Hume first made this argument, but Peter Strawson made it famous in current debates, with his agnosticism about determinism vs. free will, in favor of a Humean Naturalism that takes our moral sentiments as givens that are beyond the skepticism of logic and critical thought.

Note that Hume the Naturalist had no problem "Deriving Ought from Is" - something shown logically impossible by Hume the Skeptic.

Other glosses - Agnostic, Moral restrictivism, Naturalism

Moral Skepticism

Moral Skepticism challenges the idea that there are always rational and best answers to moral questions. Because there are various theories of morality - deontic, pragmatic, utilitarian, etc, it is easy to construct moral dilemmas and paradoxes. Moral skeptics like Walter Sinnott-Armstrong believe these are real problems in life and cannot be explained away by clever arguments.

Note that moral skepticism tends to lead to relativism and moral nihilism in the absence of objective values.

Other glosses - Moral Responsibility

N

Narrow Incompatibilism

Narrow Incompatibilism is Randolph Clarke's synonym for John Martin Fischer's concept of Semicompatibilism. Clarke distinguishes it from his term Broad Incompatibilism.

Narrow Incompatibilism is incompatible with free will, but not with moral responsibility.

Other glosses - Broad Incompatibilism, Compatibilism, Incompatibilism, Moral Responsibility, Semicompatibilism

Naturalism

Naturalism is the position that the Laws of Nature (assumed to be deterministic) apply to human beings and their actions, because humans are natural things, continuous with animals and other things that lack free will. The position originated with David Hume and has been developed in the moral responsibility debates by Paul Russell.

Naturalists tend to be revisionists on retributive punishment.

Assuming that free will is restricted to morally responsible agents is an example of the Moral restrictivism. One way of seeing the continuous nature between animals and humans is to recognize that animals, like children, have a will and freedom of action, they just lack moral responsibility.

Other glosses - Determinism, Moral restrictivism, Laws of Nature, Moral Responsibility, Restrictivism, Revisionism

Naturalistic Fallacy

G. E. Moore in Principia Ethica claimed that ethics is human, not natural. So ethical claims can not be supported by appeals to natural properties, like pleasure or utility. Moore thinks "good" cannot be defined. It is an elemental essential property.

Moore's ethical non-naturalism resembles David Hume"s denial that "ought" (human ethics) can be derived from "is" (nature).

Note the conflict with Naturalists for whom natural behaviors are moral behaviors, and "un-natural" behaviors are bad.

Other glosses - Moral restrictivism, Moral Responsibility, Naturalism

O

Ontological

Ontology is the study of real things existing in the world. A crisis in philosophy emerged when Locke and Hume, and later Kant, observed that all our knowledge comes to us through our perceptions. We cannot know the "things themselves" behind the perceptions. Moreover, our perceptions may be illusions.

The existence of real ontological chance is often denied by those who claim that randomness and probability are merely the result of human ignorance. Chance, they say is an epistemic problem, not an ontological one.

Other glosses - Epistemic, Illusion, Probability, Randomness

Origination

Origination is the idea that new causal chains can begin with an agent, something that is not predetermined to happen by events prior to the agent's deliberation (between alternative possibilities) and decision. Origination accounts for creativity.

Ted Honderich is "dismayed" because the truth of determinism requires that we give up "origination" with its promise of an open future. For him, limiting freedom to classical compatibilist voluntarism means we are not the authors of our own actions. They are not up to us.

Other glosses - Agent Causal, Alternative Possibilities, Causa Sui, Up To Us, Voluntarism

Ought From Is

David Hume famously criticized philosophers for talking about the way things are and suddenly describing the way they ought (or ought not) to be, as if the ought had been deduced from the is.

Moore's naturalistic fallacy similarly denies that ethical rules can depend on natural facts.

Other glosses - Moral restrictivism, Naturalistic Fallacy

Ought Implies Can

Ought Implies Can (sometimes abbreviated K) is the deontic principle, usually attributed to Immanuel Kant, that an agent ought to do a moral act only if she actually can do it, if she has control.

Other glosses - Control, Done Otherwise, Voluntarism

P

Possible Worlds

Gottfried Leibniz argued that necessary truths are true in all possible worlds. David Lewis appears to have believed that the truth of his counterfactuals was a result of believing that for every non-contradictory statement there is a possible world in which that statement is true. This is called modal realism. It implies the existence of infinitely many parallel universes, an idea similar to the contraversial many-world interpretations of quantum mechanics.

The astronomer David Layzer analyzes questions of free will in terms of many possible worlds.

It is a bit ironic that philosophers, who are skeptical about our ability to obtain knowledge of the real external world, are optimistic about many possible worlds.

Other glosses - Alternative Possibilities, Modal Fallacy, Quantum Mechanics

Pre-Determinism

Pre-Determinism is the idea that a strict causal determinism is true, with a causal chain of events back to the origin of the universe, and one possible future.

It is what most philosophers mean when they say that free will is compatible with determinism, and when they use determinism in the standard argument against free will.

Other glosses - Causality, Compatibilism, Determinism, Standard Argument

Principle of Alternate Possibilities

The Principle of Alternate (sic) Possibilities (or PAP) was formulated as follows in 1961 by Harry Frankfurt in order to defend compatibilism from the apparent lack of alternative possibilities in the deterministic world of classical compatibilism.

PAP: A person is morally responsible for what he has done only if he could have done otherwise.

Frankfurt maintained that PAP was false, and that agents could be free and morally responsible without alternative possibilities and the capability to do otherwise in the same circumstances.

Other glosses - Alternative Possibilities, Determinism, Done Otherwise, Moral Responsibility, Same Circumstances

Principle of Bivalence

The Principle of Bivalence is that for any proposition p, either p is true or p is false. It is the reason the standard argument against free will is framed as two horns of a dilemma. Either determinism is true or false. Most philosophers do not want to give up the idea of causal determinism, so opt to be compatibilists.

Bivalence is also known as "the law of the excluded middle." There is no middle term between true and false. This becomes the basis for the idea that there is no tertium quid or middle between chance and necessity, perceived as logical opposites.

The Principle of Bivalence is also the basis for Logical Determinism, in which the present truth of a statement implies its truth in the future.

Other glosses - Determinism, Future Contingency, Standard Argument

Probability

Probability has often been a way to deny real chance. The great mathematicians who invented the calculus of probabilities, which governs games of chance, thought that there was nothing random really going on. For them probability was merely a result of human ignorance. The problem was epistemic, not ontological.

Deterministic Laws of Nature guarantee we could predict the future, if only we had all the information needed. Laplace's demon, a supreme intelligence, could know the future, as God foreknows it, if he knew the positions and velocities of all the particles in the universe.

Today we know that the Laws of Nature are not deterministic. Not only are they probabilistic, but irreducibly random, due to the underlying quantum mechanics that has replaced classical mechanics as the proper description of the universe's fundamental particles.

The laws become arbitrarily close to certain in the limit of large numbers of particles (billiard balls, planets), leading to the illusion of perfectly deterministic laws.

Probability is the explanation for alternative possibilities and unpredictable "uncaused" causes (causa sui) that are the "free" part of "free will."

Other glosses - Alternative Possibilities, Causa Sui, Determinism, Epistemic, Foreknowledge, Illusion, Laws of Nature, Ontological, Quantum Mechanics

Q

Quantum Mechanics

The development of Quantum Mechanics in the late 1920's marked the end of physical determinism.

Quantum mechanics has replaced classical mechanics as the proper description of the universe's fundamental particles. But note that in the limit of macroscopic objects with large numbers of particles, the quantum laws correspond exactly to (i.e., become the same as) the classical laws. This is Neils Bohr's correspondence principle.

Deterministic Laws of Nature have been replaced with probabilistic laws. Quantum events can start new "causal chains" with events that are unpredictable from prior events, self-caused events that are causa sui.

Quantum phenomena are behind the generation of alternative possibilities that are the "free" part of "free will."

Other glosses - Alternative Possibilities, Causa Sui, Determinism, Laws of Nature, Probability

R

Randomness Objection

The Randomness Objection is the second horn in the traditional dilemma of free will. Either determinism is true or indeterminism is true. In neither case can there be any moral responsibility. Note that the great asymmetry between determinism and indeterminism has led philosophers to favor the kind of deterministic or causal explanations that are the apparent basis for laws of nature. But determinism is an illusion.

Indeterminism is a greater threat to moral responsibility than determinism, since it is associated with many negative ideas, such as chance. Nevertheless, many philosophers declare themselves agnostic on this objection to free will. The randomness objection is the core idea behind Peter van Inwagen's Mind Argument.

Other glosses - Agnostic, Determinism Objection, Illusion, Indeterminism, Luck Objection, Mind Argument, Standard Argument

Reactive Attitudes

Reactive Attitudes were identified by Peter Strawson as feelings that we would naturally have even if we were convinced of the truth of determinism (or indeterminism). Strawson was an early agnostic, claiming he could not make sense of either). Reactive Attitudes include gratitude and resentment, and our normal tendency to praise or blame, punish or reward. Strawson modeled his naturalist claims in the face of skepticism about free will after David Hume, who overcame his own famous skeptical views to claim ethical truths could be found in naturalism.

Other glosses - Naturalism

Reasons-Responsive

Reasons-Responsiveness describes an agent who has the kind of control needed to initiate or originate an action. Being "reasons-responsive" and taking ownership of the action means the agent can say the action was "up to me." John Martin Fischer calls this "guidance control" in the "actual sequence" of events that figure in the "Direct Argument" for source incompatibilism. Fischer's account of moral responsibility is like Thomas Aquinas' and Susan Wolf's account of free actions as those guided by reasons.

Other glosses - Actual Sequence, Control, Direct Argument, Origination, Source Incompatibilism, Up To Us

Regulative Control

John Martin Fischer separates an agent's control into two kinds. The first he calls "guidance control" - the kind of control needed to initiate or originate an action, by being "reasons-responsive" and taking ownership of the action, meaning the agent can say the action was "up to me." The other kind of control is "regulative control" - the kind needed to choose between "alternative possibilities." Fischer describes these options as happening in the "actual sequence" or "alternative sequences" of events. Derk Pereboom uses the related terms source and leeway incompatibilism.

Other glosses - Actual Sequence, Alternative Possibilities, Alternative Sequences, Control, Direct Argument, Guidance Control, Leeway Incompatibilism, Origination, Reasons-Responsive, Source Incompatibilism

Restrictivism

Restrictivist theories claim that the number of "free" actions is a tiny fraction of all actions. Robert Kane, for example limits them to rare "self-forming actions" (SFAs) in which weighty and difficult moral decisions are made. Limiting freedom to moral decisions is the moral restrictivism. Peter van Inwagen restricts free will to cases where the reasons that favor either alternative are not clearly stronger. This is the ancient liberty of indifference. Susan Wolf restricts free decisions to those made rationally according to "the True and the Good."

Other glosses - Liberty of Indifference, Self-Forming Action

Retributivism

Retributivism describes punishment that is deserved because the agent was morally responsible for the crime. Many hard incompatibilists who think free will is an illusion, and many naturalists, are revisionists calling for an end to retributive punishment.

Susan Wolf has pointed out the strange asymmetry between praise and blame. Those opposed to punishment for retributive reasons (as opposed to practical consequentialist reasons) are often in favor of praise for good deeds. This reflects the ancient Platonic view that we are responsible only for the good we do. Our errors we blame on our ignorance, which is, unfortunately, no excuse before the law.

Other glosses - Illusion, Moral Responsibility, Naturalism, Revisionism

Revisionism

Revisionists hope to change popular attitudes about free will and moral responsibility, bringing them more into line with the views of modern philosophy. A leading issue is the widely held view among current philosophers that free will is an illusion. Revisionists conclude there should be an end to retributive punishment.

Other glosses - Illusion, Moral Responsibility, Retributivism

Rule Beta

Rule Beta is Peter van Inwagen's "Third Argument" for incompatibilism. Van Inwagen argues against the compatibilism of determinism and moral responsibility. It is a Transfer Principle of unavoidability (one has no choices and can not do otherwise).

p, and no one has, or ever had, any choice about that. If p then q, and no one has, or ever had, any choice about that. Hence, q, and no one has, or ever had, any choice about that.

Rule Beta wraps the ancient and physical dilemma of determinism in analytical logical window dressing. It is identical to the Determinist Objection in the standard argument against free will.

Other glosses - Done Otherwise, Logical Fallacy, Moral Responsibility, Standard Argument, Transfer Principle

S

Same Circumstances

Determinists argue that, given the Laws of Nature and the Fixed Past, it is impossible for an agent to act differently in Exactly the Same Circumstances. Libertarians demand such Dual Rational Control and the ability to Do Otherwise as a freedom condition.

Other glosses - Done Otherwise, Fixed Past, Laws of Nature

Self-Determination

Self-Determination is the idea of a positive freedom, a freedom for actions that we originate, actions that are "up to us." Such acts constitute the essence of Free Will. This is Mortimer Adler's term, adopted also by Robert Kane. Adler called it the *Natural* Freedom of *Self-Determination.* to indicate it is a universal property. It is a Determined De-Liberation.

Other glosses - Determination, Determined De-Liberation, Origination, Self-Perfection, Self-Realization, Up to Us

Self-Forming Action

Self-Forming Actions (SFAs) are Robert Kane's idea of free actions in the distant past that contribute to our character and values. When we act out of habit today, we trace the Ultimate Responsibility (UR) for those actions back to those SFAs. Although current habitual actions may seem (adequately) determined, they are still self-determined and thus free.

We can be responsible for current actions that are essentially (viz. adequately) determined by our character and values, as long as we formed that character ourselves by earlier free Self-Forming Actions. For Kane, SFAs in turn require brains that are not deterministically caused by anything outside the agent.

Other glosses - Self-Determination, Tracing, Ultimate Responsibility

Self-Perfection

Self-Perfection is the idea from Plato to Kant that we are only free when our decisions are for reasons and we are not slaves to our passions. Mortimer Adler' called it the *Acquired* Freedom of *Self-Perfection.* to indicate it is acquired in moral development. It is also used by Robert Kane. Adler cites many theologically minded philosophers who argue that man is only perfect and free when following a divine moral law (the moral restrictivism). Sinners, they say, do not have free will, which is odd because on their account sinners are presumably responsible for evil in the world despite an omniscient, omnipotent, and benevolent God.

Other glosses - Moral Restrictivism, Restrictivism, Self-Determination, Self-Realization

Self-Realization

Self-Realization is the idea of freedom as freedom from coercions that make our actions not up to us. It is known as Freedom of Action.

Mortimer Adler' called it the *Circumstantial* Freedom of *Self-Realization.* to indicate it depends on external circumstances. Today this negative freedom recognizes internal coercions as well, such as addictions or mental disabilities. This is the classical compatibilist definition of freedom, also known as voluntarism. It is also used by Robert Kane.

Other glosses - Compatibilism, Self-Determination, Self-Perfection, Voluntarism

Semicompatibilism

Semicompatibilism is John Martin Fischer's name for the compatibilism of moral responsibility and determinism (or indeterminism). It is contrasted with classical compatibilism, the broader idea that free will is compatible with determinism.

Randolph Clarke calls these respectively Narrow and Broad Incompatibilism.

Classical compatibilists are determinists. Semicompatibilists avoid the determinist label, claiming to be agnostic about the "truth" of determinism or indeterminism. Semicompatibilism grew out of the apparent success of Harry Frankfurt's attacks on the Principle of Alternate Possibilities.

Other glosses - Agnostic, Compatibilism, Determinism, Frankfurt Examples, Indeterminism, Narrow Incompatibilism

Soft Causality

Soft Causality is the idea that most events are adequately determined by normal causes, but that some events are not precisely predictable from prior events.

Soft Causality includes occasional quantum events, which are only probabilistic and statistical. This means that they are not strictly caused by prior events, although they may be causes of subsequent events. They depend on chance in the form of irreducible quantum indeterminacy

Their unpredictability leads us to call them uncaused events, which in turn become uncaused causes (causa sui) that start new causal chains.

Other glosses - Adequate Determinism, Causality, Causa Sui, Determinism, Indeterminacy, Indeterminism

Soft Compatibilism

Soft Compatibilism is one of Alfred Mele's terms. Soft compatibilists know, as a result of quantum physics, that determinism is not true. They think that some indeterminism, in the right places, might be useful. For

soft compatibilists, the right place is in what John Martin Fischer calls the Actual Sequence, where it breaks the causal chain of determinism back to the Big Bang. This position is also known as Source Incompatibilism.

Note that soft compatibilists accept the traditional Voluntarism of Thomas Hobbes and David Hume. Even if determinism were true, they say, there would still be Freedom of Action.

Other glosses - Compatibilism, Determinism, Freedom of Action, Free Will, Hard Compatibilism, Origination, Source Incompatibilism, Voluntarism

Soft Determinism

Soft Determinism was coined by William James to describe compatibilists, who accepted the truth of determinism. They claimed free will was the voluntarism of Thomas Hobbes, the negative "freedom from" external constraints on our actions. This is called "Freedom of Action" to distinguish it from Freedom of the Will

Other glosses - Compatibilism, Determinism, Freedom of Action, Free Will, Hard Determinism, Origination, Voluntarism

Soft Incompatibilism

Soft Incompatibilism says that free will is incompatible with pre-determinism, and that pre-determinism is not true. It is preferable to the loose usage of the plain "incompatibilist" to describe a libertarian, since it is ambiguous and also used for determinists.

Soft Incompatibilism stands in contrast to Hard Incompatibilism, which maintains that pre-determinism is true and free will does not exist. It is not incompatible with an adequate determinism.

Soft Incompatibilism involves Soft Causality. Soft Incompatibilists accept occasional quantum events, which are only probabilistic and statistical, since they break strict causal chains back to the Big Bang with uncaused causes (causa sui) that start new causal chains. It resembles Al Mele's Soft Libertarianism.

Other glosses - Adequate Determinism, Causa Sui, Soft Causality, Soft Libertarianism, Pre-Determinism

Soft Libertarianism

Soft Libertarianism is one of Alfred Mele's terms. Soft libertarians think that some indeterminism, in the right place is useful. For soft libertarians , the right place is in what John Martin Fischer calls the Actual Sequence, where it breaks the causal chain of determinism back to the Big Bang. This position is also known as Source Incompatibilism.

Soft libertarianism differs from Mele's modest libertarianism in that it does not require robust alternative possibilities (APs). APs produce what John Martin Fischer calls the Alternative Sequences.

Mele also develops a model for "Daring Soft Libertarians." Daring soft libertarians, he says, especially value a power to make decisions that are not deterministically caused - a certain initiatory power. This model reaches out to Robert Kane's idea of Ultimate Responsibility, in which we can be responsible for current actions, ones that are essentially determined by our character and values, as long as we formed that character ourselves by earlier free actions that he calls Self-Forming Actions (SFA). SFA's in turn require brains that are not deterministically caused by anything outside the agent.

Other glosses - Compatibilism, Determinism, Freedom of Action, Free Will, Hard Compatibilism, Origination, Source Incompatibilism, Voluntarism

Source Incompatibilism

Source Incompatibilism or "Sourcehood" focuses on indeterminism in the "actual sequence" of events, an event that "originates" in the agent, to establish the incompatibility of determinism and moral responsibility.

Hard incompatibilists deny this indeterminism. By contrast, Leeway Incompatibilism depends on the ability to do otherwise in "alternative sequences."

Other glosses - Actual Sequence, Alternative Sequences, Consequence Argument, Direct Argument, Hard Incompatibilism, Indirect Argument, Leeway Incompatibilism, Origination

Standard Argument

The Standard Argument against Free Will is a dilemma with two horns, the Determinism Objection and the Randomness Objection.

If determinism is "true" all our actions are determined and we lack free will and moral responsibility. If indeterminism is "true" all our actions are random and we are equally unfree and not responsible.

A subtle combination of randomness and adequate determinism is required for a two-stage model of free will.

Other glosses - Basic Argument, Consequence Argument, Determinism Objection, Direct Argument, Indirect Argument, Randomness Objection

Strongest Motive

Given the alternative possibilities for action, the agent might appear to be determined to select the strongest motive. But given the complexity of an agent's character and values, motives and reasons, feelings and desires, the idea of idea of an obvious "strongest motive" has been discredited. Some philosophers say that the strongest motive was, after the fact, whatever the agent chose, reducing it to a tautology.

Other glosses - Akrasia, Alternative Possibilities, Self-Forming Action, Weakness of Will

Tracing

Tracing is the idea that an agent's responsibility (or non-responsibility) for some action or the consequence of an action is not limited to the agent's thoughts or actions at the moment immediately prior to the action or consequence, but can be traced back to earlier actions, from which responsibility can be transferred. Difficulties arise establishing that the consequences could reasonably have been foreseen by the agent.

Other glosses - Consequence Argument, Consequentialism, Moral Responsibility, Transfer Principle

Traditional Argument

The Traditional Argument for the incompatibility of determinism and moral responsibility has three steps:

1. If determinism is true, no agent could have avoided acting as she did act - could have done otherwise.

2. An agent is only responsible for actions if she could have done otherwise (the Principle of Alternative Possibilities).

3. Thus, if determinism is true, no agent is morally responsible.

Other glosses - Alternative Possibilities, Consequence Argument, Done Otherwise, Direct Argument, Incompatibilism, Moral Responsibility

Transfer Principle

A Transfer Principle says that an agent's responsibility or non-responsibility (or avoidability or unavoidability) for an action can be

transferred to the consequences of that action, or to the probable consequences (strong transfer), or to consequences that could reasonably have been foreseen by the agent (weak transfer). John Martin Fischer developed the Principle of Transfer of Non-Responsibility as a variation on Peter van Inwagen's "Third Argument" or Rule Beta. Robert Kane's Ultimate Responsibility is Transfer of Responsibility from Self-Forming Actions long ago to current actions, however automatic and habitual.

Other glosses - Consequence Argument, Moral Responsibility, Rule Beta, Self-Forming Actions, Ultimate Responsibility

U

Ultimacy

Ultimacy or the Ultimacy Condition is often used by determinists, hard incompatibilists, and illusionists to deny moral responsibility. Galen Strawson's Basic Argument is a good example of denying Ultimacy by an infinite regress of responsibility for our character.

Other glosses - Basic Argument, Consequence Argument, Responsibility, Ultimate Responsibility

Ultimate Responsibility

Ultimate Responsibility (UR) is Robert Kane's concept that we can be responsible for current actions, ones that are essentially determined by our character and values, as long as we formed that character ourselves by earlier free actions that he calls Self-Forming Actions (SFA).

Other glosses - Responsibility, Self-Forming Action

Undetermined Liberty

A decision that involves chance, which selects at random from a number of alternative possibilities that appear equally valuable or useful. When the second stage of evaluation does not produce a Determined Deliberation, the agent can "flip a coin" and yet take responsibility for the decision, however it comes out.

Note that an undetermined liberty is not random in the absolute sense of having no connection with character, values, motives, feelings, desires, etc. It is randomly chosen from within a subset of alternative possibilities that all are rational. An undetermined liberty is a liberty of indifference, but it is still a determination that is adequately determined. Robert Kane's SFAs are undetermined liberties.

Other glosses - Adequate Determinism, Determination, Determined Deliberation, Liberty of Indifference, Up To Us

Up To Us

The idea that we are the originators of our actions was first described by Aristotle in his Metaphysics and Nichomachean Ethics with the Greek phrase ἐφ’ ἡμῖν, “up to us,” or “depends on us.”

Agent causal libertarians insist that our actions begin with something inside our minds. (Aristotle had also said some actions begin ἐν ἡμῖν - “in us”.) They describe this variously as non-occurrent causation, contra-causal freedom, metaphysical freedom, a causa sui, or simply non-causal freedom.

If our actions are not “up to us,” if we feel they “happen to us,” then we cannot feel morally responsible for them.

Other glosses - Agent Causal, Moral Responsibility, Origination,

V

Volition

Volition is another word for Will. It implies the moment of decision or choice and commitment to a course of action, as distinguished from earlier moments of deliberation and evaluation of alternative possibilities. Aquinas, who identified five or more stages, called this moment the *electio* or choice.

Other glosses - Alternative Possibilities, Deliberation, Free Will, Voluntarism

Voluntarism

Voluntarism is the classical compatibilist definition of freedom as freedom from coercions that make our actions not up to us. Today this negative freedom includes internal constraints as well, such as addictions or mental disabilities.

Mortimer Adler and Robert Kane call this self-realization, contrasting it with the libertarian positive freedom of self-determination. Honderich calls it voluntariness, contrasting it with the libertarian freedom of origination, without which, he says, we are not the authors of our own actions.

Other glosses - Liberty of Spontaneity, Origination, Self-Determination, Self-Realization, Up To Us

Weakness of Will

Weakness of Will (akrasia) describes actions taken against one's better judgment. Rationalism assumes there is always a single best way to evaluate an agent's options or alternative possibilities, so that weakness of will is fundamentally irrational.

Other glosses - Akrasia, Alternative Possibilities, Strongest Motive

Yes-No Objection

The Yes-No Objection claims that Frankfurt examples can not prove that alternative possibilities do not exist, because the agent's decision to act or not to act, to do or not to do, can always wait until the last possible moment, so a hypothetical intervener would have to block alternatives ahead of time and thus constitute an external coercion that denies the agent's compatibilist voluntarism or negative freedom.

Other glosses - Alternative Possibilities, Frankfurt Examples, Information Objection, Kane-Widerker Objection, Voluntarism

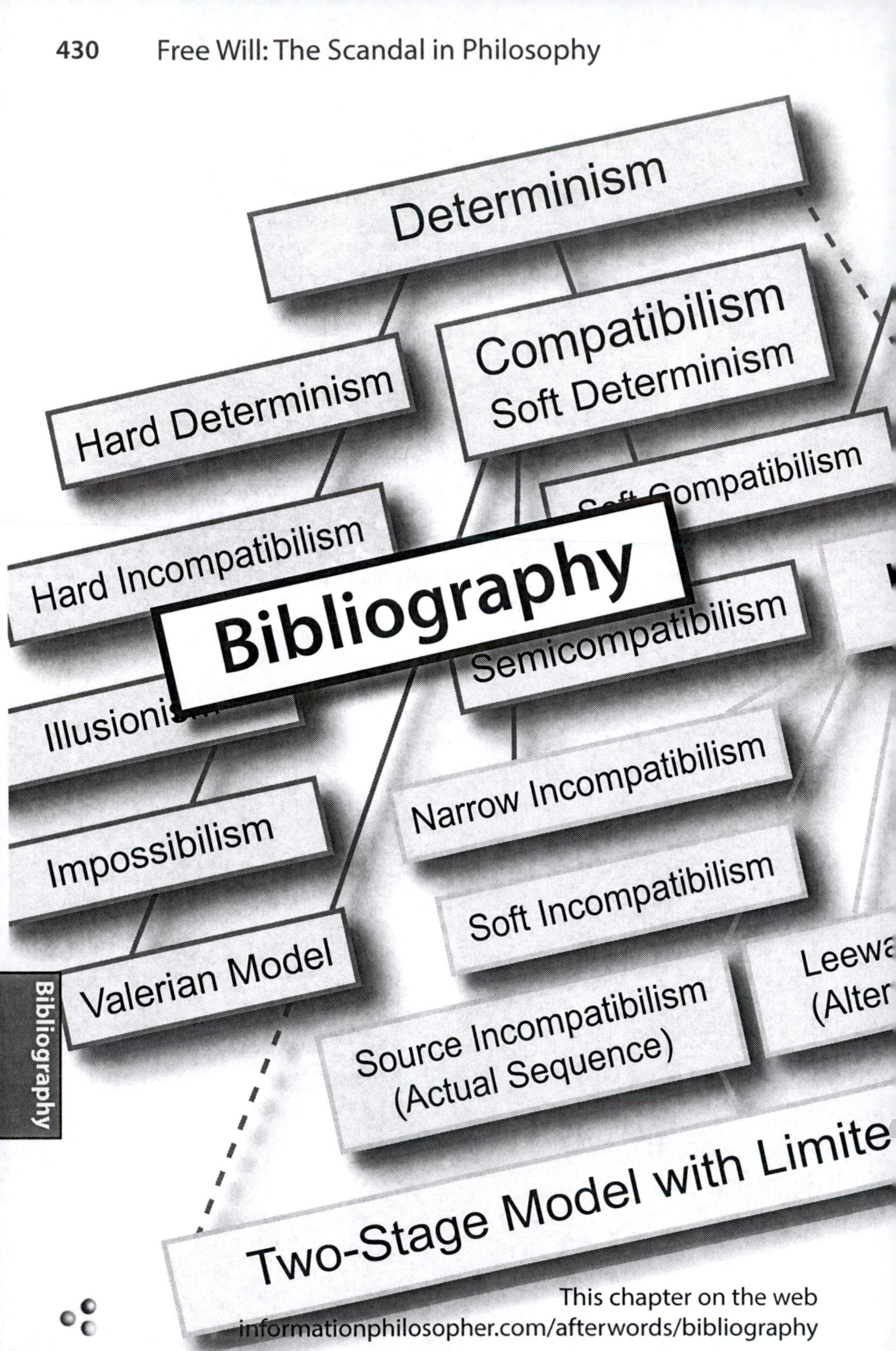

This chapter on the web
informationphilosopher.com/afterwords/bibliography

References

Adler, M.J., 1958. *The Idea of Freedom; a dialectical examination of the conceptions of freedom*, Garden City, N. Y.,: Doubleday.

________, 1961. *The Idea of Freedom*; vol. II, Garden City, N. Y.,: Doubleday.

Alberts, Bruce, et al., 2003. *Molecular Biology of the Cell*, 4th ed. New York, Garland Science, 2003.

Annas, J., 1992. *Hellenistic Philosophy of Mind*, Berkeley: University of California Press.

Anscombe, G. E. M., 1971. *Causality and Determination: an inaugural lecture*, London: Cambridge University Press.

Aristotle, 1934. *Physics II*. Cambridge, Mass.: Loeb Library 255, Harvard University Press.

________, 1935. *Metaphysics*. Cambridge, Mass.: Loeb Library 271, Harvard University Press.

Augustine. 1935. *The City of God*. Cambridge, Mass.: Loeb Library 287, Harvard University Press.

________, Benjamin, A.S. & Hackstaff, L.H., 1964. *On Free Choice of the Will*, Indianapolis,: Bobbs-Merrill.

Ayer, A.J., 1946. *Language, Truth, and Logic*, London,: V. Gollancz.

________, 1954. *Philosophical Essays*, New York, St. Martin's Press.

________, 1984. *Freedom and Morality and Other Essays*, Oxford [Oxfordshire]: Clarendon Press.

Ayers, M.R., 1968. *The Refutation of Determinism*, London: Methuen & Co.

Baer, J., J.C.Kaufman, and R.F.Baumeister., 2008. *Are We Free?: Psychology and Free Will*, Oxford: Oxford University Press.

Bailey, C., 1964. *The Greek Atomists and Epicurus: A Study*, New York: Russell & Russell.

Balaguer, Mark. 2004. 'A Coherent, Naturalistic, and Plausible Formulation of Libertarian Free Will.' *Noûs*, 38, 3, 379-406)

________, 2009. *Free Will as an Open Scientific Problem*, The MIT Press.

Baars, B.J., 1997. *In the Theater of Consciousness: The Workspace of the Mind*, New York: Oxford University Press.

________, and Nicole M. Gage 2007: *Cognition, Brain, and Consciousness: Introduction to Cognitive Neuroscience*. London: Academic Press.

Baumeister, Roy F. , Alfred Mele , and Kathleen Vohs, 2010. *Free Will and Consciousness*, Oxford: Oxford University Press.

Bell, J. 1987. *Speakable and Unspeakable in Quantum Mechanics* . Cambridge: Cambridge University Press.

Belsham, William, 1789. *Essays: Philosophical and Literary*, London: Dilly

Bergson, H., 2001. *Time and Free Will: An Essay on the Immediate Data of Consciousness*, Mineola, N.Y: Dover Publications.

Berlin, S.I., 1990. *Four Essays on Liberty*, Oxford University Press, USA.

Bernstein, M.H., 1992. *Fatalism*, Lincoln: University of Nebraska Press.

Berofsky, B., 1971. *Determinism.*, Princeton, N.J.: Princeton University Press.

________, 1966. *Free Will and Determinism*, New York: Harper & Row

________, 1988. *Freedom from Necessity: The Metaphysical Basis of Responsibility*, Routledge & Kegan Paul Books Ltd.

Bobzien, Susanne, 1998. *Determinism and Freedom in Stoic Philosophy*, Oxford: Clarendon Press.

Born, M., 1964. *Natural Philosophy of Cause and Chance*, New York: Dover Publications.

Brembs, Björn, 2010, 'Towards a scientific concept of free will as a biological trait,' *Proceedings of the Royal Society*, B (Biology), December 10.

Bremmer, Jan, 1983. *The Early Greek Concept of the Soul*, Princeton: Princeton University Press.

Broad, C. D. 1934. *Determinism, Indeterminism, and Libertarianism.* London: Routledge & Kegan Paul.

Campbell, C.A., 1967. *In Defense of Free Will*, Prometheus Books.

Campbell, Joseph Keim , M. O'Rourke , and D. Shier, 2004. *Freedom and Determinism.* Cambridge, Mass.: MIT Press.

Cassirer, Ernst. 1956. *Determinism and Indeterminism in Modern Physics.* New Haven: Yale University Press.

Chisholm, Roderick. 1964: 'Freedom and Action,' reprinted in *Freedom and Determinism.* Keith Lehrer, ed., 1966 New York: Random House

Chomsky, N., 1971. *Problems of Knowledge and Freedom*, New York: Pantheon Books.

Cicero, 1951. *De Natura Deorum*, Cambridge, MA, Harvard. Loeb Library, H. Rackham, trans

_____, 2004: *De Fato*. Cambridge, Mass.: Loeb Library 349, Harvard University Press

Clarke, R., 2003. *Libertarian Accounts of Free Will*, Oxford University Press, USA.

Clarke, S. & Vailati, E., 1998. *A Demonstration of the Being and Attributes of God and other writings*, Cambridge, U.K., Cambridge University Press.

Compton, Arthur Holly. 1931: 'The Uncertainty Principle and Free Will'. *Science*, 74, 1911.

Compton, Arthur Holly 1935: *The Freedom of Man*. New Haven: Yale University Press

Compton, Arthur Holly 1967: *The Cosmos of Arthur Holly Compton*, chapter 8,'Science and Man's Freedom.' New York: Knopf; originally published in The Atlantic Monthly, October 1957.

Conway, J. , and S. Kochen . 2006. "The free will theorem." *Foundations of Physics* 36 (10): 1441–73.

Darwin, C. G. 1931: 'Free Will as Involving Determinism'. *Science*, 73, 653.

Davidson, M., 1937. *Free Will or Determinism*, London: Watts & Co.

________, 1942. *The Free Will Controversy*, London: Watts & Co.

De Moivre, Abraham. 1756. *The Doctrine of Chances*, London.

Dennett, D.C., 1978. *Brainstorms: Philosophical Essays on Mind and Psychology*, The MIT Press.

________, 1985. *Elbow Room*, Oxford University Press.

________, 2004. *Freedom Evolves*, Penguin (Non-Classics).

Dihle, Albrecht, 1982. *The Theory of the Will in Classical Antiquity*, Berkeley: University of California Press.

Dilman, İ., 1999. *Free Will: An Historical and Philosophical Introduction*, London: Routledge.

Dirac, P.A.M., 2001. *Lectures on Quantum Mechanics*, Dover Publications.

Dobzhansky, T. G., 1956. *The Biological Basis of Human Freedom*, New York: Columbia University Press.

Dodds, E.R., 1951. *The Greeks and the Irrational*, Berkeley: University of California Press.

Double, R., 1991. *The Non-Reality of Free Will*, New York: Oxford University Press.

Doyle, Robert O., 2009. 'Free Will: it's a normal biological property, not a gift or a mystery,' *Nature*, 459 (June 2009): 1052.

________, 2010. 'Jamesian Free Will,' *William James Studies*, Vol. 5, p. 1

Dudley, J., 2011. *Aristotle's Concept of Chance*, SUNY Press.

Dworkin, G., 1970. *Determinism, Free Will, and Moral Responsibility*, Englewood Cliffs, N.J: Prentice-Hall.

Earman, John . 1986. *A Primer on Determinism*. Dordrecht, The Netherlands: D. Reidel.

Eccles, John C. 1953. *The Neurophysiological Basis of Mind*. Oxford: Oxford University Press, 271-86.

________. 1970. *Facing Reality* . New York: Springer.

Eccles, John C., 1994. *How the Self Controls Its Brain*, Springer-Verlag Telos.

Eddington, A.S., 2005 (1927). The Nature of the Physical World, Kessinger Publishing, LLC.

________, 2007 (1936). New Pathways In Science, Frazer Press.

________, 1939. The Philosophy of Physical Science : Tarner Lectures, Macmillan Co.

Edwards, Jonathan. 1969. *Freedom of the Will*. Indianapolis, Ind.: Bobbs-Merrill.

Einstein, A. , B. Podolsky , and N. Rosen . 1935. "Can quantum-mechanical description of physical reality be considered complete?" *Physical Review* 47: 777–80.

Ekstrom, L.W., 1999. *Free Will: A Philosophical Study*, Westview Press.

Erasmus, D., and M. Luther, 1988. *Discourse on Free Will*, New York: Continuum.

Farrer, A.M., 1958. *The Freedom of the Will*, London: Adam & Charles Black.

Feynman, R., 1994. *The Character of Physical Law*, Modern Library.

Fischer, John M., 1989. *God, Foreknowledge, and Freedom*, Stanford, Calif: Stanford University Press.

________, 1994. *The Metaphysics of Free Will : an essay on control*, Cambridge, Mass.: Blackwell.

________, 1995. "Libertarianism and Avoidability: A Reply to Widerker," *Faith and Philosophy* 12: 122-25.

________, 2005. *Free Will: Critical Concepts in Philosophy*, London: Routledge.

________, & Ravizza, M., 1999. *Responsibility and Control: A Theory of Moral Responsibility*, Cambridge University Press.

________, et al., 2007. *Four Views on Free Will*, Wiley-Blackwell.

Flanagan, O., 2003. *The Problem Of The Soul*, Basic Books.

Foot, Philippa. 1957: 'Free Will as Involving Determinism'. *Philosophical Review*, 76, pp. 439-50

Frank, J., 1945. *Fate and Freedom : a philosophy for free Americans*, New York: Simon and Schuster.

Franklin, R., 1969. *Freewill and Determinism: A Study of Rival Concepts of Man*, Routledge & Kegan Paul.

Frankfurt, Harry . 1969. "Alternate possibilities and moral responsibility." *Journal of Philosophy* 66: 829–39.

Frede, Michael. 2011. *A Free Will: Origins of the Notion in Ancient Thought*, U. of California Press.

Freeman, A., 2006. *Radical Externalism: Honderich's Theory of Consciousness Discussed*, Imprint Academic.

Furley, D.J., 1967. *Two Studies in the Greek Atomists*: Study II, Aristotle and Epicurus on Voluntary Action, Princeton, N.J: Princeton University Press.

Gazzaniga, Michael . 2005. "Neuroscience and the law." *Scientific American Mind* 16(1): 42–49.

Ginet, Carl . 1966. "Might we have no choice?" in *Freedom and Determinism*, ed. Keith Lehrer , 87–104. New York: Random House.

Gisin, N. "Quantum nonlocality: How does nature do it?" Science 326: 1357–58.

Glimcher, Paul W., 2003. *Decisions, Uncertainty, and the Brain*, Cambridge, MA: MIT Press.

________. et al. 2009. *Neuroeconomics: Decision Making and the Brain*, Amsterdam: Elsevier.

Greene, Joshua and Jonathan Cohen. 1990: 'For the law, neuroscience changes nothing and everything.' *Philosophical Transactions of the Royal Society of London B*, 359, 1776.

Grice, H. Paul, 1989. *Studies in the Ways of Words*, Cambridge: Harvard University Press.

Hacking, Ian, 1990. *The Taming of Chance*, Cambridge: Cambridge University Press.

________, 2006. *The Emergence of Probability*. Cambridge: Cambridge University Press.

Hadamard, J., 1945. *An Essay on the Psychology of Invention in the Mathematical Field*, Princeton: Princeton University Press.

Haji, Ishtiyaque. 1998. *Moral Appraisability*. Oxford: Oxford University Press.

Hamon, A.F., 1899. *The Universal Illusion of Free Will and Criminal Responsibility*, London: The University Press, ltd.

Hampshire, S., 1959. *Thought and Action*, London: Chatto and Windus.

________, 1965. *Freedom of the Individual*, New York: Harper & Row.

Hardie, W.F.R., 1980. *Aristotle's Ethical Theory*, Oxford: Oxford University Press.

Hare, R.M., 1963. *Freedom and Reason.*, Oxford,: Clarendon Press.

Harris, James A., 2005. *Of Liberty and Necessity: The Free Will Debate in Eighteenth-Century British Philosophy*, Oxford: Oxford University Press.

Hegel, G.W.F., 1967. *Hegel's Philosophy of Right*, London: Oxford University Press.

Heidegger, M., 1962. *Being and Time Revised*, HarperCollins Publishers.

Heil, J. & Mele, A.R., 1993. *Mental Causation*, Oxford, England: Clarendon.

Heisenberg, Martin. 2009: 'Is Free Will an Illusion?' *Nature*, 459, pp. 164-5.

Heisenberg, Werner. 1972: *Physics and Beyond: Encounters and Conversations*. New York: Harper & Row.

Hobart, R. E. 1934. 'Free Will as Involving Determination and Inconceivable Without It'. *Mind*, Vol. 43, No. 169, pp.1-27.

Hobbes, T., Bramhall, J. & Chappell, V.C., 1999. *Hobbes and Bramhall on Liberty and Necessity*, Cambridge, U.K. ;: Cambridge University Press.

Hodgson, D., 1993. *The Mind Matters: Consciousness and Choice in a Quantum World*, Oxford University Press, USA.

Hodgson, S. 1891. "Free-Will: An Analysis," *Mind*, Vol. 16, No. 62, pp. 161-180

Honderich, T., 1973. *Essays on Freedom of Action*, London: Routledge.

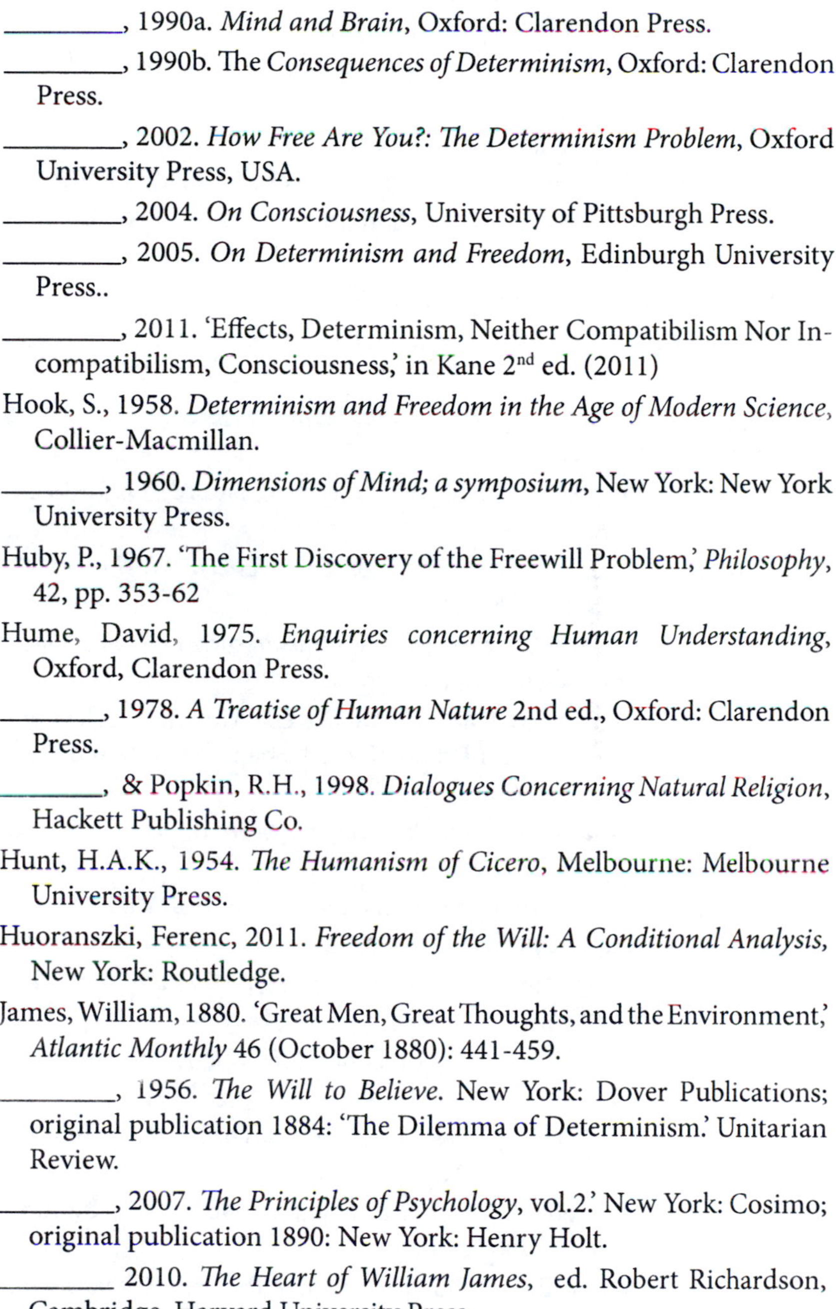

________, 1990a. *Mind and Brain*, Oxford: Clarendon Press.

________, 1990b. The *Consequences of Determinism*, Oxford: Clarendon Press.

________, 2002. *How Free Are You?: The Determinism Problem*, Oxford University Press, USA.

________, 2004. *On Consciousness*, University of Pittsburgh Press.

________, 2005. *On Determinism and Freedom*, Edinburgh University Press..

________, 2011. 'Effects, Determinism, Neither Compatibilism Nor Incompatibilism, Consciousness,' in Kane 2nd ed. (2011)

Hook, S., 1958. *Determinism and Freedom in the Age of Modern Science*, Collier-Macmillan.

________, 1960. *Dimensions of Mind; a symposium*, New York: New York University Press.

Huby, P., 1967. 'The First Discovery of the Freewill Problem,' *Philosophy*, 42, pp. 353-62

Hume, David, 1975. *Enquiries concerning Human Understanding*, Oxford, Clarendon Press.

________, 1978. *A Treatise of Human Nature* 2nd ed., Oxford: Clarendon Press.

________, & Popkin, R.H., 1998. *Dialogues Concerning Natural Religion*, Hackett Publishing Co.

Hunt, H.A.K., 1954. *The Humanism of Cicero*, Melbourne: Melbourne University Press.

Huoranszki, Ferenc, 2011. *Freedom of the Will: A Conditional Analysis*, New York: Routledge.

James, William, 1880. 'Great Men, Great Thoughts, and the Environment,' *Atlantic Monthly* 46 (October 1880): 441-459.

________, 1956. *The Will to Believe*. New York: Dover Publications; original publication 1884: 'The Dilemma of Determinism.' Unitarian Review.

________, 2007. *The Principles of Psychology*, vol.2.' New York: Cosimo; original publication 1890: New York: Henry Holt.

________ 2010. *The Heart of William James*, ed. Robert Richardson, Cambridge, Harvard University Press.

Kandel, Eric, James H. Schwarz, and Thomas M. Jessell. 2000: *Principles of Neuroscience*. New York: McGraw-Hill.

Kane, G. Stanley, 1981 *Anselm's Doctrine of Freedom and the Will*, Lewiston, NY: Edwin Mullen Press.

Kane, R., 1985. *Free Will and Values*, SUNY.

_______, 1996. *The Significance of Free Will*, Oxford University Press.

_______, 1999: "Responsibility, Luck, and Chance," *Journal of Philosophy*, 96, 5 p.225.

_______, 2001. *Free Will*, Wiley-Blackwell.

_______, 2002. *The Oxford Handbook of Free Will*, Oxford University Press, USA.

_______, 2005. *A Contemporary Introduction to Free Will*, Oxford University Press, USA.

_______, 2011. *The Oxford Handbook of Free Will*, 2nd ed., Oxford University Press, USA.

Kant, Immanuel. 1952: *Great Books of the Western World*, vol.42. Chicago: Encyclopedia Britannica

Kirk, G.S., J.E.Raven, and M.Schofield. 1983: *The Presocratic Philosophers*. Cambridge: Cambridge University Press.

Knobe, Joshua , and Shaun Nichols . 2008. "An experimental philosophy manifesto." In *Experimental Philosophy* , ed. Shaun Nichols and Joshua Knobe , 1–23. New York:

Korsgaard, Christine, 1996. *The Sources of Normativity*. Columbia University Press.

Koshland, Daniel E., Jr., 1980. *Bacterial Chemotaxis as a Model Behavioural System*. New York: Raven Press.

Laplace, Pierre-Simon, 1995. *Philosophical Essay on Probabilities*.' New York: Springer-Verlag.

Layzer, David, 1975. "The Arrow of Time," *Scientific American* 233, 6 (1975) pp.56-69.

Layzer, David, 1991. *Cosmogenesis: The Growth of Order in the Universe*, Oxford University Press, USA.

Lehrer, Keith. 1966. *Freedom and Determinism*. New York: Random House. Oxford University Press.

Lestienne, R. & Neher, E.C., 1998. *The Creative Power of Chance*. University of Illinois Press.

Levin, Michael . 2007. 'Compatibilism and Special Relativity.' *Journal of*

Philosophy 104: 433–63.

Libet, B., 1999: 'Do We Have Free Will? ' *Journal of Consciousness Studies*, 6, No. 8-9, pp. 47-57.

_______, 2004. *Mind Time*, Cambridge, MA:Harvard University Press.

Liddell, Henry George and Robert Scott. 1968: *A Greek-English Lexicon*, Oxford: Clarendon Press.

Lipton, P. 2004. 'Genetic and generic determinism: a new threat to free will?,' in *The New Brain Sciences: Perils and Prospects*, ed. D. Rees and S. Rose. Cambridge University Press, 2004, p. 89.

Locke, John., 1959 (1690). *Essay Concerning Human Understanding*, Book II, Chapter XXI, Of Power, sections 14-21 (New York, Dover, 1959), pp.319-324

Lockwood, M., 1989. *Mind, Brain and the Quantum*, Oxford: Blackwell.

_______, 2005. *The Labyrinth of Time*. New York: Oxford University Press.

Long, A. A. 1986: *Hellenistic Philosophy*, Berkeley: U. California Press,.

_______, and D. Sedley. 1987. *The Hellenistic Philosophers*, Cambridge: Cambridge University Press.

_______, 2000. *Problems in Stoicism*, New York: Continuum.

Lucas, J.R., 1970. *The Freedom of the Will*, Oxford: Clarendon.

Lucretius. 1982: *De Rerum Natura*. Cambridge, MA.: Loeb Library 181, Harvard University Press.

Mackay, D.M., 1967. *Freedom of Action in a Mechanistic Universe*, London: Cambridge University Press

Margenau, Henry. 1968. *Scientific Indeterminism and Human Freedom*.,Wimmer Lecture XX' Latrobe, Pennsylvania.: The Archabbey Press

_________, and Lawrence LeShan. 1982. *Einstein's Space and Van Gogh's Sky*, New York: Macmillan.

Mayr, Ernst., 1988. *Toward a New Philosophy of Biology*, Cambridge, MA, Harvard Belknap Press.

McFee, G., 2000. *Free Will*, Montreal: McGill-Queen's University Press.

McGinn, Colin. 1995: *Problems in Philosophy: The Limits of Inquiry*, New York: Wiley-Blackwell

Mele, A.R., 1995. *Autonomous Agents: From Self-Control to Autonomy*,

New York: Oxford University Press.

_______, 2006. *Free Will and Luck*, Oxford: Oxford University Press.

_______, 2010. *Effective Intentions: The Power of Conscious Will*, Oxford University Press, USA.

Mill, John Stuart. 2006 (1843). *A System of Logic, Rationative and Inductive*, vols. 7 and 8, *Collected Works of John Stuart Mill*, Indianapolis: Liberty Fund.

Moore, G. E. 1912. *Ethics* . Oxford: Oxford University Press.

Morgenbesser, S., 1962. *Free Will*, Englewood Cliffs, N.J: Prentice-Hall.

Munn, A.M., 1960. *Free-Will and Determinism*, Toronto: University of Toronto Press.

Murphy, Nancey , and Warren S. Brown . 2007. *Did My Neurons Make Me Do It*? Oxford: Oxford University Press.

Nagel, T., 1979. *Mortal Questions*, Cambridge: Cambridge University Press.

Nagel, T., 1986. *The View from Nowhere*, New York: Oxford University Press.

Nahmias, Eddy. 2006. 'Folk fears about freedom and responsibility: Determinism vs. reductionism.' *Journal of Cognition and Culture* 6(1–2): 215–37.

Neuringer, Allen and Greg Jensen, 2010, 'Operant Variability and Voluntary Action,' *Psychological Review*, Vol. 117, No. 3, p. 991

Nichols, Shaun, 2006. 'Folk intuitions on free will,' *Journal of Cognition and Culture* 6(1–2): 57–86.

Nietzsche, Friedrich, 1999. *Also sprach Zarathustra* I–IV, ed. by G. Colli & M. Montinari .

Nowell-Smith, P, 1948. 'Freewill and Moral Responsibility.' *Mind*, 57, pp. 45-61.

Nozick, Robert, 1981. *Philosophical Explanations*. Cambridge: Harvard University Press

O'Connor, D., 1971. *Free Will*, Anchor Books.

O'Connor, T., 1995. *Agents, Causes, and Events: Essays on Indeterminism and Free Will*, Oxford University Press, USA.

O'Connor, T., 2002. *Persons and Causes: The Metaphysics of Free Will*, Oxford University Press, USA.

O'Hear, A, 2003. *Minds and Persons*, New York: Cambridge University Press.

O'Keefe, T., 2005. *Epicurus on Freedom*, Cambridge, UK: Cambridge

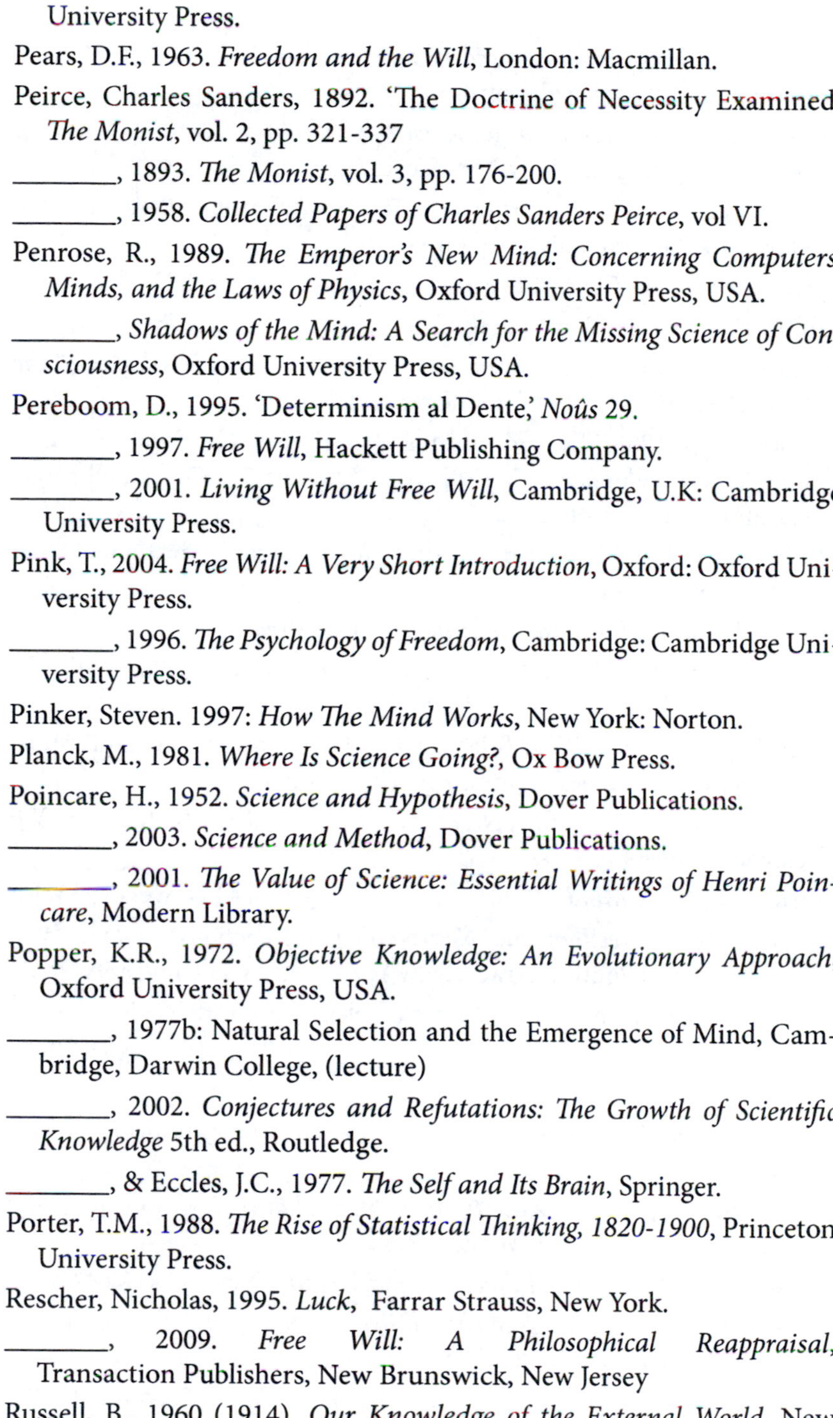

University Press.

Pears, D.F., 1963. *Freedom and the Will*, London: Macmillan.

Peirce, Charles Sanders, 1892. 'The Doctrine of Necessity Examined.' *The Monist*, vol. 2, pp. 321-337

_______, 1893. *The Monist*, vol. 3, pp. 176-200.

_______, 1958. *Collected Papers of Charles Sanders Peirce*, vol VI.

Penrose, R., 1989. *The Emperor's New Mind: Concerning Computers, Minds, and the Laws of Physics*, Oxford University Press, USA.

_______, *Shadows of the Mind: A Search for the Missing Science of Consciousness*, Oxford University Press, USA.

Pereboom, D., 1995. 'Determinism al Dente,' *Noûs* 29.

_______, 1997. *Free Will*, Hackett Publishing Company.

_______, 2001. *Living Without Free Will*, Cambridge, U.K: Cambridge University Press.

Pink, T., 2004. *Free Will: A Very Short Introduction*, Oxford: Oxford University Press.

_______, 1996. *The Psychology of Freedom*, Cambridge: Cambridge University Press.

Pinker, Steven. 1997: *How The Mind Works*, New York: Norton.

Planck, M., 1981. *Where Is Science Going?*, Ox Bow Press.

Poincare, H., 1952. *Science and Hypothesis*, Dover Publications.

_______, 2003. *Science and Method*, Dover Publications.

_______, 2001. *The Value of Science: Essential Writings of Henri Poincare*, Modern Library.

Popper, K.R., 1972. *Objective Knowledge: An Evolutionary Approach*, Oxford University Press, USA.

_______, 1977b: Natural Selection and the Emergence of Mind, Cambridge, Darwin College, (lecture)

_______, 2002. *Conjectures and Refutations: The Growth of Scientific Knowledge* 5th ed., Routledge.

_______, & Eccles, J.C., 1977. *The Self and Its Brain*, Springer.

Porter, T.M., 1988. *The Rise of Statistical Thinking, 1820-1900*, Princeton University Press.

Rescher, Nicholas, 1995. *Luck*, Farrar Strauss, New York.

_______, 2009. *Free Will: A Philosophical Reappraisal*, Transaction Publishers, New Brunswick, New Jersey

Russell, B., 1960 (1914). *Our Knowledge of the External World*, New

York, Mentor.

_______, 1936. *Determinism and Physics*, repr. in The Collected Papers of Bertrand Russell, Volume 10

Russell, P., 1995. *Freedom and Moral Sentiment: Hume's Way of Naturalizing Responsibility*, New York: Oxford University Press.

Rychlak, J.F., 1979. *Discovering Free will and Personal Responsibility*, New York: Oxford University Press.

Ryle, G., 1949. *The Concept of Mind*, New York: Barnes & Noble.

Sambursky, S., 1988. *Physics of the Stoics*, Princeton Univ Press.

Satinover, J., 2001. *The Quantum Brain: The Search for Freedom and the Next Generation of Man*, New York: J. Wiley.

Scanlon, T. M. 1988. 'The significance of choice,' in *The Tanner Lectures on Human Values*, ed. Sterling M. McMurrin, 1–35. Cambridge: Cambridge University Press.

Schelling, F.W.J.V., 1936. *Of Human Freedom*, Chicago: The Open Court Publishing Company.

Schlick, M., 2008. *Problems Of Ethics*, Nielsen Press.

Schopenhauer, A. & Kolenda, K., 1995. *On the Freedom of the Will*, Wiley-Blackwell.

Schrödinger, E., 1992. *What Is Life?*, with "Mind and Matter" and "Autobiographical Sketches", Cambridge University Press.

Schwartz, S.P., 1977. *Naming, Necessity, and Natural Kinds*, Ithaca [N.Y.]: Cornell University Press.

Searle, J. R., 1986. *Minds, Brains and Science*, Harvard University Press.

_______, 2007. *Freedom and Neurobiology: Reflections on Free Will*, Language, and Political Power, New York: Columbia University Press.

_______, 1990. *The Mystery of Consciousness*, New York Review Books.

Sharples, R., 2007. *Alexander of Aphrodisias On Fate*, Duckworth Publishers.

Simon, Herbert A. 1981: *The Sciences of the Artificial*, Cambridge, Mass: MIT Press.

Simonton, D.K., 2004. *Creativity in Science: Chance, Logic, Genius, and Zeitgeist*, Cambridge University Press.

Skinner, B.F., 1971. *Beyond Freedom and Dignity*, New York: Knopf.

Skyrms, B., 1980. *Causal Necessity : a Pragmatic Investigation of the Necessity of Laws*, New Haven: Yale University Press.

Smart, J. J. C. 1961: 'Free-Will, Praise and Blame'. *Mind*, 70, pp. 291–306.

_______, and John Haldane. 2003: *Atheism and Theism*, Malden, MA: Wiley-Blackwell

Smilansky, S., 2000. *Free Will and Illusion*, Oxford: Clarendon Press.

Snell, Bruno, 1953. *The Discovery of the Mind*, New York: Dover Publications

Sobel, J.H., 1998. *Puzzles for the Will: Fatalism, Newcomb and Samarra, Determinism and Omniscience*, Toronto: U. of Toronto Press.

Sorabji, R., 1980. *Necessity, Cause, and Blame: Perspectives on Aristotle's Theory*, Ithaca, N.Y: Cornell University Press.

Stapp, H.P., 2004. *Mind, Matter and Quantum Mechanics*, Berlin: Springer.

Stebbing, L.S., 1937. *Philosophy & the Physicists*, Dover.

Sternberg, E.J. 2007, *Are You A Machine?*, Amherst, NY: Humanity Books.

_______, 2010. *My Brain Made Me Do It*, Prometheus Books

Strawson, Galen, 1986. *Freedom and Belief*, Oxford: Clarendon Press.

_______, 1989. The Secret Connexion, Oxford: Clarendon Press.

_______, 1994. 'The Impossibility of Moral Responsibility.' *Philosophical Studies*, 75/1-2, 5-24.

Strawson, P. F., 1962. *Freedom and Resentment, and other essays*, London: Methuen ;.

_______, 1985. *Skepticism and Naturalism: some varieties*, New York: Columbia University Press.

Taylor, Christopher, and Daniel Dennett, 2002. "Who's afraid of determinism." In Kane 2002, 257–79. Oxford: Oxford University Press.

Taylor, Richard . 1962. "Fatalism." *Philosophical Review* 71(1): 56–66.

_______,1963. *Metaphysics*, Englewood Cliffs, N.J: Prentice-Hall.

_______, 1973. *Action and Purpose*, Humanities Press.

Thorp, J., 1980. *Free Will : a Defence against Neurophysiological Determinism*, London: Routledge & Kegan Paul.

Timpe, K., 2008. *Free Will: Sourcehood and Its Alternatives*, Continuum.

Trusted, J., 1984. *Free Will and Responsibility*, Oxford: Oxford University Press.

Van Inwagen, P., 1983. *An Essay on Free Will*, Oxford: Clarendon Press.

_______, 2004: 'Van Inwagen on Free Will.' in Campbell 2004

Vannevar, A.H.., 1967. *Cosmos of Arthur Holly Compton*, Knopf.

Vargas, Manuel. 2007. 2007. "Revisionism." In Fischer et al. 2007

Vihvelin, Kadri. 2007. 'Arguments for incompatibilism.' *The Stanford Encyclopedia of Philosophy*, http://plato.stanford.edu/incompatibilism-arguments/

Vohs, K. D., & Schooler, J. W. (2008). 'The Value of Believing in Free Will,' *Psychological Science*, Vol.19, No.1

Wallace, D.F., 2010. *Fate, Time, and Language: An Essay on Free Will*, Columbia University Press.

Waller, B.N., 1990. *Freedom Without Responsibility*, Philadelphia: Temple University Press.

_______, 1998. *The Natural Selection of Autonomy*, Albany, N.Y.: State University of New York Press.

Walter, H., 2001. *Neurophilosophy of Free Will: From Libertarian Illusions to a Concept of Natural Autonomy*, Cambridge, Mass: MIT Press.

Watson, Gary . 1975. "Free agency." *Journal of Philosophy* 72: 205–20.

_______, 1982. *Free Will* . New York: Oxford University Press.

Wegner, Daniel. 2002: *The Illusion of Conscious Will*. Cambridge, Mass.: MIT Press.

Weiss, P., 1950. *Man's Freedom*, Yale University Press.

Wheeler, J. A., and W. H. Zurek, 1983. *Quantum Theory and Measurement*, Princeton, N.J.: Princeton University Press.

Widerker, D. and M. McKenna., 2003. *Moral Responsibility and Alternative Possibilities*, Aldershot, Hants, England: Ashgate.

Wiener, N., 1965. *Cybernetics: or the Control and Communication in the Animal and the Machine* 2nd ed., The MIT Press.

Wiggins, David., 1973: 'Towards a Reasonable Libertarianism,' in *Essays on Freedom of Action*, ed. Ted Honderich, London, Routledge & Kegan Paul.

Williams, B.A.O., 1981. *Moral Luck: Philosophical Papers*, 1973-1980, Cambridge [Cambridgeshire]: Cambridge University Press.

Williams, C., 1980. *Free Will and Determinism: A Dialogue*, Indianapolis: Hackett Publishing Co.

Wittgenstein, L., 1993. *Philosophical Occasions*, 1912-1951, Indianapolis: Hackett Publishing Co.

Wolf, S., 1993. *Freedom within Reason*, Oxford University Press.

Free Will Anthologies

Some anthologies on free will, with contributing authors:

Hook, S. and New York University. (1958). *Determinism and Freedom in the Age of Modern Science; a philosophical symposium*. New York, New York University Press.

[Blanshard, Black, Barrett, Bridgman, Munitz, Landé, Sciama, Hart, Edwards, Hospers,Beardsley, Brandt, Chisholm, Ducasse, Hempel, Hintz, Hook, Lerner, E. Nagel, Northrop, Pap, Schultz, R. Taylor, Weiss, Wilson.]

Morgenbesser, S. and J. J. Walsh (1962). *Free Will*. Englewood Cliffs, N.J., Prentice-Hall.

[Augustine, Aquinas, Scotus, Hobbes, Mill, Foot, R.Taylor, Sartre, Broad, Aristotle, Hart.]

Berofsky, B. (1966). *Free Will and Determinism*. New York,, Harper & Row.

[Hospers, Hook, Schlick, Hobart, Foot, Campbell. Broad, Mill, Sartre, Melden, Davidson, MacIntyre, Bradley, Augustine, R. Taylor, Austin, Nowell Smith, Chisholm, Campbell, Nowell Smith.]

Lehrer, K. (1966). *Freedom and Determinism*. New York,, Random House.

[Chisholm, Danto, R.Taylor, Ginet, Sellars, Lehrer.]

Dworkin, G. (1970). *Determinism, Free Will, and Moral Responsibility*. Englewood Cliffs, N.J.,, Prentice-Hall.

[Hume, Peirce, Nagel, Reid, Campbell, De Valla, Ginet, Moore, Thomas, Broad, Lehrer, Smart.]

Honderich, T. (1973). *Essays on Freedom of Action*. London, Boston,, Routledge and Kegan Paul.

[Warnock, Watling, Wiggins, Frankfurt, Kenny, Pears, Davidson, Dennett, Honderich.]

Watson, G. (1982). *Free Will*. Oxford Oxfordshire ; New York, Oxford University Press.

[Ayer, Chisholm, Aune, Lehrer, van Inwagen, P. F. Strawson, Frankfurt, Watson, C.Taylor, Malcolm, T.Nagel.]

O'Connor, T. (1995). *Agents, Causes, and Events: Essays on Indeterminism and Free Will.* New York/Oxford , Oxford University Press.

[G.Strawson, T.Nagel, Dennett, Double, Ginet, Chisholm, Nozick, Kane, Rowe, O'Connor, Clarke, van Inwagen, Fischer, Ravizza.]

Pereboom, D. (1997). *Free Will.* Indianapolis/Cambridge, Hackett Publishing

[Aristotle, Stoics, Lucretius,Augustine, Aquinas, Hume, Kant, Ayer, P. F. Strawson, Chisholm, Frankfurt, van Inwagen, Wolf, Fischer, Pereboom, Clarke.]

Ekstrom, L. W. (2001). *Agency and Responsibility : essays on the metaphysics of freedom.* Boulder, Colo., Westview Press.

[Van Inwagen, Lewis, Fischer, Anscombe, Frankfurt, Watson, Bratman, Chisholm, Ekstrom, Kane, P. F. Strawson, Wolf, Widerker, Mele and Robb.]

Kane, R. (2002). *The Oxford Handbook of Free Will.* Oxford ; New York, Oxford University Press.

[Kane, Zagzebski, Bernstein, Hodgson, Bishop, Kapitan, van Inwagen, Berofsky, Haji, Russell, C.Taylor and Dennett, Fischer, Ekstrom, Widerker, O'Connor, Clarke, Ginet, G. Strawson, Honderich, Pereboom, Smilansky, Double, Mele, Libet, Walter.]

Kane, R. (2002). *Free Will.* Malden, MA, Blackwell Publishers.

[Skinner, Nielsen, Chisholm, Edwards, van Inwagen, Dennett, Fischer, Pereboom, Frankfurt, Wolf, Watson, O'Connor, Ginet, Kane, Hodgson, Augustine, Hasker.]

Watson, G. (2003). *Free Will.* Oxford/New York, Oxford University Press.

[Chisholm, van Inwagen, Smart, P. F. Strawson, Wiggins, Lewis, Bok, Frankfurt, Widerker, Fischer, G. Strawson, T.Nagel, O'Connor, Clarke, Kane, Watson, Scanlon, Wolf, Pettit and Smith, Albritton, Wallace.]

Campbell, J. K., M. O'Rourke, and D Shier. (2004). *Freedom and Determinism*. MIT Press.

[Earman, Lehrer, Kane, Ginet, Nelkin, Haji, Long, Arpaly, Fischer, van Inwagen, Perry, Feldman, Gier, Kjellberg, Honderich.]

Web References

Stanford Encyclopedia of Philosophy (SEP) article on *Free Will* (Timothy O'Connor)

SEP on *Incompatibilist Free Will* (Randolph Clarke)

SEP on *Causal Determinism* (Carl Hoefer)

SEP on *Incompatibilism* (Kadri Vihvelin)

SEP on *Compatibilism* (Michael McKenna)

SEP on *Moral Responsibility* (Andrew Eshleman)

Internet Encyclopedia of Philosophy (IEP) article on *Free Will* (Kevin Timpe)

IEP on *Moral Responsibility* (Garrath Williams)

Online Papers on Free Will, compiled by David Chalmers (Australian National University)

Free Will Bibliography (David Chalmers and David Bourget)

Index

A

B

C

D

E

F

G

My thanks to J. L. Speranza for editorial assistance and help with the index.

Philosophers

Mortimer Adler
Rogers Albritton
Alexander of Aphrodisias
G.E.M.Anscombe
Anselm
Thomas Aquinas
Aristotle
David Armstrong
Augustine
J.L.Austin
A.J.Ayer
Alexander Bain
Mark Balaguer
William Belsham
Henri Bergson
Isaiah Berlin
Bernard Berofsky
Susanne Bobzien
Emil du Bois-Reymond
George Boole
Émile Boutroux
F.H.Bradley
C.D.Broad
C.A.Campbell
Joseph Keim Campbell
Carneades
Ernst Cassirer
Roderick Chisholm
Chrysippus
Cicero
Randolph Clarke
Diodorus Cronus
Donald Davidson
Democritus
Daniel Dennett
René Descartes
Richard Double
Fred Dretske
John Earman
Laura Waddell Ekstrom
Epictetus
Epicurus
John Martin Fischer
Owen Flanagan
Luciano Floridi
Philippa Foot
Alfred Fouillée
Harry Frankfurt
Richard L. Franklin
Carl Ginet
Nicholas St. John Green
H. Paul Grice
Ian Hacking
Ishtiyaque Haji
Stuart Hampshire
W.F.R. Hardie
R. M. Hare
Georg W.F. Hegel
Martin Heidegger
R.E.Hobart
Thomas Hobbes
David Hodgson
Shadsworth Hodgson
Ted Honderich
Pamela Huby
David Hume
William James
Robert Kane
Immanuel Kant
Tomis Kapitan
Christine Korsgaard
Keith Lehrer
Gottfried Leibniz
Leucippus
Michael Levin
C.I.Lewis
David Lewis
Peter Lipton
John Locke
Michael Lockwood
John R. Lucas
Lucretius
James Martineau
Hugh McCann
Colin McGinn
Michael McKenna
Paul E. Meehl
Alfred Mele
John Stuart Mill
Dickinson Miller
G.E.Moore
Thomas Nagel
Friedrich Nietzsche
P.H.Nowell-Smith
Robert Nozick
William of Ockham
Timothy O'Connor
David F. Pears
Charles Sanders Peirce
Derk Pereboom
Steven Pinker
Karl Popper
H.A.Prichard
Hilary Putnam
Willard van Orman Quine
Frank Ramsey
Ayn Rand
Thomas Reid
Charles Renouvier
Nicholas Rescher
C.W.Rietdijk
Josiah Royce
Bertrand Russell
Paul Russell
Gilbert Ryle
T.M.Scanlon
Moritz Schlick
Arthur Schopenhauer
John Searle
Henry Sidgwick
Walter Sinnott-Armstrong
J.J.C.Smart
Saul Smilansky
Michael Smith
L. Susan Stebbing
George F. Stout
Galen Strawson
Peter Strawson
Eleonore Stump
Richard Taylor
Kevin Timpe
Peter van Inwagen
Manuel Vargas
John Venn
Kadri Vihvelin
Voltaire
G.H. von Wright
David Foster Wallace
R. Jay Wallace
W. G.Ward
Ted Warfield
Roy Weatherford
Alfred North Whitehead
David Widerker
David Wiggins
Ludwig Wittgenstein
Susan Wolf

Scientists

Michael Arbib
Bernard Baars
John S. Bell
Charles Bennett
Margaret Boden
David Bohm
Neils Bohr
Ludwig Boltzmann

Max Born
Stephen Brush
Leon Brillouin
Henry Thomas Buckle
Donald Campbell
Anthony Cashmore
Eric Chaisson
Jean-Pierre Changeux
Arthur Holly Compton
Charles Darwin
Abraham de Moivre
Paul Dirac
John Eccles
Arthur Stanley Eddington
Albert Einstein
Richard Feynman
GianCarlo Ghirardi
Nicolas Gisin
A.O.Gomes
Joshua Greene
Jacques Hadamard
Patrick Haggard
Martin Heisenberg
Werner Heisenberg
William Stanley Jevons
Pascual Jordan
Simon Kochen
Stephen Kosslyn
Rolf Landauer
Alfred Landé
Pierre-Simon Laplace
David Layzer
Benjamin Libet
Josef Loschmidt
Ernst Mach
Henry Margenau
James Clerk Maxwell
Ernst Mayr
Jacques Monod
Roger Penrose
Steven Pinker
Max Planck
Henri Poincaré
Adolphe Quételet
Jerome Rothstein
Erwin Schrödinger
Claude Shannon
Dean Keith Simonton
Herbert Simon
B. F. Skinner
Henry Stapp
Antoine Suarez
Leo Szilard
William Thomson
(Lord Kelvin)
John von Neumann
Daniel Wegner
Steven Weinberg
Norbert Wiener
Eugene Wigner
E. O. Wilson
Ernst Zermelo

Core Concepts

Adequate Determinism
Agent-Causality
Alternative Possibilities
Causa Sui
Causality
Certainty
Chance
Chance Not Direct Cause
The Cogito Model
Compatibilism
Comprehensive Compatibilism
Conceptual Analysis
Control
Could Do Otherwise
Creativity
Default Responsibility
De-liberation
Determination
Determination Fallacy
Determinism
Disambiguation
Either Way
Ethical Fallacy
Experimental Philosophy
Extreme Libertarianism
Event Has Many Causes
Frankfurt Cases
Free Choice
Freedom of Action
"Free Will"
Free Will Axiom
Free Will in Antiquity
Free Will Mechanisms
Free Will Requirements
Free Will Theorem
Future Contingency
Hard Incompatibilism
Illusion of Determinism
Illusionism
Impossibilism
Incompatibilism
Indeterminacy
Indeterminism
Infinities
Laplace's Demon
Libertarianism
Liberty of Indifference
Libet Experiments
Luck
Master Argument
Modest Libertarianism
Moral Responsibility
Moral Sentiments
Mysteries
Naturalism
Necessity
Noise
Non-Causality
Nonlocality
Origination
Pre-determinism
Predictability
Probability
Pseudo-Problem
Random When?/Where?
Rational Fallacy
Responsibility
Same Circumstances
Scandal
Science Advance Fallacy
Second Thoughts
Semicompatibilism
Separability
Soft Causality
Special Relativity
Standard Argument
Taxonomy
Temporal Sequence
Tertium Quid
Torn Decision
Two-Stage Models
Ultimate Responsibility
Uncertainty
Up To Us
Voluntarism

Information Philosopher books are *bridges* from the information architecture of the printed page, from well before Gutenberg and his movable-type revolution, to the information architecture of the world-wide web, to a future of knowledge instantly available on demand anywhere it is needed in the world.

Information wants to be free. Information *makes you free.*

I-Phi printed books are still material, with their traditional costs of production and distribution. But they are physical pointers and travel guides to help you navigate the virtual world of information online, which of course still requires energy for its communication, and material devices for its storage and retrieval to displays.

But the online information itself is, like the knowledge in our collective minds, neither material nor energy, but pure information, pure idea, the stuff of thought. It is as close as physical science comes to the notion of spirit, the ghost in the machine, the soul in the body.

Google

It is this spirit that information philosophy wants to set free, with the help of Google and Wikipedia, Facebook and YouTube.

At a time when one in ten living persons have a presence on the web, when the work of past intellects has been captured by Google Scholar, we have entered the age of *Information Immortality*.

YouTube

When you Google one of the concepts of information philosophy, the search results page will retrieve links to the latest versions of Information Philosopher pages online, and of course links to related pages in the Wikipedia, in the Stanford Encyclopedia of Philosophy, and links to YouTube lectures.

Thank you for purchasing this physical embodiment of our work. We put the means of intellectual production in the hands of the people.